VOLUME

OLD TESTAM

GW00385460

THE NEW COLLEGEVILLE BIBLE COMMENTARY

EXODUS

Mark S. Smith

SERIES EDITOR

Daniel Durken, O.S.B.

LITURGICAL PRESS

Collegeville, Minnesota

www.litpress.org

Nihil Obstat: Reverend Robert Harren, *Censor deputatus.*
Imprimatur: ✠ Most Reverend John F. Kinney, J.C.D., D.D., Bishop of St. Cloud, Minnesota, December 17, 2010.

Design by Ann Blattner.

Cover illustration: *Ten Commandments* by Thomas Ingmire. Copyright 2003 *The Saint John's Bible*, Order of Saint Benedict, Collegeville, Minnesota USA. Used by permission. Scripture quotations are from the New Revised Standard Version of the Bible, Catholic Edition, copyright 1989, 1993 National Council of the Churches of Christ in the United States of America. Used by permission. All rights reserved.

Photos: pages 18, 99, 123, Thinkstock.com; pages 34, 59, 84, Photos.com.

1   2   3   4   5   6   7   8   9

Library of Congress Cataloging-in-Publication Data

Smith, Mark S., 1955–
    Exodus / Mark S. Smith.
        p. cm. — (New Collegeville Bible commentary. Old Testament ; v. 3)
    Includes index.
    ISBN 978-0-8146-2837-9
    1. Bible. O.T. Exodus—Commentaries.   I. Title.
    BS1245.53.S65 2010
    222'.1207—dc22   2009036730

CONTENTS

ABBREVIATIONS

Books of the Bible

Acts—Acts of the Apostles
Amos—Amos
Bar—Baruch
1 Chr—1 Chronicles
2 Chr—2 Chronicles
Col—Colossians
1 Cor—1 Corinthians
2 Cor—2 Corinthians
Dan—Daniel
Deut—Deuteronomy
Eccl (or Qoh)—Ecclesiastes
Eph—Ephesians
Esth—Esther
Exod—Exodus
Ezek—Ezekiel
Ezra—Ezra
Gal—Galatians
Gen—Genesis
Hab—Habakkuk
Hag—Haggai
Heb—Hebrews
Hos—Hosea
Isa—Isaiah
Jas—James
Jdt—Judith
Jer—Jeremiah
Job—Job
Joel—Joel
John—John
1 John—1 John
2 John—2 John
3 John—3 John
Jonah—Jonah
Josh—Joshua
Jude—Jude
Judg—Judges
1 Kgs—1 Kings

2 Kgs—2 Kings
Lam—Lamentations
Lev—Leviticus
Luke—Luke
1 Macc—1 Maccabees
2 Macc—2 Maccabees
Mal—Malachi
Mark—Mark
Matt—Matthew
Mic—Micah
Nah—Nahum
Neh—Nehemiah
Num—Numbers
Obad—Obadiah
1 Pet—1 Peter
2 Pet—2 Peter
Phil—Philippians
Phlm—Philemon
Prov—Proverbs
Ps(s)—Psalms
Rev—Revelation
Rom—Romans
Ruth—Ruth
1 Sam—1 Samuel
2 Sam—2 Samuel
Sir—Sirach
Song—Song of Songs
1 Thess—1 Thessalonians
2 Thess—2 Thessalonians
1 Tim—1 Timothy
2 Tim—2 Timothy
Titus—Titus
Tob—Tobit
Wis—Wisdom
Zech—Zechariah
Zeph—Zephaniah

The Book of Exodus

The significance of the exodus

Exodus tells the story of Israel's divine deliverance and the freedom it gained in the covenant relationship with God on Mount Sinai. Many people think of the exodus as Israel's escape from slavery in Egypt, but freedom in the book of Exodus is not completely sealed until Israel completes the covenant with God at Mount Sinai. Freedom in Exodus is not only freedom from oppressive conditions or the evil of human power; human freedom becomes complete in the context of the covenantal relationship with the God of Israel. For the book of Exodus, to be free means not only freedom *from* evil but also freedom *through* responsible relationships *with* and *for* others, human as well as divine. Exodus expresses this twofold reality about human freedom through the geographical structure of the book: Egypt dominates the first major part (Exod 1–15), while Sinai is the focus of the second (Exod 16–40).

The book of Exodus is therefore not simply the record of physical journeys. It is also the journey of Israel and God. Following the end of Genesis, with its narrative about Jacob, his sons, and their families in Egypt, the beginning of Exodus shows how this family has become a people, the people of Israel. In the very first verse, they are collectively called "the sons of Israel." Exodus identifies Israel's origins as an oppressed people, one not at home in the foreign land of Egypt (Exod 1:8-14). It is a people heard by God (Exod 3:7) even before the divine name is revealed to them (4:29-31); God relates to Israel even before Israel knows fully who their God is and well before they enter into the formal covenant relationship (Exod 19–40). Because Israel is God's people, "the God of Israel" is one key way for identifying the Lord. From the book of Exodus on, the Lord is "the God of Israel," and knowledge of the One God in the universe, whether for the Egyptians or for other peoples, comes through Israel (Exod 7:5; 8:6, etc.). Exodus not only tells the story of Israel's identity; it also explains who God is.

The exodus provided a model for expressing Israel's collective passage from persecution to freedom in a renewed relationship with God. In the sixth century B.C., the book of Isaiah could proclaim the impending return from exile in Babylon to Jerusalem precisely as a second exodus: "In the wilderness prepare the way of the LORD! / Make straight in the wasteland a highway for our God!" (Isa 40:3). Echoing Exodus, the first-century author of the book of Wisdom addresses the problem of reward for the just and punishment for the wicked: "For by the things through which their foes [the Egyptians] were punished / they [the Israelites] in their need were benefited" (Wis 11:5). The exodus was also celebrated in Israel's worship and used as an ongoing model for exploring its relationship with God. Psalm 105 focuses on the exodus for examples of God's "wondrous deeds" (v. 5), and Psalm 106 uses the same story to illustrate Israel's failures.

The early church likewise drew on the exodus for inspiration. As Jews, the early Christians adopted and adapted Passover and Pentecost in their experience of Jesus as the Paschal Lamb (Paschal referring to Passover) and the coming of the Spirit. The imagery of the Passover is explicit in the events of Easter, as the gospels locate the events of Jesus' death and resurrection at the time of the Passover (also called the feast of Unleavened Bread). The Last Supper was evidently understood by some of the gospel writers as a Passover meal. Luke explicitly uses the language of Exodus for Jesus' passage from persecution to the exaltation of the Father (Luke 9:31). Paul uses a traditional Jewish preaching strategy in referring symbolically to human corruption as food with yeast or leavening (removed from Jewish households during the feast of Passover/Unleavened Bread): "Clear out the old yeast, so that you may become a fresh batch of dough, inasmuch as you are unleavened. For our paschal lamb, Christ, has been sacrificed. Therefore let us celebrate the feast, not with the old yeast, the yeast of malice and wickedness, but with the unleavened bread of sincerity and truth" (1 Cor 5:7-8).

The Christian use of the imagery of Weeks may not be as obvious for the feast of Pentecost, but it is there in a very deep way. Following seven weeks after Passover, Weeks celebrates the giving of the Law through Moses in order to guide the Jewish people. So too in a parallel way, following fifty days after Easter, Pentecost celebrates the giving of the Spirit through the figure of Jesus in order to guide the Christian community. The coming of the Spirit in fire on Pentecost Sunday (Acts 2:2-3) echoes the fire of God blazing on Mount Sinai (Exod 19:18).

Passover, commanded as one of three annual pilgrimage feasts, becomes the occasion for retelling and reliving the exodus, and this celebration is complete in the pilgrimage feast of Weeks (Pentecost), which in late biblical tradition celebrates the giving of the covenant and law on Mount Sinai.

Exodus tells its audience that Passover is a feast "which your future genera-tions will celebrate with pilgrimage to the LORD . . . as a statute forever" (12:14). The book is designed not simply to convey information about the past; it also invites readers to participate in this event for themselves. Ac-cordingly, Exodus was intended to be both informative and performative: it provides information about where Israel's ancestors came from and who they were; and it invites participation by their descendants to ritually per-form this identity story for themselves.

The later Jewish celebration of the Passover beautifully captures the performative spirit of the book of Exodus: the identity story of the Israelite ancestors becomes the identity story of their Jewish descendants forever. The Jewish retelling of the Passover story says, "In each generation, every person should feel as though he or she had actually been redeemed from Egypt, as it is said [quoting Exod 13:8]: 'You should tell your children on that day, saying, "It is because of what the Lord did for me when I went free out of Egypt."' For the Holy One (Blessed be He) redeemed not only our ancestors; He redeemed us with them." The past is not simply celebrated in the present, nor is the past merely the model for the present. The present experience is the reality shaped and informed by the past event.

Thanks to the early church's Jewish foundations, Christians participate in their own way in this narrative of freedom and relationship with the God of Israel. In their eucharistic meal, Christians experience the ancient events surrounding the Last Supper as a living, present reality made pos-sible through Jesus' mystical presence. Reading the book of Exodus, too, was meant to be a "sacramental" experience: not simply a reading of some past events, but a reading of present reality informed and shaped by the foundational events of the past.

Historical background of the exodus

Egyptian records are as silent as the Sphinx regarding the event of the exodus. Yet it is not surprising that Moses' dealings with Pharaoh do not get even a footnote in Egyptian history. Egyptian texts serve to exalt the glory of the Pharaohs and their deities. Moreover, from the Egyptians' perspective the Israelites were a relatively unimportant group, one that merited their attention only years after the event of the exodus. (There is only one reference to Israel in Egyptian records before the time of David and Solomon.)

The lack of Egyptian evidence is hardly proof that the exodus did not happen at least in some form. As the famous scholarly dictum expresses the point, "Absence of evidence is not evidence of absence." It is plausible that despite Egyptian silence about it, the exodus took place (even if the biblical memory elaborated the event). There are reasons to think that a historical event might lie behind the biblical account. It has been long noted that the names of Moses, Aaron, Hur, Merari, and Phinehas are Egyptian in origin and not Hebrew (Moses' name is related to the Egyptian element contained in the name of the Pharaoh Thut-mose, "the god Thut is born"). Some scholars would regard it as odd for these Egyptian names to be in the Israelite record if some major contact with Egyptian culture had not been a part of the Israelite historical experience. A further argument has also been marshaled in support of seeing an event behind the book of Exodus. If the exodus was originally a "made-up story," it seems odd to many that a people would have concocted a story of slavery for their origins (kingship in Mesopotamia, in contrast, was thought to have descended from heaven). Because of these considerations, a number of scholars see some historical kernel embedded in the exodus account.

The skepticism of some scholars about the exodus event helps all researchers to be as honest as possible in examining historical claims. Scholarship reminds us that the book of Exodus, as handed down to us, was written hundreds of years after the events that it narrates. As a result, the precise nature of the historical kernel is impossible to discern from the biblical record. Did the exodus involve as many people as the 600,000 Israelite males, "not counting the children" or the "crowd of mixed ancestry," as claimed in Exodus 12:37-38 (compare the 603,550 of Num 1:46 and the 601,730 of Num 26:51)? Did God really intervene miraculously at the Sea of Reeds by creating walls of waters through which the Israelites crossed (Exod 14:22), or did it involve a more naturalistic picture of an escape attributed to God's saving power (Exod 15)? Did the exodus really take place all at once, or could it have involved multiple departures, with different memories as to the routes taken (possibly with even different interpretations attached to them)? Was the God of the exodus really Yahweh, or was it El (cf. Num 24:8) before the two deities were identified (cf. Exod 6:2-3)?

Such questions lay beyond the grasp of historians to answer clearly. Instead, the biblical record as it now stands expresses Israelite faith in a single exodus event made possible by the God of Israel. There are many layers of material in the text of Exodus, identified by many scholars according the so-called Documentary Hypothesis. This theory holds that four sources of the Pentateuch (the first five books of the Old Testament) as well as their arrangement together by one or more later scribes were produced during the reigns of the Israelite kings and afterward. These multiple levels alert us to the fact that the book of Exodus itself contains not only the record of

Israelites leaving Egypt but also several interpretations of the event. For example, the crossing of the sea in the poem of Exodus 15 looks natural, but the prose account of the same event in Exodus 14 contains elements that might be characterized as supernatural. Both natural and supernatural are expressions of faith in a God who has the power and will to redeem. Our biblical text combines event and interpretation.

The setting of the exodus

Although neither Egyptian records nor the biblical accounts provide any historical report in the modern sense of the term, there are some indications about the setting of the exodus in the Bible. Most scholars place the exodus in the thirteenth century B.C. According to these scholars, the Pharaoh who oppressed the Israelites was Rameses II (sometimes called Rameses the Great), the great builder who ruled around 1290 to 1224 B.C. One reason given for this view is the testimony in Exodus 1:11 that refers to the supply city of Raamses, which this Pharaoh is thought to have had built. It is known that Rameses II established his capital in the Nile Delta and that the term "city of Raamses" was not used after 1100 B.C.

Exodus 1–2 suggests a more complicated picture, if it is historically accurate. These chapters refer to three Egyptian kings: one who knew Joseph; a second who did not (1:8) and who oppressed the Israelites (1:8-14); and a third who continued the Israelites' slavery while Moses was in Midian (2:23). Rameses II is sometimes thought to be the Pharaoh of the exodus for whom the Israelites help build the store-cities mentioned in Exodus 1:11 and that it was his predecessor with whom Joseph and his family enjoyed such good relations. Other authorities would identify Rameses II as both the oppressor and the Pharaoh of the exodus as a single Pharaoh. Either way, the exodus would have occurred around 1250 B.C.

In contrast, other scholars wish to date these events to the fifteenth century B.C., in part based on 1 Kings 6:1, which dates the exodus to 480 years before Solomon's construction of the temple (ca. 970 B.C.). If this date were to be preferred, then it would be possible to situate the exodus against the backdrop of Egyptian records that complain about the activities of foreign Habiru; some scholars would like to identify them with the biblical word Hebrews, but many other scholars dispute this equation. Despite these uncertainties, most scholars still prefer a date in the thirteenth century. At the same time, one must openly admit that the precise dates are simply not known.

Literary forms, structure, and features

Modern readers often come to the Bible with the expectation that it provides accurate historical reporting of the events it depicts; it is often thought that the divine inspiration of the Bible guarantees its historical accuracy. Yet the book of Exodus is not history writing in the modern sense of the term. It includes a wide variety of genres or types of literature: genealogies (in chs. 1 and 6); stories of various sorts, including the call narrative of Moses (chs. 3–4), the plague stories (chs. 7–11), a poem (ch. 15), the travelogues and complaint narratives (chs. 15–17), and the story of Moses' intercession with God after the worship of the Golden Calf (chs. 32–34); commandments (chs. 20–23) and priestly instructions for worship (chs. 25–31 and 35–40). The variety of literary genres suggests that the exodus events were sources of reflection at various points in Israel's tradition. The core message proclaiming divine redemption of Israel from Egyptian oppression and the salvation of the eternal covenant on Sinai was celebrated throughout Israel's history. Scholarly analysis of Exodus has led commentators to see the book itself as the product of such reflection on the foundational events in Egypt and Sinai.

Within the book, scholars have discerned not only different genres but also different styles, vocabulary, and perspectives belonging to various writers or traditions. For decades, the dominant theory used to explain these differences was the Documentary Hypothesis, which holds that four sources of the Pentateuch as well as their arrangement together by one or more later scribal editors were produced during the reigns of the Israelite kings and afterwards. Other theories emphasizing different concurrent traditions in dialogue with one another have been proposed as well.

Whatever approach proves true, it is evident that priestly concerns mark the prescriptions in chapters 25–31 and their execution in chapters 35–40. Moreover, priestly emphasis on the figure of Aaron (the prototype for the chief priest), for example, in Exodus 6:13–7:6 (over and above 4:10-17) likewise suggests a priestly hand. Accordingly, we may see the priestly concern for priestly personnel and space (often abbreviated as P) in these chapters and elsewhere (for example, in the priestly description of the tabernacle, etc., in chs. 25–31 and 35–40). This priestly tradition probably extended over a long period of time, from at least the eighth century down through the period following the return from exile in Babylon, when priestly rule governed the internal workings of Israel under the Persian Empire.

The other narrative material in Exodus, according to the Documentary Hypothesis (also called "source-criticism"), was divided into three other sources: the Yahwist (J), whose popular, suspenseful storytelling was produced in Judah anywhere from the tenth century to the sixth; the Elohist (E), a northern source with its emphasis on the fear (or better, reverence) of God, variously dated to the ninth through seventh century, and familiar with the prophetic milieu that produced the Elijah and Elisha stories of 1 Kings 17–2 Kings 13; and the Deuteronomist (dtr), a source identified largely based on similarities with the book of Deuteronomy (for example, in the Passover prescription in Exod 13). Material to be attributed to the Deuteronomist editor is relatively rare, and the E source is often tightly worked into the J material (in fact, one may represent the redaction of the other). Some scholars have further divided priestly material into priestly texts (P) and "Holiness School" (H) texts that have terms and expressions found in the Holiness Code of Leviticus 17–26 rather than other priestly material.

Without getting bogged down in the technical details of this source-criticism, for the purposes of this commentary it is sufficient to understand that the book of Exodus basically divides into priestly material (P and H) on the one hand and non-priestly material on the other (JE with some of the Deuteronomist material occasionally included) as well as regulations that may not derive from any of these sources. In the commentary these sources are mentioned, but issues about sources do not dominate the discussion.

There is an important theological value in noting the diversity of authors and their styles. It shows that ancient Israel cherished a variety of literary means to present its story: what is entertaining (the dramatic poem of Exod 15, or the suspenseful stories of the J source) as well as what is perhaps a bit shocking to modern sensibilities (for example, Moses as magician or his marriage to a non-Israelite) are preserved along with the morally uplifting tenor of E's theme of fear of God and with priestly narrative and ritual. Furthermore, these layers of material show that the biblical tradition reflected more and more deeply on the events that shaped the identity of ancient Israel. Finally, the tradition retained the variety of viewpoints expressed in the book. As a result, the canonized book preserves not only a record of past events but also the history of Israel's dialogue over their meaning.

Despite their variety, the genres (or categories) and sources (or traditions) did not result in a haphazard collection of material. Instead, the material now contained in Exodus passed through the hands of various scribal editors who shaped it in a way intended to provide a sense of literary balance and religious connection. The final editors seem to have belonged to the priestly tradition in ancient Israel. These priestly editors of Exodus placed a tremendous emphasis on Mount Sinai as the site of God's definitive revelation and covenant. As a result, priestly material dominates in the Sinai covenant not only in Exodus 25–31 and 35–40 but also the entire priestly book of Leviticus.

These priestly editors also seem to be responsible for the placement of the older poem into chapter 15. This piece of poetry marks the book's thematic midpoint between Egypt, the land of slavery, and Sinai, the mountain of freedom. As the book's fulcrum, the poem helps to create a literary balance that relates the Egypt story beforehand to the Sinai covenant afterwards. As a result, the journey of Moses to the mountain of God in chapter 2 seems to anticipate the journey of Moses and the people to the mountain of God in chapters 15–18. Both journeys are modeled on the audience's experience of making pilgrimage journeys to sanctuaries that were traditionally regarded as the mountain of God (for example, Ps 15:1 referring to Jerusalem as God's "holy mountain"). Similarly, the two divine calls of Moses and his confrontations with Pharaoh in Exodus 3–15 seem to structurally echo the two sets of covenant tablets in Exodus 19–40. In the case of both, the initial effort fails, only to be followed by a second effort that is successful. Moses' initial call in chapters 3–4 is followed by an unsuccessful meeting with Pharaoh, a turn of events reversed following Moses' second call in chapters 6–7. Similarly, the Israelites' worship of the golden calf in chapter 32 represents an initial failure (signaled by Moses' smashing of the first set of tablets), evidently reversed with the second set of tablets. As a result of this priestly handling of various older texts, there emerges a picture of divine care for Israel which does not end on the first try. Instead, despite initial failure because of human resistance, God persistently works for Israel's deliverance.

Finally, it is important to note that the ancient authors and editors of Exodus often used language that deliberately echoes other passages in Scripture, especially the book of Genesis. The effect of such verbal resonances often indicates a pattern of divine purpose and redemption from the beginning of creation through the Sinai covenant (e. g., the Genesis creation story echoed in Exod 1 and 39–40). These writers enjoyed a high level of literary sophistication. Some of the techniques that they used and the religious message which they intended to convey through these techniques are noted in the commentary.

The sort of scholarly discussion involved with the Documentary Hypothesis and its four sources can be difficult to handle as readers try to read the Bible for spiritual benefit. It may be helpful to think of such scholarly notions as indicating that behind the Bible is a long tradition that discussed and wrestled with the hard issues: Does God care? What is the nature of God? How does Israel know God? How should Israel respond to God's actions in its midst and in the world? Out of this tradition emerged a number of voices: some prophetic (this seems to be the view of E); others priestly in concern and tone (so the P source or tradition). The prophetic and priestly voices had long been associated with God's own voices, while others, such as the material associated with J, show the hallmarks of a more popular voice, one that might not have been viewed as originally revelatory. Yet in time these voices were melded into a single literary progression that presented an original divine word as the last word.

The ongoing message of the exodus

The exodus story continues to inspire readers of the Bible. Throughout Jewish communities around the world and in Israel, the exodus is the single most celebrated holiday. The exodus story in the Passover meal returns Jewish families year in and year out to its fundamental message that God brought Israel out of oppression and into an eternal covenant. The story has provided inspiration and calls to action through various episodes of oppression against Jews.

The influence of the exodus story runs deep also in the church's struggle for justice in various parts of the world. In Central and South America, liberation theology has used the exodus story to understand and work against political oppression. Liberation theology applies the ancient story of Israel's bondage and subsequent deliverance to the circumstances of exploitation that have characterized a great deal of Latin American history, including the actions of the church itself. Closer to home in churches in the United States, the exodus story has continued to move people to justice, again within and outside the church. Time and time again, Martin Luther King Jr. returned to the story of the exodus to exhort his audiences to work for freedom in their communities. On the night before he died, Reverend King at a church in Memphis delivered a speech that would become famous, "I've Been to the Mountaintop." Responding to a hypothetical question from God Almighty as to what age he would like to live in, Reverend King begins, "I would take my mental flight by Egypt, and I would watch God's children in their magnificent trek from the dark dungeons of Egypt through, or rather, across the Red Sea, through the wilderness, on toward the Promised Land. And in spite of its magnificence, I wouldn't stop there." In Reverend King's speech the struggle for freedom did not end with the exodus but is part of human history down to his own time with his struggle for civil rights. For Reverend King, the time of the exodus that ultimately mattered was his own time; and so too it is for us now. The exodus is not only an ancient story of a great, divine deliverance. It is also today's story, calling all people to work against oppression and to participate in a covenant relationship with one another and with God.

The Book of Exodus

I. Introduction:
The Oppression of the Israelites
in Egypt

1 **Jacob's Descendants in Egypt.** [1]These are the names of the sons of Israel who, accompanied by their households, entered into Egypt with Jacob: [2]Reuben, Simeon, Levi and Judah; [3]Issachar, Zebulun and Benjamin; [4]Dan and Naphtali; Gad and Asher. [5]The total number of Jacob's direct descendants was seventy. Joseph was already in Egypt.

[6]Now Joseph and all his brothers and that whole generation died. [7]But the Israelites were fruitful and prolific. They multiplied and became so very numerous that the land was filled with them.

PART I: OUT OF EGYPT

Exodus (1:1–15:21)

The first part of Exodus relates the beginnings of Israel as a people, Moses' origins and his relationship to the people, and God's redemption of the people from slavery in Egypt. The various sources or traditions embedded in the book explore many questions: How did the Israelites become slaves in Egypt? How did Moses become their leader? What did it take for Moses to be leader? How did Moses deal with Pharaoh? What finally made Pharaoh agree to release the Israelites? What happened at the Reed Sea as they departed? What did God do for them at the Sea?

1:1-7 Israel in Egypt

This introduction begins by listing "the sons of Israel" (an expression for the Israelites). Verses 1-5 briefly retell the story of Jacob (Israel) traveling with his household down to Egypt, a story that refers back to Genesis 46. Verse 6 refers to the end of Genesis 50, with the death of Joseph. The mention of the earlier circumstances of Jacob and Joseph reminds readers of God's earlier deliverance of the family from the famine in Canaan, and it sets the

▶ This symbol indicates a cross reference number in the *Catechism of the Catholic Church*. See page 141 for number citations.

15

The Oppression. [8]Then a new king, who knew nothing of Joseph, rose to power in Egypt. [9]He said to his people, "See! The Israelite people have multiplied and become more numerous than we are! [10]Come, let us deal shrewdly with them to stop their increase; otherwise, in time of war they too may join our enemies to fight against us, and so leave the land."

[11]Accordingly, they set supervisors over the Israelites to oppress them with forced labor. Thus they had to build for Pharaoh the garrison cities of Pithom and Raamses. [12]Yet the more they were oppressed, the more they multiplied and spread, so that the Egyptians began to loathe the Israelites. [13]So the Egyptians reduced the Israelites to cruel slavery, [14]making life bitter for them with hard

stage for Exodus' story of danger and redemption. These verses provide further information about the Israelites in Egypt. They are "fruitful and prolific . . . the land was filled with them," which is an echo of the divine command in the Priestly (P) creation story of Genesis 1:28 ("Be fertile and multiply; fill the earth . . ."). The genealogy and the echo of the priestly passage of Genesis 1:28 suggest that the priestly tradition provided this introduction to the exodus story. The priestly prose of Exodus is thought to have been written any time during the end of the monarchy, the exile in Babylon, or after the return to the land under Persian authority. Apart from some brief exceptions, all these periods were ones of significant testing of Israelite faith. The introduction faces these difficulties and offers an expression of encouragement and a sign of hope that the divine promise made to Abraham (Gen 17) began to be fulfilled in Egypt and will continue to come to pass despite difficult circumstances.

1:8-14 The oppression of God's people

The passage introduces new circumstances between Egyptians and Israelites, mentioned at the beginning and end of the unit (vv. 7-8 and 13). Like a new boss or political leader who does not recognize earlier working relationships or ways of doing things, the new pharaoh introduces a note of tension into the scene. Both his lack of a prior relationship with Joseph and Israel's increased growth fuel fear in the new pharaoh. Despite the Israelites' positive relationship with his predecessor, the new pharaoh expresses his fear of a potential threat of an alliance with outsiders in wartime. It is unclear why Pharaoh thinks such things about the Israelites, but because he speaks his words "to his people" (instead of just saying them to himself), the pharaoh sets up a divide between himself and his people over and against the Israelites; perhaps he perceives them as outsiders. Fear of outsiders was a common theme of Egyptian texts of the New Kingdom, and it may serve as reason enough. Yet this is only implicit (v. 9); readers are left in the dark as

labor, at mortar and brick and all kinds of field work—cruelly oppressed in all their labor.

Command to the Midwives. [15]The king of Egypt told the Hebrew midwives, one of whom was called Shiphrah and the other Puah, [16]"When you act as midwives for the Hebrew women, look on the birthstool: if it is a boy, kill him; but if it is a girl, she may live." [17]The midwives, however, feared God; they did not do as the king of Egypt had ordered them, but let the boys live. [18]So the king of Egypt summoned the midwives and asked them, "Why have you done this, allowing the boys to live?" [19]The midwives answered Pharaoh, "The Hebrew women are not like the Egyptian women. They are robust and give birth before the midwife arrives." [20]Therefore God dealt well with the midwives; and the people multiplied and grew very numerous. [21]And because the midwives feared God, God built up families for them. [22]Pharaoh then commanded all his people, "Throw into the Nile every boy that is born, but you may let all the girls live."

---

to any further reasoning behind Pharaoh's thinking. By leaving unanswered the question as to why one in a position of superior power comes to fear the Israelites, the story opens with a heightened level of anxiety.

The Egyptians join Pharaoh in taking action against the Israelites (1:11-14). Enslavement provides a profitable mechanism of control, and it leads to an increased death rate. The story, however, gives no reason for the choice of slavery as the response to the perceived threat (and in any event, the readers of this story know that it will not work). The story introduces an Egyptian flavor into the story in referring to Egyptian store-cities by name. Raamses was a city built by Rameses II; it is generally identified with Qantir. Its full name in Egyptian was "Houses of Rameses, Beloved of the god Amun, great of victories." Pithom means "House [or domain, i.e., estate] of the god, Atum"; its location is debated. Yet even within the difficult circumstances, the divine promise was not thwarted, as the Israelites "multiplied and spread" (v. 12). At this point, Pharaoh's fear has become the dread of the Egyptians as a whole. In a sense, the Egyptians and the Israelites are mysteries to one another. The Israelites have no understanding of why they are enslaved, and the Egyptians do not understand why the Israelites continue to grow despite enslavement. The gaps in understanding generate an unresolved tension. With the new threat of danger introduced, the remainder of part 1 of the book continuously builds toward its resolution.

1:15-22 From enslavement to the threat of genocide

In verses 15-16 Pharaoh decides to act against the Israelite population increase by forcing the help of two Israelite midwives, Shiphrah ("Beauty") and Puah ("Girl"?). The episode reflects what many critics regard as a motif

2 **Birth and Adoption of Moses.** ¹Now a man of the house of Levi married a Levite woman, ²and the woman conceived and bore a son. Seeing what a fine child he was, she hid him for three months. ³But when she could no longer hide him, she took a papyrus basket, daubed it with bitumen and pitch, and putting the child in it, placed it among the reeds on the bank of the Nile. ⁴His sister stationed herself at a distance to find out what would happen to him.

⁵Then Pharaoh's daughter came down to bathe at the Nile, while her attendants walked along the bank of the Nile. Noticing the basket among the reeds, she sent her handmaid to fetch it. ⁶On opening it, she looked, and there

---

of the Elohist (E) source, the fear or reverence of God (see Gen 20:11; Exod 20:20). It is this emphasis on fear of God (v. 17) that leads to the midwives' civil disobedience. Before any male leadership appears in Exodus, the two women know how to act rightly without God's telling them, even in the most difficult of circumstances. Thanks to the midwives, the people of Israel continue to increase (v. 20), a reward that is highlighted for their households (v. 21). The narrative introduces God into the story for the first time, in this case not as a divine agent acting center stage but as standing behind the scene while the two women act courageously. Failing to enlist the aid of the two midwives, Pharaoh turns to his own people to have every male Israelite drowned (v. 22). While Pharaoh needs the help of others to carry out his will, God's will is enacted without any divine action taken.

The passage reads nicely in a straightforward manner, yet it also creates a structure which arranges phrases in an inverted series of parallels (called chiasms):

A Pharaoh's directive to the midwives to kill the male infants
(vv. 15-16)
    B The midwives' fear of God and their refusal to obey Pharaoh
    (v. 17)
        C Pharaoh's reaction to the midwives' refusal and the
        midwives' response (vv. 18-19)
        C' God's reaction to their refusal and the effect on the people
        (v. 20)
    B' The midwives' fear of God and their reward (v. 21)
A' Pharaoh's command to his people to kill the male infants (v. 22)

One basic contrast reflected in this structure is the vast superiority of the Israelites to any power wielded by Pharaoh. Even humble Israelite midwives are presented as outsmarting the Pharaoh, who has aspirations to divinity. These women are the first model of spirituality presented in

19

Head of the southernmost colossus of Rameses II, Temple of Rames

was a baby boy crying! She was moved with pity for him and said, "It is one of the Hebrews' children." ⁷Then his sister asked Pharaoh's daughter, "Shall I go and summon a Hebrew woman to nurse the child for you?" ⁸Pharaoh's daughter answered her, "Go." So the young woman went and called the child's own mother. ⁹Pharaoh's daughter said to her, "Take this child and nurse him for me, and I will pay your wages." So the woman took the child and nursed him. ¹⁰When the child grew, she brought him to Pharaoh's daughter, and he became

Exodus. They do not receive communication from God, yet they know what is right and they act on this knowledge. Here they differ not only from Moses and Aaron later in Exodus but also from the male models of Genesis: Abraham, who enjoys direct communication with God; Isaac, who shows no such initiative or brave act as do the midwives; and Jacob, who struggles with God. As the midwives do not enjoy communication with God yet know how to act rightly, they are emblematic not only of women but of Israelites in general. The Bible's human models of spirituality differ rather dramatically, yet God chooses to work through all of them.

2:1-10 The birth and salvation of Moses

This passage highlights the role of women in Israel's salvation, for the unnamed women help Moses survive. Being born to parents of the priestly tribe of Levi (v. 1), Moses stands within the ranks of priestly leadership. (This non-priestly passage does not seem to have a tradition of the parents' names, unlike Moses' priestly genealogy in Exod 6:20, which gives Amram and Jochebed as their names.) Moses' mother sees that Moses is "fine," or, literally, "good" (apparently echoing priestly creation language in Gen 1:4, 10, 18, 21, 31), and she bravely hides her son (v. 2), an act that again reflects the female courage. Her hiding Moses in a "basket" also echoes the story of Noah. The Hebrew word chosen for "basket" in verse 3 is the same word for Noah's ark in Genesis 6–9; these are the only biblical passages that use this word. The word choice suggests that like Noah's ark, Moses passes through the threatening waters and survives. His passage through the waters also anticipates his passage with the Israelites through the sea in Exodus 14–15. With him at this point in his life (v. 4) is his sister; here she goes unnamed, but later she is Miriam, who will lead the singing with the women of Israel after the Israelites pass through the sea (Exod 15:20-21). In Exodus 2:4 Moses' sister shows a concern that captures and directs the audience's concern for Moses: what will happen to him?

In verse 5 yet another female acts on Moses' behalf. This time Pharaoh's daughter enters the picture. Opening the basket (v. 6), she sees the baby crying, perhaps anticipating the cries of Israelites later in this chapter

her son. She named him Moses; for she said, "I drew him out of the water."

Moses' Flight to Midian. [11]On one occasion, after Moses had grown up, when he had gone out to his kinsmen and witnessed their forced labor, he saw an Egyptian striking a Hebrew, one of his own kinsmen. [12]Looking about and seeing no one, he struck down the Egyptian and hid him in the sand. [13]The next day he went out again, and now two Hebrews were fighting! So he asked the culprit, "Why are you striking your companion?" [14]But he replied, "Who has appointed you ruler and judge over us? Are you thinking of killing me as you killed the Egyptian?" Then Moses became afraid and thought, "The affair must certainly be known." [15]When Pharaoh heard of the affair, he sought to kill

---

(v. 23). Her compassion for the baby crosses ethnic boundaries, and she reverses the will of her father in saving Moses; she recognizes that the baby is a "Hebrew" (a term sometimes used by non-Israelites for Israelites). In verse 7 Moses' sister returns to the story at just the right moment to offer to find a nurse, and the passage comes full circle in reintroducing Moses' mother in verse 8. Moses' mother returns to her maternal role in verse 9. Together all of these women act heroically in saving the human hero from destruction.

The name given to Moses in verse 10 offers a summary of the action in this section. His name makes a wordplay on the Hebrew word "to draw" (*mšh). The name is actually Egyptian (as in the name Thut-mose). The "cultural amnesia" about the origins of Moses' name suggests that his Egyptian background or experience may bear some kernel of historical authenticity. The Hebrew interpretation given to Moses' name aims to proclaim the message of divine salvation from life-threatening peril represented by the waters (cf. 2 Sam 22:17 and Ps 18:17 where the same word is used in David's describing his divine rescue from the waters of the underworld).

As in the preceding passage, this one uses a structure that highlights the role of the women in the action:

    A Moses' parents and his birth
        B His mother hides him in a basket
            C The sister positions herself
                D The princess finds him
            C' The sister makes an offer
        B' The mother becomes his nurse
    A' Moses is adopted and named

The structure highlights Moses' salvation through the Egyptian princess (D), flanked by the help of his sister (C and C') and his mother (B and B').

Moses. But Moses fled from Pharaoh and went to the land of Midian. There he sat down by a well.

¹⁶Now the priest of Midian had seven daughters, and they came to draw water and fill the troughs to water their father's flock. ¹⁷But shepherds came and drove them away. So Moses rose up in their defense and watered their flock. ¹⁸When they returned to their father Reuel, he said to them, "How is it you have returned so soon today?" ¹⁹They answered, "An Egyptian delivered us from the shepherds. He even drew water for us and watered the flock!" ²⁰"Where is he?" he asked his daughters. "Why did you leave the man there? Invite him to have something to eat." ²¹Moses agreed to stay with him, and the man gave Moses his daughter Zipporah in marriage. ²²She

The story of Moses' miraculous delivery enjoys important parallels in ancient Middle Eastern literature. The birth legend of Sargon, which was current during the later part of Israel's monarchy, may even have inspired this account of Moses. According to the legend of Sargon, his mother (a priestess, perhaps not permitted to have children) places him in a basket of rushes that she seals with bitumen. After he is found and drawn out (by Aqqi, drawer of water), he was adopted and later becomes king. The similarities between the baby stories of Sargon and Moses are quite striking. The biblical story further stresses the role of the various women in advancing the divine plan.

2:11-22 From manslaughter to Midian

These passages link Moses' life to the destiny of his people. Faced with the conflict between an Egyptian taskmaster and a Hebrew slave, the adult Moses is moved to intervene (vv. 11-12). The text presents the act neutrally, neither praising nor condemning it, and the author evidently presupposed that an Israelite audience would assume that Moses is siding with his "kindred" (as he calls them in 4:18) and against his adopted people. Moses' effort to conceal his crime is unsuccessful. When he intervenes a second time, this time between "two Hebrews," they question his authority (a motif that will be picked up again in Exod 16–17 when the people quarrel with him in the wilderness). Now he knows that his crime is known (v. 14). Knowledge of the deed reaches Pharaoh, who seeks justice of "a life for a life." Facing the possibility of a death sentence, Moses flees to the land of Midian (v. 15).

Other figures of ancient Middle Eastern literature leave their homeland for refuge in the wilds of Syria-Palestine, for example, Sinuhe of Egypt and Idrimi of Alalakh; in both cases, such journeys eventuate in their elevation back at home. Sinuhe in particular flees Egypt, lives with a tent-dwelling Bedouin and marries his daughter, and later returns to Egypt. The same is true of Moses. His deed stands in some contrast to the midwives' of the

conceived and bore a son, whom he named Gershom; for he said, "I am a stranger residing in a foreign land."

II. The Call and Commission of Moses

The Burning Bush. [23]A long time passed, during which the king of Egypt died. The Israelites groaned under their bondage and cried out, and from their bondage their cry for help went up to God. [24]God heard their moaning and God was mindful of his covenant with Abraham, Isaac and Jacob. [25]God saw the Israelites, and God knew. . . .

3 [1] Meanwhile Moses was tending the flock of his father-in-law Jethro, the priest of Midian. Leading the flock beyond the wilderness, he came to the mountain of God, Horeb. [2]There the angel of the LORD appeared to him as fire flaming out of a bush. When he looked, although the bush was on fire, it was not being consumed. [3]So Moses decided, "I must turn aside to look at this remarkable sight. Why does the bush not burn up?" [4]When the LORD saw that he had turned aside to look, God called out to him from the bush: Moses! Moses! He answered, "Here I am." [5]God said: Do not come near! Remove your sandals from your feet, for the place where you stand is holy ground. [6]I am the God of your father, he continued, the

---

preceding chapter: where they fear God (1:17), he fears for his life (2:14). Where their deed of saving Israelite life is regarded as a righteous act rewarded by God, Moses' deed of killing an Egyptian is relatively ambiguous in its moral quality, and it leads to self-imposed exile. Despite mixed signals, the divine plan proceeds toward Midian.

The land of Midian was a desert area located in the northwest corner of modern-day Saudi Arabia (reflected in St. Paul's mention of "Sinai, a mountain in Arabia," in Gal 4:25). In early biblical tradition the area, which is designated by a number of names (Seir, Teman, Paran, and Edom), is associated with God's southern mountain of Sinai (cf. Judg 5:4-5; Deut 33:2; Ps 68:9; Hab 3:3, 7). Moses is said to dwell there for some amount of time before he comes and sits at a well, a traditional site of meetings between men and women, where he meets Reuel's seven daughters (cf. Rebecca in Gen 24:15 and Rachel in 29:10). Their father is called Jethro in Exodus 3:1; 4:18; and 18:1; in Judges 4:11 he is named Hobab, but Numbers 10:29 regards Hobab as the son of Reuel. In the case of Judges 4:11 and Numbers 10:29 there seems to be some conflicting recollection about Hobab's identity; in contrast, both Reuel and Jethro are names only for Moses' father-in-law. Attempts have been made to see one of these two names as a mistake, either in the tradition or because of a scribal error. Another possibility is to regard Reuel as a tribal name and Jethro as the man's specific name. It is also possible that multiple traditions for the name existed.

God of Abraham, the God of Isaac, and the God of Jacob. Moses hid his face, for he was afraid to look at God.

The Call and Commission of Moses. [7]But the LORD said: I have witnessed the affliction of my people in Egypt and have heard their cry against their taskmasters, so I know well what they are suffering. [8]Therefore I have come down to rescue them from the power of the Egyptians and lead them up from that land into a good and spacious land, a land flowing with milk and honey, the country of the Canaanites, the Hittites, the Amorites, the Perizzites, the Girgashites, the Hivites and the Jebusites. [9]Now indeed the outcry of the Israelites has reached me, and I have seen how the Egyptians are oppressing them. [10]Now, go! I am sending you to Pharaoh to bring my people, the Israelites, out of Egypt.

[11]But Moses said to God, "Who am I that I should go to Pharaoh and bring the Israelites out of Egypt?" [12]God answered: I will be with you; and this will be your sign that I have sent you. When you have brought the people out of Egypt, you will serve God at this mountain. [13]"But," said Moses to God, "if I go to the Israelites and say to them, 'The God of your ancestors has sent me to you,' and they ask me, 'What is his name?' what do I tell them?" [14]God replied to Moses: I am who I am. Then he added: This is what you will tell the Israelites: I AM has sent me to you.

[15]God spoke further to Moses: This is what you will say to the Israelites: The LORD, the God of your ancestors, the God of Abraham, the God of Isaac, and the God of Jacob, has sent me to you.

This is my name forever;
this is my title for all
generations.

[16]Go and gather the elders of the Israelites, and tell them, The Lord, the God of your ancestors, the God of Abraham,

---

After Moses helps the sisters fend off intruders, he is invited to their father's household (vv. 17-21). This sort of story was evidently quite popular. The Egyptian tale of Sinuhe narrates the hospitality that the hero receives from a local leader in Syria-Palestine, followed by marriage to one of his daughters. In Moses' case, hospitality leads to his marriage to Zipporah and the birth of their son, Gershom, whose name emblemizes Moses' situation as a "stranger residing in a foreign land." Moses' marriage echoes an ancient tradition linking the Midianites with the Israelites. Early, the Midianites were probably traders allied and intermarried with Israelites; later this positive relationship turned hostile (see Judg 6–7).

2:23–3:22 The burning bush and the call of Moses

The scene goes back to Egypt with information that the king of Egypt died (v. 23). The slavery of the Israelites continues despite the change of pharaohs, and as a result, the Israelites groan and cry out to God, who hears and recalls the covenant with the patriarchs (vv. 23-24). This presentation

Isaac, and Jacob, has appeared to me and said: I have observed you and what is being done to you in Egypt; [17]so I have decided to lead you up out of your affliction in Egypt into the land of the Canaanites, the Hittites, the Amorites, the

---

recalls the communal liturgy of lamentation in the psalms that ask God to hear their prayer and remember the covenant (e.g., Ps 74, in particular v. 20). The prayer is thought to go up to God in heaven (v. 23), who then hears the prayer and is reminded of the covenant (v. 24). The model for such prayer is human petition made to a superior in the treaty or covenant relationship, who then is reminded of the urgent matter. As the superior party, God pays attention to the prayer of the Israelites; God is said to see them and know (v. 25). The phrasing is a bit awkward in English (note the inconclusive dots at the end of v. 25), but the verb "to know" is a hallmark of covenantal language, indicating that God, the overlord of Israel, is now prepared to act on behalf of the treaty-vassal, the Israelites. In setting the stage for the call of Moses, these verses hint that he will carry out God's response to the Israelite crisis in Egypt.

The narrative returns to Midian, where Moses works for his father-in-law. The brief mention of Jethro as a priest (3:1) may be intended to suggest an appropriate marriage for Moses since he comes from a priestly family. Tending the family sheep, Moses journeys to the mountain of God, here called Horeb. This name appears in the E and D traditions, their alternative to the better-known name of Sinai (found in the J and P traditions). Moses has arrived unknowingly at a site of divine presence represented by a bush that burns but is not burned up ("consumed," v. 2). Moses does not initially see anything more than a natural wonder, inspiring his curiosity (v. 3).

An "angel of the Lord" then appears in the burning bush, reflecting a traditional idea about angels appearing with fire—the angel and the fire in the call story of Gideon in Judges 6:21-22, or the appearance of the angel and the fire to Manoah and his wife in Judges 13:20. Whereas in these cases this association is made to confirm a revelation at the end of the story, for Moses such a revelation is signaled as a hallmark at the outset of the story. Moreover, this particular story adds the specific word for the bush, *seneh*, which was apparently chosen (by J) to connect to the name of Mount Sinai and the fiery appearance of God on the mountain (see 19:18). Moses' journey to the mountain anticipates both his journey with the people to the same mountain of God in chapters 15–18 and the experience of the divine that follows.

Moses' experience of the burning bush is the first element in a pattern of call stories of leaders such as Gideon (Judg 6) and the prophets, Samuel

Perizzites, the Girgashites, the Hivites and the Jebusites, a land flowing with milk and honey. [18]They will listen to you. Then you and the elders of Israel will go to the king of Egypt and say to him: The Lord, the God of the Hebrews, has come

---

(1 Sam 3), Isaiah (ch. 6), Ezekiel (chs. 1–3) and Jeremiah (ch. 1). These narratives often begin with some experience or contact with the divine. In Moses' case this is the burning bush (in Isaiah's it is the vision of the enthroned God and the burning seraphim). This initial experience is followed in varying order by a divine address informing the figure about the job description (or commission); the would-be leader's objection to being called (often citing some personal inadequacy as an excuse, for Isaiah his feeling of unholiness, for Jeremiah his not knowing how to speak because of his young age); and the divine response of assurance and a sign meant to aid the leader.

For an ancient Israelite audience, the application of this format to Moses would serve to emphasize that he is chosen by God like other leaders, especially prophets. Additional details in Exodus 3–4 will suggest further that Moses was not only prophetic but also greater than all the prophets who would come after him (Deut 34:10). Moreover, the elaborate extension of the prophetic objection and of the divine reassurance in Exodus 3–4 serves a variety of purposes, including showing Moses' humility (cf. Num 12:3: "very humble, more than anyone else on earth") and revealing the character of God.

The discussion between the divine and Moses that ensues from verse 4 can be somewhat confusing, as it switches so much between "Lord" and "God" (not to mention the angel who drops out of the scene). The Documentary Hypothesis considers this alternation one of the hallmarks of different sources ("the Lord" in J, and "God" in both E and P). Whatever the precise literary development lying behind this passage, it may be simpler to regard it as a combination of JE. In context, it would seem that "Yahweh" (the translation "the Lord" is actually a traditional substitute used out of reverence for the actual name of God) is the name of the deity who serves as "the god," specifically in the role called "the God of your father" (3:6), or the family god who accompanies and protects the clan. In the ancient Middle East, the family god was often identified with a high god; for ancient Israel, the Lord often served in both capacities.

The deity twice calls the name of Moses (v. 4), just as with the call of Samuel (1 Sam 3:10); Moses responds "Here I am," just as Isaiah responds (Isa 6:8; cf. 1 Sam 3:4, 6, 8). Warning Moses, God then informs him about the location as a sacred site and commands him to remove his footwear (v. 5), now a traditional practice for Muslims when entering mosques. God

to meet us. So now, let us go a three days' journey in the wilderness to offer sacrifice to the Lord, our God. ¹⁹Yet I know that the king of Egypt will not allow you to go unless his hand is forced. ²⁰So I will stretch out my hand and strike

---

provides identification through the chain of time back to Abraham, Isaac, and Jacob. Shielding his face in fear, Moses understands the fiery bush to be the chosen medium of the divine presence. Moses' concern is echoed by Isaiah, who laments: "Woe is me, I am doomed! . . . my eyes have seen the King, the LORD of hosts!" (Isa 6:5). This fear is familiar from other experiences of "seeing God" (Gen 32:31 and Judg 6:22-23; 13:20-22). To see the divine, it was believed, was to run the risk of death, and to be able to do so was viewed as a mark of divine approval. This belief was rooted in popular conceptions of divine purity that regarded holiness not only as absence of impurity and unholiness but also as a dangerous power intolerant of unholiness. Yet unlike the stories of other leaders, Moses' call shows no concern about holiness or about the danger of seeing God. The absence of such concerns marks Moses as a man unlike others. The response additionally anticipates Moses' later experience of seeing God on the mountain (Exod 24:11; 33:20).

God continues with the description of the past divine relationship to Israel and leads up to Moses' new job description (vv. 7-10). The cry of the Israelites first mentioned in 2:23-24 is now acknowledged by God; it serves as a framing motif in verses 7 and 9 around God's stated purpose in verse 8: to rescue them and lead them to the land of the ancestors. This divine speech concludes with Moses' designation as the divinely sent instrument of this plan (v. 10). Prophets are said to be sent in order to speak on God's behalf (Jer 1:7; 26:12, 15), and Moses' speeches directed against Pharaoh and the Egyptians are similar to prophetic oracles against foreign nations. Yet Moses' job description involves more than speaking. He is sent to the Israelites, like angels sent to help or accompany God's human servants (Gen 48:16; Exod 23:20-22, 23; Tob 5–6). The cumulative effect of the presentation of Moses is to elevate him to a status as close to God as is humanly possible without calling him "divine" or a "god."

Yet such an exaltation does not inspire pride or confidence in Moses. Instead, his dialogue with God in verses 11-14 opens with a question of modesty, "Who am I that . . . ?" A similar formulation conveying humility appears in Psalm 8:5 ("What are humans that . . . ?"), where God's universe overawes the speaker, who feels his modest place within this wondrous creation. The initial divine response is one of the assurances of the divine presence. It is backed up further by an unusual sign. Most biblical "signs"

Egypt with all the wondrous deeds I will do in its midst. After that he will let you go. ²¹I will even make the Egyptians so well-disposed toward this people that, when you go, you will not go empty-handed. ²²Every woman will ask her

---

are ones perceptible and operative in the present (see 4:1-17), but the "proof" given in verse 12 involves the future. Here the anticipation of the return to the mountain in Exodus 19 is made explicit, and it says something further about Moses' mission: it is not only to lead out of Egypt but also to bring the people to God at the mountain. With verse 13 Moses presents a new objection concerned with the response he will get from the Israelites.

The divine response in verse 14 picks up from the assurance God provided in verse 12: both start with the same form "I will be/I am." Yet the response in verse 14 gives the full divine identity: "I am who I am" is the one who has sent Moses (connecting with the end of v. 13). The presentation presupposes that the name derives from the verb "to be"; Yahweh ("the Lord" in translation) is the third-person form, while the form given in verse 14 is first person. Accordingly, the first-person formulation given here is perhaps not the literal name of the Lord (which is the third-person form, meaning either "He is/will be" or "He causes/will cause to be," possibly a way of expressing the divine role of creation). In context, it is a first-person explanation of the name, conveying the point that the being of God means *being with*, conveying divine involvement and participation with those human parties in relationship to this God.

The Lord confirms this name for eternity as the one and only divine name, unlike any other name or title. As a result, "The Lord" now heads up the references to the "God of your ancestors" (vv. 15, 16; 4:5). The name is expressive of God having "observed" (v. 16) the Israelites, and it helps to explain the divine effort to rescue Israel from Egypt and to lead the people to the land of the Canaanites, etc. (returning full circle to vv. 7-8). God predicts the acceptance of Moses' message to the elders, and together with them Moses is told how to carry out his commission, namely, to go before Pharaoh with the elders to plead for permission to journey in the wilderness to worship God (vv. 18-19). The three-day time period matches the three encampments between Egypt and Sinai in 15:27; 16:1; 17:1; and 19:2. God concludes this speech with a second prediction, that Pharaoh will not let the Israelites go until God exercises divine power. Like a victorious army that takes spoils from an enemy, the Israelites will go with goods taken from the Egyptians, goods that will serve for proper offerings (vv. 21-22). The phrase, "you will not go empty-handed" (v. 21), echoes the command for Israelite pilgrims to bring goods as proper offerings for the three major annual feasts (23:15).

neighbor and the resident alien in her house for silver and gold articles and for clothing, and you will put them on your sons and daughters. So you will plunder the Egyptians.

4 ¹"But," objected Moses, "suppose they do not believe me or listen to me? For they may say, 'The LORD did not appear to you.'" ²The LORD said to him: What is in your hand? "A staff," he answered. ³God said: Throw it on the ground. So he threw it on the ground and it became a snake, and Moses backed away from it. ⁴Then the LORD said to Moses: Now stretch out your hand and take hold of its tail. So he stretched out his hand and took hold of it, and it became a staff in his hand. ⁵That is so they will believe that the LORD, the God of their ancestors, the God of Abraham, the God of Isaac, and the God of Jacob, did appear to you.

⁶Again the LORD said to him: Put your hand into the fold of your garment. So he put his hand into the fold of his garment, and when he drew it out, there

4:1-17 Further objections and divine assurances

After two rounds of question and answer, Moses persists with his reservations. In this third round, Moses backs up to the rejection he fears from the people (vv. 1-9). In order to allay his concerns about being regarded as a fraud ("The LORD did not appear to you"), the Lord offers Moses three powerful signs. Though considered beyond the capability of most people, they are common for magicians and not supernatural. Magical acts were not uncommon for older Israelite prophets such as Elijah and Elisha, whose powers Moses later manifests (see 15:22-27).

In the fourth round of dialogue (vv. 10-17) Moses raises another objection: that he is unable to speak. Jeremiah (1:6) offers a similar excuse. In Jeremiah's case he is too young to know how to speak well, but Moses claims to be "slow of speech and tongue," perhaps a speech impediment. Moses does not deny his relationship to the Lord in referring to himself as "your servant" (v. 10), but he acknowledges his inadequacy in speech. The Lord responds that such bodily capacities are divinely given (v. 11) and that the Lord will assist Moses in speaking (v. 12; similarly in Jer 1:7-9).

Continuing his objection, Moses angers the Lord, who offers an alternative strategy of employing his brother Aaron to serve as his spokesperson, while Moses stands in the role of "God" toward him (v. 16), namely, in telling him what to say. The two brothers will serve as a team whom the Lord will aid (vv. 15-16). Here divine anger does not issue in punishment or rebuke from the Lord; instead, it moves the Lord to undertake a new strategy that works with human limitations. Biblical heroes are often deeply flawed individuals rather than ideal heroes; the divine choice of leaders often involves selecting ordinary individuals called to do extraordinary things on behalf of the people.

was his hand covered with scales, like snowflakes. [7]Then God said: Put your hand back into the fold of your garment. So he put his hand back into the fold of his garment, and when he drew it out, there it was again like his own flesh. [8]If they do not believe you or pay attention to the message of the first sign, they should believe the message of the second sign. [9]And if they do not believe even these two signs and do not listen to you, take some water from the Nile and pour it on the dry land. The water you take from the Nile will become blood on the dry land.

Aaron's Office as Assistant. [10]Moses, however, said to the LORD, "If you please, my Lord, I have never been eloquent, neither in the past nor now that you have spoken to your servant; but I am slow of speech and tongue." [11]The LORD said to him: Who gives one person speech? Who makes another mute or deaf, seeing or blind? Is it not I, the LORD? [12]Now go, I will assist you in speaking and teach you what you are to say. [13]But he said, "If you please, my Lord, send someone else!" [14]Then the LORD became angry with Moses and said: I know there is your brother, Aaron the Levite, who is a good speaker; even now he is on his way to meet you. When he sees you, he will truly be glad. [15]You will speak to him and put the words in his mouth. I will assist both you and him in speaking and teach you both what you are to do. [16]He will speak to the people for you: he will be your spokesman, and you will be as God to him. [17]Take this staff in your hand; with it you are to perform the signs.

Moses' Return to Egypt. [18]After this Moses returned to Jethro his father-in-law and said to him, "Let me return to my kindred in Egypt, to see whether they are still living." Jethro replied to Moses, "Go in peace." [19]Then the LORD said to Moses in Midian: Return to Egypt, for all those who sought your life are dead. [20]So Moses took his wife and his sons, mounted them on the donkey, and started back to the land of Egypt. Moses took the staff of God with him. [21]The LORD said to Moses: On your return to Egypt, see that you perform before Pharaoh all the wonders I have put in your power. But I will harden his heart and he will not let the people go. [22]So you will say to Pharaoh, Thus says the LORD: Israel is my son, my firstborn. [23]I said to you: Let my son go, that he may serve me. Since you refused to let

---

The extended call narrative of 3:1–4:17 presents the identity and character of both God and Moses. The divine identity is communicated in the name, itself an expression of divine care and concern for Israel. Moses' responses show humility as his heroic quality, and in turn the Lord's response to his self-perceived limitations shows divine compassion willing to bend to human weakness.

4:18-23 From Midian back to Egypt

Moses respectfully asks permission from his father-in-law to return to his people in Egypt (cf. Jacob's request to Laban in Gen 30:25). Moses does

him go, I will kill your son, your first-born.

²⁴ On the journey, at a place where they spent the night, the LORD came upon Moses and sought to put him to death. ²⁵ But Zipporah took a piece of flint and cut off her son's foreskin and, touching his feet, she said, "Surely you are a spouse of blood to me." ²⁶So God let Moses alone. At that time she said,

---

not mention his experience of God, but his words reflect a concern for the life-threatening effects of Egyptian slavery on his people. Speaking again to Moses, the Lord declares that it is safe to return to Egypt since "those who sought your life are dead" (v. 19); this opposition was principally identified in 2:15 as Pharaoh. Perhaps another pharaoh was thought to have assumed the throne in the interim, but the text does not clarify this matter. Moses sets out with his household, using a donkey for transportation (like "Asiatics" depicted in Egyptian art). With the reference to the staff (v. 20), the Lord's speech (vv. 21-23) to Moses about his mission begins with the wonders to be worked. These will not move Pharaoh, whose heart, we are told for the first time in verse 21, God "will harden."

In biblical thought the heart was regarded as the seat of intellectual, moral, and spiritual faculties, and so "hardening" suggests a lack of proper functioning, in Pharaoh's case a lack of compassion or reason. The idea that God would harden Pharaoh's heart (in 7:3; 9:12; 10:1, 20, 27; 11:10) and then punish him with plagues seems unfair, yet the motif is complicated. Over the course of the first five plagues, it is Pharaoh who is said to be obstinate (7:13, 14, 22; 8:11, 15, 28; 9:7, 34-35), not God who makes him so. When Pharaoh hardens his heart, the story (often J) stresses his responsibility. God's hardening or stiffening his heart over the course of the last five plagues (in E and P) indicates Pharaoh's habitual, irreversible attitude as well as divine control over the chain of events. Divine involvement also evokes an atmosphere of warfare (cf. Josh 11:20: "For it was the LORD's doing to make their hearts obstinate to meet Israel in battle," but literally, "It was from the Lord to stiffen their heart . . ."). First Samuel 6:6 cites the hardening of Pharaoh's heart as an object lesson to Israel's enemies, the Philistines. The divine speech anticipates a struggle to the death (Exod 12), with the death of the firstborn son as retribution for enslaving God's metaphorical "firstborn," a term that expresses Israel's special relationship to God. The notion of this conflict as a war continues in Exodus 14–15, with Pharaoh and his army pursuing the enemy Israel saved by its warrior-god. The plagues as "holy war" is also suggested by Israel being designated by army terms: "company by company" (6:26; 12:51), "armies, my people the Israelites" (7:4; cf. 12:41), "your armies" (12:17).

"A spouse of blood," in regard to the circumcision.

²⁷The Lord said to Aaron: Go into the wilderness to meet Moses. So he went; when meeting him at the mountain of God, he kissed him. ²⁸Moses told Aaron everything the Lord had sent him to say, and all the signs he had commanded him to do. ²⁹Then Moses and Aaron went and gathered all the elders of the Israelites. ³⁰Aaron told them everything the Lord had said to Moses, and he performed the signs before the people. ³¹The people believed, and when they heard that the Lord had observed the Israelites and had seen their affliction, they knelt and bowed down.

5 Pharaoh's Hardness of Heart. ¹Afterwards, Moses and Aaron went to Pharaoh and said, "Thus says the Lord, the God of Israel: Let my people go, that they may hold a feast for me in the wilderness." ²Pharaoh answered, "Who is the Lord, that I should obey him and let Israel go? I do not know the Lord, and I will not let Israel go." ³They replied,

4:24-31 Meeting in the desert

The circumstances and motivations for the circumcision in verses 24-26 are hard to understand. The circumcision may use older ideas associated with adult circumcision (that accompanies marriage—hence "spouse of blood"—perhaps to avert demonic threats thought to menace the occasion) in order to express the idea that as Moses returns to the scene of his crime of manslaughter (2:12), he still bears bloodguilt considered punishable by divine retribution. In any case, the scene brands Moses in his identity before exercising his divinely appointed role (cf. Jacob's wrestling with the unnamed divine figure in Gen 32:24-32).

The setting of this conflict may confuse modern readers, since Moses has left the mountain here, only to be described back on "the mountain of God" in verse 27. Contrary to expectations, biblical narrative does not always follow linear order; instead, it sometimes is ordered thematically. In the case of verses 24-26 the theme of circumcision is associated with the notion of the firstborn son mentioned in verses 22-23 (cf. circumcision in 12:43-49 followed by the theme of the firstborn in 13:1-2, 11-15). The meeting of Moses and Aaron in verses 27-31 sets up the structure of authority between the brothers. The passage then moves without comment to Egypt. In this context Aaron operates as spokesperson; it would also seem that he, and not Moses, performs the signs. As a result, the people believe, and they bow down after learning not simply about divine power but of divine compassion for their suffering.

5:1–6:1 Pharaoh versus Moses

Six short scenes set into motion the events that increase the severity of the Israelites' situation. The *first* (vv. 1-5) involves Moses' message and

"The God of the Hebrews has come to meet us. Let us go a three days' journey in the wilderness, that we may offer sacrifice to the LORD, our God, so that he does not strike us with the plague or the sword." ⁴The king of Egypt answered them, "Why, Moses and Aaron, do you make the people neglect their work? Off to your labors!" ⁵Pharaoh continued, "Look how they are already more numerous than the people of the land, and yet you would give them rest from their labors!"

⁶That very day Pharaoh gave the taskmasters of the people and their foremen this order: ⁷"You shall no longer supply the people with straw for their brickmaking as before. Let them go and gather their own straw! ⁸Yet you shall levy upon them the same quota of bricks as they made previously. Do not reduce it. They are lazy; that is why they are crying, 'Let us go to offer sacrifice to our God.' ⁹Increase the work for the men, so that they attend to it and not to deceitful words."

¹⁰So the taskmasters of the people and their foremen went out and told the people, "Thus says Pharaoh, 'I will not provide you with straw. ¹¹Go and get your own straw from wherever you can find it. But there will not be the slightest reduction in your work.'" ¹²The people, then, scattered throughout the land of

Pharaoh's response. As with the prophetic style of his call in 3:1–4:17, Moses is presented like biblical prophets. His message begins by stressing the commission's divine origin and authority ("Thus says the LORD, the God of Israel") and is followed by the message proper ("Let my people go . . ."). Compared with the ultimate outcome of the plague stories, Moses' request for permission for proper worship (and not complete freedom from Egypt) appears modest. Yet Pharaoh's response is not simply to question the significance of Moses' God and deny the request.

The *second* scene (vv. 6-9) shows an increased work quota for the Israelite slaves. They are to continue to make bricks with straw that they themselves must now gather. Straw is a necessary element that served as a binder; it is thought that the acid released by the decay of the straw further enhanced the cohesion of the bricks. (Egyptian villagers today make bricks by piling mud bricks in large square stacks that can be burned from fire made in the hollow area left inside.) The increased labor is to put thoughts of departure out of the slaves' minds.

The *third* scene (vv. 10-13) depicts the taskmasters' aggression in implementing the royal order. It results in the people's failure to comply, which leads to the *fourth* scene of Israelite foremen getting flogged and complaining (vv. 14-18). The passage seems to blame Pharaoh ("you" in v. 16), but the Hebrew wording aims the point indirectly at "your people," namely, the Egyptian taskmasters enforcing his command. The royal response is to repeat the original directive.

Egypt to gather stubble for straw, [13]while the taskmasters kept driving them on, saying, "Finish your work, the same daily amount as when the straw was supplied to you." [14]The Israelite foremen, whom the taskmasters of Pharaoh had placed over them, were beaten, and were asked, "Why have you not completed your prescribed amount of bricks yesterday and today, as before?"

Complaint of the Foremen. [15]Then the Israelite foremen came and cried out to Pharaoh: "Why do you treat your servants in this manner? [16]No straw is supplied to your servants, and still we are told, 'Make bricks!' Look how your servants are beaten! It is you who are at fault." [17]He answered, "Lazy! You are lazy! That is why you keep saying, 'Let us go and offer sacrifice to the LORD.' [18]Now off to work! No straw will be supplied to you, but you must supply your quota of bricks."

[19]The Israelite foremen realized they were in trouble, having been told, "Do not reduce your daily amount of bricks!" [20]So when they left Pharaoh they assailed Moses and Aaron, who were waiting to meet them, [21]and said to them, "The LORD look upon you and judge! You have made us offensive to Pharaoh and his servants, putting a sword into their hands to kill us."

Renewal of God's Promise. [22]Then Moses again had recourse to the LORD and said, "LORD, why have you treated this people badly? And why did you send me? [23]From the time I went to Pharaoh to speak in your name, he has treated this people badly, and you have done nothing to rescue your people."

[1]The LORD answered Moses: Now you will see what I will do to Pharaoh. For by a strong hand, he will let them go; by a strong hand, he will drive them from his land.

The *fifth* scene (vv. 19-21) returns the story back to Moses, now faced with failure. The foremen's wish that God judge between them and Moses (v. 21) does not challenge God or God's power; they question Moses' commission from God, which should have been successful; instead, it has only made the Israelites' situation worse. The *sixth* scene (5:22–6:1) brings Moses back to God, who redirects the lament of the Israelites. This speech before God exhibits a further characteristic of Israelite prophets (such as Jeremiah) who not only deliver divine messages to human parties but also plead human concerns before the Almighty. Here Moses pleads the case of the Israelites and his own case as well. The divine response in 6:1 is not to deny Moses' concerns but to demonstrate divine power. This final section provides a transition between the failure of this section and the renewed commission of Moses in 6:2–7:7.

6:2–7:7 The recommissioning of Moses

Up to this point the story consists mainly of JE passages. They are largely *descriptive*: they evoke an earlier era of Israelite origins and life. They offer a good suspenseful story with entertaining details (such as Moses' magical

The Karnak temple complex at Luxor, Egypt, with over 25 temples and chapels built over 1,300 years beginning in the 16th century B.C. by 30 successive pharoahs

Confirmation of the Promise to the Ancestors. ²Then God spoke to Moses, and said to him: I am the LORD. ³As God the Almighty I appeared to Abraham, Isaac, and Jacob, but by my name, LORD, I did not make myself known to them. ⁴I also established my covenant with them, to give them the land of Canaan, the land in which they were residing as aliens. ⁵Now that I have heard the groaning of the Israelites, whom the Egyptians have reduced to slavery, I am mindful of my covenant. ⁶Therefore, say to the Israelites: I am the LORD. I will free you from the burdens of the Egyptians and will deliver you from their slavery. I will redeem you by my outstretched arm and with mighty acts of judgment. ⁷I will take you as my own people, and I will be your God; and you will know that I, the LORD, am your God who has freed you from the burdens of the Egyptians ⁸and I will bring you into the land which I swore to give to Abraham, Isaac, and Jacob. I will give it to you as your own possession—I, the LORD! ⁹But when Moses told this to the Israelites, they would not listen to him because of their dejection and hard slavery.

¹⁰Then the LORD spoke to Moses: ¹¹Go, tell Pharaoh, king of Egypt, to let the Israelites leave his land. ¹²However, Moses protested to the LORD, "If the Israelites did not listen to me, how is it possible that Pharaoh will listen to me, poor speaker that I am!" ¹³But the LORD spoke to Moses and Aaron regarding the Israelites and Pharaoh, king of Egypt, and charged them to bring the Israelites out of the land of Egypt.

Genealogy of Moses and Aaron. ¹⁴These are the heads of their ancestral houses. The sons of Reuben, the firstborn of Israel: Hanoch, Pallu, Hezron and Carmi; these are the clans of Reuben. ¹⁵The sons of Simeon: Jemuel, Jamin, Ohad, Jachin, Zohar and Shaul, the son of a Canaanite woman; these are the clans of Simeon. ¹⁶These are the names of the sons of Levi, in their genealogical order: Gershon, Kohath and Merari. Levi lived one hundred and thirty-seven years.

¹⁷The sons of Gershon, by their clans: Libni and Shimei. ¹⁸The sons of Kohath: Amram, Izhar, Hebron and Uzziel. Kohath lived one hundred and thirty-three years. ¹⁹The sons of Merari: Mahli and

staff) or exotic elements (including the mysterious circumcision). At this point in the story, priestly compositions are added to the mix. Priestly narratives bear a *prescriptive* force: they often relate what is supposed to be taught and then followed, according to the priestly view. Matters such as the high status of Aaron and the miraculous character of divine power come to the fore in these compositions. In the narrative context of 6:2-13, Moses receives a recommissioning that enhances his capabilities following the failures related in chapter 5. From the perspective of the sources, this priestly version repeats many of the themes found in the earlier JE commission in 3:1–4:17 and adds some priestly thematic emphases. (In a sense, the priestly commission offers a sort of inner-biblical commentary on the JE commission.)

Mushi. These are the clans of Levi in their genealogical order.

[20]Amram married his aunt Jochebed, who bore him Aaron, Moses, and Miriam. Amram lived one hundred and thirty-seven years. [21]The sons of Izhar: Korah, Nepheg and Zichri. [22]The sons of Uzziel: Mishael, Elzaphan and Sithri. [23]Aaron married Elisheba, Amminadab's daughter, the sister of Nahshon; she bore him Nadab, Abihu, Eleazar and Ithamar. [24]The sons of Korah: Assir, Elkanah and Abiasaph. These are the clans of the Korahites. [25]Eleazar, Aaron's son, married one of Putiel's daughters, who bore him Phinehas. These are the heads of the ancestral houses of the Levites by their clans. [26]These are the Aaron and the Moses to whom the LORD said, "Bring the Israelites out from the land of Egypt,

---

Verses 2-10 lay out Moses' commission again in prophetic style. As expected of the priestly narrative, the divine name switches back to God (cf. "LORD" in preceding J material), since it is only at this point that the divine name is being revealed, according to the view of the priestly tradition. The divine self-identification acknowledges both the equation of this deity with "the God of the fathers" and the fact that the proper name of the deity had not been revealed before. For the priestly tradition the revelation of the divine name marks a new era of revelation, one that will culminate in the second half of Exodus with the giving of the covenant on Mount Sinai. Compared with the JE history of the divine relationship with the patriarchs in 3:4-10, which verses 3-5 closely parallel, the priestly source here adds the distinctive theme of the covenant. For priestly theology this is the most important event of world history (see 31:18); after Sinai, Israel and the world are changed forever. Verses 6-8 state the central meaning of the covenant: it binds God and people together, with divine destiny cast with Israel forever, and so the Lord is about to act miraculously on its behalf. With the commission, the people believed and then Moses was rebuffed by Pharaoh; this time, the people now rebuff Moses (v. 9).

Verses 10 and 28, together with verses 13 and 26, form a frame around the genealogy that follows, with verse 28 through 7:7 continuing the story of the commission. This technique of repetition (vv. 10 and 28; 13 and 26) is sometimes used by scribes to insert material, in this case the genealogy of Moses and Aaron. Genealogies do not normally belong with a commission; the priestly genealogy inserted at this point traces the line of Moses and Aaron in order to connect their origins with the lines of the priesthood as known to ancient Israelites. For the priestly tradition, Aaron was thought of as the model chief priest, and his high priestly line was traced through Phinehas and Eleazar (v. 25), as opposed to the Korahites (v. 24), considered a lesser priestly family and known from the books of Psalms and Chronicles

company by company." ²⁷They are the ones who spoke to Pharaoh, king of Egypt, to bring the Israelites out of Egypt—the same Moses and Aaron.

²⁸When the LORD spoke to Moses in the land of Egypt ²⁹the LORD said to Moses: I am the LORD. Say to Pharaoh, king of Egypt, all that I tell you. ³⁰But Moses protested to the LORD, "Since I am a poor speaker, how is it possible that Pharaoh will listen to me?"

7 ¹The LORD answered Moses: See! I have made you a god to Pharaoh, and Aaron your brother will be your prophet. ²You will speak all that I command you. In turn, your brother Aaron will tell Pharaoh to let the Israelites go out of his land. ³Yet I will make Pharaoh so headstrong that, despite the many signs and wonders that I work in the land of Egypt, ⁴Pharaoh will not listen to you. Therefore I will lay my hand on Egypt and with mighty acts of judgment I will bring my armies, my people the Israelites, out of the land of Egypt. ⁵All Egyptians will know that I am the LORD, when I stretch out my hand against Egypt and bring the Israelites out of their midst.

⁶This, then, is what Moses and Aaron did. They did exactly as the LORD had commanded them. ⁷Moses was eighty years old, and Aaron eighty-three, when they spoke to Pharaoh.

III. The Contest with Pharaoh

The Staff Turned into a Serpent. ⁸The LORD spoke to Moses and Aaron: ⁹When Pharaoh demands of you, "Produce a sign or wonder," you will say to

---

as temple singers. This priestly view of Aaron's priesthood became the established norm in the Jerusalem temple in the postexilic period.

Exodus 6:28–7:7 echoes the conversation in 4:10-17. It repeats the divine commission and Moses' objection about his speech, but this time the priestly account introduces two themes: the Lord promises divine power in a manner never seen before, and it will show not just Israel but also Egypt who the Lord is. The One God is to be known not just by Israel but also by foreigners, with power wielded only by this One God. In this way the priestly version of Moses' commission adds a monotheistic perspective to the earlier JE rendering of Moses' commission. The section ends by mentioning the advanced years of Moses and Aaron. The two begin their important life's work at ages when most have long completed theirs. Is this intended to highlight the heroic nature of the two men, or does it signal the strength and support that God gives them? According to Deuteronomy 34:7, Moses' strength lasted right up to his death at 120 years of age.

7:8-13 Last chance before the plagues

The renewed conflict is a competition between Moses and Aaron, on one side, and the Egyptian magicians, on the other. It involves not supernatural signs but the sort of magic that the Egyptians are capable of performing. It is

Aaron: "Take your staff and throw it down before Pharaoh, and it will turn into a serpent." [10]Then Moses and Aaron went to Pharaoh and did just as the LORD had commanded. Aaron threw his staff down before Pharaoh and his servants, and it turned into a serpent. [11]Pharaoh, in turn, summoned the wise men and the sorcerers, and they also, the magicians of Egypt, did the same thing by their magic arts. [12]Each one threw down his staff, and they turned into serpents. But Aaron's staff swallowed their staffs. [13]Pharaoh, however, hardened his heart and would not listen to them, just as the LORD had foretold.

First Plague: Water Turned into Blood. [14]Then the LORD said to Moses: Pharaoh is obstinate in refusing to let the people go. [15]In the morning, just when he sets out for the water, go to Pharaoh and present yourself by the bank of the Nile, holding in your hand the staff that turned into a snake. [16]Say to him: The LORD, the God of the Hebrews, sent me to you with the message: Let my people go to serve me in the wilderness. But as yet you have not listened. [17]Thus says the LORD: This is how you will know that I am the LORD. With the staff here in my hand, I will strike the water in the Nile and it will be changed into blood.

interesting that magic here is no religious issue, as the two Israelite leaders are presented as superior magicians. This section introduces the so-called ten plagues, which are rendered in various ways in the Bible. In matching poetic parallel lines, Psalm 78 has only six or seven plagues, and Psalm 105 enumerates seven plagues in a slightly different order. Exodus 10:2 implies that these traditions were transmitted orally, and some variation is to be expected from processes of transmission that involved a combination of written and oral modes that possibly influenced one another. Scripture's truth lies not in its specific historical detail as much as its moral truth (2 Tim 3:16: "for teaching, for refutation, for correction, and for training in righteousness").

7:14-25 First plague

The first plague involves turning the Nile into blood, a traditional sign of trouble in ancient Egyptian literature. Chaotic conditions in Egypt are characterized by one Egyptian wisdom text (the Admonitions of Ipuwer): "the river is blood" and "as one drinks from it, one . . . thirsts for water." Natural explanations for the first plague have been long sought in the Nile's reddish appearance in the summer months due to reddish particles of soil and/or flagellates flowing to Egypt from the Sudan. If correct, it would suggest that the ten plagues take place roughly over a single year, as they apparently end with Passover in the following spring.

This plague shows Egyptian magicians performing the same feats as Moses and Aaron (see also 7:11). The initial plagues were not understood

¹⁸The fish in the Nile will die, and the Nile itself will stink so that the Egyptians will be unable to drink water from the Nile.

¹⁹The LORD then spoke to Moses: Speak to Aaron: Take your staff and stretch out your hand over the waters of Egypt—its streams, its canals, its ponds, and all its supplies of water—that they may become blood. There will be blood throughout the land of Egypt, even in the wooden pails and stone jars.

²⁰This, then, is what Moses and Aaron did, exactly as the LORD had commanded. Aaron raised his staff and struck the waters in the Nile in full view of Pharaoh and his servants, and all the water in the Nile was changed into blood. ²¹The fish in the Nile died, and the Nile itself stank so that the Egyptians could not drink water from it. There was blood throughout the land of Egypt. ²²But the Egyptian magicians did the same by their magic arts. So Pharaoh hardened his heart and would not listen to them, just as the LORD had said. ²³Pharaoh turned away and went into his house, with no concern even for this. ²⁴All the Egyptians had to dig round about the Nile for drinking water, since they could not drink any water from the Nile.

Second Plague: the Frogs. ²⁵Seven days passed after the LORD had struck

as "supernatural" in the sense of coming from outside the natural order; instead, they were within the power of superior magicians (v. 22). Egyptian texts record wondrous tricks of legendary magicians. A late Egyptian text (Setne Khamwas II and Si-Osire) describes a competition between Egyptian and Nubian magicians; if the Nubians prove successful, then water would take on the color of blood (turning water into blood is a common ancient Middle Eastern theme). Verse 22 also pokes fun at the Egyptian magicians: in their zeal to show off their power, they add to the Nile's destruction.

In the story of the first plague God fights the Egyptians on their own terms in order to show the Israelites the ultimate source of the magic of Moses and Aaron (v. 17). The two appear every bit as much as prophets commanded to deliver a divine accusation against Egypt; in Ezekiel 29 the prophet is ordered to face Pharaoh and Egypt and announce a divine punishment that kills the Nile's fish (cf. Isa 19). The scene of Moses and Aaron versus the Egyptian magicians highlights the question as to whether God or Pharaoh is more powerful, and perhaps by implication, which one is really divine.

It has been thought that various plagues imply a polemic against different Egyptian deities and therefore against Egyptian polytheism in general, since in Egyptian culture different deities were associated with the Nile and its inundation, with frogs, etc. For Exodus 8:22-23 and Numbers 33:4 (cf. Exod 12:12), the plagues represent the Lord's judgment against not just the Egyptians but also their gods. It is unclear whether Israelite authors

the Nile. [26]Then the Lord said to Moses: Go to Pharaoh and tell him: Thus says the Lord: Let my people go to serve me. [27]If you refuse to let them go, then I will send a plague of frogs over all your territory. [28]The Nile will teem with frogs. They will come up and enter into your palace and into your bedroom and onto your bed, into the houses of your servants, too, and among your people, even into your ovens and your kneading bowls. [29]The frogs will come up over you and your people and all your servants.

8 [1]The Lord then spoke to Moses: Speak to Aaron: Stretch out your hand with your staff over the streams, the canals, and the ponds, and make frogs overrun the land of Egypt. [2]So Aaron stretched out his hand over the waters of Egypt, and the frogs came up and covered the land of Egypt. [3]But the magicians did the same by their magic arts and made frogs overrun the land of Egypt.

[4]Then Pharaoh summoned Moses and Aaron and said, "Pray to the Lord to remove the frogs from me and my people, and I will let the people go to sacrifice to the Lord." [5]Moses answered Pharaoh, "Please designate for me the time when I am to pray for you and your servants and your people, to get rid of the frogs from you and your houses. They will be left only in the Nile." [6]"Tomorrow," he said. Then Moses replied, "It will be as you have said, so that you may know that there is none like the Lord, our God. [7]The frogs will leave you and your houses, your servants and your people; they will be left only in the Nile."

[8]After Moses and Aaron left Pharaoh's presence, Moses cried out to the Lord on account of the frogs that he had inflicted on Pharaoh; [9]and the Lord did as Moses had asked. The frogs died off in the houses, the courtyards, and the fields. [10]Heaps of them were piled up, and the land stank. [11]But when Pharaoh saw there was a respite, he became obstinate and would not listen to them, just as the Lord had said.

Third Plague: the Gnats. [12]Thereupon the Lord spoke to Moses: Speak to Aaron: Stretch out your staff and

---

had this level of knowledge about such Egyptian religious matters, but the possibility cannot be ruled out.

7:26–8:11 Second plague

This plague may have been inspired by frogs known to invade the land during the Nile's inundation in September and October. In the context of the story, the first plague sets off a chain reaction: as a result of the fouling of the Nile, frogs invade the land in massive proportions. The frogs that "come up" (v. 29; cf. the river "will teem" with frogs in v. 28) may resonate as a just punishment against the Egyptians who tried to kill Israelites, who were "fruitful" and "filling" the land (1:7). Once again the Egyptian magicians add to the destruction, and again Moses is shown to be superior, this time in being able to end it. Unlike the first plague, the second induces Pharaoh to relent, if only temporarily.

strike the dust of the earth, and it will turn into gnats throughout the land of Egypt. [13]They did so. Aaron stretched out his hand with his staff and struck the dust of the earth, and gnats came upon human being and beast alike. All the dust of the earth turned into gnats throughout the land of Egypt. [14]Though the magicians did the same thing to produce gnats by their magic arts, they could not do so. The gnats were on human being and beast alike, [15]and the magicians said to Pharaoh, "This is the finger of God." Yet Pharaoh hardened his heart and would not listen to them, just as the LORD had said.

Fourth Plague: the Flies. [16]Then the LORD spoke to Moses: Early tomorrow morning present yourself to Pharaoh when he sets out toward the water, and say to him: Thus says the LORD: Let my people go to serve me. [17]For if you do not let my people go, I will send swarms of flies upon you and your servants and your people and your houses. The houses of the Egyptians and the very ground on which they stand will be filled with swarms of flies. [18]But on that day I will make an exception of the land of Goshen, where my people are, and no swarms of flies will be there, so that you may know that I the LORD am in the midst of the land. [19]I will make a distinction between my people and your people. This sign will take place tomorrow. [20]This the LORD did. Thick swarms of flies entered the house of Pharaoh and the houses of his servants; throughout Egypt the land was devastated on account of the swarms of flies.

[21]Then Pharaoh summoned Moses and Aaron and said, "Go sacrifice to your God within the land." [22]But Moses replied, "It is not right to do so, for what we sacrifice to the LORD, our God, is abhorrent to the Egyptians. If we sacrifice

8:12-15 Third plague

The plague of gnats may have been suggested by mosquitoes reproducing quickly in pools of water left by the Nile following its inundation, but the story presents this plague in terms of dust turning into gnats. The picture evokes the image of a dust storm transforming into gnats. In this brief plague story the Egyptian competition finally recognizes the divine power behind Moses' superior ability: "This is the finger of God" (v. 15). Once again Pharaoh does not respond (as with the first plague, but not the second).

8:16-28 Fourth plague

The plague of flies is similar to the preceding, and Psalm 78:45 does not distinguish them, speaking only of "insects," placed in matching poetic lines with the frogs (before them and not after). Psalm 105:31 speaks of "flies" and "gnats" in matching poetic terms, suggesting that for this psalm the two together represented a single plague. The authors of the exodus story evidently understood the poetic parallelism of "gnats" and "flies" as sepa-

what is abhorrent to the Egyptians before their very eyes, will they not stone us? [23]We must go a three days' journey in the wilderness and sacrifice to the LORD, our God, as he commands us." [24]Pharaoh said, "I will let you go to sacrifice to the LORD, your God, in the wilderness, provided that you do not go too far away. Pray for me." [25]Moses answered, "As soon as I leave you I will pray to the LORD that the swarms of flies may depart tomorrow from Pharaoh, his servants, and his people. Pharaoh, however, must not act deceitfully again and refuse to let the people go to sacrifice to the LORD." [26]When Moses left Pharaoh, he prayed to the LORD; [27]and the LORD did as Moses had asked, removing the swarms of flies from Pharaoh, his servants, and his people. Not one remained.

[28]But once more Pharaoh became obstinate and would not let the people go.

9 Fifth Plague: the Pestilence. [1]Then the LORD said to Moses: Go to Pharaoh and tell him: Thus says the LORD, the God of the Hebrews: Let my people go to serve me. [2]For if you refuse to let them go and persist in holding them, [3]the hand of the LORD will strike your livestock in the field—your horses, donkeys, camels, herds and flocks—with a very severe pestilence. [4]But the LORD will distinguish between the livestock of Israel and that of Egypt, so that nothing belonging to the Israelites will die. [5]And the LORD set a definite time, saying: Tomorrow the LORD will do this in the land. [6]And on the next day the LORD did it. All the livestock of the Egyptians died, but not one animal belonging to

---

rate plagues. (This reading might also help to explain the relative brevity of the third plague.) This plague marks a new level of drama in the story. Verse 18 introduces a new element: the Lord will protect the Israelites from the effects of this plague. (Readers may perhaps assume that the same was true of the previous plagues, but the story does not address the issue.) This new element is aimed at helping to persuade Pharaoh, who enters into negotiations with Moses and Aaron for the first time. Verse 21 shows Pharaoh offering limited concessions. As a result, Moses ends the plague only to have Pharaoh stubbornly refuse once again.

9:1-7 Fifth plague

Pestilence here applies specifically to livestock plague. In Habakkuk 3:5 pestilence personified appears as one of the Lord's destructive agents. Here pestilence is regarded as the smiting by God's "hand" (in the ancient world, diseases are described as the "hand" of destructive deities). Underlying the presentation of the destruction of land and animals is the idea that their well-being depends on the righteousness of its human inhabitants (Lev 26; Deut 28). The distinction made between Egypt and Israel continues, and no negotiations defuse the tension that only continues to rise.

the Israelites died. [7]But although Pharaoh found upon inquiry that not even so much as one of the livestock of the Israelites had died, he remained obstinate and would not let the people go.

Sixth Plague: the Boils. [8]So the LORD said to Moses and Aaron: Each of you take handfuls of soot from a kiln, and in the presence of Pharaoh let Moses scatter it toward the sky. [9]It will turn into fine dust over the whole land of Egypt and cause festering boils on human being and beast alike throughout the land of Egypt.

[10]So they took the soot from a kiln and appeared before Pharaoh. When Moses scattered it toward the sky, it caused festering boils on human being and beast alike. [11]Because of the boils the magicians could not stand in Moses' presence, for there were boils on the magicians as well as on the rest of the Egyptians. [12]But the LORD hardened Pharaoh's heart, and he would not listen to them, just as the LORD had said to Moses.

Seventh Plague: the Hail. [13]Then the LORD spoke to Moses: Early tomorrow morning present yourself to Pharaoh and say to him: Thus says the LORD, the God of the Hebrews: Let my people go to serve me, [14]for this time I will unleash all my blows upon you and your servants and your people, so that you may know that there is none like me anywhere on earth. [15]For by now I should have stretched out my hand and struck you and your people with such pestilence that you would have vanished from the earth. [16]But this is why I have let you survive: to show you my power and to make my name resound throughout the earth! [17]Will you continue to

---

9:8-12 Sixth plague

The plague of boils is the first to afflict humans as well as livestock. Boils afflict the knees and legs, according to Deuteronomy 28:35. Boils may refer to skin inflammations (the Hebrew literally means "to be hot"), and their "festering" suggests malignant pustules that characterize anthrax. In Deuteronomy 28:27 boils are associated specifically with Egypt. It is to be noted that Aaron's role in this plague is minimal when compared with the other plagues where Moses and he function as a team. The story of the boils brings the Egyptian magicians back into the picture, but this time they do not copy Moses and Aaron in creating the plague; instead, for the first time they are said to be afflicted with the plague. Their mention here perhaps caps the middle set of plagues four through six, just as the magicians' special role in acknowledging God in the third plague provides a fitting climax to the first three plagues. After plague six, the magicians drop out of the narrative.

9:13-35 Seventh plague

The plague of hail makes the conflict seem less like a human drama. Instead, the next three plagues shift the story's focus away from the com-

exalt yourself over my people and not let them go? [18]At this time tomorrow, therefore, I am going to rain down such fierce hail as there has never been in Egypt from the day it was founded up to the present. [19]Therefore, order your livestock and whatever else you have in the open fields to be brought to a place of safety. Whatever human being or animal is found in the fields and is not brought to shelter will die when the hail comes down upon them. [20]Those of Pharaoh's servants who feared the word of the Lord hurried their servants and their livestock off to shelter. [21]But those who did not pay attention to the word of the Lord left their servants and their livestock in the fields.

[22]The Lord then said to Moses: Stretch out your hand toward the sky, that hail may fall upon the entire land of Egypt, on human being and beast alike and all the vegetation of the fields in the land of Egypt. [23]So Moses stretched out his staff toward the sky, and the Lord sent forth peals of thunder and hail. Lightning flashed toward the earth, and the Lord rained down hail upon the land of Egypt. [24]There was hail and lightning flashing here and there through the hail, and the hail was so fierce that nothing like it had been seen in Egypt since it became a nation. [25]Throughout the land of Egypt the hail struck down everything in the fields, human being and beast alike; it struck down all the vegetation of the fields and splintered every tree in the fields. [26]Only in the land of Goshen, where the Israelites were, was there no hail.

[27]Then Pharaoh sent for Moses and Aaron and said to them, "I have sinned this time! The Lord is the just one, and I and my people are the ones at fault. [28]Pray to the Lord! Enough of the thunder and hail! I will let you go; you need stay no longer." [29]Moses replied to him, "As soon as I leave the city I will extend my hands to the Lord; the thunder will cease, and there will be no more hail so that you may know that the earth belongs to the Lord. [30]But as for you and your servants, I know that you do not yet fear the Lord God."

[31]Now the flax and the barley were ruined, because the barley was in ear and the flax in bud. [32]But the wheat and the spelt were not ruined, for they grow later.

[33]When Moses had left Pharaoh and gone out of the city, he extended his hands to the Lord. The thunder and the hail ceased, and the rain no longer poured down upon the earth. [34]But Pharaoh, seeing that the rain and the hail and the thunder had ceased, sinned again and became obstinate, both he and his servants. [35]In the hardness of his

---

petition between Moses and Aaron and the Egyptian magicians. It moves the drama from the water and land to the heavens. As a result, the third set of three plagues offers an almost apocalyptic conflict between God and Pharaoh. This shift heightens the divine agenda, moving from a simple request for proper worship to the divine cosmic plan to "unleash all my blows upon" all the Egyptians in order that Pharaoh will learn there is no one like the God of Israel (v. 14). Up to this point God has spared them only

heart, Pharaoh would not let the Israelites go, just as the LORD had said through
Moses.

10 **Eighth Plague: the Locusts.**
[1]Then the LORD said to Moses:
Go to Pharaoh, for I have made him and
his servants obstinate in order that I may
perform these signs of mine among them
[2]and that you may recount to your son
and grandson how I made a fool of the
Egyptians and what signs I did among
them, so that you may know that I am
the LORD.

[3]So Moses and Aaron went to Pharaoh and told him, "Thus says the LORD,
the God of the Hebrews: How long will
you refuse to submit to me? Let my
people go to serve me. [4]For if you refuse
to let my people go, tomorrow I will
bring locusts into your territory. [5]They
will cover the surface of the earth, so that
the earth itself will not be visible. They
will eat up the remnant you saved un-
damaged from the hail, as well as all the
trees that are growing in your fields.
[6]They will fill your houses and the
houses of your servants and of all the
Egyptians—something your parents and
your grandparents have not seen from
the day they appeared on this soil until
today." With that he turned and left Pharaoh.

[7]But Pharaoh's servants said to him,
"How long will he be a snare for us? Let

---

in order to demonstrate the cosmic power of this deity (v. 16). The warning
is unlike anything that came before, as all the Egyptians are given a chance
to respond in bringing in their livestock from the fields. Here Pharaoh more
than concedes; he admits fault (v. 27). Yet the tension only builds, as Pharaoh once again refuses (v. 35).

The plague involves a massive rainstorm (v. 33). In Psalm 78:47 the
plague of hail is combined with frost, and in Psalm 105:32 hail comes with
lightning. Hail is common to Israel and its immediate neighbors, less so
in Egypt. In some contexts it is combined with burning sulfur (Gen 19:24),
there evoking the east wind storm (called the *khamsin* in Arabic) blowing
off the desert from the east during the dry season. Verses 31-32 give one of
the few clues as to the time of year imagined by the authors, after the flax
and barley ripened but before the wheat crop comes in. In Egypt, flax comes
in late January and barley in February. This description implies a rain after
the normal rainy season (roughly October to March) and moving into the
dry weather season (approximately April to September). For ancient Israelites the lateness of the rain would be considered extraordinary, possibly a
sign of divine intervention (1 Sam 6:10). Here it serves as one of the Lord's
weapons (Josh 10:11; Isa 30:30; Ps 18:13-14).

10:1-20 Eighth plague

No longer aimed simply at persuading the Israelites or the Egyptians,
the plague of locusts is to teach the descendants of the Israelites (v. 2). This

the people go to serve the LORD, their God. Do you not yet realize that Egypt is being destroyed?" [8]So Moses and Aaron were brought back to Pharaoh, who said to them, "Go, serve the LORD, your God. But who exactly will go?" [9]Moses answered, "With our young and old we must go; with our sons and daughters, with our flocks and herds we must go. It is a pilgrimage feast of the LORD for us." [10]"The LORD help you," Pharaoh replied, "if I let your little ones go with you! Clearly, you have some evil in mind. [11]By no means! Just you men go and serve the LORD. After all, that is what you have been asking for." With that they were driven from Pharaoh's presence.

[12]The LORD then said to Moses: Stretch out your hand over the land of Egypt for the locusts, that they may come upon it and eat up all the land's vegetation, whatever the hail has left. [13]So Moses stretched out his staff over the land of Egypt, and the LORD drove an east wind over the land all that day and all night. When it was morning, the east wind brought the locusts. [14]The locusts came up over the whole land of Egypt and settled down over all its territory. Never before had there been such a fierce swarm of locusts, nor will there ever be again. [15]They covered the surface of the whole land, so that it became black. They ate up all the vegetation in the land and all the fruit of the trees the hail had spared. Nothing green was left on any tree or plant in the fields throughout the land of Egypt.

[16]Pharaoh hurriedly summoned Moses and Aaron and said, "I have sinned against the LORD, your God, and against you. [17]But now, do forgive me my sin only this once, and pray to the LORD, your God, only to take this death from me." [18]When Moses left Pharaoh, he prayed to the LORD, [19]and the LORD caused the wind to shift to a very strong west wind, which took up the locusts and hurled them into the Red Sea. Not a single locust remained within the whole territory of Egypt. [20]Yet the LORD

---

theme anticipates the celebration of Passover in Exodus 12–13. Here, for the first time, Pharaoh's own servants plead for the Israelites' release (v. 7); Pharaoh is presented as the only Egyptian who still needs convincing. He again negotiates with Moses and Aaron, but to no avail; also for the first time, the story depicts Pharaoh's suspicions about some hidden agenda on the part of Moses and Aaron (vv. 8-11).

A massive east windstorm (v. 13) brings the locusts, which were a major problem all around the ancient Middle East. The poetic traditions of the plagues are no less graphic: in Psalm 78:46 locusts are paired in poetic parallelism with "the caterpillar," and in Psalm 105:34-35 with "grasshoppers." Psalm 78:46 mentions the locusts in the context of a harvest, and Psalm 105:35 mentions the destruction of crops; the authors seem to have in mind the destruction of the spring or summer harvests. The book of Joel likewise describes a locust plague in the context of an east windstorm. Verse 19 uses

hardened Pharaoh's heart, and he would not let the Israelites go.

Ninth Plague: the Darkness. [21]Then the Lord said to Moses: Stretch out your hand toward the sky, that over the land of Egypt there may be such darkness that one can feel it. [22]So Moses stretched out his hand toward the sky, and there was dense darkness throughout the land of Egypt for three days. [23]People could not see one another, nor could they get up from where they were, for three days. But all the Israelites had light where they lived.

[24]Pharaoh then summoned Moses and Aaron and said, "Go, serve the Lord. Only your flocks and herds will be detained. Even your little ones may go with you." [25]But Moses replied, "You also must give us sacrifices and burnt offerings to make to the Lord, our God. [26]Our livestock also must go with us. Not an animal must be left behind, for some of them we will select for service to the Lord, our God; but we will not know with which ones we are to serve the Lord until we arrive there." [27]But the Lord hardened Pharaoh's heart, and he was unwilling to let them go. [28]Pharaoh said to Moses, "Leave me, and see to it that you do not see my face again! For the day you do see my face you will die!" [29]Moses replied, "You are right! I will never see your face again."

---

the western wind (literally "sea-wind") to drive off the destructive locusts into the Reed Sea, anticipating the hurling of the Egyptians into this body of water in Exodus 14. The presentation of the east wind likewise heralds the dry wind mentioned in the account of the crossing of the sea (14:21). Israel's experience of westerly rainstorms and dry east windstorms helped to inform its story of Egypt's destruction.

10:21-29 Ninth plague

The plague of darkness is not mentioned in Psalms 78 and 105. The preceding plague (10:15) mentions the covering of the entire land, while this one blankets the entire sky (10:21-22). A late Egyptian text (Setne Khamwas II and Si-Osire) similarly presents a magician casting darkness over Pharaoh's court. Like the preceding plague, this one presupposes the picture of a massive *khamsin*, the destructive east wind darkening the sky (Joel 2:2, 10; 3:4; 4:15). Perhaps because of the massive severity of this plague, Pharaoh again attempts to negotiate with Moses (v. 24). He refuses the request to release the Israelites' animals, ironic given that they are needed for the sacrifice (vv. 25-26). Ultimately Pharaoh refuses, increasing the tension by refusing future audiences with Moses (vv. 27-29). This plague ends with a stalemate that requires a different sort of persuasion.

11:1-10 Tenth plague

The command from God declares not that the Pharaoh will simply let the Israelites go but that he will drive them away (v. 1). They are to depart with

11 **Tenth Plague: the Death of the Firstborn.** ¹Then the LORD spoke to Moses: One more plague I will bring upon Pharaoh and upon Egypt. After that he will let you depart. In fact, when he finally lets you go, he will drive you away. ²Instruct the people that every man is to ask his neighbor, and every woman her neighbor, for silver and gold articles and for clothing. ³The LORD indeed made the Egyptians well-disposed toward the people; Moses himself was very highly regarded by Pharaoh's servants and the people in the land of Egypt.

⁴Moses then said, "Thus says the LORD: About midnight I will go forth through Egypt. ⁵Every firstborn in the land of Egypt will die, from the firstborn of Pharaoh who sits on his throne to the firstborn of the slave-girl who is at the handmill, as well as all the firstborn of

---

goods from the Egyptians (v. 2) due to their positive attitude toward them (v. 3); the picture might suggest spoils of war. This plague is different from all the others because the death of the firstborn is the only plague presented as the result of direct divine intervention and not an act of nature (v. 4).

The various plagues were evidently understood as three sets of three, or triads, capped by the tenth and final plague. The first triad is marked by the Egyptian magicians' admission of "the finger of God" (8:15), the second by the same magicians suffering from the plague (9:11), and the third by Pharaoh's isolation in his deadlock with Moses and Aaron (10:28). Each triad moves the conflict to a higher level of dramatic tension. The first triad operates mostly on a basic human level of which Egyptian magicians are nearly as capable as Moses and Aaron. The second triad adds the idea of divine protection of the Israelites from the plagues. The last set of three plagues moves the drama from the human level between the Egyptian magicians and Moses and Aaron to a cosmic plane of conflict between Pharaoh and God. In the tenth plague God's force and intervention reach a climax.

In verses 4-10 the divine message about the tenth plague is delivered to Pharaoh without description of his response. The message shows the ultimate effects of Pharaoh's refusal: all Egyptian firstborn will die because of him. The firstborn extends to male offspring of people and animals, as well as crops, which serve as offerings to God (see 4:23; 13:12; cf. 22:28-29, 34:19-20). In the case of Israelite human firstborns, a further ritual provides for their redemption (Exod 34:19-20; see also Num 3:40-51). Such ritual borrows from the literal notion of redemption as financial compensation paid to get a family member out of slavery entered into because of debt (cf. Exod 22:2). The presentation is metaphorically dense: Israel's salvation (which literally refers to military help) is here understood as God's exercising the divine right to Egyptian firstborns without their recourse to

the animals. ⁶Then there will be loud wailing throughout the land of Egypt, such as has never been, nor will ever be again. ⁷But among all the Israelites, among human beings and animals alike, not even a dog will growl, so that you may know that the LORD distinguishes between Egypt and Israel. ⁸All these servants of yours will then come down to me and bow down before me, saying: Leave, you and all your followers! Then I will depart." With that he left Pharaoh's presence in hot anger.

⁹The LORD said to Moses: Pharaoh will not listen to you so that my wonders may be multiplied in the land of Egypt. ¹⁰Thus, although Moses and Aaron performed all these wonders in Pharaoh's

---

financial redemption. In Numbers 3:12-13 and 8:17-18 the Lord's slaying of the Egyptian firstborn appears as an explanation for when the Israelite practice of firstborn redemption started. These passages give the impression that the Israelite tradition of the tenth plague was celebrated in the ritual of redeeming the firstborn. The exodus story connects the narrative of the Egyptian's destruction of their firstborn to Passover.

In the context of the story, because of Pharaoh's refusal to release Israel, the Lord's firstborn son (4:22; cf. Hos 11:1), the Egyptians will experience the destruction of their own firstborn with no possibility of redemption (see Num 3:12-13). Sacrificial imagery appears in other descriptions of Israelite warfare (Isa 34, especially v. 6). Under oppressive conditions, war can show that a deity is both willing and able to act on behalf of Israelites, who call to this deity for help and call this deity "the God of Israel." This ultimate sacrifice will reverse the situation between the Israelites and the Egyptians. Before it was the Israelites who cried from their suffering (Exod 3:7, 9); now it is to be the Egyptians' turn (11:6). There will be no sign of hostility against the Israelites: "not even a dog will growl" at them (v. 7). As a result, the Egyptians will act like the "servants" to Israel (just as the Israelites had been Egypt's servants), and they will beg them to leave (v. 8). Moses departs from Pharaoh's presence not with fear or disappointment but with "hot anger," evidently mirroring God's own attitude against Pharaoh (v. 8). Although the quoted words of verses 4-8 begins as God's speech that Moses is to deliver to Pharaoh, in verse 8 Moses is the one referred to as "me," the one to whom the Egyptians will come and beg, implying overlap in the identity of God and Moses (cf. 7:1, where the Lord predicts that Moses will be "a god to Pharaoh"). A brief divine report (11:9) and a narrative notice (v. 10) indicate that Pharaoh refuses. A description of Pharaoh's response is delayed until 12:29-36, after the description of the Passover ritual (12:1-28).

presence, the LORD hardened Pharaoh's heart, and he would not let the Israelites go from his land.

12 **The Passover Ritual Prescribed.** [1]The LORD said to Moses and Aaron in the land of Egypt: [2]This month will stand at the head of your calendar; you will reckon it the first month of the year. [3]Tell the whole community of Israel: On the tenth of this month every family must procure for itself a lamb, one apiece for each household. [4]If a household is too small for a lamb, it along with its nearest neighbor will procure one, and apportion the lamb's cost in proportion to the number of persons, according to what each household consumes. [5]Your lamb must be a year-old male and without blemish. You may take it from either the sheep or the goats. [6]You will keep it until the fourteenth day of this month, and then, with the whole community of Israel assembled, it will be slaughtered during the evening twilight. [7]They will take some of its blood and apply it to the two doorposts and the lintel of the houses in which they eat it. [8]They will consume its meat that same night, eating it roasted with unleavened bread and bitter herbs. [9]Do not eat any of it raw or even boiled in water, but roasted, with its head and shanks and inner organs. [10]You must not keep any of it beyond the morning; whatever is left over in the morning must be burned up.

[11]This is how you are to eat it: with your loins girt, sandals on your feet and

---

12:1-20 The Passover ritual (initial description)

This chapter contains a complex set of materials centered on Passover. The core description of the holiday in verses 1-10 is followed by a series of elaborations, verses 11-13, 14-20, 21-27. Verses 11-13 and 21-27 are somewhat redundant, suggesting two versions of the ritual instructions for this festival. Like a magnet, this chapter attracted various texts originating from different traditions (vv. 1-20 = P, possibly the specific priestly tradition of the Holiness Code [H] of Lev 17–26; vv. 21-28, 29-39 = J[E]; vv. 43-49 = P, possibly H, similar to Num 9:11-12; cf. 13:3-13 = dtr).

The initial part of the Passover ritual is marked by time: Passover occurs in the first month of the year, specifically on the tenth day (vv. 2-3). With Passover the story enters into the holy time of the spring pilgrimage feast, suggesting that this is the time when God acts on Israel's behalf. This sacred time lasts through the book of Exodus, as the covenant on Mount Sinai (Exod 19:1) corresponds to the time of the feast of Weeks (Pentecost). The next pieces of ritual information concern the sacrificial animal and the setting of this ritual in homes (v. 3). According to verse 5, the animal may be the young of a sheep or of a goat (in colloquial English a "kid"). The blood of the animal is a significant element of the ritual (v. 7). The meat of the animal is to be eaten with unleavened bread and bitter herbs (v. 8). The description reflects the domestic setting of Passover, designed to overcome

51

your staff in hand, you will eat it in a hurry. It is the Lord's Passover. [12]For on this same night I will go through Egypt, striking down every firstborn in the land, human being and beast alike, and executing judgment on all the gods of Egypt—I, the Lord! [13]But for you the blood will mark the houses where you are. Seeing the blood, I will pass over you; thereby, when I strike the land of Egypt, no destructive blow will come upon you.

[14]This day will be a day of remembrance for you, which your future generations will celebrate with pilgrimage to the Lord; you will celebrate it as a statute forever. [15]For seven days you must eat unleavened bread. From the very first day you will have your houses clear of all leaven. For whoever eats leavened bread from the first day to the seventh will be cut off from Israel. [16]On the first day you will hold a sacred assembly, and likewise on the seventh. On these days no sort of work shall be done, except to prepare the food that everyone needs. [17]Keep, then, the custom of the unleavened bread, since it was on this very day that I brought your armies out of the land of Egypt. You must observe this day throughout your generations as a statute forever. [18]From the evening of the fourteenth day of the first month

the limits of any family's poverty ("too small," v. 4). The ritual prescription also reflects the understanding of Passover as a national holiday ("the whole community of Israel assembled," v. 6), elsewhere listed as one of the three great pilgrimage feasts to the temple (Exod 23:14-17; Lev 23:4-14; Num 28:16-25).

Verses 11-13 elaborate on the unleavened bread and the blood. Verses 11-12 link those celebrating the ritual of Passover with the Israelite ancestors who experienced the first Passover. The departure from Egypt serves as an explanation for the Passover celebration. Verses 12-13 describe the Lord as the direct executor of the plague. (An alternative interpretation appears in the J version of vv. 21-23.) Verses 14-20 contain provisions designed specifically for the feast of Unleavened Bread, without reference to Passover. (The well-known interpretation of the unleavened bread as a remembrance of the haste with which the Israelites had to leave Egypt does not appear here, but in the narrative of 12:24 and 39.) The two feasts are thought to have been originally separate but were linked at an early point in Israel's history.

12:21-28 Passover instructions revisited

The instructions here vary from verses 1-20. Verse 21 does not specify the animals (cf. 12:5), with the Hebrew for "lambs" being generic for small animals of the flock. Verse 22 adds hyssop as the instrument for applying the blood. Because of its thin branches, hyssop was suitable for use in ritual cleansing (Lev 14:4; Num 19:6; cf. Ps 51:9). The detailed location given for the blood (v. 22) and the "destroyer" (v. 23) may point to an old belief that

until the evening of the twenty-first day of this month you will eat unleavened bread. [19]For seven days no leaven may be found in your houses; for anyone, a resident alien or a native, who eats leavened food will be cut off from the community of Israel. [20]You shall eat nothing leavened; wherever you dwell you may eat only unleavened bread.

Promulgation of the Passover. [21]Moses summoned all the elders of Israel and said to them, "Go and procure lambs for your families, and slaughter the Passover victims. [22]Then take a bunch of hyssop, and dipping it in the blood that is in the basin, apply some of this blood to the lintel and the two doorposts. And none of you shall go outdoors until morning. [23]For when the LORD goes by to strike down the Egyptians, seeing the blood on the lintel and the two doorposts, the LORD will pass over that door and not let the destroyer come into your houses to strike you down.

[24]"You will keep this practice forever as a statute for yourselves and your descendants. [25]Thus, when you have entered the land which the LORD will give you as he promised, you must observe this rite. [26]When your children ask you, 'What does this rite of yours mean?' [27]you will reply, 'It is the Passover sacrifice for the LORD, who passed over the houses of the Israelites in Egypt; when he struck down the Egyptians, he delivered our houses.'"

Then the people knelt and bowed down, [28]and the Israelites went and did exactly as the LORD had commanded Moses and Aaron.

---

paschal blood averts the springtime demonic power that kills its victims, except where the ritual commanded by God prevents execution. Although an older tradition might have held that the demon thinks that, because of the blood, the inhabitants of those houses are already dead, in the context of the exodus story the blood was regarded as purifying the houses, which become zones of holiness repellent to demonic force and attractive to the Lord.

The Hebrew word *pasach* seems to mean "to shield" in Isaiah 31:5, and the idea of the Lord's protection is explicit in Exodus 12:13, 23. In Psalm 78:49 the plagues, generally regarded as the unleashing of divine "fiery breath, / roar, fury, and distress," are personified as divine "storming messengers of death." The idea of the divine "destroyer" also underlies the two divine figures with the Lord who "destroy" Sodom and Gomorrah (Gen 19:13; cf. 1 Chr 21:15; according to Isa 54:16 God created this "destroyer"). These passages show considerable imagery of the destructive east wind (Ps 35:5), and this spring-summer wind perhaps inspired the destructive dimension of this divine figure, whose force was modeled on the military units called "raiders" ("strike forces" in colloquial English) in 1 Samuel 13:17; 14:15. The destroyer embodies the power of death passing by under God's authority (cf. Isa 28:18-19). Exodus 12:13 and 23 present the divine

Death of the Firstborn. ²⁹And so at midnight the LORD struck down every firstborn in the land of Egypt, from the firstborn of Pharaoh sitting on his throne to the firstborn of the prisoner in the dungeon, as well as all the firstborn of the animals. ³⁰Pharaoh arose in the night, he and all his servants and all the Egyptians; and there was loud wailing throughout Egypt, for there was not a house without its dead.

Permission to Depart. ³¹During the night Pharaoh summoned Moses and Aaron and said, "Leave my people at once, you and the Israelites! Go and serve the LORD as you said. ³²Take your flocks, too, and your herds, as you said, and go; and bless me, too!"

³³The Egyptians, in a hurry to send them away from the land, urged the people on, for they said, "All of us will die!" ³⁴The people, therefore, took their dough before it was leavened, in their kneading bowls wrapped in their cloaks on their shoulders. ³⁵And the Israelites did as Moses had commanded: they asked the Egyptians for articles of silver and gold and for clothing. ³⁶Indeed the LORD had made the Egyptians so well-disposed toward the people that they let them have whatever they asked for. And so they despoiled the Egyptians.

Departure from Egypt. ³⁷The Israelites set out from Rameses for Succoth, about six hundred thousand men on foot, not counting the children. ³⁸A crowd of mixed ancestry also went up with them, with livestock in great abundance, both flocks and herds. ³⁹The dough they had brought out of Egypt

---

destruction in different ways, but both differ from the later idea of devils or Satan. Verses 24-27 add a ritual instruction addressed to Israel's descendants; they are to ask questions and provide answers about the meaning of the ritual, which infuses events with meaning. The people's compliance in verses 27-28 echoes their compliance in 4:31.

12:29-36 The story resumes

With the prescriptions for Passover laid out, the narrative picks up again. This section fulfills the divine words of 11:5-8: destruction of the Egyptian firstborn results in lamentation; in turn, Pharaoh demands the Israelites' departure. Verses 33-36 add the Egyptian people to the picture. Missing from the ritual prescriptions is the detail that the Israelites should take their dough before it was leavened (12:34). Verses 35-36 echo the divine words of 11:1-3 regarding the Egyptians providing the Israelites with goods. Given the resonances between 11:1-8 and 12:29-36 (as well as the crossing pattern or "chiasm" achieved by their reversal of sections), the two passages form a literary frame around 12:1-28, highlighting its importance.

12:37-42 The beginning of the departure

As recalled in Numbers 33:5, the first stage in the journey from Egypt to Sinai involves the trip from Raamses to Succoth (v. 37). The number of six

they baked into unleavened loaves. It was not leavened, because they had been driven out of Egypt and could not wait. They did not even prepare food for the journey.

⁴⁰The time the Israelites had stayed in Egypt was four hundred and thirty years. ⁴¹At the end of four hundred and thirty years, on this very date, all the armies of the LORD left the land of Egypt. ⁴²This was a night of vigil for the LORD, when he brought them out of the land of Egypt; so on this night all Israelites must keep a vigil for the LORD throughout their generations.

Law of the Passover. ⁴³The LORD said to Moses and Aaron: This is the Passover statute. No foreigner may eat of it. ⁴⁴However, every slave bought for money you will circumcise; then he may eat of it. ⁴⁵But no tenant or hired worker may eat of it. ⁴⁶It must be eaten in one house; you may not take any of its meat outside the house. You shall not break any of its bones. ⁴⁷The whole community of Israel must celebrate this feast. ⁴⁸If any alien residing among you would celebrate the Passover for the LORD, all his males must be circumcised, and then he may join in its celebration just like the natives. But no one who is uncircumcised may eat of it. ⁴⁹There will be one law for the native and for the alien residing among you.

⁵⁰All the Israelites did exactly as the LORD had commanded Moses and Aaron. ⁵¹On that same day the LORD brought the Israelites out of the land of Egypt company by company.

---

hundred thousand Israelite males, "not counting the children" or the "crowd of mixed ancestry" in verses 37-38 (cf. Num 1 and 26), has been doubted by scholars; some prefer to view the word "thousand" instead as a homonym (words spelled and pronounced alike but different in meaning) for "clan" or "unit." The narrative refers in v. 39 to the unleavened dough mentioned in verse 34; the duplication may suggest that the two units were not written down by the same author. In verses 40-41 the chronological notice of 430 years spent in Egypt contrasts with the 400 years offered for the same period in Genesis 15:13 (cf. the 480 years that 1 Kgs 6:1 counts from the time of the exodus until the building of the temple); it would seem that these numbers represent a reckoning of generations (generally twenty years in biblical terms). With these sorts of numbers, ancient scribes were perhaps trying to make sense of the vagaries in the historical record that they inherited.

Verse 42 closes the unit by underscoring the relationship between the ancient event of the Passover and its ritual celebration in the time of its author.

12:43-51 Passover: Further regulations

Verse 19 had mentioned the possibility of the problem with a "resident alien," but had not fully clarified his status in the actual celebration; verses 43-49 address the matter of the "foreigner." This style of inserting or adding

13 **Consecration of Firstborn.** [1]The LORD spoke to Moses and said: [2]Consecrate to me every firstborn; whatever opens the womb among the Israelites, whether of human being or beast, belongs to me.

[3]Moses said to the people, "Remember this day on which you came out of Egypt, out of a house of slavery. For it was with a strong hand that the LORD brought you out from there. Nothing made with leaven may be eaten. [4]This day on which you are going out is in the month of Abib. [5]Therefore, when the LORD, your God, has brought you into the land of the Canaanites, the Hittites, the Amorites, the Perrizites, the Girgashites, the Hivites, and the Jebusites, which he swore to your ancestors to give you, a land flowing with milk and honey, you will perform the following service in this month. [6]For seven days you will eat unleavened bread, and the seventh day will also be a festival to the LORD. [7]Unleavened bread may be eaten during the seven days, but nothing leavened

---

paragraphs of material to the core of the ritual (itself embedded within the larger narrative) suggests a growing priestly corpus of texts, which further clarify issues as needed. Verse 46 adds a note about the manner of eating the meal; it must take place in the house, and eating may not go as far as breaking the animal's bones (to get at the marrow for further nourishment?), a directive quoted as prophetic of Jesus' crucifixion in John's Gospel (19:36).

The team of Moses and Aaron suggests a priestly hand for this section, which adds specifications about the participants in the Passover celebration. Ancient Israelite households could include non-Israelites (specifically servants), and the priestly tradition here clarifies who is eligible to participate in the Passover. Verse 51 virtually repeats verse 41, picking up the story line of verses 37-41. This technique of repetition is used by scribes to insert material, in this case the regulations of verses 43-50.

13:1-16 Unleavened bread

Using language closer to the book of Deuteronomy than to priestly tradition, this presentation focuses on the redemption of the firstborn (vv. 1-2, 11-16) and the feast of Unleavened Bread (3-10). In this version Passover is not mentioned at all. Redemption of the firstborn represents a ritual strategy (see 11:4-10) to avoid the practice of child sacrifice known among Israel's neighbors and evidently in early Israel as well (Isa 30:33; Mic 6:7; cf. Ezek 20:25-26). The sacrifice of the firstborn son endured as a powerful image, one that would heavily inform the Christian presentation of Jesus as the Son of the Father.

For several decades scholars have viewed Passover and Unleavened Bread as unrelated festivals: Passover has been thought to have originated as a spring rite to ensure the protection of the group and its flocks against

and no leaven may be found in your possession in all your territory. [8]And on that day you will explain to your son, 'This is because of what the LORD did for me when I came out of Egypt.' [9]It will be like a sign on your hand and a reminder on your forehead, so that the teaching of the LORD will be on your lips: with a strong hand the LORD brought you out of Egypt. [10]You will keep this statute at its appointed time from year to year.

[11]"When the LORD, your God, has brought you into the land of the Canaanites, just as he swore to you and your ancestors, and gives it to you, [12]you will dedicate to the LORD every newborn that opens the womb; and every firstborn male of your animals will belong to the LORD. [13]Every firstborn of a donkey you will ransom with a sheep. If you do not ransom it, you will break its neck. Every human firstborn of your sons you must ransom. [14]And when your son asks you later on, 'What does this mean?' you will tell him, 'With a strong hand the LORD brought us out of Egypt, out of a house of slavery. [15]When Pharaoh stubbornly refused to let us go, the LORD killed every firstborn in the land of Egypt, the firstborn of human being and beast alike. That is why I sacrifice to the LORD every male that opens the womb, and why I ransom every firstborn of my sons.' [16]It will be like

death as they move to summer pasture, while Unleavened Bread has been interpreted as ritual for a settled agrarian community celebrating the first spring grain harvest. Israelites, however, took care of both flocks and crops, and participated in the festivals of spring associated with their care (just as they celebrated a group of holidays in the early fall, at the end of the dry season and just as the rainy season is to commence). The shift from the rainy season to the dry season in the spring brought potential threats to both flocks and crops, and the rituals of this period may have been designed to ward off dangers associated with the east wind (including pestilence, locusts, darkness, and death), captured in the personification of the destroyer (12:23). The Passover story perhaps moves from plagues associated most directly with Egypt (in particular, the first three or four plagues) closer to the Israelite experience at home.

Throughout its history Passover–Unleavened Bread remained largely a family affair, even as it served as one of the three pilgrimage festivals. After the Roman destruction of the Jerusalem temple in A.D. 70, Passover–Unleavened Bread remained preeminently a family celebration. The Samaritan community, which traces its origins to the northern kingdom of Israel, today adheres to the ancient tradition of family sacrifice spelled out in Exodus 12. Although sacrifices stopped in Jewish tradition following the temple's destruction, Passover celebrations ritually remember this sacrifice by including an animal bone on the Passover plate. The Last Supper was

a sign on your hand and a band on your forehead that with a strong hand the LORD brought us out of Egypt."

IV. The Deliverance of the Israelites from Pharaoh and Victory at the Sea

Toward the Red Sea. [17]Now, when Pharaoh let the people go, God did not lead them by way of the Philistines' land, though this was the nearest; for God said: If the people see that they have to fight, they might change their minds and return to Egypt. [18]Instead, God rerouted them toward the Red Sea by way of the wilderness road, and the Israelites went up out of the land of Egypt arrayed for battle. [19]Moses also took Joseph's bones with him, for Joseph had made the Israelites take a solemn oath, saying, "God will surely take care of you, and you must bring my bones up with you from here."

[20]Setting out from Succoth, they camped at Etham near the edge of the wilderness.

[21]The LORD preceded them, in the daytime by means of a column of cloud to show them the way, and at night by

---

understood as a Passover meal by three of the gospel writers (Matt 26:17; Mark 14:1; Luke 22:1, 7, 11, 15; cf. John 13:1).

Christianity further reinterpreted various aspects of Passover ritual. The unleavened bread and wine are the elements transformed by the Eucharist into the body and blood of Christ. Jesus himself becomes the sacrificial "paschal" Lamb of God who takes away the sin of the world (John 1:29, 36; 1 Pet 1:19; Rev 5:6-14; 17:14). The English word "paschal" derives from Jewish Aramaic *pascha*, itself derived from the biblical Hebrew word for Passover, *pesach*. Jesus as the sacrificial lamb (Acts 8:32) was modeled on Isaiah 53:7's application of this notion to a prophetic figure. Paul makes a classic rabbinic move in using unleavened bread as a symbol of personal renewal, thanks to Jesus the paschal lamb (1 Cor 5:7-8). The bitter herbs endure in the Jewish Passover as a powerful reminder of the Israelites' bitter life in Egypt.

As these examples show, the Jewish use of these symbols, as well as their Christian reuses, gains meaning when considered in the larger context of the ancient Israelite-Jewish sacrificial system prior to the temple's destruction. In more recent decades, Christians have been invited into Jewish homes to celebrate the Passover meal, helping Christians to appreciate Judaism in itself as well as the Jewish background of Jesus and the Christianity inspired by his life, death, and resurrection.

The Passover instructions in 13:1-16 capture the personal side of the exodus, as it is commanded that the child shall be instructed that this is "what the LORD did *for me*" and "so that the teaching of the LORD will be on *your lips*" (vv. 8-9; emphasis added). For Jews of each generation, to remember (v. 3) is to reexperience the exodus for themselves (v. 8). This is to

Statue of brewer in ancient Egypt

means of a column of fire to give them light. Thus they could travel both day and night. ²²Neither the column of cloud by day nor the column of fire by night ever left its place in front of the people.

14 ¹Then the LORD spoke to Moses: ²Speak to the Israelites: Let them turn about and camp before Pi-hahiroth, between Migdol and the sea. Camp in front of Baal-zephon, just opposite, by the sea. ³Pharaoh will then say, "The Israelites are wandering about aimlessly in the land. The wilderness has closed in on them." ⁴I will so harden Pharaoh's heart that he will pursue them. Thus I will receive glory through Pharaoh and all his army, and the Egyptians will know that I am the LORD.

This the Israelites did. ⁵When it was reported to the king of Egypt that the people had fled, Pharaoh and his servants had a change of heart about the people. "What in the world have we done!" they said. "We have released Israel from our service!" ⁶So Pharaoh harnessed his chariots and took his army with him. ⁷He took six hundred select chariots and all the chariots of Egypt, with officers on all of them. ⁸The LORD hardened the heart of Pharaoh, king of Egypt, so that he pursued the Israelites while they were going out in triumph.

---

be recalled with the help of memory aid devices put on the hand and head (vv. 9, 16), comparable to amulets in the ancient world, but without magical incantations (cf. Deut 11:18). This Passover memory from one generation to the next is expressed in the title of the Jewish Haggadah, the book used for the Passover ritual meal, which derived from the biblical expression in verse 8, "you will explain" (*wehiggadta*).

13:17–14:9 Succoth to the sea

The route taken by the Israelites does not follow the direct route "by way of the Philistines' land" (v. 17); instead, God directs them toward the sea. Following the early Greek translators, the NABRE translation renders this sea as the "Red Sea" (v. 18), but the Hebrew word involved better suits either "Reed Sea" or "Sea of the Edge." "Reed Sea" would point to the marshes at the north of the Nile Delta or perhaps even the Gulf of Aqaba (cf. 23:31), while "Sea of the Edge" evokes a watery peripheral area. The march is couched in military language as Israel goes "arrayed for battle" (v. 18).

The passage mentions "Joseph's bones" (v. 19), in fulfillment of the oath in Genesis 50:24-25 and anticipating their interment at Shechem. For an Israelite audience these bones would have evoked the connection of the Shechem sanctuary with the patriarchs Joseph and Jacob. For that was the holy place where Jacob earlier "set up an altar there and invoked 'El, the God of Israel'" (Gen 33:20) and where the bones will be ultimately buried (Josh 24:32). Verse 20 then includes a geographical reference of the type found in 12:37 and paralleled in Numbers 33:6. The list in Numbers 33 may

⁹The Egyptians pursued them—all Pharaoh's horses, his chariots, his horsemen, and his army—and caught up with them as they lay encamped by the sea, at Pi-hahiroth, in front of Baal-zephon.

Crossing the Red Sea. ¹⁰Now Pharaoh was near when the Israelites looked up and saw that the Egyptians had set out after them. Greatly frightened, the Israelites cried out to the LORD. ¹¹To Moses they said, "Were there no burial places in Egypt that you brought us to die in the wilderness? What have you done to us, bringing us out of Egypt? ¹²Did we not tell you this in Egypt, when we said, 'Leave us alone that we may serve the Egyptians'? Far better for us to serve the Egyptians than to die in the wilderness." ¹³But Moses answered the people, "Do not fear! Stand your ground and see the victory the LORD will win for you today. For these Egyptians whom you see today you will never see again. ¹⁴The LORD will fight for you; you have only to keep still."

¹⁵Then the LORD said to Moses: Why are you crying out to me? Tell the Israelites to set out. ¹⁶And you, lift up your staff and stretch out your hand over the sea, and split it in two, that the Israelites may pass through the sea on dry land. ¹⁷But I will harden the hearts of the Egyptians so that they will go in after them, and I will receive glory through Pharaoh and all his army, his chariots and his horsemen. ¹⁸The Egyptians will know that I am the LORD, when I receive glory through Pharaoh, his chariots, and his horsemen.

¹⁹The angel of God, who had been leading Israel's army, now moved and went around behind them. And the

---

have provided the names for the stops made by the Israelites in the books of Exodus and Numbers. The columns of fire and cloud (v. 21), dramatic signs of divine presence and protection (Isa 4:5), anticipate one version of the battle at the sea in 14:11-31. Finally, 14:1-10 presents the Egyptians mobilized as a military force, this time obstinate beyond belief and ultimately for the sake of God's glory (v. 4).

Much speculation has gone into the route taken by the Israelites. A journey across the north of the Sinai Peninsula has been thought to underlie the place names (13:20, also 14:1-2), since the only known place name is Baal-zephon, believed to be located about twenty-seven miles south-southwest of modern Port Said (on the Mediterranean Sea). The mention of the "wilderness road" in 13:18 had been thought to suggest a way farther south. Some scholars speculate further as to whether different Israelite groups or tribes went by different routes, but such reconstructions lie beyond any known evidence. During the period of these texts' writing, accurate information about the route may have been unknown.

14:10-31 A double version of the crossing

The frightened, lamenting Israelites caught between the Egyptians and the sea set the stage for the Lord's military action (vv. 10-14). The better-known

column of cloud, moving from in front of them, took up its place behind them, [20]so that it came between the Egyptian army and that of Israel. And when it became dark, the cloud illumined the night; and so the rival camps did not come any closer together all night long. [21]Then Moses stretched out his hand over the sea; and the LORD drove back the sea with a strong east wind all night long and turned the sea into dry ground. The waters were split, [22]so that the Israelites entered into the midst of the sea on dry land, with the water as a wall to their right and to their left.

Rout of the Egyptians. [23]The Egyptians followed in pursuit after them—all Pharaoh's horses and chariots and horsemen—into the midst of the sea. [24]But during the watch just before dawn, the LORD looked down from a column of fiery cloud upon the Egyptian army and threw it into a panic; [25]and he so clogged their chariot wheels that they could drive only with difficulty. With that the Egyptians said, "Let us flee from Israel, because the LORD is fighting for them against Egypt."

[26]Then the LORD spoke to Moses: Stretch out your hand over the sea, that the water may flow back upon the Egyptians, upon their chariots and their horsemen. [27]So Moses stretched out his hand over the sea, and at daybreak the sea returned to its normal flow. The Egyptians were fleeing head on toward it when the LORD cast the Egyptians into the midst of the sea. [28]As the water flowed back, it covered the chariots and the horsemen. Of all Pharaoh's army which had followed the Israelites into the sea, not even one escaped. [29]But the Israelites had walked on dry land through the midst of the sea, with the water as a wall to their right and to their left. [30]Thus the LORD saved Israel on that day from the power of Egypt. When Israel saw the Egyptians lying dead on the seashore [31]and saw the great power that the LORD had shown against Egypt, the people feared the LORD. They believed in the LORD and in Moses his servant.

---

version of the victory presents it as a miraculous splitting of the sea. This version (usually considered priestly) begins in verses 15-18 with the divine command to Moses to part the waters. The Egyptians will be obstinate and learn the lesson of who the true God is. This version continues in verses 21-23 with the execution of the command and its supernatural effect. With the Egyptians following the Israelites (v. 23), the Lord instructs Moses again to stretch out his hand for the waters to return (vv. 26-27a) to engulf the Egyptians (v. 28). This version, summarized in verse 29, stresses the miraculous divine help (cf. Ps 78:13: "He split the sea and led them across, / piling up the waters rigid as walls"; see also Neh 9:11a; Isa 63:11-14). This presentation closely resembles the Israelites crossing the Jordan (Josh 3–4, esp. 4:23; the two may have influenced one another). This version, dramatically rendered in the Hollywood movie *The Ten Commandments*, is not the complete story in Exodus 14, however.

15 ¹Then Moses and the Israelites sang this song to the LORD:

I will sing to the LORD, for he is
gloriously triumphant;
horse and chariot he has cast
into the sea.
²My strength and my refuge is the
LORD,
and he has become my savior.
This is my God, I praise him;
the God of my father, I extol
him.

³The LORD is a warrior,
LORD is his name!
⁴Pharaoh's chariots and army he
hurled into the sea;

Another version, often attributed to JE (vv. 19-20, 21b, 24-25, 27b, 30-31), involves the help of an angel and the column of cloud (see 13:21-22; Josh 24:7). Together they protect the Israelites by separating the two camps. The Lord uses the east wind (v. 21a) to allow the Israelites to move forward at the sea. With the Egyptians in hot pursuit, the Lord throws them into a panic. Their wheels get clogged in the mud and they try to retreat (vv. 24-25), but the Lord hurls them into the sea. This natural account evidently takes place at the edge of the sea (not in the middle of it), resulting in the Egyptians "lying dead on the seashore" (v. 30). This version seems to inform the mention in Numbers 20:16. Partially similar to this version is Psalm 106, which stresses the drying of the sea through a divine roar (v. 9; cf. Ps 105, with no crossing of the sea).

15:1-21 The song at the sea

The poetic song celebrates the victory (v. 1). With its numerous ancient Hebrew grammatical features, the poem offers the oldest surviving witness to the victory at the sea, and the later JE and P authors used it to craft their own prose accounts. The poem has three parts: verses 1b-8 offer an initial picture of divine victory, verses 9-12 recapitulate verses 4-8, and verses 13-18 shift the focus away from the battle to events after the victory. The initial section presents God as the divine warrior who saves Israel (vv. 1-2). In its literal sense, to save is a military image. The Lord is also the personal deity of the family, "the God of my father" (vv. 2-3). It is this God who throws Pharaoh and his military force into the sea, with the water piling up on them (vv. 4-8). The picture focuses not on the Israelites' progression through the sea but on the drowning Egyptians. How this exactly took place is not spelled out (which is not expected of a poem). To reconcile the versions requires one to reinterpret the piling up of the water as happening during the Israelites' movement (as they are in 14:22), even though the Israelites are not mentioned in this part of the poem.

the elite of his officers were
drowned in the Red Sea.
⁵The flood waters covered them,
they sank into the depths like a
stone.
⁶Your right hand, O Lord,
magnificent in power,
your right hand, O Lord,
shattered the enemy.
⁷In your great majesty you over-
threw your adversaries;
you loosed your wrath to
consume them like
stubble.
⁸At the blast of your nostrils the
waters piled up,
the flowing waters stood like a
mound,
the flood waters foamed in the
midst of the sea.
⁹The enemy boasted, "I will pursue
and overtake them;

The enemy is presented as an individual warrior who wrongly believes the victory to be already his, but just then the divine power in the wind defeats him (vv. 9-10). Verse 10, like verse 8, suggests a picture of drowning Egyptians. The poem asks a hymnic question that suggests no god compares with the Lord (v. 11). Other gods are known to Israel, yet only the Lord acts for Israel, and no other god can rival this one. This account concludes with the enemy ending up in the "earth" (v. 12), which can mean either "world" or "underworld." Context suggests the underworld, though not the fiery hell of later tradition but a shadowy sort of postmortem existence.

Verses 13-18 shift the focus to post-victory events. The victory is complete with the people at the Lord's "mountain" (v. 17). This is also a victory insofar as it panics the other peoples in Canaan and its environs (v. 15). Accordingly, this section of verses 13-18 balances the victory over the Egyptians in verses 1-12; both show the Lord as the warrior-king. Verses 19-21 present a sequel of song. Verse 19 reiterates the priestly summary of the events at the sea (cf. 14:22), followed by Miriam and the women breaking into song, apparently the same one (vv. 20-21). The quote of the first line of the poem (v. 1b compared with v. 21) may suggest that the women answer in song not just with one line but with the contents of the whole poem. Moses' sister, who went unidentified in 2:4, 7-9, is named here as Miriam and as Aaron's sister. She is provided with the important title of prophet. The use of the title in this context perhaps suggests that hymnic celebration by the people is a prophetic witness to God (like the psalms in later tradition).

The poem stands in its present position as a sequel to the battle. Poems in narrative contexts offer a sort of punctuation point to events; the shift to poetry marks their great importance. Finally, the poem functions as a pivotal point: verses 1-12 look back to events surrounding the departure from

I will divide the spoils and have
my fill of them;
I will draw my sword; my hand
will despoil them!"
¹⁰When you blew with your breath,
the sea covered them;
like lead they sank in the mighty
waters.
¹¹Who is like you among the gods,
O LORD?
Who is like you, magnificent
among the holy ones?
Awe-inspiring in deeds of renown,
worker of wonders,
¹²when you stretched out your
right hand, the earth
swallowed them!

¹³In your love you led the people
you redeemed;
in your strength you guided
them to your holy
dwelling.
¹⁴The peoples heard and quaked;
anguish gripped the dwellers in
Philistia.
¹⁵Then were the chieftains of Edom
dismayed,
the nobles of Moab seized by
trembling;
All the inhabitants of Canaan
melted away;
¹⁶terror and dread fell upon
them.

Egypt while verses 13-18 anticipate coming events, namely, the journey to God's mountain. Exodus 15 originally celebrated the exodus tradition at a shrine in the land (which would account for the peoples in and around the land in v. 15); the language in verses 13, 16-18 is used for sanctuaries (cf. Ps 78:54-55, with v. 60 suggesting Shiloh). Placed in its new context in Exodus by priestly tradition, the poem anticipates the journey to Mount Sinai (Exod 19:1) and not a shrine in the land. The poem's placement constitutes a priestly reinterpretation of its meaning.

The prose and poetic versions all treat the scene as a battle conflict. Unlike chapter 14, the poem does not mention Moses or his holding his hand over the sea. Nor is there any reference to an angel, the divine cloud, or the nighttime setting of the conflict. Yet the prose versions are literarily dependent on the poetic version. The east wind in 14:21a reflects the poetic rendering of the same wind in 15:8 and 10, and the image of the waters standing like a mound in 15:8 evidently inspired the priestly reading of the walls of water to the Israelites' left and the right in 14:22.

The tradition of composition reflected by these connections presupposed that authenticity was based not on eyewitness testimony to the event but on the capacity of the witness to proclaim God's victorious nature on Israel's behalf. One more supernatural, the two others more natural, all three versions attest to God's glory. The result was a collection of different viewpoints from different times, set in a literary progression that could speak to Israelites across time. This may contradict modern ideas about

By the might of your arm they became silent like stone, while your people, LORD, passed over, while the people whom you created passed over.	[17]You brought them in, you planted them on the mountain that is your own— The place you made the base of your throne, LORD,

truth in the Bible, that only one original version can be true, or that to be true it must be a historically original eyewitness account. Yet these are not biblical ideas about truth (note that texts like Ps 18 and 2 Sam 22 contain both cosmic and naturalistic presentations of an event). The versions in Exodus 14–15 witness to the truth that against powerful evils in this world, the Lord has the capacity and desire to act on Israel's behalf.

PART II: FROM EGYPT TO SINAI

15:22–40:38

This part begins with the movement to God's mountain by Moses and the Israelites (15:22 through ch. 18). After arriving at the mountain, they enter into the covenant with God (chs. 19–31). This covenant fails on the first try as the Israelites fall into idolatry with the golden calf (ch. 32). A second set of tablets is made, and the threat of the failed covenant is averted (chs. 33–34). This covenant includes both the Ten Commandments (ch. 20) and the Covenant Code (chs. 21–23). The collections of commandments in Exodus widely differ in form and function: the Ten Commandments of chapter 20 are general in formulation; the Covenant Code in Exodus 21–23 deals mostly with civil and religious matters often in the form of case law; and Exodus 25–31, 35–40 consist of priestly instructions for the sanctuary, sacrifices, priestly vestments, and other cultic provisions.

These collections are set in a single literary progression designed to suggest that all of them belong to a single covenant on Mount Sinai. This literary presentation of the collections stresses their eternal source, yet it is evident that the different collections came from different times and backgrounds. To illustrate this apparent contradiction, three different calendars of holidays show ongoing additions and modifications (Exod 23:14-17; 34:18-26; Lev 23; cf. Deut 16), yet appear as part of the same Sinai covenant. This is a paradox: commandments both early and later in the order of human time now belong to a single ancient divine order. The covenant is eternal and timeless yet also added to over time.

the sanctuary, LORD, your hands established.
¹⁸May the LORD reign forever and ever!

¹⁹When Pharaoh's horses and chariots and horsemen entered the sea, the LORD made the waters of the sea flow back upon them, though the Israelites walked on dry land through the midst of the sea. ²⁰Then the prophet Miriam, Aaron's sister, took a tambourine in her hand, while all the women went out after her with tambourines, dancing; ²¹and she responded to them:

Sing to the LORD, for he is
gloriously triumphant;
horse and chariot he has cast
into the sea.

V. The Journey in the Wilderness to Sinai

At Marah and Elim. ²²Then Moses led Israel forward from the Red Sea, and they marched out to the wilderness of Shur. After traveling for three days through the wilderness without finding water, ²³they arrived at Marah, where they could not drink its water, because it was too bitter. Hence this place was called Marah. ²⁴As the people grumbled against Moses, saying, "What are we to drink?" ²⁵he cried out to the LORD, who pointed out to him a piece of wood. When he threw it into the water, the water became fresh.

It was here that God, in making statutes and ordinances for them, put them to the test. ²⁶He said: If you listen closely to the voice of the LORD, your God, and do what is right in his eyes: if you heed his commandments and keep all his statutes, I will not afflict you with any of the diseases with which I afflicted the Egyptians; for I, the LORD, am your healer.

²⁷Then they came to Elim, where there were twelve springs of water and seventy palm trees, and they camped there near the water.

15:22-27 Conflict at Marah and Elim

Exodus 15:22–18:27 contains a series of episodes that take place at three places listed in the travel itinerary in Numbers 33. These episodes, including 15:22-27, often begin with an Israelite complaint about the situation (this motif begins back in 14:10-14). In Exodus the needs voiced by Israelite complaints are not regarded as unwarranted. Instead, they show the Lord's benevolent care for a people who do not fully grasp the divine plan or capacity to save Israel. These episodes are regarded as a series of tests for the Israelites (Exod 15:25; 16:4; cf. 20:20). The book of Numbers resumes and sharpens these stories of the Israelites' complaints after they leave Sinai (Num 11–21); there the emphasis falls on the Israelites as sinners. Exodus is the book of promise moving toward the Sinai covenant, while Numbers is the book of disappointment in the old generation that fails the tests.

Exodus 15:22–18:27 stresses divine concern during the Israelite journey toward Mount Sinai, echoing the same journey made by Moses alone at the outset of Exodus. The place name of Marah ("bitter") inspired the story of

16 **The Wilderness of Sin.** ¹Having set out from Elim, the whole Israelite community came into the wilderness of Sin, which is between Elim and Sinai, on the fifteenth day of the second month after their departure from the land of Egypt. ²Here in the wilderness the whole Israelite community grumbled against Moses and Aaron. ³The Israelites said to them, "If only we had died at the LORD's hand in the land of Egypt, as we sat by our kettles of meat and ate our fill of bread! But you have led us into this wilderness to make this whole assembly die of famine!"

The Quail and the Manna. ⁴Then the LORD said to Moses: I am going to rain down bread from heaven for you. Each day the people are to go out and gather their daily portion; thus will I test them, to see whether they follow my instructions or not. ⁵On the sixth day, however, when they prepare what they bring in, let it be twice as much as they gather on the other days. ⁶So Moses and Aaron told all the Israelites, "At evening you will know that it was the LORD who brought you out of the land of Egypt; ⁷and in the morning you will see the glory of the LORD, when he hears your grumbling against him. But who are we that you should grumble against us?" ⁸And Moses said, "When the LORD gives you meat to eat in the evening and in the morning your fill of bread, and hears the grumbling you utter against him, who then are we? Your grumbling is not against us, but against the LORD."

⁹Then Moses said to Aaron, "Tell the whole Israelite community: Approach the LORD, for he has heard your grumbling." ¹⁰But while Aaron was speaking to the whole Israelite community, they turned in the direction of the wilderness, and there the glory of the LORD appeared in the cloud! ¹¹The LORD said to Moses: ¹²I have heard the grumbling of the Israelites. Tell them: In the evening twilight you will eat meat, and in the morning you will have your fill of bread, and then you will know that I, the LORD, am your God.

"bitter" water (v. 23); this verse provides a folk explanation for the name of the place. The miracle (v. 25) recalls the prophetic figure of Elisha, who "heals" bad water (2 Kgs 2:19-22); the association with healing appears in verse 26 (cf. Ezek 47:12 for water and healing). As the channel of divine healing, Moses is the preeminent prophet (see Exod 3–4, 6–7). Underlying the complaint stories is the Lord's providing food and drink for his prophet Moses in the wilderness; Elijah in the wilderness similarly receives divine provisions (1 Kgs 17:1-6). As these comparisons suggest, E sees Moses as a prophet like Elijah, only greater (see Exod 33–34). In the context of the complaint stories in Exodus, the Israelites benefit from the Lord's regard for the prophet.

16:1-36 The manna and the quail

The stop in the wilderness of Sin (v. 1) is the setting for this complaint story (primarily P). The preceding episode is a classic story of providing

¹³In the evening, quail came up and covered the camp. In the morning there was a layer of dew all about the camp, ¹⁴and when the layer of dew evaporated, fine flakes were on the surface of the wilderness, fine flakes like hoarfrost on the ground. ¹⁵On seeing it, the Israelites asked one another, "What is this?" for they did not know what it was. But Moses told them, "It is the bread which the LORD has given you to eat.

Regulations Regarding the Manna. ¹⁶"Now, this is what the LORD has commanded. Gather as much of it as each needs to eat, an omer for each person for as many of you as there are, each of you providing for those in your own tent." ¹⁷The Israelites did so. Some gathered a large and some a small amount. ¹⁸But when they measured it out by the omer, the one who had gathered a large amount did not have too much, and the one who had gathered a small amount did not have too little. They gathered as much as each needed to eat. ¹⁹Moses said to them, "Let no one leave any of it over until morning." ²⁰But they did not listen to Moses, and some kept a part of it over until morning, and it became wormy and stank. Therefore Moses was angry with them.

²¹Morning after morning they gathered it, as much as each needed to eat; but when the sun grew hot, it melted away. ²²On the sixth day they gathered twice as much food, two omers for each person. When all the leaders of the community came and reported this to Moses,

---

water; this one addresses the problem of not having food in the wilderness. Like the recurring complaint over water in the wilderness, the manna-quail theme appears elsewhere (for quail as a replacement for the manna, see Num 11:5-6, 31-33). Manna was the secretion of insects living on the tamarisk tree and is said to be prized by Bedouin for its sweetness (see Exod 16:14, 31). Quail migrate to Europe in the spring and return in the fall when they can be captured. Verses 1-15 show the solicitous care of the Lord, who appears to the Israelites. "[T]he glory of the LORD . . . in the cloud" (v. 10) reflects a priestly picture of the divine presence in the temple (cf. Exod 19, esp. v. 9; the divine glory in Isa 6). A folk explanation for the word manna is provided in verse 15; the Israelites ask "What is this?" (Hebrew, *man hu'*). In this largely priestly passage, the manna becomes the occasion for a spiritual test over working on the sabbath (vv. 16-30; cf. Deut 8:2-3; Ezek 20:10-13).

A final commandment in verses 32-33, perhaps authored by an additional priestly hand, shows the manna as a memorial to the Lord's care for the forty years of Israelite journey in the wilderness (in contrast, the quail was not provided over the course of the forty years; see Deut 8:3, 16 and Neh 9). With verse 36 a later writer or editor added a sentence to correlate the ephah, perhaps a unit of measure better known to the audience of his time, with the measurement of the omer mentioned in verse 32.

²³he told them, "That is what the Lord has prescribed. Tomorrow is a day of rest, a holy sabbath of the Lord. Whatever you want to bake, bake; whatever you want to boil, boil; but whatever is left put away and keep until the morning." ²⁴When they put it away until the morning, as Moses commanded, it did not stink nor were there worms in it. ²⁵Moses then said, "Eat it today, for today is the sabbath of the Lord. Today you will not find any in the field. ²⁶Six days you will gather it, but on the seventh day, the sabbath, it will not be there." ²⁷Still, on the seventh day some of the people went out to gather it, but they did not find any. ²⁸Then the Lord said to Moses: How long will you refuse to keep my commandments and my instructions? ²⁹Take note! The Lord has given you the sabbath. That is why on the sixth day he gives you food for two days. Each of you stay where you are and let no one go out on the seventh day. ³⁰After that the people rested on the seventh day.

³¹The house of Israel named this food manna. It was like coriander seed, white, and it tasted like wafers made with honey.

³²Moses said, "This is what the Lord has commanded. Keep a full omer of it for your future generations, so that they may see the food I gave you to eat in the wilderness when I brought you out of the land of Egypt." ³³Moses then told Aaron, "Take a jar and put a full omer of manna in it. Then place it before the Lord to keep it for your future generations." ³⁴As the Lord had commanded Moses, Aaron placed it in front of the covenant to keep it.

³⁵The Israelites ate the manna for forty years, until they came to settled land; they ate the manna until they came to the borders of Canaan. ³⁶(An omer is one tenth of an ephah.)

17 Water from the Rock. ¹From the wilderness of Sin the whole Israelite community journeyed by stages, as the Lord directed, and encamped at Rephidim.

But there was no water for the people to drink, ²and so they quarreled with Moses and said, "Give us water to drink." Moses replied to them, "Why do you quarrel with me? Why do you put the Lord to a test?" ³Here, then, in their thirst for water, the people grumbled against Moses, saying, "Why then did you bring us up out of Egypt? To have us die of thirst with our children and our livestock?" ⁴So Moses cried out to the Lord, "What shall I do with this people? A little more and they will stone me!" ⁵The Lord answered Moses: Go on ahead of the people, and take along with you some of the elders of Israel, holding in your hand, as you go, the staff with which you struck the Nile. ⁶I will be

17:1-46 Water from the rock and the Amalekites

In the next stop at Rephidim, two episodes take place. First is another episode regarding water (see 15:22-27), largely an E narrative (possibly with J material) fronted by the P itinerary notice in verse 1a. The story line of water needed by the Israelites is paralleled quite closely in an episode about Samson (Judg 15:18-19). The wilderness stories of this sort add the idea of

standing there in front of you on the rock in Horeb. Strike the rock, and the water will flow from it for the people to drink. Moses did this, in the sight of the elders of Israel. ⁷The place was named Massah and Meribah, because the Israelites quarreled there and tested the Lord, saying, "Is the Lord in our midst or not?"

Battle with Amalek. ⁸Then Amalek ▷ came and waged war against Israel in Rephidim. ⁹So Moses said to Joshua, "Choose some men for us, and tomorrow go out and engage Amalek in battle. I will be standing on top of the hill with the staff of God in my hand." ¹⁰Joshua did as Moses told him: he engaged Amalek in battle while Moses, Aaron, and

God's testing the Israelites found in 15:25 and 16:4 (cf. Ps 81:8), which is turned on its head with the Israelites testing God (vv. 2, 7; cf. Num 14:22, "put me to the test ten times"). Both sorts of testing were a teaching theme at sanctuaries, especially northern shrines (Pss 78:18, 41, 56; 81:8; 95:9; 106:14; cf. the preaching theme about wilderness as a "honeymoon period" among prophets of the northern tradition, Hos 2:17, Jer 2:2).

These complaint stories also stress Moses as a prophetic mediator between the Lord and the people. Moses pleads before the Lord, who answers with the command to strike the rock (vv. 5-6). Verse 6 suggests that the episode takes place at Horeb (= Sinai in J and P). The episode (v. 7) then locates this episode at Massah (literally, "test") and Meribah ("contention"). In the rain-starved Middle East, water was a source of strife (see Exod 2:17; Judg 7:24), and the names of some springs reflect competition (Gen 14:7; 26:18-33). Deuteronomy 33:8 as well as Psalms 81:8 and 95:7-11 associate Massah and Meribah with the complaint tradition. The section ends on the assumption that the people are satisfied and Moses acts correctly; in contrast, Numbers 20:11-13, the replay of this episode, dramatizes Moses' disobedience, which prevents him from entering the Promised Land. The different handling of this story idea in Exodus versus Numbers reflects the contrasting purposes of the two books: graciousness in Exodus, disappointment in Numbers.

Reconciling the place names in this section is a problem. The priestly editor of Exodus 17:1-7 locates Massah and Meribah at the stop at Rephidim (v. 1a), evidently because of the framework of place names he is apparently using; Numbers 33 locates the complaint about water there (v. 14). This list, however, does not mention Massah and Meribah or Horeb. Massah and Meribah are known in the northern tradition (Ps 81), and it is not surprising to find them in E material.

The reference to the Massah-Meribah incident "in Horeb" (v. 6) is confusing, since this is the mountain of God (Sinai in J and P). The theory that

Hur climbed to the top of the hill. ¹¹As long as Moses kept his hands raised up, Israel had the better of the fight, but when he let his hands rest, Amalek had the better of the fight. ¹²Moses' hands, however, grew tired; so they took a rock and put it under him and he sat on it. Meanwhile Aaron and Hur supported his hands, one on one side and one on the other, so that his hands remained steady until sunset. ¹³And Joshua defeated Amalek and his people with the sword.

¹⁴Then the Lord said to Moses: Write this down in a book as something to be remembered, and recite it to Joshua: I will completely blot out the memory of Amalek from under the heavens. ¹⁵Moses built an altar there, which he named Yahweh-nissi; ¹⁶for he said, "Take up the

---

"in Horeb" is a later addition makes little sense, given the later tradition's presentation of the Israelites arriving at Sinai in 19:1. Instead, Massah and Meribah in the tradition known to E were apparently located at or near Horeb (cf. Meribath-kadesh in context with Sinai in Deut 33:1-2). Exodus 17:1b-7 was perhaps relocated to the pre-Sinai wilderness because the association of Massah and Meribah with Horeb-Sinai was unknown to the priestly writer of verse 1a, for whom the complaint episodes traditionally occurred in the wilderness (see also Num 27:14). For the biblical writers (especially the priestly tradition), themes influenced the representation of geography: Egypt was the land of slavery and death, the desert was a place of divine care for human anxiety and neediness, and Sinai was the Mount Everest of divine revelation.

The placement of the battle with the Amalekites (vv. 8-16, E) was perhaps suggested by their living in the territory generally south of Israel. As camel nomads and traders, they interacted with the Israelites. Before the monarchy the two enjoyed good relations at some times (Judg 5:14a, literally "Ephraim whose root is in Amalek"). With the royal exercise of territorial control (1 Sam 15:6-7; 27:8-9; 30:1-2; 2 Sam 8:12), conflict with the Amalekites ensued, perhaps over economic turf, which influenced monarchic period renderings of the Amalekites as Israel's enemies (see also Judg 6:3, 33; 7:12). This view of military conflict with the Amalekites informs Exodus 17:8-16. The first part of the story (vv. 8-13) focuses on the battle proper, anticipating Joshua's later leadership in the biblical book bearing his name. Unlike the prophetic (E) or priestly treatments of Moses elsewhere, in this E piece Moses channels divine power, apparently reflecting what prophets accompanying armies into battle were thought to contribute in military conflicts. The second part (vv. 14-16) serves as a commemoration of the victory yet paradoxically contains a divine command to blot out the memory of Amalek (also Deut 25:17-19).

banner of the Lord! The Lord has a war against Amalek through the ages."

18 **Meeting with Jethro.** ¹Now Moses' father-in-law Jethro, the priest of Midian, heard of all that God had done for Moses and for his people Israel: how the Lord had brought Israel out of Egypt. ²So his father-in-law Jethro took along Zipporah, Moses' wife—now this was after Moses had sent her back—³and her two sons. One of these was named Gershom; for he said, "I am a resident alien in a foreign land." ⁴The other was named Eliezer; for he said, "The God of my father is my help; he has rescued me from Pharaoh's sword." ⁵Together with Moses' wife and sons, then, his father-in-law Jethro came to him in the wilderness where he was encamped at the mountain of God, ⁶and he sent word to Moses, "I, your father-in-law Jethro, am coming to you, along with your wife and her two sons."

⁷Moses went out to meet his father-in-law, bowed down, and then kissed him. Having greeted each other, they went into the tent. ⁸Moses then told his father-in-law of all that the Lord had done to Pharaoh and the Egyptians for the sake of Israel, and of all the hardships that had beset them on their journey, and how the Lord had rescued them. ⁹Jethro rejoiced over all the goodness that the Lord had shown Israel in rescuing them from the power of the Egyptians. ¹⁰"Blessed be the Lord," he said, "who has rescued you from the power of the Egyptians and of Pharaoh. ¹¹Now I know that the Lord is greater than all the gods; for he rescued the people from the power of the Egyptians when they treated them arrogantly."

18:1-27 Moses and Jethro

Tacked onto the stories situated at Rephidim in chapter 17, chapter 18 (E) describes a meeting between Moses and his father-in-law, here called Jethro (but Reuel in 2:18). His Midian background reflects an older, friendly relationship between the Midianites and Israelites, despite later enmity (cf. Num 25:16-18; 31:1-12; Judg 6–8). The description of Moses' family (vv. 1-6) echoes Exodus 2. The explanation of Gershom's name in 2:22 ("I am a resident alien in a foreign land") is repeated in 18:3, which adds the meaning of the name of Moses' second son, Eliezer ("The God of my father is my help"). The appearance of the second son reflects the passage of time since Exodus 1–2.

These connections also highlight the parallel between Moses' journey to Midian in chapters 1–2 and his journey with the Israelites in chapters 15–18. As with 17:6, verse 5 locates the episode "at the mountain of God," evidently a sign of an older E tradition that located this story at the mountain in the wilderness (P distinguishes the wilderness episodes from the events at the mountain). The initial meeting continues with Moses' witness to divine care and power, and Jethro's joy at the news and belief in the Lord, followed by a covenant meal (vv. 7-12); these features are suggestive of the E source of

¹²Then Jethro, the father-in-law of Moses, brought a burnt offering and sacrifices for God, and Aaron came with all the elders of Israel to share with Moses' father-in-law in the meal before God.

Appointment of Minor Judges. ¹³The next day Moses sat in judgment for the people, while they stood around him from morning until evening. ¹⁴When Moses' father-in-law saw all that he was doing for the people, he asked, "What is this business that you are conducting for the people? Why do you sit alone while all the people have to stand about you from morning till evening?" ¹⁵Moses answered his father-in-law, "The people come to me to consult God. ¹⁶Whenever they have a disagreement, they come to me to have me settle the matter between them and make known to them God's statutes and instructions."

¹⁷"What you are doing is not wise," Moses' father-in-law replied. ¹⁸"You will surely wear yourself out, both you and these people with you. The task is too heavy for you; you cannot do it alone. ¹⁹ Now, listen to me, and I will give you some advice, and may God be with you. Act as the people's representative before God, and bring their disputes to God. ²⁰Enlighten them in regard to the statutes and instructions, showing them how they are to conduct themselves and what they are to do. ²¹But you should also look among all the people for able and God-fearing men, trustworthy men who hate dishonest gain, and set them over the people as commanders of thousands, of hundreds, of fifties, and of tens. ²²Let these render decisions for the people in all routine cases. Every important case they should refer to you, but every lesser case they can settle themselves. Lighten your burden by letting them bear it with you! ²³If you do this, and God so commands you, you will be able to stand the strain, and all these people, too, will go home content."

²⁴Moses listened to his father-in-law and did all that he had said. ²⁵He picked

---

the northern kingdom (cf. 2 Kgs 5:15). Verse 12 shows Jethro acting in his priestly role (v. 1) in preparing the covenant meal for Moses, Aaron, and the elders. Given Jethro's Midianite background and the later tradition's relative silence about him, the tradition about him in E material bears signs of authenticity, even if it was elaborated.

Verses 13-27 seem to presuppose a large, sedentary population. The judicial appointments to be made are "God-fearing" (v. 21), reflecting E's theme of reverence for God (1:17, 21). It has been suggested that this passage reflects judicial appointments made during the reign of King Jehoshaphat (2 Chr 19:4-11). The judicial system balances the military mobilization of chapter 17. For the E material represented in chapters 17–18, the tradition of Horeb involved the establishment of a Levitical priesthood, an army with Joshua (17:8-13), a judiciary (ch. 18), writings (possibly including holy battles) to be read and remembered (17:14), a covenant meal at the mountain (18:5, 7-12)—in short, many of the basic ingredients of a covenant

out able men from all Israel and put them in charge of the people as commanders of thousands, of hundreds, of fifties, and of tens. ²⁶They rendered decisions for the people in all routine cases. The more difficult cases they referred to Moses, but all the lesser cases they settled themselves. ²⁷Then Moses said farewell to his father-in-law, who went off to his own country.

VI. Covenant and Legislation at Mount Sinai

19 **Arrival at Sinai.** ¹In the third month after the Israelites' departure from the land of Egypt, on the first day, they came to the wilderness of Sinai. ²After they made the journey from Rephidim and entered the wilderness of Sinai, they then pitched camp in the wilderness.

While Israel was encamped there in front of the mountain, ³Moses went up to the mountain of God. Then the LORD called to him from the mountain, saying: This is what you will say to the house of Jacob; tell the Israelites: ⁴You have seen how I treated the Egyptians and how I bore you up on eagles' wings and brought you to myself. ⁵Now, if you obey me completely and keep my covenant, you will be my treasured possession among all peoples, though all the earth is mine. ⁶You will be to me a kingdom of priests, a holy nation. That is what you must tell the Israelites. ⁷So

with God. These mountain episodes fulfill the promise made in 3:12 (also E). This earlier E tradition of covenant making at the divine mountain was obscured in part by the priestly tradition, which positioned these episodes after its own wilderness traditions (in chs. 15 and 16) and incorporated other E episodes at Horeb into the priestly organization of material set at Sinai in chapters 19 and following. For the priestly tradition, the Israelites arrive at Sinai in the next section.

19:1-2 Arrival at Sinai

With this section dawns a new day in the history of the Israelite people; in fact, it is the central moment of world history for the priestly tradition in particular and for Judaism in general. Sinai looms as the Mount Everest of the covenant and torah (teaching, often rendered "law"), overshadowing and shaping later Jewish traditions. Already in pre-rabbinic Judaism, covenant giving was celebrated at the feast of Weeks (though the exact day was debated at this time, e. g., Jubilees 6:17). Christian tradition echoes this association in celebrating the Spirit's coming at the same time on Pentecost (Acts 2). The coming of the Spirit in "tongues as of fire" (Acts 2:3) echoes the fiery divine appearance (theophany) in Exodus 19:18.

Chapter 19 is introduced by a double itinerary notice (vv. 1-2a), which locates the Israelites' arrival at the time of Weeks (Pentecost). Unlike the association of Passover with the departure from Egypt in Exodus 12–13,

Moses went and summoned the elders of the people. When he set before them all that the LORD had ordered him to tell them, [8]all the people answered together, "Everything the LORD has said, we will do." Then Moses brought back to the LORD the response of the people.

[9]The LORD said to Moses: I am coming to you now in a dense cloud, so that when the people hear me speaking with you, they will also remain faithful to you.

When Moses, then, had reported the response of the people to the LORD, [10]the LORD said to Moses: Go to the people and have them sanctify themselves today and tomorrow. Have them wash their garments [11]and be ready for the third day; for on the third day the LORD will come down on Mount Sinai in the sight of all the people. [12]Set limits for the people all around, saying: Take care not to go up the mountain, or even to touch its edge. All who touch the mountain must be put to death. [13]No hand shall touch them, but they must be stoned to death or killed with arrows. Whether human being or beast, they must not be allowed to live. Only when the ram's horn sounds may they go up on the mountain. [14]Then Moses came down from the mountain to the people and had them sanctify themselves, and they washed their garments. [15]He said to the people, "Be ready for the third day. Do not approach a woman."

The Great Theophany. [16]On the morning of the third day there were peals of thunder and lightning, and a heavy cloud over the mountain, and a very loud blast of the shofar, so that all the people in the camp trembled. [17]But Moses led the people out of the camp to meet God, and they stationed them-

---

Weeks is not mentioned here. The priestly itinerary notices are deliberate, and sacred times are very much in evidence with Passover in Exodus 12–13 and in Numbers 10; it seems odd for priestly tradition to omit reference to Weeks in Exodus 19 (unless it was reticent to fuel the debate over the feast's precise date). In any case, the Jewish association of the covenant with Weeks predates rabbinic Judaism or Christianity (e. g., Jubilees 6:17).

The exact location of Sinai is unknown. Later tradition locates it at Jebel Musa in the southern Sinai Peninsula, but Paul and other Jewish writers located it "in Arabia" (Gal 4:25), which accords with older poetic references to Sinai used sometimes in conjunction with Seir, Edom, and Teman (Deut 33:1-2; Judg 5:4-5; cf. Ps 68:8; Hab 3:3, 7), all thought to be located to the southeast of ancient Judah and not in the Sinai Peninsula. Later disagreements suggest that Sinai's location was forgotten or disputed, perhaps even within the biblical period.

19:2-25 Meeting the Lord

Because of its initial position at Sinai, chapter 19 constitutes an important presentation of the relationship of God and Israel. The divine speech of

selves at the foot of the mountain. [18]Now Mount Sinai was completely enveloped in smoke, because the LORD had come down upon it in fire. The smoke rose from it as though from a kiln, and the whole mountain trembled violently. [19]The blast of the shofar grew louder and louder, while Moses was speaking and God was answering him with thunder. [20]When the LORD came down upon Mount Sinai, to the top of the mountain, the LORD summoned Moses to the top of the mountain, and Moses went up.

[21]Then the LORD told Moses: Go down and warn the people not to break through to the LORD in order to see him; otherwise many of them will be struck down. [22]For their part, the priests, who approach the LORD must sanctify themselves; else the LORD will break out in anger against them. [23]But Moses said to the LORD, "The people cannot go up to Mount Sinai, for you yourself warned us, saying: Set limits around the mountain to make it sacred." [24]So the LORD said to him: Go down and come up

verses 3b-8 has been thought to derive from an older poetic piece. Given its resonances with Deuteronomy, this passage is attributed by other scholars to the Deuteronomist editor, but the later priestly tradition may have incorporated older elements, whatever their origin. Verses 4-6 contain a series of memorable expressions for the covenant relationship. The journey from Egypt to Sinai is couched in terms of the Lord bearing the Israelites "on eagles' wings" (v. 4). The image, known also from Deuteronomy 32:11, at once conveys majestic power and care.

The covenant relationship is to make Israel into God's "treasured possession" (v. 5), an economic expression referring to one's personal financial accumulation (1 Chr 29:3; Eccl 2:8). In this metaphorical usage, Israel has special value for the Lord. The covenant relationship will result in Israel's transformation into "a kingdom of priests, a holy nation" (v. 6). This metaphorical application of the priestly status to the wider community is not a challenge to the traditional priesthood but a recognition of the people's special character to partake of divine holiness (cf. Isa 61:6). The people accept the terms of the divine mandate for them, which is reported to the Lord (vv. 7-8).

In verses 9-15 (JE), Moses, the covenant mediator, is to prepare the Israelites for their meeting with God. The ritual preparations and the precise details regarding observing distance from the mountain to which the divine glory is to come suggest a priestly model of liturgy. It also ties into the earlier description of Israel as "a kingdom of priests, a holy nation." The third day signals the arrival of the Lord in the thunderstorm (vv. 16-19, JE). The result is the divine mountain blanketed in smoke, which at once signals yet hides the divine presence. Corresponding to the natural effects

along with Aaron. But do not let the priests and the people break through to come up to the LORD; else he will break out against them." ²⁵So Moses went down to the people and spoke to them.

20 The Ten Commandments. ¹Then God spoke all these words:

²I am the LORD your God, who brought you out of the land of Egypt, out of the house of slavery. ³You shall not have other gods beside me. ⁴You shall not make for yourself an idol or a likeness of anything in the heavens above or on the earth below or in the waters beneath the earth; ⁵you shall not bow down before them or serve them. For I, the LORD, your God, am a jealous God, inflicting punishment for their ancestors' wickedness on the children of those who hate me, down to the third and fourth generation; ⁶but showing love down to the thousandth generation of those who love me and keep my commandments.

⁷You shall not invoke the name of the LORD, your God, in vain. For the LORD

of the thunder is the human trumpet blasts: both announce the coming of the Lord to the mountain. Precisely because of the common experience of the rainstorm in ancient Israel as well as its paradoxical quality, the storm served as a wonderful expression for the Lord's appearance.

Verses 20-25 (J) report the second encounter between Moses and the Lord. Whereas before the encounter was verbal (v. 3), this one envisions a divine fire (v. 18), which "came down . . . to the top of the mountain" (v. 20). A common way of making divine appearances (theophany) in the ancient Middle East, divine fire appears in the poetic description of the divine appearance at Sinai in Deuteronomy 33:2. As in Exodus 19–20, divine fire precedes the giving of teaching (Deut 33:4). The desire of the people "to see" the Lord (v. 21), also expressed in liturgical contexts (Ps 42:3), was thought to be reserved for the upright (Ps 11:7). As the restrictions imposed in Exodus 19:20-25 suggest, the divine presence was regarded as potentially deadly to the unworthy who see God (Gen 16:13; 32:31; Judg 13:22; cf. Judg 6:22). The sacred space is delimited according to priestly norms: Moses and Aaron enter into the divine presence, while the lesser priests and people are commanded: "Set limits around the mountain" (v. 23). Holiness is not simply the absence of fault or sin; it is also a positive power proportioned within the community according to priestly rank. The description of the divine presence, the restrictions placed on the Israelites, and their desire to "see God" are heavily liturgical in sensibility. The book of Exodus is religious literature inspired on several levels by religious experience.

20:1-26 The Ten Commandments

Framed by theophany on either side (19:16-19; 20:18-21), the Ten Commandments (more accurately, the Ten Sayings or Words) are unlike either

will not leave unpunished anyone who invokes his name in vain.

◄ ⁸Remember the sabbath day—keep it holy. ⁹Six days you may labor and do all your work, ¹⁰but the seventh day is a sabbath of the LORD your God. You shall not do any work, either you, your son or your daughter, your male or female slave, your work animal, or the resident alien within your gates. ¹¹For in six days ► the LORD made the heavens and the earth, the sea and all that is in them; but on the seventh day he rested. That is why the LORD has blessed the sabbath day and made it holy.

¹²Honor your father and your mother, ► that you may have a long life in the land the LORD your God is giving you.

---

the civil and religious regulations of Exodus 21–23 or the priestly instructional literature in Exodus 25–31. They provide general statements applicable to a variety of circumstances. Some are provided with motivations (e.g., v. 11, with a priestly justification; cf. the Deuteronomistic motivation provided in Deut 5:15). The variations between the two versions of the Ten Commandments in Exodus 20 and Deuteronomy 5 point to a tradition later modified separately by priestly and Deuteronomistic hands. These may not postdate the Ten Commandments by much, but they may represent distillation and elaboration of earlier material, reflecting the traditional ethos of Israelite society based on family units and their inherited land.

Despite consensus about their number, the Ten Commandments are divided differently. Jewish and Protestant traditions view verses 3-4 as two different commandments (Judaism takes v. 2 as the beginning of the first commandment) and follow Exodus 20:17 in taking the rule of coveting as a single commandment. Catholic tradition regards verses 1-6 as the first commandment and follows Deuteronomy 5:21 in treating coveting as two commandments.

Verse 2 details the background of God's relationship to Israel. Many scholars compare this introduction and the obligations that follow it to ancient Middle Eastern treaties between kings and their vassals. This treaty style (which is more heavily marked in Deut) presupposes a royal model of relationship that binds the Divine Lord and Israel as overlord and servant. Verse 3 has been understood as a monotheistic declaration of belief in only one God (NABRE "beside me"), but the Hebrew expression (literally, "before me") suggests a prohibition against any worship of another god; the issue concerns cultic practice, which is to lead to proper regard of only the Lord. Within the context of treaty imagery, Israel is to serve only one divine Lord.

Verse 4 forbids images of any sort, but verse 5 restricts the prohibition to religious images. As "a jealous God" (v. 5), the Lord has a singular claim

◄ ¹³You shall not kill.

◄ ¹⁴You shall not commit adultery.

◄ ¹⁵You shall not steal.

◄ ¹⁶You shall not bear false witness against your neighbor.

◄ ¹⁷You shall not covet your neighbor's house. You shall not covet your neighbor's wife, his male or female slave, his ox or donkey, or anything that belongs to your neighbor.

Moses Accepted as Mediator. ¹⁸Now as all the people witnessed the thunder and lightning, the blast of the shofar and the mountain smoking, they became afraid and trembled. So they took up a position farther away ¹⁹and said to Moses, "You speak to us, and we will listen; but do not let God speak to us, or we shall die." ²⁰Moses answered the ► people, "Do not be afraid, for God has

on Israel, which demonstrates its loyalty through the body language of worship (cf. the corresponding command made in terms of verbal prayer, 23:13). The biblical period witnessed a debate over whether a form of the Lord was perceptible, for example, Numbers 12:8 versus Deuteronomy 4:15-18. The latter connects its denial of a form to God to the prohibition against images. The motivation clause in verses 5b-6 appears in longer form in 34:6-7, reflecting an older liturgical context.

Prohibition against the improper invocation of the divine name (v. 7) may include a number of abuses, such as cursing and swearing by the divine name in blasphemy (Lev 24:10-11; cf. Middle Assyrian Palace Decree 10). The divine name was regarded as sacred, reflected by the substitution of the word "Lord" in the early Greek translation of the Bible and in many later Bible translations, including the NABRE. In the Dead Sea Scrolls, sometimes the divine name was written in archaic Hebrew letters, at other times only with four dots. This substitution illustrates why calling Jesus "Lord" was scandalous by Jewish standards of the time.

The sabbath law in its form here (vv. 8-11) is the first of two "positive" commandments (i.e., what to do versus what not to do). The elaboration reflects priestly influence (Exod 16:25-30; 31:12-17), with its connection to the priestly creation story known from Genesis 1. The term refers to cessation from work, and the sabbath provision perhaps originated not to rest after a week's time but to mark cessation from labor after six days of harvesting. For this reason the sabbath rule in Exodus 23:12 follows regulations pertaining to harvesting, and in Exodus 34:20-25 it stands between the regulation for bringing offerings at the pilgrimage feasts and their listing (cf. the Mesad Yeshavyahu inscription).

The sabbath cessation fits with the lunar reckoning of the year, in particular for the months of the spring and fall major harvests, which is reflected by the phrase "new moon and sabbath" (Isa 1:13; Amos 8:5; cf. 2

come only to test you and put the fear of him upon you so you do not sin." ²¹So the people remained at a distance, while Moses approached the dark cloud where God was.

The Covenant Code. ²²The LORD said to Moses: This is what you will say to the Israelites: You have seen for yourselves that I have spoken to you from heaven. ²³You shall not make alongside of me gods of silver, nor shall you make for yourselves gods of gold. ²⁴An altar of earth make for me, and sacrifice upon it your burnt offerings and communion sacrifices, your sheep and your oxen. In every place where I cause my name to be invoked I will come to you and bless you. ²⁵But if you make an altar of stone for me, do not build it of cut stone, for by putting a chisel to it you profane it. ²⁶You shall not ascend to my altar by steps, lest your nakedness be exposed.

Kgs 4:23). The seven-day celebration of Passover and Booths (Lev 23:6, 34; Num 28:17; 29:12) corresponds to the week-long effort involved in the harvests. This may explain why the sabbath, although it was distinguished from holidays in priestly reckoning, begins priestly calendars (Lev 23; Num 28–29). In the sixth-century book of Ezekiel, the new moon would be separated from the sabbath (46:1), which would be sanctified on a weekly basis (cf. Ezek 20:20; 44:24). The seventh year of land rest (Exod 23:11) and the jubilee year (Lev 25) of rest for the land may have developed as an extension of the harvest sabbath and not the weekly sabbath. Later development of the sabbath's significance is here enshrined at the original moment of the Sinai covenant.

The second "positive" commandment is to honor one's parents (v. 12). Extending into adulthood, this responsibility included not hitting parents (21:15; cf. Code of Hammurabi 195) or cursing them (21:17). Honoring parents included honoring their memory, perhaps including offerings to them in their afterlife. Traditionally verses 2-12 have been counted as five commandments in the Lord's honor, with honoring parents considered an extension of divine respect.

The last five commandments govern human relations. Verse 13 outlaws murder (not warfare or capital punishment). Verse 14 forbids adultery, namely, sexual relations involving a married woman and any man (cf. Code of Hammurabi 129). Married men were permitted sexual relations with prostitutes (Gen 38; Hos 4:14 rejects this double standard); regulations governing sexual relations with single women do not specify married versus single men (e.g., Exod 22:15; Deut 22:22). The commandment not to steal (v. 15) covers theft of goods (including slaves). "False witness" (v. 16), a legal problem in Israel (1 Kgs 21), perhaps was expanded to include lying (Hos 4:2) and slander (Lev 19:16). The last commandment (v. 17) may cover a

21 **Laws Regarding Slaves.** ¹These are the ordinances you shall lay before them. ² When you purchase a Hebrew slave, he is to serve you for six years, but in the seventh year he shall leave as a free person without any payment. ³If he comes into service alone, he shall leave alone; if he comes with a wife, his wife shall leave with him. ⁴But if his master gives him a wife and she bears him sons or daughters, the woman and her children belong to her master and the man shall leave alone. ⁵If, however, the slave declares, 'I love my master and my wife and children; I will not leave as a free person,' ⁶his master shall bring him to God and there, at the door or doorpost, he shall pierce his ear with an awl, thus keeping him as his slave forever.

⁷When a man sells his daughter as a slave, she shall not go free as male slaves do. ⁸But if she displeases her master, who had designated her for himself, he shall let her be redeemed. He has no right to sell her to a foreign people, since he has broken faith with her. ⁹If he designates her for his son, he shall treat her according to the ordinance for daughters. ¹⁰If he takes another wife, he shall not withhold her food, her clothing, or her conjugal rights. ¹¹If he does not do these three things for her, she may leave without cost, without any payment.

covetous disposition (cf. Code of Hammurabi 25) as well as actions taken in efforts to seize another's property (cf. Mic 2:1-2). In this listing, women hold a status just above slaves and animals.

The storm of the divine glory resumes in verses 18-19. According to the story, the storm as occurs during the giving of the Ten Commandments. The presentation adds dramatic effect by describing the people's reaction. They are frightened by the thunder and lightning, and their speech shows fear at hearing the divine speech (v. 19); the divine words are presented as being heard as thunder (cf. "voice" is thunder in Ps 29:3-8). This is to test and inspire reverence in Israel (v. 20); only Moses can withstand the full brunt of the divine presence (v. 21). Verses 22-26 add miscellaneous instructions about proper worship. Some scholars view this section as the beginning of the Covenant Code of Exodus 21–23, though verses 22-26 hardly look like an opening, in contrast to 21:1. Nonetheless, the section (esp. v. 22) functions to connect the Covenant Code to the Sinai theophany of chapter 20.

21:1-11 Regulations about slaves

Verse 1 uses a standard opening formula (as in 35:1; Deut 1:1; 4:45; cf. Exod 19:6; 36:21). It signals the start of a collection called the Covenant Code (based on the expression "book of the covenant" in 24:7). At its core are regulations governing property loss and damage (21:33–22:14), framed by rules concerning the social realm (21:12-32 and 22:15–23:9), with 23:10-33 perhaps added as a closing exhortation. Like the great law codes of ancient

Personal Injury. [12]Whoever strikes someone a mortal blow must be put to death. [13]However, regarding the one who did not hunt another down, but God caused death to happen by his hand, I will set apart for you a place to which that one may flee. [14]But when someone kills a neighbor after maliciously scheming to do so, you must take him even from my altar and put

Middle Eastern societies, the code reflects a patriarchal society engaged in agriculture; social identity was based not on the individual but on the multigenerational family and its inherited land. The regulations strongly correspond in form, content, and principle to ancient Middle Eastern law codes, such as the Code of Hammurabi (also spelled Hammurapi). The Covenant Code mostly follows ancient Middle Eastern legal tradition, reflected in the citations below to law codes from Mesopotamia. Contrary to common perception, the laws in the Covenant Code do not show a generally higher moral standard in Israel as opposed to its neighbors; in some cases, the more humanitarian ruling occurs in the extra-biblical material. Provisions for the poor and noncitizens (22:20-24) are poignant, but they compare with the concern shown the "commoner" in Mesopotamian law codes, which, unlike the Covenant Code, provide some concrete rulings on their behalf. Women and descendants of slaves will find little noble and uplifting in the Covenant Code. Like its monotheistic ideal, Israel's moral sensibilities developed over time.

Exodus 21:1-11 reflect standard rulings for the ancient world (cf. Code of Hammurabi 117–19); only later would the tradition outlaw Israelite slaves (Deut 15:12-15; Jer 34:8-10). In verses 1-6, a male slave may go free in the seventh year (like an indentured servant), but various conditions are placed on family members. If a slave chooses not to go free, he is brought "to God" at the door and marked as a "slave forever" (v. 6). The word "God" may be also translated "divine ones," perhaps household gods (or deceased ancestors?) who participate in marking the slave as a permanent member of the household (see 22:27). In an attempt to stem potential abuses, regulations (21:7-11) nonetheless show women's terrible vulnerability in the patriarchal structure: they could be sold by their fathers, they do not go free like male slaves (v. 7), and they may suffer the difficulties of polygamy (v. 10). An alternative for some women in dire economic trouble was prostitution (see 38:8).

21:12-32 Personal injury law

This section addresses damages and conditions involving the death penalty (cf. Code of Hammurabi 195–214). It does not provide procedures for ascertaining guilt, but largely assumes it. Verses 13-14 distinguish conditions

him to death. [15]Whoever strikes father or mother shall be put to death.

[16]A kidnaper, whether he sells the person or the person is found in his possession, shall be put to death.

[17]Whoever curses father or mother shall be put to death.

[18]When men quarrel and one strikes the other with a stone or with his fist, not mortally, but enough to put him in bed, [19]the one who struck the blow shall be acquitted, provided the other can get up and walk around with the help of his staff. Still, he must compensate him for his recovery time and make provision for his complete healing.

[20]When someone strikes his male or female slave with a rod so that the slave dies under his hand, the act shall certainly be avenged. [21]If, however, the

---

between accidents ("God caused death to happen," v. 13) and premeditated murder (v. 14). Other cases result in the death penalty (vv. 15-19), including kidnapping (Code of Hammurabi 14). The means used ("stone or . . . fist," v. 18, as opposed to a lethal weapon, such as a sword or knife) are considered an indicator of intent. Since some Mesopotamian law codes at times permit payment instead of the death penalty in cases involving persons of higher social status than their victims, Israel's silence at such a "solution" has been taken as a higher moral standard; it may instead reflect a less stratified society in Israel. Additional provisions hold damage to slaves to a lower standard than injury to free persons (vv. 20-21). Miscarriage due to injury merits a fine (v. 22; Sumerian Laws 1–2, Code of Hammurabi 209–13). Damage is viewed from a patriarchal perspective: the loss is incurred by the male head of the household and damages are paid to him.

Otherwise, the standard for justice is premised on the logic of equivalence summarized in what is called the *lex talionis* ("life for life, eye for eye . . . ," vv. 23-25; cf. Gen 9:6; Lev 24:17-22; Judg 15:11): the severity of punishment is to be proportionate to the magnitude of the crime's damage. This principle runs from the Code of Hammurabi to modern Western norms of justice. It has been wrongly thought to reflect Old Testament legalism because of the contrast drawn in Matthew 5:38-39 between the Old Testament *lex talionis* and the supposedly "higher" New Testament norm. Matthew's gospel, however, is not addressing civil case law but personal interactions, and no "Christian" society relies on the Christian standard for adjudicating legal cases.

The formulation of correspondence in verses 23-25 is almost poetic; here it is not applied literally in cases of mutilations, which issue instead in compensation, as reflected in verses 26-27 (cf. Lev 24:19-20; Code of Hammurabi 196–208). Without forbidding physical abuse by slave owners, the

85

Moses looks over the Promised Land. Wood engraving.

slave survives for a day or two, he is not to be punished, since the slave is his own property.

²²When men have a fight and hurt a pregnant woman, so that she suffers a miscarriage, but no further injury, the guilty one shall be fined as much as the woman's husband demands of him, and he shall pay in the presence of the judges. ²³But if injury ensues, you shall give life for life, ²⁴eye for eye, tooth for tooth, hand for hand, foot for foot, ²⁵burn for burn, wound for wound, stripe for stripe.

²⁶When someone strikes his male or female slave in the eye and destroys the use of the eye, he shall let the slave go free in compensation for the eye. ²⁷If he knocks out a tooth of his male or female slave, he shall let the slave go free in compensation for the tooth.

²⁸When an ox gores a man or a woman to death, the ox must be stoned; its meat may not be eaten. The owner of the ox, however, shall be free of blame. ²⁹But if an ox was previously in the habit of gor-ing people and its owner, though warned, would not watch it; should it then kill a man or a woman, not only must the ox be stoned, but its owner also must be put to death. ³⁰If, however, a fine is imposed on him, he must pay in ransom for his life whatever amount is imposed on him. ³¹This ordinance applies if it is a boy or a girl that the ox gores. ³²But if it is a male or a female slave that it gores, he must pay the owner of the slave thirty shekels of silver, and the ox must be stoned.

Property Damage. ³³When someone uncovers or digs a cistern and does not cover it over again, should an ox or a donkey fall into it, ³⁴the owner of the cistern must make good by restoring the value of the animal to its owner, but the dead animal he may keep.

³⁵When one man's ox hurts another's ox and it dies, they shall sell the live ox and divide this money as well as the dead animal equally between them. ³⁶But if it was known that the ox was previously in the habit of goring and its

two provisions penalize it. Verses 28-32 address the problem of an ox that gores others (Laws of Eshnunna 53; Code of Hammurabi 250–51; cf. Sumerian Laws 10). The responsibility for the ox's behavior belongs ultimately to the owner (v. 29). This section presupposes a patriarchal hierarchy, with free men at the top, women in the middle, and slaves and animals ("living property") at the bottom.

21:33–22:14 Property loss

Shifting from damage by oxen (vv. 28-32) to damage to oxen (vv. 33-36), this section continues the idea of payment of like for damage of like ("an ox for an ox," v. 36); verse 37, however, requires a higher compensation, possibly as a deterrent. Exodus 22:1-14 addresses loss due to theft, accident, and negligence. Verses 1-2 defend the right of the homeowner against a thief caught at night, but not during daytime when it would be easier to detain him (Job 24:15b-16). A thief may enter servitude to cover the debt incurred

owner would not watch it, he must make full restitution, an ox for an ox; but the dead animal he may keep.

[37]When someone steals an ox or a sheep and slaughters or sells it, he shall restore five oxen for the one ox, and four sheep for the one sheep.

22 [1][If a thief is caught in the act of housebreaking and beaten to death, there is no bloodguilt involved. [2]But if after sunrise he is thus beaten, there is bloodguilt.] He must make full restitution. If he has nothing, he shall be sold to pay for his theft. [3]If what he stole is found alive in his possession, be it an ox, a donkey or a sheep, he shall make twofold restitution.

[4]When someone causes a field or a vineyard to be grazed over, by sending his cattle to graze in another's field, he must make restitution with the best produce of his own field or vineyard. [5]If a fire breaks out, catches on to thorn bushes, and consumes shocked grain, standing grain, or the field itself, the one who started the fire must make full restitution.

Trusts and Loans. [6]When someone gives money or articles to another for safekeeping and they are stolen from the latter's house, the thief, if caught, must make twofold restitution. [7]If the thief is not caught, the owner of the house shall be brought to God, to swear that he himself did not lay hands on his neighbor's property. [8]In every case of dishonest appropriation, whether it be about an ox, or a donkey, or a sheep, or a garment, or anything else that has disappeared, where another claims that the thing is his, the claim of both parties shall be brought before God; the one whom God convicts must make twofold restitution to the other.

[9]When someone gives an ass, or an ox, or a sheep, or any other animal to another for safekeeping, if it dies, or is maimed or snatched away, without anyone witnessing the fact, [10]there shall be an oath before the LORD between the two of them that the guardian did not lay hands on his neighbor's property; the owner must accept the oath, and no restitution is to be made. [11]But if the guardian has actually stolen from it, then he must make restitution to the owner. [12]If it has been killed by a wild beast, let him bring it as evidence; he need not make restitution for the mangled animal.

[13]When someone borrows an animal from a neighbor, if it is maimed or dies while the owner is not present, that one must make restitution. [14]But if the owner

---

by legal penalty (v. 2; cf. the death penalty in Code of Hammurabi 21). The compensation required in verse 3 perhaps acts as a deterrent in cutting down on the thief's margin of profitability.

Though liable to unintended damage, burning fires to destroy stubble and thorns in fields and vineyards (vv. 4-5) was common agricultural practice and a well-known metaphor for divine destruction (e.g., Isa 5:24; 9:18; 10:17; 27:2-4; 33:11-12). Without banks or safety deposit boxes, ancients used neighbors to safeguard "money" (silver, not currency or coinage, which began in the Middle East in the sixth century) or property (vv. 6-12; cf. Code of Hammurabi 122–25). The procedures include an appeal to God in the

is present, that one need not make restitution. If it was hired, this was covered by the price of its hire.

Social Laws. [15]When a man seduces a virgin who is not betrothed, and lies with her, he shall make her his wife by paying the bride price. [16]If her father refuses to give her to him, he must still pay him the bride price for virgins.

[17]You shall not let a woman who practices sorcery live.

[18]Anyone who lies with an animal shall be put to death.

[19]Whoever sacrifices to any god, except to the LORD alone, shall be put under the ban.

[20]You shall not oppress or afflict a resident alien, for you were once aliens residing in the land of Egypt. [21]You shall not wrong any widow or orphan. [22]If ever you wrong them and they cry out to me, I will surely listen to their cry. [23]My wrath will flare up, and I will kill you with the sword; then your own wives will be widows, and your children orphans.

[24]If you lend money to my people, the poor among you, you must not be like a money lender; you must not demand interest from them. [25]If you take your neighbor's cloak as a pledge, you shall return it to him before sunset; [26]for this is his only covering; it is the cloak for his body. What will he sleep in? If he cries out to me, I will listen; for I am compassionate.

[27]You shall not despise God, nor curse a leader of your people.

[28]You shall not delay the offering of your harvest and your press. You shall give me the firstborn of your sons. [29]You must do the same with your oxen and

---

form of an oath taken in God's name, perhaps at a shrine (cf. 20:7). Verses 13-14 add rules about borrowing and hiring the use of an animal.

22:15–23:9 Social regulations

This passage shifts from property loss to social matters, which also include damages potentially incurred by the household patriarch. Premarital sexual intercourse between a man—married or single—and an unengaged single woman potentially is not forbidden but it may damage the household's welfare. This situation (vv. 15-16) is somewhat similar to Genesis 34. Both reflect the perception that a "virgin" (v. 15), literally an unmarried or married woman who has not yet born children (Joel 1:8), needs protection from men (cf. Ruth 2:9, 22; Songs 8:8-9), sometimes even to the point of rape (Sumerian Laws 7–8). Marriage is a financial arrangement involving a "bride price" (v. 15) paid to the woman's father (1 Sam 18), whether or not he allows her to marry (cf. Code of Hammurabi 159–64).

Sorcery, bestiality, and sacrifice to multiple deities were known in ancient Middle Eastern cultures, including Israel (vv. 17-19). Sorcery, legislated in neighboring cultures (e.g., Code of Hammurabi 2), refers primarily to spells to harm others, and not to divination (cf. Num 23:23). The formula-

your sheep; for seven days the firstling may stay with its mother, but on the eighth day you must give it to me.

³⁰You shall be a people sacred to me. Flesh torn to pieces in the field you shall not eat; you must throw it to the dogs.

23 ¹You shall not repeat a false report. Do not join your hand with the wicked to be a witness supporting violence. ²You shall not follow the crowd in doing wrong. When testifying in a lawsuit, you shall not follow the crowd in perverting justice. ³You shall not favor the poor in a lawsuit.

⁴When you come upon your enemy's ox or donkey going astray, you must see to it that it is returned. ⁵When you notice the donkey of one who hates you lying down under its burden, you should not desert him; you must help him with it.

⁶You shall not pervert justice for the needy among you in a lawsuit. ⁷You shall keep away from anything dishonest. The innocent and the just you shall not put to death, for I will not acquit the guilty. ⁸Never take a bribe, for a bribe blinds the clear-sighted and distorts the words of the just. ⁹You shall not oppress

---

tion in Hebrew refers to a female practitioner; magical acts performed by a female are also singled out in neo-Babylonian laws (7). Hittite laws (187–88, 199–200) and Middle Assyrian laws (199, 200) forbid bestiality with cows, sheep, pigs, or dogs. The lines of what was considered idolatry in Israel shifted over time, and strictures against worshiping other deities reflect the attitudes of those who made the rules, and not necessarily the view of the entire culture.

Rules show concern for weaker groups in the society, namely, the non-citizen who lives in Israel as well as the widow and the orphan (vv. 20-23; see Prov 23:10-11). The Bible reflects the ancient Middle Eastern norm. The three categories lack a patriarch who provides for and protects them. The poignant cases in verses 24-26 (cf. Prov 22:22-23) show a concern for the poor comparable to the "commoner" defended in Mesopotamian law codes. Cloaks taken as pledges must be returned by nightfall so that the poor can keep themselves warm (Job 22:6; Prov 20:16; 27:13; Amos 2:8; a seventh-century Israelite inscription from Mesad Yeshavyahu). When the family unit fails to provide, the system is designed to compensate. More-over, justice is more than just compensation for individual loss; it advocates care for the weaker in society who, if necessary, have recourse to God, who will hear their cry. In the Covenant Code, these high ideals lack concrete punishment or motivation to help the poor.

The ordinances of verses 27-30 overlap between the religious and social spheres, but ancient Israelites did not conceptually separate the two. Second Samuel 16:1-12 illustrates the reviling (v. 27) that even "a leader" could experience. In 22:27 the word "God" may be an honorific title for "judges"

a resident alien; you well know how it feels to be an alien, since you were once aliens yourselves in the land of Egypt.

Religious Laws. [10]For six years you may sow your land and gather in its produce. [11]But the seventh year you shall let the land lie untilled and fallow, that the poor of your people may eat of it and their leftovers the wild animals may eat. So also shall you do in regard to your vineyard and your olive grove.

[12]For six days you may do your work, but on the seventh day you must rest, that your ox and your donkey may have rest, and that the son of your maidservant and the resident alien may be refreshed. [13]Give heed to all that I have told you.

You shall not mention the name of any other god; it shall not be heard from your lips.

[14]Three times a year you shall celebrate a pilgrim feast to me. [15]You shall keep the feast of Unleavened Bread. As I have commanded you, you must eat unleavened bread for seven days at the

---

(or perhaps the household "gods"). Verses 28-29 offer no distinction in the treatment of human or animal firstborns. Child sacrifice was a known Israelite practice (Isa 30:33; Mic 6:7), though later it was not followed (Ezek 20:25-26). Human firstborns could be redeemed with an animal (Exod 34:19-20). Verse 30 includes an old dietary restriction against eating the meat of an animal carcass. Divine self-reference ("to me") in verses 28-30 is unusual in the Covenant Code; it perhaps adds the authority of the divine persona to the prohibition's force.

Exodus 23:1-9 addresses behavior in lawsuits. Verses 1-3 cover individual testimony as well as conspiracy with others. They also extend to wrongful favoritism of the poor (see also Lev 19:15; Deut 1:17). Verses 4-5 require neighborly help, even for someone "who hates you." This is not simply an emotional designation but refers to someone outside the kin group or someone otherwise lacking a social bond to the addressee. The legal context may seem odd for this regulation, but it offers safeguards against accusations of theft. In the Hittite laws (later version of 45) the return of a lost animal is treated under livestock theft rules. Someone "who hates you" may be more prone to suspect theft, and so it is strongly advisable to be neighborly under such circumstances. Verses 6-9 apparently address judges (cf. 18:13-27). The famous command, "Justice, justice alone shall you pursue" (Deut 16:20), belongs to a legal section concerning judges. Bribes could be a problem.

23:10-33 Religious law

Land use and animal labor are tied to the sabbatical year and the sabbath (vv. 10-12; see Exod 20:8-11). Israelites are expected to keep the sabbath on the same day, but it is unclear whether all are to observe the sabbatical year

appointed time in the month of Abib, for it was then that you came out of Egypt. No one shall appear before me empty-handed. [16]You shall also keep the feast of the grain harvest with the first fruits of the crop that you sow in the field; and finally, the feast of Ingathering at the end of the year, when you collect your produce from the fields. [17]Three times a year shall all your men appear before the LORD God.

[18]You shall not offer the blood of my sacrifice with anything leavened; nor shall the fat of my feast be kept overnight till the next day. [19]The choicest first fruits of your soil you shall bring to the house of the LORD, your God.

You shall not boil a young goat in its mother's milk.

Reward of Fidelity. [20]See, I am sending an angel before you, to guard you on the way and bring you to the place I have prepared. [21]Be attentive to him and obey him. Do not rebel against him, for he will not forgive your sin. My authority is within him. [22]If you obey him and carry out all I tell you, I will be an enemy to your enemies and a foe to your foes.

[23]My angel will go before you and bring you to the Amorites, Hittites, Perizzites, Canaanites, Hivites and Jebusites; and I will wipe them out. [24]Therefore, you shall not bow down to their gods and serve them, nor shall you act as they

---

in the same year or whether all the fields of a single Israelite must lie fallow in the same year. The regulations are not simply ecological in providing for a term of fallow land; the provisions are also "conservationist" with respect to people and animals in aiding both the poor and noncitizens ("the resident alien") as well as one's "living property," animals and servants. These provisions have no explicit religious association, but elsewhere they are treated in more religious terms, which may explain the rationale for their inclusion here.

A provision to invoke only the name of the Lord and not those of other gods (cf. body language of homage forbidden in the Ten Commandments, 20:5) heads up calendar of holidays (vv. 14-17). These are the three pilgrimage feasts when males are to bring their produce as offerings to the Lord (v. 17; also not "empty-handed," v. 15). Males are required; women could be excused for cause (Hannah stays home to nurse her baby Samuel, in 1 Sam 1). This calendar lacks provisions for Passover with the feast of Unleavened Bread (see Exod 12–13). Passover was perhaps still a separate home celebration at the time of the Covenant Code (cf. 2 Kgs 23:21-23). The grain harvest here (v. 16) does not have a religious connection with the giving of the Covenant at Sinai; this was probably a postexilic association. The same applies to the feast of Ingathering (v. 17), which later is connected with the wandering in the wilderness. Further provisions (for example, the Day of Atonement) are added in other versions of the annual calendar

do; rather, you must demolish them and smash their sacred stones. ²⁵You shall serve the Lord, your God; then he will bless your food and drink, and I will remove sickness from your midst; ²⁶no woman in your land will be barren or miscarry; and I will give you a full span of life.

²⁷I will have the terror of me precede you, so that I will throw into panic every nation you reach. I will make all your enemies turn from you in flight, ²⁸and ahead of you I will send hornets to drive the Hivites, Canaanites and Hittites out of your way. ²⁹But I will not drive them all out before you in one year, lest the land become desolate and the wild animals multiply against you. ³⁰Little by little I will drive them out before you, until you have grown numerous enough to take possession of the land. ³¹I will set your boundaries from the Red Sea to the sea of the Philistines, and from the wilderness to the Euphrates; all who dwell in this land I will hand over to you and you shall drive them out before you. ³²You shall not make a covenant with them or their gods. ³³They must not live in your land. For if you serve their gods, this will become a snare to you.

---

commanded on Mount Sinai (Exod 34:18-26; Lev 23; Deut 16), yet other additions are made to the cultic calendar commanded in the wilderness (Num 28–29). Historical progression of the Jewish calendar did not end with the Pentateuch; Purim was added in the Persian period (Esth 9), and Hannukah was included in the Maccabean era (1 Macc 4:36-60).

The provisions in verses 18-19 are connected to Unleavened Bread and the produce for the three pilgrimage festivals in verses 14-17. Blood in sacrifices is addressed in the priestly Holiness Code, which provides a rationale: "the life of the flesh is in the blood" (Lev 17:11; cf. 19:26). When animal consumption shifts from shrines to family communities, the associated provision for avoiding blood carries over (Deut 15:19-23).

The provision not to boil a kid in its mother's milk (v. 19) was once interpreted as an Israelite reaction against Canaanite practice, but this idea was based on a Ugaritic text now understood differently. The placement of this provision with the annual calendar may suggest that the dietary rules generally were to maintain temple holiness (cf. Exod 34:26); such provisions were perhaps followed in homes, though probably not at the same level (cf. Deut 14:21). The rule of verse 19 (and related passages), perhaps inspired by economic strategy (to maintain either the mother or her kid as a source of benefit) or humanitarian concerns (cf. 22:29), became the basis for separating milk (dairy) and meat products in Jewish dietary practice.

23:20-33 Promise of divine protection

This passage concerns divine protection on the journey to the land. In this E speech, the Horeb covenant is nearing conclusion, and travel to the

24 **Ratification of the Covenant.** ¹Moses himself was told: Come up to the LORD, you and Aaron, with Nadab, Abihu, and seventy of the elders of Israel. You shall bow down at a distance. ²Moses alone is to come close to the LORD; the others shall not come close, and the people shall not come up with them.

³When Moses came to the people and related all the words and ordinances of the LORD, they all answered with one voice, "We will do everything that the LORD has told us." ⁴Moses then wrote down all the words of the LORD and, rising early in the morning, he built at the foot of the mountain an altar and twelve sacred stones for the twelve tribes of Israel. ⁵Then, having sent young men of the Israelites to offer burnt offerings and sacrifice young bulls as communion offerings to the LORD, ⁶Moses took half of the blood and put it in large bowls; the other half he splashed on the altar. ⁷Taking the book of the covenant, he read it aloud to the people, who answered, "All that the LORD has said, we will hear and do." ⁸Then he took the blood and splashed it on the people, saying, "This is the blood of the covenant which the LORD has made with you according to all these words."

⁹Moses then went up with Aaron, Nadab, Abihu, and seventy elders of Israel, ¹⁰and they beheld the God of Israel. Under his feet there appeared to be sapphire tilework, as clear as the sky itself. ¹¹Yet he did not lay a hand on these chosen Israelites. They saw God, and they ate and drank.

Promised Land lies on the horizon. In context, it links the Covenant Code to the following narrative. For E, the angel would serve the expected role of divine accompaniment, fueled with the firepower of the divine name ("my authority," literally "my name," v. 21; cf. Ps 29:2). The angel reinforced with the name represents the Lord in battle (vv. 22, 23, 27; cf. Isa 30:27). Proclamations of divine victory over the peoples of the Promised Land (vv. 23, 27-31) preface commands to avoid them and their gods (vv. 24-26, 32-33).

24:1-11 Covenant meal

Verses 1-2 specify the company Moses is to bring, but only he is to come near the Lord. The others are to bow down to the Lord from afar, language used in royal letters to denote the submission of a vassal to his overlord. Because verses 9-11 again name those who are to accompany Moses, commentators suggest that these verses originally followed verses 1-2. This theory assumes verses 3-8 as a second version of covenant renewal, with reading the law, its acknowledgment by the people, and blood manipulation ritual. In context, verses 1-11 (JE) are designed to be read as a single version that functions to show the acceptance of the Ten Commandments and the Covenant Code: in verse 3, "words" refer to the Ten Commandments (20:1) and "ordinances" to the Covenant Code (21:1). In verse 8 blood binds the

Moses on the Mountain. ¹²The LORD said to Moses: Come up to me on the mountain and, while you are there, I will give you the stone tablets on which I have written the commandments intended for their instruction. ¹³So Moses set out with Joshua, his assistant, and went up to the mountain of God. ¹⁴He told the elders, "Wait here for us until we return to you. Aaron and Hur are with you. Anyone with a complaint should approach them." ¹⁵Moses went up the mountain. Then the cloud covered the mountain. ¹⁶The glory of the LORD settled upon Mount Sinai. The cloud covered it for six days, and on the seventh day he called to Moses from the midst of the cloud. ¹⁷To the Israelites the glory of the LORD was seen as a consuming fire on the top of the mountain. ¹⁸But Moses entered into the midst of the cloud and went up on the mountain. He was on the mountain for forty days and forty nights.

---

people and God (symbolized by the altar, v. 6). Verses 9-11 in context serve to seal the covenant of verses 3-8.

The company mentioned in verse 1 may advance to enjoy the vision of God in verses 9-10 (cf. 19:20-25), a biblical example of mystical experience and forerunner to what Catholic tradition calls the "beatific vision" in heaven. They look up through the floor of the heavenly palace and see God's feet (presumably resting on a divine footstool before the heavenly throne on which God sits enthroned; cf. Isa 6:1; 66:1). The "sapphire tilework" (v. 10) refers to the stonework of the heavenly palace (cf. the sapphire in the heavenly throne in Ezek 1:26). Sapphire evokes the color of the heavens (the word also means skies), as suggested by the simile at the end of verse 10. Verse 11 reflects the common belief that only the righteous may see God and live (see 19:20-25). The picture closes with a covenant meal, a eucharistic communion, on the mountain (Exod 18:12).

Verses 12-15a (E) follow unevenly from verses 1-11. In verse 12 Moses is ordered up the mountain, but according to verses 9-11 he is there already, and the word for regulations in verse 12 differs from the terms used in verse 3. In general, ancient and modern readers can read such shifts without noticing; they show a high capacity to read ambiguity out of a text presented as a single work. In context, this section narrates how Moses receives the written form of the commandments. He already has a "book" (more exactly, "a document"), but a permanent copy in the form of "stone tablets" is to be given to Moses (v. 12).

Clay tablets were the norm; standing stones (such as the Code of Hammurabi) served for public display of writing. The tablets, however, are of conventional scale, given so that Moses carries them down the mountain (Exod 32:15). A seventh-century rectangular stone tablet about eleven inches

25 **Collection of Materials.** ¹The LORD spoke to Moses: ²Speak to the Israelites: Let them receive contributions for me. From each you shall receive the contribution that their hearts prompt them to give me. ³These are the contributions you shall accept from them: gold, silver, and bronze; ⁴violet, purple, and scarlet yarn; fine linen and goat hair; ⁵rams' skins dyed red, and tahash skins; acacia wood; ⁶oil for the light; spices for the anointing oil and for the fragrant incense; ⁷onyx stones and other gems for mounting on the ephod and the breastpiece. ⁸They are to make a sanctuary for me, that I may dwell in their midst. ⁹According to all that I show you regarding the pattern of the tabernacle and the pattern of its furnishings, so you are to make it.

---

square has Aramaic writing on one side; the two tablets inscribed on both sides (32:15) could have contained the contents of the Ten Commandments. The ark is also the correct size for tablets (see 25:10, 15). The idea of the tablets was apparently created with the scale of the Ten Commandments in mind.

Verses 15b-18 (P) shift into priestly imagery of divine glory and the formula of seven days. Presupposing the covenant context of verses 1-15a, the description of the glory in verses 15b-18 anticipates the tabernacle's construction in Exodus 25–31, a mechanism for maintaining holy, divine presence in the midst of a people that sometimes sins. The divine glory and the tabernacle are linked in the book's finale in chapter 40 (Exod 24:15-17 parallels 40:34-35; cf. Lev 1:1; 9:6, 23-24). Verses 15b-18 also anticipate the story of the golden calf in Exodus 32. Instructions to Aaron and Hur to adjudicate disputes (v. 14) foreshadow Aaron's role in the calf story (32:1-3), and Moses is up on the mountain for forty days (v. 18) at the time of the beginning of chapter 32 (v. 1). These connections provide "narrative room" for including Exodus 25–31 in the Sinai covenant, and the two tablets mentioned at either end (24:12; 31:18) frame the chapters and connect them to the larger story line.

25:1-9 The collection of materials

The first phase in the standard format for the construction of sanctuaries involves instructions for gathering building materials, the actual building and furnishing of the tabernacle or temple; these appear in the priestly chapters 25–31 (to be carried out in chs. 35–40). This section shows priestly adaptations to the older biblical and ancient Middle Eastern pattern that appears in Solomon's temple in Jerusalem (1 Kgs 5–8) as well as the palace of the storm god Baal (the Ugaritic Baal Cycle). A command is given to take up a collection from the Israelites for the various materials needed (vv. 1-7).

◄ **Plan of the Ark.** [10]You shall make an ark of acacia wood, two and a half cubits long, one and a half cubits wide, and one and a half cubits high. [11]Plate it inside and outside with pure gold, and put a molding of gold around the top of it. [12]Cast four gold rings and put them on the four supports of the ark, two rings on one side and two on the opposite side. [13]Then make poles of acacia wood and plate them with gold. [14]These poles you are to put through the rings on the sides of the ark, for carrying it; [15]they must remain in the rings of the ark and never be withdrawn. [16]In the ark you are ► to put the covenant which I will give you.

[17]You shall then make a cover of pure gold, two and a half cubits long, and one and a half cubits wide. [18]Make two cherubim of beaten gold for the two ends of the cover; [19]make one cherub at one end, and the other at the other end, of one piece with the cover, at each end. [20]The cherubim shall have their wings spread out above, sheltering the cover with

The metal and wood are for furnishings and tent frames, the cloth materials for the tent curtains, the stones for the priestly vestments.

A first-person divine speech explains the sanctuary's purpose: it is for the Lord to dwell in its midst (v. 8). A transition from named materials to instructions for construction refers to the "pattern of the tabernacle" (v. 9), the model to be followed in the construction (25:40; 26:30). Like Moses' vision, King Gudea of Lagash has a vision showing the pattern of the temple commanded by his patron-god. Though following a traditional motif of building stories, these passages show that, for Israel, Moses was a leader who possessed prophetic capabilities.

25:10-22 The ark

The wooden box of the ark, gold plated inside and out, measures about 3.75 feet in length, and 2.5 feet in width and height (v. 10). The attached rings and poles (vv. 12-15) equip the ark for being carried. Gold plate expresses the ideal that the furnishings of the gods consist of gold. The ark is to provide storage for the tablets (vv. 16, 21), a purpose mentioned also for them in the Jerusalem temple (1 Kgs 8:9). The ark was imagined as God's footstool (1 Chr 28:2), but this may be an old idea. In an Egyptian-Hittite treaty, the copy of the treaty is deposited "beneath the feet" of the patron gods of the contracting parties. In contrast to this idea in the Jerusalem tradition, the Shiloh tradition recalls "the ark of the LORD of hosts, who is enthroned upon the cherubim" (1 Sam 4:4).

The ark's measurements are the same for the "propitiatory" (the gold cover known as the "mercy seat" where the presence of God was believed to dwell) placed on top of it, flanked by cherubim with outstretched wings (vv. 17-21). According to 1 Kings 6:19-28, the cherubim throne without the

them; they shall face each other, with their faces looking toward the cover. [21]This cover you shall then place on top of the ark. In the ark itself you are to put the covenant which I will give you. [22]There I will meet you and there, from above the cover, between the two cherubim on the ark of the covenant, I will tell you all that I command you regarding the Israelites.

The Table. [23]You shall also make a table of acacia wood, two cubits long, a cubit wide, and a cubit and a half high. [24]Plate it with pure gold and make a molding of gold around it. [25]Make a frame for it, a handbreadth high, and make a molding of gold around the frame. [26]You shall also make four rings of gold for it and fasten them at the four corners, one at each leg. [27]The rings shall be alongside the frame as holders for the poles to carry the table. [28]These poles for carrying the table you shall make of acacia wood and plate with gold. [29]You shall make its plates and cups, as well as its pitchers and bowls for pouring libations;

---

ark or propitiatory appears in the holy of holies in the Jerusalem temple. Biblical cherubim are not the winged babies depicted in Western art but large creatures of the mixed form of a human's head, an eagle's wings, and a lion's body (cf. Ezek 1:6-11; 10:14-22) who protect the abode of their divine masters. Cherubim guard the garden of Eden (Gen 3:24), and they mark the walls of the Jerusalem temple (1 Kgs 6:29-32; cf. Ezek 41:18-19). In 2 Samuel 22:11 (Ps 18:11) the Lord rides his cherub on the wind. Two cherubs make up two sides of a royal throne on a piece of ivory from Megiddo; the comparison suggests that the ark had a propitiatory function as a throne, with the Lord as divine king. Adding the sizes of the ark and the propitiatory heights, the seat of the throne stands five feet in height and conjures a picture of a superhuman-size divine king.

"Propitiatory" is the same word as *kippur* ("atonement," a metaphor from the word "to clean, purge"), as in the name of the holiday, Yom Kippur ("Day of Atonement"). It implies a place where the deity cleanses the priests' sins. The context explains the propitiatory's function as the site where the Lord addresses the priests to "tell you all that I command you regarding the Israelites" (v. 22; cf. 40:20). A broader revelatory function appears in Psalm 80:2, which asks the Lord to "From your throne upon the cherubim reveal yourself." Unmentioned outside of priestly contexts (except 1 Chr 28:11), the propitiatory may reflect a priestly understanding of the cover placed on the ark.

25:23-40 The table and menorah

The table is to be constructed with gold and equipment for being carried as well as an accompanying set of dishes (vv. 23-29). The table is designed

make them of pure gold. ³⁰On the table you shall always keep showbread set before me.

The Menorah. ³¹You shall make a menorah of pure beaten gold—its shaft and branches—with its cups and knobs and petals springing directly from it. ³²Six branches are to extend from its sides, three branches on one side, and three on the other. ³³On one branch there are to be three cups, shaped like almond blossoms, each with its knob and petals; on the opposite branch there are to be three cups, shaped like almond blossoms, each with its knob and petals; and so for the six branches that extend from the menorah. ³⁴On the menorah there are to be four cups, shaped like almond blossoms, with their knobs and petals. ³⁵The six branches that go out from the menorah are to have a knob under each pair. ³⁶Their knobs and branches shall so

for the placement of the "showbread" always set before the Lord (v. 30). Replenished every sabbath, these loaves of unleavened bread are twelve in number for the twelve tribes of Israel (Lev 24:5-9; cf. 1 Sam 21:2-7). The gold stand (vv. 31-40) holds seven lamps (cf. the ten lampstands in Solomon's temple, 1 Kgs 7:49; and the lamp taken in the sacking of the temple depicted on the Arch of Titus in Rome). These are equipped with items used to remove burned wicks (v. 38).

The temple's menorah is commemorated in Jewish tradition by the seven-branched "menorah" lit for the holiday of Hanukkah. The menorah has branches, blossoms, and petals, all of which suggest the image of a tree, possibly evoking or replacing the sacred tree. In Israel one sacred tree symbolized a goddess by the same name (*asherah*), and later the tree symbolizes the personified female wisdom (Prov 3:18). Cherubs flank trees in the temple walls (1 Kgs 6:29-32). The menorah also served as an "eternal light" (Exod 27:20; Lev 24:2-3), and its seven branches may have evoked the seven heavenly bodies, perhaps understood as the hosts of the Lord, the divine assembly of angelic powers.

The showbread and other items reflect the idea that offerings are food consumed by people and their God in a communion mediated by priests, a norm in ancient Middle Eastern religion and evident in biblical characterizations of sacrifices as the Lord's food (e.g., Lev 3:11; 21:6, 8, 17, 21; for God consuming offerings in fire, see Lev 9:22-24). This human representation of God was not transcended in biblical religion, as shown by criticism of the idea (see Pss 40:7; 50:8-15, 23; 51:18; Isa 1:10-17; Jer 7:21-22; Hos 6:6; Amos 5:21-25; Mic 6:6-8). This criticism does not call for abolishing sacrifice but for a deeper understanding of the meaning of the sacrificial system. Along with prayers and body language (gestures and postures), sacrifice represents part of a communication system expressing the covenant relationship be-

Arch of Titus, Rome. Relief depicting the carrying off of the menorah and other spoils of war by the Romans.

spring from it that the whole will form a single piece of pure beaten gold. ³⁷ You shall then make seven lamps for it and so set up the lamps that they give their light on the space in front of the menorah. ³⁸These, as well as the trimming shears and trays, must be of pure gold. ³⁹Use a talent of pure gold for the menorah and all these utensils. ⁴⁰See that you make them according to the pattern shown you on the mountain.

26 **The Tent Cloth.** ¹The tabernacle itself you shall make out of ten sheets woven of fine linen twined and of violet, purple, and scarlet yarn, with cherubim embroidered on them. ²The length of each shall be twenty-eight cubits, and the width four cubits; all the sheets shall be of the same size. ³Five of the sheets are to be joined one to another; and the same for the other five. ⁴Make loops of violet yarn along the edge of the end sheet in one set, and the same along the edge of the end sheet in the other set. ⁵Make fifty loops along the edge of the end sheet in the first set, and fifty loops along the edge of the corresponding sheet in the second set, and so placed that the loops are directly opposite each other. ⁶Then make fifty clasps of gold and join the two sets of sheets, so that the tabernacle forms one whole.

⁷Also make sheets woven of goat hair for a tent over the tabernacle. Make eleven such sheets; ⁸the length of each shall be thirty cubits, and the width four cubits: all eleven sheets shall be of the same size. ⁹Join five of the sheets into one set, and the other six sheets into another set. Use the sixth sheet double at the front of the tent. ¹⁰Make fifty loops along the edge of the end sheet in one set, and fifty loops along the edge of the end sheet in the second set. ¹¹Also make fifty bronze clasps and put them into the loops, to join the tent into one whole. ¹²There will be an extra half sheet of tent covering, which shall be allowed to hang down over the rear of the tabernacle. ¹³Likewise, the sheets of the tent will have an extra cubit's length to be left hanging down on either side of the tabernacle to cover it. ¹⁴Over the tent itself make a covering of rams' skins dyed red, and above that, a covering of tahash skins.

The Framework. ¹⁵You shall make frames for the tabernacle, acacia-wood uprights. ¹⁶The length of each frame is to be ten cubits, and its width one and a

---

tween human vassals and their divine king; the terms for sacrifices include "tribute" and other payment owed the divine overlord. Critiques call for understanding sacrifice as an offering of the self to the Lord.

26:1-37 The sanctuary

The items in chapter 25 are to be housed in the structure mandated in this chapter. Behind the temple traditions at Jerusalem and Shiloh and the Exodus tabernacle stands a long line of tent-tabernacle shrines going back to the pre-Israelite tradition (the Baal Cycle), which portrays the god El issuing decrees from his tent-home. From the second millennium site of Mari to modern Bedouin culture, large tents have been used, sometimes for sacred

half cubits. [17]Each frame shall have two arms joined one to another; so you are to make all the frames of the tabernacle. [18]Make the frames of the tabernacle as follows: twenty frames on the south side, [19]with forty silver pedestals under the twenty frames, two pedestals under each frame for its two arms; [20]twenty frames on the other side of the tabernacle, the north side, [21]with their forty silver pedestals, two pedestals under each frame. [22]At the rear of the tabernacle, to the west, six frames, [23]and two frames for the corners of the tabernacle, at its rear. [24]These two shall be double at the bottom, and likewise double at the top, to the first ring. That is how both corner frames are to be made. [25]Thus, there shall be eight frames, with their sixteen silver pedestals, two pedestals under each frame. [26]Also make bars of acacia wood: five for the frames on one side of the tabernacle, [27]five for those on the other side, and five for those at the rear, to the west. [28]The center bar, at the middle of the frames, shall reach across from end to end. [29]Plate the frames with gold, and make gold rings on them as holders for the bars, which are also to be plated with gold. [30]You shall set up the tabernacle according to its plan, which you were shown on the mountain.

The Veils. [31]You shall make a veil woven of violet, purple, and scarlet yarn, and of fine linen twined, with cherubim embroidered on it. [32]It is to be hung on four gold-plated columns of acacia wood, which shall have gold hooks and shall rest on four silver pedestals. [33]Hang the veil from clasps. The ark of the covenant you shall bring inside, behind this veil which divides the holy place from the holy of holies. [34]Set the cover on the ark of the covenant in the holy of holies.

[35]Outside the veil you shall place the table and the menorah, the latter on the south side of the tabernacle, opposite the

purposes. In the priestly conception here, the sanctuary is a portable tent half the size of Solomon's temple (1 Kgs 6:2, 16-17). It is implicitly identified with and thereby supersedes the tent of meeting in the E tradition (see Exod 33:7-11 and 40:34-38). Sheets of cloth are sewn together to make two large sheets joined together by means of clasps and loops (vv. 1-6) and woven with the image of the cherubim (compare the cherubim on the temple walls, 1 Kgs 6:29-32). Sheets woven of goat hair overlay the cloth sheets of verses 1-6 and hang down on both sides (vv. 7-13). Dyed ram skins cover the whole structure of wooden frames, which form a rectangular structure, about forty-five feet long, fifteen feet wide, and open to the east (vv. 15-29). In addition, one veil (vv. 31-37) is over the entrance and another inside splits the interior space between an outer area ("the holy place") and an area in the back ("the holy of holies"). The outer area is for the divine table setting and menorah (v. 35), while "the holy of holies" (a way of expressing superlative degree in Hebrew, so "the holiest place") is the space reserved for the propitiatory and the ark (v. 34). The model for this structure is the

table, which is to be put on the north side. ³⁶For the entrance of the tent make a variegated curtain of violet, purple, and scarlet yarn and of fine linen twined. ³⁷Make five columns of acacia wood for this curtain; plate them with gold, with their hooks of gold; and cast five bronze pedestals for them.

27 **The Altar for Burnt Offerings.** ¹You shall make an altar of acacia wood, on a square, five cubits long and five cubits wide; it shall be three cubits high. ²At the four corners make horns that are of one piece with the altar. You shall then plate it with bronze. ³Make pots for removing the ashes, as well as shovels, basins, forks, and fire pans; all these utensils you shall make of bronze. ⁴Make for it a grating, a bronze network; make four bronze rings for it, one at each of its four corners. ⁵Put it down around the altar, on the ground. This network is to be half as high as the altar. ⁶You shall also make poles of acacia wood for the altar, and plate them with bronze. ⁷These poles are to be put through the rings, so that they are on either side of the altar when it is carried. ⁸Make the altar itself

in the form of a hollow box. Just as it was shown you on the mountain, so it is to be made.

Court of the Tabernacle. ⁹You shall also make a court for the tabernacle. On the south side the court shall have hangings, of fine linen twined, a hundred cubits long, ¹⁰with twenty columns and twenty pedestals of bronze; the hooks and bands on the columns shall be of silver. ¹¹On the north side there shall be similar hangings, a hundred cubits long, with twenty columns and twenty pedestals of bronze; the hooks and bands on the columns shall be of silver. ¹²On the west side, across the width of the court, there shall be hangings, fifty cubits long, with ten columns and ten pedestals. ¹³The width of the court on the east side shall be fifty cubits. ¹⁴On one side there shall be hangings to the extent of fifteen cubits, with three columns and three pedestals; ¹⁵on the other side there shall be hangings to the extent of fifteen cubits, with three columns and three pedestals.

¹⁶At the gate of the court there shall be a variegated curtain, twenty cubits long, woven of violet, purple, and scarlet

---

interior space of temples and shrines, regarded as palaces of the divine king with back spaces of the "holy of holies," the divine throne-room served by the king's servants, the priests. The colors of the clothes used (v. 1) recall the colors of the high priest's garments (Exod 28:5).

27:1-21 The altar and the courtyard

Today, altars are located inside churches, but in ancient Israel the altar was located outside the temple building in a courtyard area accessible to the people. The altar (vv. 1-8), about 7.5 feet in length and width and about 4.5 feet high, is a hollow wood box with bronze plating (cf. Exod 20:24). The altar's horns (v. 2) are marked with blood in sacrifices (29:12), and an offering for God could be brought to the altar and bound to its horns (Ps 118:27). The horns were also grasped by persons seeking asylum at the sanctuary

yarn and of fine linen twined. It shall have four columns and four pedestals.

¹⁷All the columns around the court shall have bands and hooks of silver, and pedestals of bronze. ¹⁸The court is to be one hundred cubits long, fifty cubits wide, and five cubits high. Fine linen twined must be used, and the pedestals must be of bronze. ¹⁹All the fittings of the tabernacle, whatever be their use, as well as all its tent pegs and all the tent pegs of the court, must be of bronze.

Oil for the Lamps. ²⁰You shall command the Israelites to bring you clear oil of crushed olives, to be used for the light, so that you may keep lamps burning always. ²¹From evening to morning Aaron and his sons shall maintain them before the LORD in the tent of meeting, outside the veil which hangs in front of the covenant. This shall be a perpetual statute for the Israelites throughout their generations.

28 The Priestly Vestments. ¹Have your brother Aaron, and with him his sons, brought to you, from among the Israelites, that they may be my priests: Nadab and Abihu, Eleazar and Ithamar, Aaron's sons. ²For the glorious adornment of your brother Aaron you shall have sacred vestments made. ³Therefore, tell the various artisans whom I have endowed with skill to make vestments for Aaron to consecrate him as my priest. ⁴These are the vestments they shall make: a breastpiece, an ephod, a robe, a brocade tunic, a turban, and a sash. In making these sacred vestments which your brother Aaron and his sons are to wear in serving as my priests, ⁵they shall use gold, violet, purple, and scarlet yarn and fine linen.

(see Exod 21:13-14; 1 Kgs 1:50; 2:28; cf. Num 35). In these instances, the horns are a contact point with the divine. Horns generally denote power and belong to the symbolism of several gods, which is perhaps reflected in the altar's horns (cf. ox imagery for God, Num 24:8).

The enclosure (vv. 9-19) functions as an uncovered outside courtyard for the altar. A note (vv. 20-21) is added about oil, which was extracted by pounding the olives in a mortar rather than grinding and then passed through a strainer (and thereby free of dregs, hence "clear"). How the priesthood conceived the sacrificial process is spelled out in Leviticus 9:22-24: following his blessing of the people and various sacrifices, Aaron along with Moses would enter and exit the tabernacle, blessing the people. Then the divine glory would be revealed to the people through the divine presence producing fire that consumes the offering; at the sight of the fire the people would respond in worship (Exod 25:23-40; 29:43-46; cf. Sir 50).

28:1-43 Priestly vestments

Aaron and his sons in 27:21 connect to their mention in 28:1. For the priestly writer, Aaron's family was the preeminent priestly line (in contrast to the Korahites and other lesser Levitical priests, regarded by P as worthy

The Ephod and Breastpiece. [6]The ephod they shall make of gold thread and of violet, purple, and scarlet yarn, embroidered on cloth of fine linen twined. [7]It shall have a pair of shoulder straps joined to its two upper ends. [8]The embroidered belt of the ephod shall extend out from it and, like it, be made of gold thread, of violet, purple, and scarlet yarn, and of fine linen twined.

[9]Get two onyx stones and engrave on them the names of the sons of Israel: [10]six of their names on one stone, and the names of the remaining six on the other stone, in the order of their birth. [11]As a gem-cutter engraves a seal, so shall you have the two stones engraved with the names of the sons of Israel and then mounted in gold filigree work. [12]Set these two stones on the shoulder straps of the ephod as memorial stones of the sons of Israel. Thus Aaron shall bear their names on his shoulders as a reminder before the LORD. [13]Make filigree rosettes of gold, [14]as well as two chains of pure gold, twisted like cords, and fasten the cordlike chains to the filigree rosettes.

[15]The breastpiece of decision you shall also have made, embroidered like the ephod with gold thread and violet, purple, and scarlet yarn on cloth of fine linen twined. [16]It is to be square when folded double, a span high and a span wide. [17] On it you shall mount four rows of precious stones: in the first row, a carnelian, a topaz, and an emerald; [18]in the second row, a garnet, a sapphire, and a beryl; [19]in the third row, a jacinth, an agate, and an amethyst; [20]in the fourth row, a chrysolite, an onyx, and a jasper. These stones are to be mounted in gold filigree work, [21]twelve of them to match the names of the sons of Israel, each stone engraved like a seal with the name of one of the twelve tribes.

[22]When the chains of pure gold, twisted like cords, have been made for the breastpiece, [23]you shall then make two rings of gold for it and fasten them to the two upper ends of the breastpiece. [24]The gold cords are then to be fastened to the two rings at the upper ends of the breastpiece, [25]the other two ends of the cords being fastened in front to the two filigree rosettes which are attached to the shoulder straps of the ephod. [26]Make two other rings of gold and put them on the two lower ends of the breastpiece, on its edge that faces the ephod. [27]Then

---

not of high sacrificial service but of temple duties considered of lesser importance; see 6:10-27). The items to be made are listed (v. 4) before the materials to be used (v. 5). The priestly garments correspond in color to the tabernacle's cloth, suggesting a color-coded identification of the priests with the service in the sanctuary (27:16). Many of the garments and their colors echo royal dress (39:30 calls the plate a "diadem").

The ephod (vv. 6-12) was an ancient robe of priests (1 Sam 21:10; cf. 1 Sam 2:18; 22:18; 2 Sam 6:14). Fastened to the ephod was a robe to be worn over the priest's chest (vv. 13-35). Because the priest is the representative of the twelve tribes, his clothing bears two stones inscribed with those names "as a reminder before the LORD" (v. 12). The priest serves as mediator, bearing

make two more rings of gold and fasten them to the bottom of the shoulder straps next to where they join the ephod in front, just above its embroidered belt. [28]Violet ribbons shall bind the rings of the breastpiece to the rings of the ephod, so that the breastpiece will stay right above the embroidered belt of the ephod and not swing loose from it.

[29]Whenever Aaron enters the sanctuary, he will thus bear the names of the sons of Israel on the breastpiece of decision over his heart as a constant reminder before the Lord. [30]In this breastpiece of decision you shall put the Urim and Thummim, that they may be over Aaron's heart whenever he enters the presence of the Lord. Thus he shall always bear the decisions for the Israelites over his heart in the presence of the Lord.

Other Vestments. [31]The robe of the ephod you shall make entirely of violet material. [32]It shall have an opening for the head in the center, and around this opening there shall be a selvage, woven as at the opening of a shirt, to keep it from being torn. [33]At the hem at the bottom you shall make pomegranates, woven of violet, purple, and scarlet yarn and fine linen twined, with gold bells between them; [34]a gold bell, a pomegranate, a gold bell, a pomegranate, all around the hem of the robe. [35]Aaron shall wear it when ministering, that its sound may be heard as he enters and leaves the Lord's presence in the sanctuary; else he will die.

[36]You shall also make a plate of pure gold and engrave on it, as on a seal engraving, "Sacred to the Lord." [37]This plate is to be tied over the turban with a violet ribbon in such a way that it rests on the front of the turban, [38]over Aaron's forehead. Since Aaron bears whatever guilt the Israelites may incur in consecrating any of their sacred gifts, this plate must always be over his forehead, so that they may find favor with the Lord.

---

a reminder and offerings of the Israelites before the Lord and in turn the Lord's commands to the people.

Priests also convey to the people the Lord's oracles via the Urim and Thummim (v. 30), mentioned several times in the Bible (Lev 8:8; Num 27:21; Deut 33:8; 1 Sam 28:6; Ezra 2:63; Neh 7:65; cf. Septuagint of 1 Sam 14:31). Worn over the priest's heart in "the breastpiece of decision," these stones are used in a divinatory practice to indicate answers to questions posed to them. A Mesopotamian text describes a "shining" divinatory stone like the Urim ("Light"). A Mesopotamian myth tells of divinatory stone called "true word stone," similar to the Thummim ("Truth").

Worn on the priest's head was a gold plate secured to his miter and inscribed (vv. 36-38) with the formula, "Sacred to the Lord," found also in Zechariah 14:20 (cf. Ezek 48:14). Pertinent in view of the pomegranates of verse 33 is an excavated pomegranate written with these very words. The priests are so marked as living vessels of holiness.

³⁹The tunic of fine linen shall be brocaded. The turban shall be made of fine linen. The sash shall be of variegated work.

⁴⁰Likewise, for the glorious adornment of Aaron's sons you shall have tunics and sashes and skullcaps made, for glorious splendor. ⁴¹With these you shall clothe your brother Aaron and his sons. Anoint and install them, consecrating them as my priests. ⁴²You must also make linen pants for them, to cover their naked flesh from their loins to their thighs. ⁴³Aaron and his sons shall wear them whenever they go into the tent of meeting or approach the altar to minister in the sanctuary, lest they incur guilt and die. This shall be a perpetual ordinance for him and for his descendants.

29 **Consecration of the Priests.** ¹This is the rite you shall perform in consecrating them as my priests. Procure a young bull and two unblemished rams. ²With bran flour make unleavened cakes mixed with oil, and unleavened wafers spread with oil, ³and put them in a basket. Take the basket of them along with the bull and the two rams. ⁴Aaron and his sons you shall also bring to the entrance of the tent of meeting, and there wash them with water. ⁵Take the vestments and clothe Aaron with the tunic, the robe of the ephod, the ephod itself, and the breastpiece, fastening the embroidered belt of the ephod around him. ⁶Put the turban on his head, the sacred diadem on the turban. ⁷Then take the anointing oil and pour it on his head, and anoint him. ⁸Bring forward his sons also and clothe them with the tunics, ⁹gird them with the sashes, and tie the skullcaps on them. Thus shall the priesthood be theirs by a perpetual statute, and thus shall you install Aaron and his sons.

Installation Sacrifices. ¹⁰Now bring forward the bull in front of the tent of meeting. There Aaron and his sons shall

The new clothing along with an ordination ritual (v. 41) prepares the priests for service in the sanctuary. Anointing was a common ritual marker to denote the new, elevated status of new priests or royalty. "Ordain" is here literally "filling the hands" (perhaps referring to priestly instruments placed in a new inductee's hand at the time of his ordination), an old idiomatic expression designating priestly consecration (Lev 21:10; Num 3:3; Judg 17:5, 12; 1 Kgs 13:33; 2 Chr 13:9). The chapter closes with a description of additional garments (vv. 39-43). "The clothes that make the man" in this case communicate priestly identity (see Num 20:22-29). The high priest, exiting the tent in his magnificent robes and making offerings with his brother priests, would be remembered as glorious, comparable to the shining sun and the moon (Sir 50:6).

29:1-46 Priestly consecration

Aaron's induction mentioned in 28:41 involves three ritual steps: purification offerings and washing (vv. 1-4), clothing (vv. 5-6), and anointing (v. 7). The other priests are to follow Aaron's lead (vv. 8-9; see also Lev

lay their hands on its head. ¹¹Then slaughter the bull before the Lord, at the entrance of the tent of meeting. ¹²Take some of its blood and with your finger put it on the horns of the altar. All the rest of the blood you shall pour out at the base of the altar. ¹³All the fat that covers its inner organs, as well as the lobe of its liver and its two kidneys, together with the fat that is on them, you shall take and burn on the altar. ¹⁴But the meat and hide and dung of the bull you must burn up outside the camp, since this is a purification offering.

¹⁵Then take one of the rams, and after Aaron and his sons have laid their hands on its head, ¹⁶slaughter it. The blood you shall take and splash on all the sides of the altar. ¹⁷Cut the ram into pieces; you shall wash its inner organs and shanks and put them with the pieces and with the head. ¹⁸Then you shall burn the entire ram on the altar, since it is a burnt offering, a sweet-smelling oblation to the Lord.

¹⁹After this take the other ram, and when Aaron and his sons have laid their hands on its head, ²⁰slaughter it. Some of its blood you shall take and put on the tip of Aaron's right ear and on the tips of his sons' right ears and on the thumbs of their right hands and the great toes of their right feet. Splash the rest of the blood on all the sides of the altar. ²¹Then take some of the blood that is on the altar, together with some of the anointing oil, and sprinkle this on Aaron and his vestments, as well as on his sons and their vestments, that he and his sons and their vestments may be sacred.

²²Now, from this ram you shall take its fat: its fatty tail, the fat that covers its inner organs, the lobe of its liver, its two kidneys with the fat that is on them, and its right thigh, since this is the ram for installation; ²³then, out of the basket of unleavened food that you have set before the Lord, you shall take one of the loaves of bread, one of the cakes made with oil, and one of the wafers. ²⁴All these things you shall put into the hands of Aaron and his sons, so that they may raise them as an elevated offering before the Lord. ²⁵After you receive them back from their hands, you shall burn them on top of the burnt offering on the altar

8:1-38). Purification is a prerequisite for entering into the holy area of the tabernacle. The offerings, laid out in verses 10-28 (cf. Lev 1–7), distinguish between their purpose, manner, and material. The "purification offering" (v. 14), reflecting its purpose to purify of sin, uses blood toward that end; the interior organs and fat go as offerings to the Lord, and the rest is burned outside the camp. The "burnt offering" (v. 18) refers to the manner of the offering as completely made to the Lord, with the blood on the altar and the entire animal burned on the altar, but the name for this offering in Hebrew denotes its purpose as literally "one that ascends" to heaven in order to gain the Lord's attention. Washing (v. 17) offerings of meat is ancient (see 1 Sam 2:13-17; cf. Ezek 46:19-23's vision of the priestly kitchens in the temple for cooking offerings). The "ram for installation" (v. 22) provides blood of

as a sweet-smelling oblation to the LORD. [26]Finally, take the brisket of Aaron's installation ram and raise it as an elevated offering before the LORD; this is to be your own portion.

[27]Thus shall you set aside the brisket of whatever elevated offering is raised, as well as the thigh of whatever contribution is raised up, whether this be the installation ram or anything else belonging to Aaron or to his sons. [28]Such things are due to Aaron and his sons from the Israelites by a perpetual statute as a contribution. From their communion offerings, too, the Israelites shall make a contribution, their contribution to the LORD.

[29]The sacred vestments of Aaron shall be passed down to his sons after him, that in them they may be anointed and installed. [30]The son who succeeds him as priest and who is to enter the tent of meeting to minister in the sanctuary shall be clothed with them for seven days.

[31]You shall take the installation ram and boil its meat in a holy place. [32]At the entrance of the tent of meeting Aaron and his sons shall eat the meat of the ram and the bread that is in the basket. [33]They themselves are to eat of these things by which atonement was made at their installation and consecration; but no un-authorized person may eat of them, since they are sacred. [34]If some of the meat of the installation sacrifice or some of the bread remains over on the next day, this remnant you must burn up; it is not to be eaten, since it is sacred.

[35]Carry out all these commands in regard to Aaron and his sons just as I have given them to you. Seven days you shall spend installing them, [36]sacrificing a bull each day as a purification offering, to make atonement. Thus you shall purify the altar by purging it, and you shall anoint it in order to consecrate it. [37]Seven days you shall spend in purging the altar and in consecrating it. Then the altar will be most sacred, and whatever touches it will become sacred.

[38]Now, this is what you shall regularly offer on the altar: two yearling lambs as the sacrifice established for each day; [39]one lamb in the morning and the other lamb at the evening twilight. [40]With the first lamb there shall be a tenth of an ephah of bran flour mixed with a fourth of a hin of oil of crushed olives and, as its libation, a fourth of a hin of wine. [41]The other lamb you shall offer at the evening twilight, with the same grain offering and libation as in the morning. You shall offer this as a sweet-smelling

---

purification for the priests (on their right ears, vv. 19-20; cf. Lev 14:14), for the altar (v. 20), and then in a mixture with oil for all the priests as well as their vestments (v. 21).

The rest of this meat, combined with cereal offerings, shows how priestly income derived from offerings: the Lord receives the generally less (humanly) edible inner organs and the priests receive the meat of the brisket (vv. 22-27; cf. Lev 7:28-34). The division of sacrificial income is mandated also for "elevated offerings" and "communion offerings" (vv. 27-28); the first term refers to an act of elevation signifying the transfer of items to priestly use, while the second means greetings or good, peaceful relations between

oblation to the LORD. [42]Throughout your generations this regular burnt offering shall be made before the LORD at the entrance of the tent of meeting, where I will meet you and speak to you.

[43]There, at the altar, I will meet the Israelites; hence, it will be made sacred by my glory. [44]Thus I will consecrate the tent of meeting and the altar, just as I also consecrate Aaron and his sons to be my priests. [45]I will dwell in the midst of the Israelites and will be their God. [46]They shall know that I, the LORD, am their God who brought them out of the land of Egypt, so that I, the LORD, their God, might dwell among them.

30 **Altar of Incense.** [1]For burning incense you shall make an altar of acacia wood, [2]with a square surface, a cubit long, a cubit wide, and two cubits high, with horns that are of one piece with it. [3]Its grate on top, its walls on all four sides, and its horns you shall plate with pure gold. Put a gold molding around it. [4]Underneath the molding you shall put gold rings, two on one side and two on the opposite side, as holders for the poles used in carrying it. [5]Make the poles, too, of acacia wood and plate them with gold. [6]This altar you are to place in front of the veil that hangs before the ark of the covenant where I will meet you.

[7]On it Aaron shall burn fragrant incense. Morning after morning, when he prepares the lamps, [8]and again in the evening twilight, when he lights the lamps, he shall burn incense. Throughout your generations this shall be the regular incense offering before the LORD. [9]On this altar you shall not offer up any profane incense, or any burnt offering or grain offering; nor shall you pour out a libation upon it. [10]Once a year Aaron shall purge its horns. Throughout your generations he is to purge it once a year with the blood of the atoning purification offering. This altar is most sacred to the LORD.

Census Tax. [11]The LORD also told Moses: [12]When you take a census of the Israelites who are to be enrolled, each

---

the Lord and the offerer (see Lev 3). In addition to the priests, their vestments are anointed and ordained for the seven-day ritual, which focuses on the altar's purification through offerings (vv. 29-30, 35-42). Verse 37 reflects the understanding that holiness can be conveyed by contact. These rituals relate the human mechanics involved, but the first-person divine speech (vv. 43-46) explains their religious significance: the ritual site and its priestly officiants are consecrated by the Lord's presence experienced in the ritual. As a result, the Lord will meet Israel at the altar and dwell in its midst. Through this experience, the Israelites will come to the knowledge of God begun by the exodus (cf. 6:7; 7:4-5).

30:1-38 Final ritual ordinances

The incense altar (vv. 1-10) follows the regulations for sacrifices in chapter 29. It is to provide a sweet smell of aromatic smoke specially reserved for the deity (Lev 4:7). Unlike the bronze altar (Exod 27:1-8), this one is

one, as he is enrolled, shall give the Lord a ransom for his life, so that no plague may come upon them for being enrolled. ¹³This is what everyone who is enrolled must pay: a half-shekel, according to the standard of the sanctuary shekel—twenty gerahs to the shekel—a half-shekel contribution to the Lord. ¹⁴Everyone who is enrolled, of twenty years or more, must give the contribution to the Lord. ¹⁵The rich need not give more, nor shall the poor give less, than a half-shekel in this contribution to the Lord to pay the ransom for their lives. ¹⁶When you receive this ransom money from the Israelites, you shall donate it to the service of the tent of meeting, that there it may be a reminder of the Israelites before the Lord of the ransom paid for their lives.

The Basin. ¹⁷The Lord told Moses: ¹⁸For ablutions you shall make a bronze basin with a bronze stand. Place it between the tent of meeting and the altar, and put water in it. ¹⁹Aaron and his sons shall use it in washing their hands and feet. ²⁰When they are about to enter the tent of meeting, they must wash with water, lest they die. Likewise when they approach the altar to minister, to offer an oblation to the Lord, ²¹they must wash their hands and feet, lest they die. This shall be a perpetual statute for him and his descendants throughout their generations.

The Anointing Oil. ²²The Lord told Moses: ²³Take the finest spices: five hundred shekels of free-flowing myrrh; half that amount, that is, two hundred and fifty shekels, of fragrant cinnamon; two hundred and fifty shekels of fragrant cane; ²⁴five hundred shekels of cassia— all according to the standard of the sanctuary shekel; together with a hin of olive oil; ²⁵and blend them into sacred anointing oil, perfumed ointment expertly prepared. With this sacred anointing oil

---

gold, corresponding to the gold altar in Solomon's temple (1 Kgs 6:22) used for burning incense (2 Chr 26:16). Sites from the period of Israel's kings have yielded forty-five limestone altars, thirty-three horned and twelve unhorned; they were apparently used for burning incense. The incense altar is reserved for the atonement rite of Yom Kippur (v. 10; cf. Lev 16:18). A census tax (vv. 11-16) is mandated for all in the community.

"Ransom" (v. 12) is an economic application of the word used for "atoning" in verse 10 (also related to the word for "propitiatory"), here for buying a person's life out of debt, conceptualized as a payment owed to God, which if unmet may result in divine plague. The words "atoning" in verse 10 and "ransom" in verse 12 help to explain the placement of the census tax in this context of ritual purification. The "service of the tent of meeting" (v. 16) could refer to priestly service in general or to the work of construction (as in 39:32); the former seems preferable, given the future use imagined for the other items here.

The bronze basin (vv. 17-21; cf. 1 Sam 2:14) is used for priestly washing (cf. 40:30-32), like the laver belonging to Solomon's temple (2 Chr 4:6). Yet

²⁶you shall anoint the tent of meeting and the ark of the covenant, ²⁷the table and all its utensils, the menorah and its utensils, the altar of incense ²⁸and the altar for burnt offerings with all its utensils, and the basin with its stand. ²⁹When you have consecrated them, they shall be most sacred; whatever touches them shall be sacred. ³⁰Aaron and his sons you shall also anoint and consecrate as my priests. ³¹Tell the Israelites: As sacred anointing oil this shall belong to me throughout your generations. ³²It may not be used in any ordinary anointing of the body, nor may you make any other oil of a like mixture. It is sacred, and shall be treated as sacred by you. ³³Whoever prepares a perfume like this, or whoever puts any of this on an unauthorized person, shall be cut off from his people.

The Incense. ³⁴The LORD told Moses: Take these aromatic substances: storax and onycha and galbanum, these and pure frankincense in equal parts; ³⁵and blend them into incense. This fragrant powder, expertly prepared, is to be salted and so kept pure and sacred. ³⁶Grind some of it into fine dust and put this before the covenant in the tent of meeting where I will meet you. This incense shall be treated as most sacred by you. ³⁷You may not make incense of a like mixture for yourselves; you must treat it as sacred to the LORD. ³⁸Whoever makes an incense like this for his own enjoyment of its fragrance, shall be cut off from his people.

31 **Choice of Artisans.** ¹The LORD said to Moses: ²See, I have singled out Bezalel, son of Uri, son of Hur,

according to 1 Kings 7:23-26, the laver in front of Solomon's temple was the bronze "sea," which was far too large for washing, probably a symbol of the divine victory over the cosmic sea celebrated at the temple (cf. Ps 29); this old religious theme is not transmitted by the Exodus tradition of the laver, which prefers a purpose and scale suitable for priestly use.

The anointing oil (vv. 22-33) is to be applied to the tent and its various items, symbolizing their consecration like the anointing of priests and their vestments (28:41; 29:29). Forbidden to laypersons, it is not for "any ordinary anointing" (v. 32), as it is composed of imported aromatic substances from southern Arabia, Somalia, and various places in Asia. As valuable trade items (cf. Gen 37:25), they were stored in the royal treasury (2 Kgs 20:13). Their mixing required professional expertise (v. 25). The incense (vv. 34-38) too is made up of imported spices. Frankincense (v. 34) and myrrh (v. 23) are gum resins deriving from trees growing in the southern Arabian Peninsula and Somalia. The subject of the incense connects the end of the chapter to its opening topic of the incense altar in verses 1-10.

31:1-11 Choice of artisans

The selection of craftsmen is a standard element in ancient building stories, especially in the Bible and texts from nearer neighboring areas

of the tribe of Judah, ³and I have filled him with a divine spirit of skill and understanding and knowledge in every craft: ⁴in the production of embroidery, in making things of gold, silver, or bronze, ⁵in cutting and mounting precious stones, in carving wood, and in every other craft. ⁶As his assistant I myself have appointed Oholiab, son of Ahisamach, of the tribe of Dan. I have also endowed all the experts with the necessary skill to make all the things I have commanded you: ⁷the tent of meeting, the ark of the covenant with its cover, all the furnishings of the tent, ⁸the table with its utensils, the pure gold menorah with all its utensils, the altar of incense, ⁹the altar for burnt offerings with all its utensils, the basin with its stand, ¹⁰the service cloths, the sacred vestments for Aaron the priest, the vestments for his sons in their ministry, ¹¹the anointing oil, and the fragrant incense for the sanctuary. According to all I have commanded you, so shall they do.

Sabbath Laws. ¹²The Lord said to Moses: ¹³You must also tell the Israelites: Keep my sabbaths, for that is to be the sign between you and me throughout the generations, to show that it is I, the Lord, who make you holy. ¹⁴Therefore, you must keep the sabbath for it is holiness for you. Whoever desecrates it shall be put to death. If anyone does work on that day, that person must be cut off from the people. ¹⁵Six days there are for doing work, but the seventh day is the sabbath of complete rest, holy to the Lord. Anyone who does work on the sabbath day shall be put to death. ¹⁶So shall the Israelites observe the sabbath, keeping it throughout their generations as an everlasting covenant. ¹⁷Between me and the Israelites it is to be an everlasting sign; for in six days the Lord made the heavens and the earth, but on the seventh day he rested at his ease.

¹⁸When the Lord had finished speaking to Moses on Mount Sinai, he gave him the two tablets of the covenant, the

---

(e.g., the Ugaritic Baal Cycle). Sometimes the divine spirit is regarded as supernatural, but in verse 3 it is the divine spirit of knowledge and skill that goes into craftsmanship, including embroidery, metalwork, working in precious stones, and wood carving (v. 4-5). The names of the craftsmen, Bezalel (v. 2) and his assistant Oholiab (v. 6), relate to the task at hand. Bezalel means "in the shadow [or protection] of God," which suggests the tabernacle's function in providing divine aid. Oholiab means "the tent of the father" or "the father is my tent," suggesting the paternal divine care embodied by the tent of meeting (v. 7). Verses 7-11 offer a recapitulation of chapters 25–31 in listing all the items commanded in them.

31:12-18 The sabbath and the tablets

The building instructions end with the sabbath observance. Like the week of six days of work followed by the sabbath, so too the labor commanded in the preceding sections culminates in a final command to keep

stone tablets inscribed by God's own finger.

VII. Israel's Apostasy and God's Renewal of the Cocenant

32 **The Golden Calf.** [1]When the people saw that Moses was delayed in coming down from the mountain, they gathered around Aaron and said to him, "Come, make us a god who will go before us; as for that man Moses who brought us out of the land of Egypt, we do not know what has happened to him." [2]Aaron replied, "Take off the golden earrings that your wives, your sons, and your daughters are wearing, and bring them to me." [3]So all the people took off their earrings and brought them to Aaron.

[4]He received their offering, and fashioning it with a tool, made a molten calf. Then they cried out, "These are your gods, Israel, who brought you up from the land of Egypt." [5]On seeing this, Aaron built an altar in front of the calf and proclaimed, "Tomorrow is a feast of the LORD." [6]Early the next day the people sacrificed burnt offerings and brought communion sacrifices. Then they sat down to eat and drink, and rose up to revel.

[7]Then the LORD said to Moses: Go down at once because your people, whom you brought out of the land of Egypt, have acted corruptly. [8]They have quickly turned aside from the way I commanded them, making for

---

the sabbath. The creation account known from Genesis 2:2-3 is given as the sabbath's rationale (for discussion, see Exod 16 and 20:8-11). Ceasing from work provides "ease" (v. 17) or, more precisely, a person's refreshment. Unlike other discussions of the sabbath, this one regards the sabbath as a sign of "an everlasting covenant" (v. 16) and "an everlasting sign" (v. 17). The sabbath thus represents the climax of the eternal covenants made with Noah (Gen 9:8-17) and Abraham (Gen 17:9-14).

The sign of the rainbow for Noah's covenant is perceptible by humanity, which is included under this covenant. The sign of the covenant with Abraham is circumcision, which marks him along with his male descendants. The sign of the Sinai covenant for the priestly tradition is specified to Israelite observance of the sabbath. Just as the sabbath represents the week's culmination, it completes and crowns the Sinai covenant for the priestly tradition. The mention of the divinely written tablets (v. 18; see 32:16; 34:1, 28) offers a narrative endpoint for Exodus 25–31, and it picks up the context of the story back in 24:12-18.

32:1-35 The golden calf

The narrative of Exodus 32–34 differs from the priestly instructions of Exodus 25–31, yet both may be viewed in terms of the ancient Middle Eastern pattern of building stories, which interrupt the construction project with an insurrection that must be subdued. The story is largely E or JE with

themselves a molten calf and bowing down to it, sacrificing to it and crying out, "These are your gods, Israel, who brought you up from the land of Egypt!" ⁹I have seen this people, how stiff-necked they are, continued the LORD to Moses. ¹⁰Let me alone, then, that my anger may burn against them to consume them. Then I will make of you a great nation.

¹¹But Moses implored the LORD, his God, saying, "Why, O LORD, should your anger burn against your people, whom you brought out of the land of Egypt with great power and with a strong hand? ¹²Why should the Egyptians say, 'With evil intent he brought them out, that he might kill them in the mountains and wipe them off the face of the earth'? Turn from your burning wrath; change your mind about punishing your people. ¹³Remember your servants Abraham, Isaac, and Israel, and how you swore to them by your own self, saying, 'I will make your descendants as numerous as the stars in the sky; and all this land that I promised, I will give your descendants as their perpetual heritage.'" ¹⁴So the LORD changed his mind about the punishment he had threatened to inflict on his people.

¹⁵Moses then turned and came down the mountain with the two tablets of the covenant in his hands, tablets that were

---

a handful of priestly additions apparent. Despite the difficulty posed for analysis, the complexity of this section with its varied traditions is witness to the importance attached to this point in Israel's covenant with God. With the priestly placement of the story between chapters 25–31 and 35–40, and with further priestly additions, the priestly tradition molds older material to illustrate the priestly understanding of the covenant.

In its present priestly form, the story demonstrates the need for the tabernacle; it serves as a means for God to dwell in the midst of Israel despite the vast gulf between divine holiness and human sinning illustrated by chapters 32–34. The tabernacle preserves boundaries between God and the Israelites even as God is in their midst. The various sacrificial rituals provide a means for purifying sin as it arises. As an example of covenant-threatening sin and the divine desire to rectify it, the golden calf story powerfully dramatizes the relationships of the Lord and Moses on one side and Moses and the people on the other.

Behind chapters 32–34 stands a long complex tradition. The idolatry of the golden calf is not straightforward, especially if the calf is to be regarded not as an attempt to represent a god but as a support for the divine throne (like the cherubim in 25:10-22). Prophets such as Hosea (13:2), however, criticize the young bull as a symbol of idolatry, perhaps suggesting then that the people did not always distinguish between the deity and the symbol of the calf.

written on both sides, front and back. [16]The tablets were made by God; the writing was the writing of God, engraved on the tablets. [17]Now, when Joshua heard the noise of the people shouting, he said to Moses, "That sounds like a battle in the camp." [18]But Moses answered,

> "It is not the noise of victory,
>   it is not the noise of defeat;
>   the sound I hear is singing."

[19]As he drew near the camp, he saw the calf and the dancing. Then Moses' anger burned, and he threw the tablets down and broke them on the base of the mountain. [20]Taking the calf they had made, he burned it in the fire and then ground it down to powder, which he scattered on the water and made the Israelites drink.

[21]Moses asked Aaron, "What did this people do to you that you should lead them into a grave sin?" [22]Aaron replied, "Do not let my lord be angry. You know how the people are prone to evil. [23]They said to me, 'Make us a god to go before us; as for this man Moses who brought us out of the land of Egypt, we do not know what has happened to him.' [24]So I told them, 'Whoever is wearing gold, take it off.' They gave it to me, and I threw it into the fire, and this calf came out."

[25]Moses saw that the people were running wild because Aaron had lost control—to the secret delight of their foes. [26]Moses stood at the gate of the camp and shouted, "Whoever is for the

---

Hosea's criticism is directed at the calf symbol that was set up by Jeroboam I (ca. 931–910). As the first king of the northern kingdom after Solomon, he erected a young bull image at his two royal shrines at Dan and Bethel (1 Kgs 12:26-32) so that northerners would make their pilgrimages to northern shrines instead of the traditionally important site of the Jerusalem temple, which was favored by the southerm kingdom. Jeroboam did not think of himself as setting up idols to other gods, but he used a form of imagery in order to distinguish his royal sanctuaries from the Jerusalem temple, which used the symbol of the cherubim.

The golden calf story is related to Jeroboam's calves. Following the contribution of the people, Aaron—in Moses' absence on the mountain—accepts their offering and makes "a molten calf" (vv. 1-4). The people respond (v. 4) with an identification of the calf as "your gods, Israel, who brought you up from the land of Egypt," the very same line used in Jeroboam's shrines (see v. 8; 1 Kgs 12:28). The word "gods" here is ambiguous; it may also mean "God." Aaron proclaims a feast of holocausts and peace offerings in honor of the Lord (vv. 5-6; Lev 1, 3), indicating that the calf is not dedicated to another god. Instead, the idolatry may lie in a confusion of symbol and deity, in other words, an idolatrous symbol used for the right God. The divine response (vv. 7-10) suggests that it is Moses who brought the Israelites out of Egypt (v. 7) and not the calf (v. 8). The sin may not be

115

LORD, come to me!" All the Levites then rallied to him, [27]and he told them, "Thus says the LORD, the God of Israel: Each of you put your sword on your hip! Go back and forth through the camp, from gate to gate, and kill your brothers, your friends, your neighbors!" [28]The Levites did as Moses had commanded, and that day about three thousand of the people fell. [29]Then Moses said, "Today you are installed as priests for the LORD, for you went against your own sons and brothers, to bring a blessing upon yourselves this day."

The Atonement. [30]On the next day Moses said to the people, "You have committed a grave sin. Now I will go up to the LORD; perhaps I may be able to make atonement for your sin." [31]So Moses returned to the LORD and said,

---

so much apostasy against God as against his choice of a leader in Moses, who then responds in the classic role of covenant mediator, imploring God in prayer (vv. 11-13). The prayer (v. 12) draws on traditional lament asking why the foreign nation such as the Egyptians should impugn God's relationship with Israel (Pss 79:10; 115:2). Moses also appeals to the divine promise to the patriarchs (v. 13). As a result, the Lord relents (v. 14), but this does not solve the problem at hand.

In the next section, Moses seems ignorant of the idolatry. Carrying the tablets down the mountain (vv. 15-16), Moses is unaware of the activity in the camp below, and in this version, Joshua accompanies Moses (cf. 24:12). The noise sounds like "a battle in the camp," in other words, "noise of victory" (vv. 17-18; cf. the victory celebration in Isa 9:2). Moses then sees the calf and the dancing (v. 19). His wrath here mirrors the divine wrath displayed in verses 7-14. Verses 1-14 and verses 15-20 were alternative versions sewn together, achieving a larger thematic whole regarding divine and human anger as responses to sin. Moses breaks the tablets, symbolizing the breaking of the covenant relationship, and he instructs the Israelites in a ritual for completely destroying the calf (vv. 19-20; cf. Num 5:12-31; the Ugaritic Baal Cycle's description of the goddess Anat destroying the god, Mot).

Moses interrogates Aaron for his side of the story (vv. 21-24). Aaron excuses himself as responding to the people and offers the further explanation that the calf "came out" from the fire as if on its own power (v. 24); yet the verb may be—or may be a pun on—"come out" as a technical term of metallurgy (Prov 25:4; cf. English expression of how "a cake turns out"). Moses summons the Levites to purge the camp of sinners (vv. 25-29).

The story then describes the process of Israel's atonement for Israel, another prayer by Moses offering to be the mediator in place of the people (vv. 30-32). He would prefer to see himself rather than the people stricken from the heavenly book that keeps a record of good and bad human deeds

"Ah, this people has committed a grave sin in making a god of gold for themselves! ³²Now if you would only forgive their sin! But if you will not, then blot me out of the book that you have written." ³³The Lord answered Moses: Only the one who has sinned against me will I blot out of my book. ³⁴Now, go and lead the people where I have told you. See, my angel will go before you. When it is time for me to punish, I will punish them for their sin.

³⁵Thus the Lord struck the people for making the calf, the one that Aaron made.

33 ¹The Lord spoke to Moses: Go! You and the people whom you have brought up from the land of Egypt are to go up from here to the land about which I swore to Abraham, Isaac, and Jacob: I will give it to your descendants. ²Driving out the Canaanites, Amorites, Hittites, Perizzites, Hivites and Jebusites, I will send an angel before you ³to a land flowing with milk and honey. But I myself will not go up in your company, because you are a stiff-necked people; otherwise I might consume you on the way. ⁴When the people heard this painful news, they mourned, and no one wore any ornaments.

⁵The Lord spoke to Moses: Speak to the Israelites: You are a stiff-necked people. Were I to go up in your company even for a moment, I would destroy you. Now off with your ornaments! Let me

---

(Ps 69:29; cf. Dan 7:10). A divine promise to destroy only those who have sinned is at odds with the earlier verses presenting the people as a whole participating in the revelry. Such a distinction recalls a liturgical setting of prayer that God postpone divine judgment; Israel averts the evil decree, for now.

The divine answer also states that an angel will lead the people. At this point, such a divine statement seems a favorable omen, a positive promise. In context here it also sets up the question of the nature of divine presence that chapters 33–34 address. Overall these chapters show a polemic directed against the priestly line of Aaron in favor of the Levitical priests, perhaps by priests of Shiloh who disapproved of Jeroboam's shrines (cf. the story praising a comparable action taken by the descendant of Aaron in Num 25:6-13). Yet chapters 32–34 are also concerned more broadly with important questions of divine presence and sin. How can a holy God move forward with Israel as it sins?

33:1-11 Moses in the middle

Chapter 32 illustrates the need for human mediation between God and the people: how now shall God accompany Israel to the Promised Land? Chapters 33–34 answer this question with a masterpiece structured with thematically inverted sections (chiasm) to dramatize Moses' crucial role

think what to do with you. ⁶So, from Mount Horeb onward, the Israelites stripped off their ornaments.

Moses' Intimacy with God. ⁷Moses used to pitch a tent outside the camp at some distance. It was called the tent of meeting. Anyone who wished to consult the LORD would go to the tent of meeting outside the camp. ⁸Whenever Moses went out to the tent, the people would all rise and stand at the entrance of their own tents, watching Moses until he entered the tent. ⁹As Moses entered the tent, the column of cloud would come down and stand at its entrance while the LORD spoke with Moses. ¹⁰On seeing the column of cloud stand at the entrance of the tent, all the people would rise and bow down at

---

in convincing God to help Israel and in representing the divine presence to Israel:

> A: 33:1-11 An angel to accompany the Israelites (vv. 1-6); Moses' mediation (vv. 7-11)
>> B: 33:12-17 Moses' intercession
>>> C: 33:18-23 Moses asks to see God
>>> C': 34:1-8 Moses sees God
>> B': 34:8-9 Moses' intercession
> A': 34:10-35 The Lord to accompany the Israelites (vv. 10-28); Moses' new mediation (vv. 29-35)

Exodus 33:1-11 (marked A in the chiasm above) continues the theme of angelic accompaniment from 32:33-34, but here it is an insufficient sign of presence contrasted with the actual divine presence. The scene (vv. 1-6), which draws on Deuteronomistic language used elsewhere for the Promised Land and for the foreign peoples there, ends with the Israelites in mourning ("no one wore any ornaments," v. 4, see v. 6). Verses 7-11 stop the story momentarily to describe how God and Moses used to interact at the tent of meeting. After noting that anyone could go to the tent in order "to consult the LORD" (v. 7), Moses, along with Joshua, is said to enter it (vv. 8-11). As a mark of Moses' special favor, the divine column of cloud descends over the tent (this E tradition of the tent will be superseded by the priestly tradition's "tabernacle, with its tent," 35:11; see 40:34-38). The Lord is said to speak face-to-face with Moses, establishing a proximity with the divine unachieved by any other mortal. This passage falls just short of stating that Moses sees God. According to an older tradition, Moses does see God (cf. 24:11; cf. Moses and God directly speaking with direct vision in Num 12:8). This chapter modifies and explores this notion and its significance for Israel's relationship with God.

the entrance of their own tents. [11]The Lord used to speak to Moses face to face, as a person speaks to a friend. Moses would then return to the camp, but his young assistant, Joshua, son of Nun, never left the tent. [12]Moses said to the Lord, "See, you are telling me: Lead this people. But you have not let me know whom you will send with me. Yet you have said: You are my intimate friend; You have found favor with me. [13]Now, if I have found favor with you, please let me know your ways so that, in knowing you, I may continue to find favor with you. See, this nation is indeed your own people. [14]The Lord answered: I myself

33:12-17 (B) Moses' intercession

The dialogue alternates between Moses and God in a manner not seen in Scripture since Abraham. Moses, as the Lord's "intimate friend" who has found divine favor, frames this section (vv. 12, 17); it is this special relationship, and not the Israelites themselves, that motivates the Lord's willingness to accompany them. Moses appeals to his special relationship with God and complains that God has not told him whom God will send with him (vv. 12-13). God has mentioned the angel (v. 2); perhaps Moses' returning to the issue represents an indirect way of suggesting that an angel is not good enough. The divine response (v. 14), agreeing to God's very self instead, seems to answer the implicit request for divine rather than angelic accompaniment. In his statement (v. 15), does Moses detect divine reluctance? Moses pursues the implication: divine absence implies divine disfavor (v. 16). God restates his agreement to Moses' request and reiterates Moses' favor with God (v. 17).

33:18-23 (C) Moses' request to see God

Moses pursues his special relationship with the Lord in asking to see the divine glory (v. 18). The Lord responds with an offer of divine beauty accompanied by a pronouncement of the divine name (v. 19), yet Moses is denied direct vision of the divine face (v. 20). Instead, God offers a partial vision, the sight of the divine back as the divine glory passes by (v. 23; cf. Jer 18:17).

This scene recalls the prophet Elijah, who travels forty days to Mount Horeb following his conflict with idolaters (1 Kgs 18–19). Moses in similar fashion has been on the mountain for forty days during the Israelite idolatry (Exod 32; cf. 24:18; 34:18). Moses' experience (vv. 22-23) echoes other features of Elijah's experience of God on Mount Horeb. Just as Elijah goes to the entrance of the cave to experience God (1 Kgs 19:13), so Moses will station himself on the rock (v. 22). Just as the Lord passes by Elijah (1 Kgs 19:11), so too Moses is to experience the Lord passing by (vv. 19, 22). Whereas Elijah covers his eyes (1 Kgs 19:13), God covers Moses' sight with the divine hand

will go along, to give you rest. [15]Moses replied, "If you are not going yourself, do not make us go up from here. [16]For how can it be known that I and your people have found favor with you, except by your going with us? Then we, your people and I, will be singled out from every other people on the surface of the earth." [17]The Lord said to Moses: This request, too, which you have made, I will carry out, because you have found favor with me and you are my intimate friend.

◄   [18]Then Moses said, "Please let me see
◄ your glory!" [19]The Lord answered: I will make all my goodness pass before you,

and I will proclaim my name, "Lord," before you; I who show favor to whom I will, I who grant mercy to whom I will. [20]But you cannot see my face, for no one can see me and live. [21]Here, continued the Lord, is a place near me where you shall station yourself on the rock. [22]When my glory passes I will set you in the cleft of the rock and will cover you with my hand until I have passed by. [23]Then I will remove my hand, so that you may see my back; but my face may not be seen.

34 **Renewal of the Tablets.** [1]The Lord said to Moses: "Cut two stone tablets like the former, that I may

---

(vv. 22-23). Revelation to both figures expresses the ineffable quality of the divine. For as close as Elijah gets, the Lord is—contrary to older biblical revelations of God—not in the wind, nor in the earthquake nor in the fire but in "a light silent sound" (1 Kgs 19:11-12), a medium mysterious yet appropriate for a prophet who speaks as God's agent.

For the northern E tradition of this passage, Moses was the prophet of the original covenant, Elijah its fiery enforcer. Malachi 3:22-24 mentions Moses, the prophet of the ancient covenant on Horeb, with Elijah, a figure of the prophet who heralds the coming day of the Lord. The ancient and future covenant prophets in the Old Testament inform the New Testament understanding of John the Baptist as an Elijah figure who heralds the coming of Jesus the Lord (e.g., Matt 11:10, combining Mal 3:1 with Exod 23:20); in this way, the end of the Old Testament connects to the start of the New Testament. Given the parallels between Elijah and Moses, the tradition of 1 Kings 18–19 informed Exodus 33's prophetic picture of Moses, greater than even the great Elijah. Yet the chapter is more complex. Moses can witness divine glory, beauty, and name, but not God's face. By drawing on Israelite liturgy (Pss 27:4; 13; 29:2; 42:3), these terms connect the audience's experience with Moses' desire for communion with God. Moses' greatness is more than being greater than Elijah; he also nearly attains the ideal of Israelite pilgrimage feasts—divine presence and vision of God.

34:1-8 (C') Moses and God

This section does not describe the divine manifestation first but returns to the tablets (v. 1). The placement of the tablets before the theophany points

write on them the words which were on the former tablets that you broke. ²Get ready for tomorrow morning, when you are to go up Mount Sinai and there present yourself to me on the top of the mountain. ³No one shall come up with you, and let no one even be seen on any part of the mountain; even the sheep and the cattle are not to graze in front of this mountain." ⁴Moses then cut two stone tablets like the former, and early the next morning he went up Mount Sinai as the Lord had commanded him, taking in his hand the two stone tablets.

⁵The Lord came down in a cloud and stood with him there and proclaimed the name, "Lord." ⁶So the Lord passed before him and proclaimed: The Lord, the Lord, a God gracious and merciful, slow to anger and abounding in love and fidelity, ⁷continuing his love for a thousand generations, and forgiving wickedness, rebellion, and sin; yet not declaring the guilty guiltless, but bringing punishment for their parents' wickedness on children and children's children to the third and fourth generation! ⁸Moses at once knelt and bowed down to the ground. ⁹Then he said, "If I find favor with you, Lord, please, Lord, come along in our company. This is indeed a stiff-necked people; yet pardon our wickedness and sins, and claim us as your own."

Religious Laws. ¹⁰The Lord said: Here is the covenant I will make. Before all your people I will perform marvels never before done in any nation anywhere on earth, so that all the people among whom you live may see the work of the Lord. Awe-inspiring are the deeds I will perform with you! ¹¹As for you, observe what I am commanding you today.

See, I am about to drive out before you the Amorites, Canaanites, Hittites, Perizzites, Hivites and Jebusites. ¹²Take care not to make a covenant with the inhabitants of the land that you are to enter; lest they become a snare among you. ¹³Tear down their altars; smash their sacred stones, and cut down their

---

to an additional sign of Moses' greatness. His divine communion advances Israel's covenant with the Lord; Moses and the covenant literally go together in this section (vv. 2-4). The narrative (vv. 5-9) then offers a unique moment of liturgical transcendence. In the cloud denoting the paradox of presence hidden from view, "the Lord . . . stood with him" and proclaimed the divine name to him (v. 5). The presentation has a liturgical atmosphere like the Day of Atonement, when the high priest is said to pronounce the divine name (cf. Sir 50:20, Mishnah, Yoma 6.2, and Sotah 7.6). The proclamation of divine attributes (vv. 6-7) is likewise the stuff of prayer (Neh 9:17; Pss 86:15; 99:8; cf. Num 14:17-18), showing hope for divine compassion even as divine justice is acknowledged.

34:8-9 (B') Moses' response

Continuing the liturgical picture, Moses bows down in worship (v. 8). Moses again asks for the Lord to accompany the people (v. 9). Despite its

121

asherahs. ¹⁴You shall not bow down to any other god, for the LORD—"Jealous" his name—is a jealous God. ¹⁵Do not make a covenant with the inhabitants of the land; else, when they prostitute themselves with their gods and sacrifice to them, one of them may invite you and you may partake of the sacrifice. ¹⁶And when you take their daughters as wives for your sons, and their daughters prostitute themselves with their gods, they will make your sons do the same.

¹⁷You shall not make for yourselves molten gods.

¹⁸You shall keep the festival of Unleavened Bread. For seven days at the appointed time in the month of Abib you are to eat unleavened bread, as I commanded you; for in the month of Abib you came out of Egypt.

¹⁹To me belongs every male that opens the womb among all your livestock, whether in the herd or in the flock. ²⁰The firstling of a donkey you shall redeem with a lamb; if you do not redeem it, you must break its neck. The firstborn among your sons you shall redeem.

No one shall appear before me empty-handed.

²¹Six days you may labor, but on the seventh day you shall rest; even during the seasons of plowing and harvesting you must rest.

²²You shall keep the feast of Weeks with the first fruits of the wheat harvest, likewise, the feast of the Ingathering at the close of the year. ²³Three times a year all your men shall appear before the Lord, the LORD God of Israel. ²⁴Since I will drive out the nations before you and enlarge your territory, no one will covet your land when you go up three times a year to appear before the LORD, your God.

²⁵You shall not offer me the blood of sacrifice with anything leavened, nor shall the sacrifice of the Passover feast be kept overnight for the next day.

²⁶The choicest first fruits of your soil you shall bring to the house of the LORD, your God.

You shall not boil a young goat in its mother's milk.

Radiance of Moses' Face. ²⁷Then the LORD said to Moses: Write down these words, for in accordance with these words I have made a covenant with you and with Israel. ²⁸So Moses was there with the LORD for forty days and forty nights, without eating any food or drinking any water, and he wrote on the tablets the words of the covenant, the ten words.

²⁹As Moses came down from Mount Sinai with the two tablets of the covenant in his hands, he did not know that

---

brevity, this section echoes the dialogue over divine accompaniment in chapter 33 (cf. 34:9 with 33:3, 5). This interlude also provides an introduction to the refashioning of the commandments. Divine presence is premised on the commandments.

34:10-35 (A') The terms of the covenant

The commandments to be written on the second set of tablets include variants of three of the Ten Commandments (20:2-17): prohibitions against

Needle monument in the Karnak Temple at Luxor, Egypt

the skin of his face had become radiant while he spoke with the LORD. [30]When Aaron, then, and the other Israelites saw Moses and noticed how radiant the skin of his face had become, they were afraid to come near him. [31]Only after Moses called to them did Aaron and all the leaders of the community come back to him. Moses then spoke to them. [32]Later, all the Israelites came up to him, and he enjoined on them all that the LORD had told him on Mount Sinai. [33]When Moses finished speaking with them, he put a veil over his face. [34]Whenever Moses entered the presence of the LORD to speak with him, he removed the veil until he came out again. On coming out, he would tell the Israelites all that he had been commanded. [35]Then the Israelites would see that the skin of Moses'

worship of other deities (v. 14) and against making "molten gods" (v. 17) as well as the sabbath requirement (v. 21). The commandments are otherwise a cultic calendar (vv. 18-25) that compares with 23:12-19. The passage gives the impression of being a second Ten Commandments (v. 28), but it combines some of the Ten Commandments with material from the calendar of pilgrimage festivals in Exodus 23. This new form of the Ten Commandments (v. 28) presents an implicit claim that the regulations of the Covenant Code in Exodus 21–23 hold the same divine authority as the original Ten Commandments in Exodus 20.

Moses writes down the commandments, echoing his earlier forty-day stay on the mountain (vv. 27-28; cf. 24:12, 18). He returns, burnished with the frightening radiance of the divine presence (vv. 29-31). Moses summons the people and presents the commandments: the mediator and the commandments go together (v. 32). As a new way to mediate (vv. 33-35), the veil is removed whenever Moses meets with God and he speaks to the Israelites; otherwise, his face is veiled. The divine radiance is imprinted on Moses, and the divine word is heard by him; in turn, he conveys the divine presence and word to the people. Overall, Exodus 32–34 places Moses at the center of God's relationship with Israel. It partially identifies Moses with God, whom Moses can partially glimpse, and it separates him from the people in his special service as the bearer of the divine presence. No golden calf or any other lifeless image can symbolize the divine. Moses becomes the living icon of the God alive in Israel's life. While these chapters mark a highpoint in the story, one final moment of divine glory awaits at the end of Exodus.

35:1–36:7 Sabbath, contribution, and craftsmen

Shifting from the JE story back to the priestly dwelling construction, the next major stage in the building pattern is the execution of the divine

face was radiant; so he would again put the veil over his face until he went in to speak with the LORD.

VIII. The Building of the Tabernacle and the Descent of God's Glory Upon It

35 **Sabbath Regulations.** [1]Moses assembled the whole Israelite community and said to them, "These are the words the LORD has commanded to be observed. [2]On six days work may be done, but the seventh day shall be holy to you as the sabbath of complete rest to the LORD. Anyone who does work on that day shall be put to death. [3]You shall not even light a fire in any of your dwellings on the sabbath day."

Collection of Materials. [4]Moses said to the whole Israelite community, "This is what the LORD has commanded: [5]Receive from among you contributions for the LORD. Everyone, as his heart prompts him, shall bring, as a contribution to the LORD, gold, silver, and bronze; [6]violet, purple, and scarlet yarn; fine linen and goat hair; [7]rams' skins dyed red, and tahash skins; acacia wood; [8]oil for the light; spices for the anointing oil and for the fragrant incense; [9]onyx stones and other gems for mounting on the ephod and on the breastpiece.

Call for Artisans. [10]"Let every artisan among you come and make all that the LORD has commanded: [11]the tabernacle, with its tent, its covering, its clasps, its frames, its bars, its columns, and its pedestals; [12]the ark, with its poles, the cover, and the curtain veil; [13]the table, with its poles and all its utensils, and the showbread; [14]the menorah, with its utensils, the lamps, and the oil for the light; [15]the altar of incense, with its poles; the anointing oil, and the fragrant incense; the entrance curtain for the entrance of the tabernacle; [16]the altar for burnt offerings, with its bronze grating, its poles, and all its utensils; the basin, with its stand; [17]the hangings of the court, with their columns and pedestals; the curtain for the gate of the court; [18]the tent pegs for the tabernacle and for the court, with their ropes; [19]the service cloths for use in the sanctuary; the sacred vestments for Aaron, the priest, and the vestments for his sons in their ministry."

The Contribution. [20]When the whole Israelite community left Moses' presence, [21]all, as their hearts moved them and their spirit prompted, brought a contribution to the LORD for the work of the tent of meeting, for all its services, and for the sacred vestments. [22]Both the men and the women, all as their heart prompted them, brought brooches, earrings, rings, necklaces, and various other gold articles. Everyone who could

---

instructions. The command to observe the sabbath (vv. 1-3) is a priestly modification of this standard pattern. Two standard preparations for building commands follow: the command to secure materials (vv. 4-9) and the execution (vv. 20-29), and the summoning of craftsmen reiterated (vv. 10-19) and the execution (35:30–36:7). These topics connect to the beginning and end of chapters 25–31: sabbath (vv. 1-3) and craftsmen (vv. 10-19) connect the end of the commands (ch. 31) with the beginning of their execution,

presented an offering of gold to the LORD. [23]Everyone who happened to have violet, purple, or scarlet yarn, fine linen or goat hair, rams' skins dyed red or tahash skins, brought them. [24]Whoever could make a contribution of silver or bronze offered it to the LORD; and everyone who happened to have acacia wood for any part of the work, brought it. [25]All the women who were expert spinners brought hand-spun violet, purple, and scarlet yarn and fine linen thread. [26]All the women, as their hearts and skills moved them, spun goat hair. [27]The tribal leaders brought onyx stones and other gems for mounting on the ephod and on the breastpiece; [28]as well as spices, and oil for the light, anointing oil, and fragrant incense. [29]Every Israelite man and woman brought to the LORD such voluntary offerings as they thought best, for the various kinds of work which the LORD, through Moses, had commanded to be done.

The Artisans. [30]Moses said to the Israelites: "See, the LORD has singled out Bezalel, son of Uri, son of Hur, of the tribe of Judah, [31]and has filled him with a divine spirit of skill and understanding and knowledge in every craft: [32]in the production of embroidery, in making things of gold, silver, or bronze, [33]in cutting and mounting precious stones, in carving wood, and in every other craft. [34]He has also given both him and Oholiab, son of Ahisamach, of the tribe of Dan, the ability to teach others. [35]He has endowed them with skill to execute all types of work: engraving, embroidering, the making of variegated cloth of violet, purple, and scarlet yarn and fine linen thread, weaving, and all other arts and crafts.

36 [1]"Bezalel, therefore, will set to work with Oholiab and with all the artisans whom the LORD has endowed with skill and understanding in knowing how to do all the work for the service of the sanctuary, just as the LORD has commanded."

[2]Moses then called Bezalel and Oholiab and all the other artisans whom the LORD had endowed with skill, men whose hearts moved them to come and do the work. [3]They received from Moses all the contributions which the Israelites had brought for the work to be done for the sanctuary service. Still, morning after morning the people continued to bring their voluntary offerings to Moses. [4]Thereupon all the artisans who were doing the work for the sanctuary came from the work each was doing, [5]and told Moses, "The people are bringing much more than is needed to carry out the work which the LORD has commanded us to do." [6]Moses, therefore, ordered a proclamation to be made throughout the camp: "Let neither man nor woman make any more contributions for the sanctuary." So the people stopped bringing their offerings; [7]there was already enough at hand, and more than enough, to complete the work to be done.

The Tent Cloth and Coverings. [8]The various artisans who were doing the work made the tabernacle with its ten sheets woven of fine linen twined, hav-

---

while the discussion of materials (vv. 4-9) connects to the beginning of the commands (25:3-7). The mention of the sabbath here adds a limitation on the use of fire (v. 3).

ing cherubim embroidered on them with violet, purple, and scarlet yarn. [9]The length of each sheet was twenty-eight cubits, and the width four cubits; all the sheets were the same size. [10]Five of the sheets were joined together, edge to edge; and the other five sheets likewise, edge to edge. [11]Loops of violet yarn were made along the edge of the end sheet in the first set, and the same along the edge of the end sheet in the second set. [12]Fifty loops were thus put on one inner sheet, and fifty loops on the inner sheet in the other set, with the loops directly opposite each other. [13]Then fifty clasps of gold were made, with which the sheets were joined so that the tabernacle formed one whole.

[14]Sheets of goat hair were also woven as a tent over the tabernacle. Eleven such sheets were made. [15]The length of each sheet was thirty cubits and the width four cubits; all eleven sheets were the same size. [16]Five of these sheets were joined into one set, and the other six sheets into another set. [17]Fifty loops were made along the edge of the end sheet in one set, and fifty loops along the edge of the corresponding sheet in the other set. [18]Fifty bronze clasps were made with which the tent was joined so that it formed one whole. [19]A covering for the tent was made of rams' skins dyed red and, above that, a covering of tahash skins.

The Framework. [20]Frames were made for the tabernacle, acacia-wood uprights. [21]The length of each frame was ten cubits, and the width one and a half cubits. [22]Each frame had two arms, fastening them one to another. In this way all the frames of the tabernacle were made. [23]The frames for the tabernacle were made as follows: twenty frames on the south side, [24]with forty silver pedestals under the twenty frames, two pedestals under each frame for its two arms; [25]twenty frames on the other side of the tabernacle, the north side, [26]with their forty silver pedestals, two pedestals under each frame. [27]At the rear of the tabernacle, to the west, six frames were made, [28]and two frames were made for the corners of the tabernacle, at its rear. [29]These were double at the bottom, and likewise double at the top, to the first ring. That is how both corner frames were made. [30]Thus, there were eight frames, with their sixteen silver pedestals, two pedestals under each frame. [31]Bars of acacia wood were also made, five for the frames on one side of the tabernacle, [32]five for those on the other side, and five for those at the rear, to the west. [33]The center bar, at the middle of the frames, was made to reach across from end to end. [34]The frames were plated with gold, and gold rings were made on them as holders for the bars, which were also plated with gold.

The Veil. [35]The veil was made of violet, purple, and scarlet yarn, and of fine linen twined, with cherubim embroidered on it. [36]Four gold-plated columns of acacia wood, with gold hooks,

36:8–39:43 Execution of the instructions

The next major component of building stories is the construction of the items commanded (chs. 25–31). The tabernacle's construction (ch. 36) precedes the making of the ark, table, and the menorah (chs. 37–38) that go

were made for it, and four silver pedestals were cast for them.

³⁷The curtain for the entrance of the tent was made of violet, purple, and scarlet yarn, and of fine linen twined, woven in a variegated manner. ³⁸Its five columns, with their hooks as well as their capitals and bands, were plated with gold; their five pedestals were of bronze.

37 The Ark. ¹Bezalel made the ark of acacia wood, two and a half cubits long, one and a half cubits wide, and one and a half cubits high. ²The inside and outside were plated with gold, and a molding of gold was put around it. ³Four gold rings were cast for its four supports, two rings on one side and two on the opposite side. ⁴Poles of acacia wood were made and plated with gold; ⁵these poles were put through the rings on the sides of the ark, for carrying it.

⁶The cover was made of pure gold, two and a half cubits long and one and a half cubits wide. ⁷Two cherubim of beaten gold were made for the two ends of the cover; ⁸one cherub was at one end, the other at the other end, made of one piece with the cover, at each end. ⁹The cherubim had their wings spread out above, sheltering the cover. They faced each other, with their faces looking toward the cover.

The Table. ¹⁰The table was made of acacia wood, two cubits long, a cubit wide, and a cubit and a half high. ¹¹It was plated with pure gold, and a molding of gold was put around it. ¹²A frame a handbreadth high was also put around it, with a molding of gold around the frame. ¹³Four rings of gold were cast for it and fastened at the four corners, one at each leg. ¹⁴The rings were alongside the frame as holders for the poles to carry the table. ¹⁵These poles for carrying the table were made of acacia wood and plated with gold. ¹⁶The vessels that were set on the table, its plates and cups, as well as its pitchers and bowls for pouring libations, were made of pure gold.

The Menorah. ¹⁷The menorah was made of pure beaten gold—its shaft and branches—with its cups and knobs and petals springing directly from it. ¹⁸Six branches extended from its sides, three branches on one side and three on the other. ¹⁹On one branch there were three cups, shaped like almond blossoms, each with its knob and petals; on the opposite branch there were three cups, shaped like almond blossoms, each with its knob and petals; and so for the six branches that extended from the menorah. ²⁰On the menorah there were four cups, shaped like almond blossoms, with their knobs and petals. ²¹The six branches that went out from the menorah had a knob under each pair. ²²The knobs and branches so sprang from it

---

inside it, in contrast to the commands for them (chs. 25–26). The progression is from the outside inward. This section largely follows chapters 25–31 with the emphasis that the final product corresponds to the instructions. For the tent cloth, coverings, wood frames, and veils (36:8-38), see 26:1-29, 31-37. For the ark with the propitiatory, table, and menorah (37:1-24), see 25:10-39. For the altar of incense (37:25-28), the anointing oil, and fragrant incense (37:29),

that the whole formed but a single piece of pure beaten gold. [23]Its seven lamps, as well as its trimming shears and trays, were made of pure gold. [24]A talent of pure gold was used for the menorah and its various utensils.

The Altar of Incense. [25]The altar of incense was made of acacia wood, on a square, a cubit long, a cubit wide, and two cubits high, having horns that sprang directly from it. [26]Its grate on top, its walls on all four sides, and its horns were plated with pure gold; and a gold molding was put around it. [27]Underneath the molding gold rings were placed, two on one side and two on the opposite side, as holders for the poles used in carrying it. [28]The poles, too, were made of acacia wood and plated with gold.

[29]The sacred anointing oil and the fragrant incense were prepared in their pure form by a perfumer.

38 **The Altar for Burnt Offerings.** [1]The altar for burnt offerings was made of acacia wood, on a square, five cubits long and five cubits wide; its height was three cubits. [2]At the four corners horns were made that sprang directly from the altar. It was then plated with bronze. [3]All the utensils of the altar, the pots, shovels, basins, forks and fire pans, were likewise made of bronze. [4]A grating, a bronze network, was made for the altar and placed around it, on the ground, half as high as the altar itself. [5]Four rings were cast for the four corners of the bronze grating, as holders for the poles, [6]which were made of acacia wood

and plated with bronze. [7]The poles were put through the rings on the sides of the altar for carrying it. The altar was made in the form of a hollow box.

[8]The bronze basin, with its bronze stand, was made from the mirrors of the women who served at the entrance of the tent of meeting.

The Court of the Tabernacle. [9]The court was made as follows. On the south side the hangings of the court were of fine linen twined, a hundred cubits long, [10]with twenty columns and twenty pedestals of bronze, the hooks and bands of the columns being of silver. [11]On the north side there were similar hangings, a hundred cubits long, with twenty columns and twenty pedestals of bronze; the hooks and bands of the columns were of silver. [12]On the west side there were hangings, fifty cubits long, with ten columns and ten pedestals; the hooks and bands of the columns were of silver. [13]On the east side the court was fifty cubits. [14]On one side there were hangings to the extent of fifteen cubits, with three columns and three pedestals; [15]on the other side, beyond the gate of the court, there were likewise hangings to the extent of fifteen cubits, with three columns and three pedestals. [16]The hangings on all sides of the court were woven of fine linen twined. [17]The pedestals of the columns were of bronze, while the hooks and bands of the columns were of silver; the capitals were silver-plated, and all the columns of the court were banded with silver.

---

see 30:1-6, 23-25, 34-36. For the priestly vestments (39:1-31), see 28:1-43. For the census tax (30:11-16), see 38:21-31, which adds a balance sheet for the amount of metals used for the various items of the tabernacle.

¹⁸At the gate of the court there was a variegated curtain, woven of violet, purple, and scarlet yarn and of fine linen twined, twenty cubits long and five cubits wide, in keeping with the hangings of the court. ¹⁹There were four columns and four pedestals of bronze for it, while their hooks were of silver, and their capitals and their bands silver-plated. ²⁰All the tent pegs for the tabernacle and for the court around it were of bronze.

Amount of Metal Used. ²¹The following is an account of the various amounts used on the tabernacle, the tabernacle of the covenant, drawn up at the command of Moses by the Levites under the direction of Ithamar, son of Aaron the priest. ²²However, it was Bezalel, son of Uri, son of Hur, of the tribe of Judah, who made all that the LORD commanded Moses, ²³and he was assisted by Oholiab, son of Ahisamach, of the tribe of Dan, who was an engraver, an embroiderer, and a weaver of variegated cloth of violet, purple, and scarlet yarn and of fine linen.

²⁴All the gold used in the entire construction of the sanctuary, having previously been given as an offering, amounted to twenty-nine talents and seven hundred and thirty shekels, according to the standard of the sanctuary shekel. ²⁵The silver of those of the community who were enrolled was one hundred talents and one thousand seven hundred and seventy-five shekels, according to the standard of the sanctuary

shekel; ²⁶one bekah apiece, that is, a half-shekel, according to the standard of the sanctuary shekel, was received from everyone who was enrolled, of twenty years or more, namely, six hundred and three thousand five hundred and fifty men. ²⁷One hundred talents of silver were used for casting the pedestals of the sanctuary and the pedestals of the veil, one talent for each pedestal, or one hundred talents for the one hundred pedestals. ²⁸The remaining one thousand seven hundred and seventy-five shekels were used for making the hooks on the columns, for plating the capitals, and for banding them with silver. ²⁹The bronze, given as an offering, amounted to seventy talents and two thousand four hundred shekels. ³⁰With this were made the pedestals at the entrance of the tent of meeting, the bronze altar with its bronze gratings, and all the utensils of the altar, ³¹the pedestals around the court, the pedestals at the gate of the court, and all the tent pegs for the tabernacle and for the court around it.

39 **The Priestly Vestments.** ¹With violet, purple, and scarlet yarn were woven the service cloths for use in the sanctuary, as well as the sacred vestments for Aaron, as the LORD had commanded Moses.

²The ephod was woven of gold thread and of violet, purple, and scarlet yarn and of fine linen twined. ³Gold was first hammered into gold leaf and then cut up into threads, which were woven with the

---

Exodus 38:8 adds that the bronze basin (30:18-21) is made from the mirrors of the women who serve at the entrance of the tent. The service is unspecified, but the parallel in 1 Samuel 2:22 suggests it is sexual in nature. In the latter verse, Eli's sons "were behaving promiscuously" with women

violet, purple, and scarlet yarn into an embroidered pattern on the fine linen. [4]Shoulder straps were made for it and joined to its two upper ends. [5]The embroidered belt on the ephod extended out from it, and like it, was made of gold thread, of violet, purple, and scarlet yarn, and of fine linen twined, as the LORD had commanded Moses. [6]The onyx stones were prepared and mounted in gold filigree work; they were engraved like seal engravings with the names of the sons of Israel. [7]These stones were set on the shoulder straps of the ephod as memorial stones of the sons of Israel, just as the LORD had commanded Moses.

[8]The breastpiece was embroidered like the ephod, with gold thread and violet, purple, and scarlet yarn on cloth of fine linen twined. [9]It was square and folded double, a span high and a span wide in its folded form. [10]Four rows of precious stones were mounted on it: in the first row a carnelian, a topaz, and an emerald; [11]in the second row, a garnet, a sapphire, and a beryl; [12]in the third row a jacinth, an agate, and an amethyst; [13]in the fourth row a chrysolite, an onyx, and a jasper. They were mounted in gold filigree work. [14]These stones were twelve, to match the names of the sons of Israel, and each stone was engraved like a seal with the name of one of the twelve tribes.

[15]Chains of pure gold, twisted like cords, were made for the breastpiece, [16]together with two gold filigree rosettes and two gold rings. The two rings were fastened to the two upper ends of the breastpiece. [17]The two gold chains were then fastened to the two rings at the ends of the breastpiece. [18]The other two ends of the two chains were fastened in front to the two filigree rosettes, which were attached to the shoulder straps of the ephod. [19]Two other gold rings were made and put on the two lower ends of the breastpiece, on the edge facing the ephod. [20]Two more gold rings were made and fastened to the bottom of the two shoulder straps next to where they joined the ephod in front, just above its embroidered belt. [21]Violet ribbons bound the rings of the breastpiece to the rings of the ephod, so that the breastpiece stayed right above the embroidered belt of the ephod and did not swing loose from it. All this was just as the LORD had commanded Moses.

Other Vestments. [22]The robe of the ephod was woven entirely of violet yarn, [23]with an opening in its center like the opening of a shirt, with selvage around the opening to keep it from being torn. [24]At the hem of the robe pomegranates were made of violet, purple, and scarlet yarn and of fine linen twined; [25]bells of pure gold were also made and put between the pomegranates all around the hem of the robe: [26]a bell, a pomegranate, a bell, a pomegranate, all around the hem of the robe which was to be worn

---

(literally, "lying with the women") at the Shiloh sanctuary. The sexual offense was evidently neither rape nor failure to pay for sex, but sexual relations considered improper for priests (Lev 21, esp. v. 7). In Genesis 38:15-24, Tamar, disguised as a "sacred" woman, is also called a prostitute. Sexual relations evidently transpired around sanctuaries (cf. Hos 4:13-15; Amos

in performing the ministry—all this, just as the Lord had commanded Moses.

²⁷For Aaron and his sons there were also woven tunics of fine linen; ²⁸the turban of fine linen; the ornate skullcaps of fine linen; linen pants of fine linen twined; ²⁹and sashes of variegated work made of fine linen twined and of violet, purple, and scarlet yarn, as the Lord had commanded Moses. ³⁰The plate of the sacred diadem was made of pure gold and inscribed, as on a seal engraving: "Sacred to the Lord." ³¹It was tied over the turban with a violet ribbon, as the Lord had commanded Moses.

Presentation of the Work to Moses. ³²Thus the entire work of the tabernacle of the tent of meeting was completed. The Israelites did the work just as the Lord had commanded Moses; so it was done. ³³They then brought to Moses the tabernacle, the tent with all its furnishings, the clasps, the frames, the bars, the columns, the pedestals, ³⁴the covering of rams' skins dyed red, the covering of tahash skins, the curtain veil; ³⁵the ark of the covenant with its poles, the cover, ³⁶the table with all its utensils and the showbread, ³⁷the pure gold menorah with its lamps set up on it and with all its utensils, the oil for the light, ³⁸the golden altar, the anointing oil, the fragrant incense; the curtain for the entrance of the tent, ³⁹the altar of bronze with its bronze grating, its poles and all its utensils, the basin with its stand, ⁴⁰the hangings of the court with their columns and pedestals, the curtain for the gate of the court with its ropes and tent pegs, all the equipment for the service of the tabernacle of the tent of meeting; ⁴¹the service cloths for use in the sanctuary, the sacred vestments for Aaron the priest, and the vestments to be worn by his sons in their ministry. ⁴²Just as the Lord had commanded Moses, so the Israelites had carried out all the work. ⁴³So when Moses saw that all the work was done just as the Lord had commanded, he blessed them.

40 Setting up the Tabernacle. ¹Then the Lord said to Moses: ²On the ▸

7:17) and were perhaps sponsored by them in order to generate revenue (cf. Lev. 19:29; 21:9). Women of families in deep economic trouble had limited options; prostitution was one alternative, slavery another (Exod 21:7).

The items made are now brought to Moses (39:32-43). Their listing (vv. 33-41) is framed by the statement that the Israelites did the work just as it had been commanded (vv. 32, 42). The paragraph ends with a deliberate echo of the Genesis creation story: Moses' seeing the work and blessing it (v. 43) echoes God's looking at all that God had made (Gen 1:31) and blessing the work of creation (Gen 2:3). This resonance sets up an implicit comparison between cosmic creation and the divine dwelling.

40:1-38 Conclusion

The last major element in building stories involves the structure's dedication, culminating in the deity's entry into the newly built abode. The

first day of the first month you shall set up the tabernacle of the tent of meeting. ³Put the ark of the covenant in it, and screen off the ark with the veil. ⁴Bring in the table and set it. Then bring in the menorah and set up the lamps on it. ⁵Put the golden altar of incense in front of the ark of the covenant, and hang the curtain at the entrance of the tabernacle. ⁶Put the altar for burnt offerings in front of the entrance of the tabernacle of the tent of meeting. ⁷Place the basin between the tent of meeting and the altar, and put water in it. ⁸Set up the court round about, and put the curtain at the gate of the court.

⁹Take the anointing oil and anoint the tabernacle and everything in it, consecrating it and all its furnishings, so that it will be sacred. ¹⁰Anoint the altar for burnt offerings and all its utensils, consecrating it, so that it will be most sacred. ¹¹Likewise, anoint the basin with its stand, and thus consecrate it.

---

divine speech (vv. 2-15) opens with an important date (v. 2): the first day of the first month is New Year (Rosh Hashanah), later symbolizing creation and renovation of the world. In context here, the completion of the tabernacle marks a moment of new creation. The items are to be brought into the erected tabernacle (vv. 2-8). The order of items begins with the ark, the item belonging in the most sacred area of the tabernacle, and then proceeds from inside to outside. All the items are to be anointed (vv. 9-11) in order to mark their elevated, holy status. The priestly personnel to serve the tabernacle are also to be anointed (vv. 12-15). Reflecting its hereditary nature, the priesthood is a family household consisting of a priestly "father" and his "sons" (Sir 50:12-13). It is also "a perpetual priesthood," serving as maintainer and sign of the "eternal covenant" with Israel.

The final instructions (vv. 2-15) are matched by their implementation (vv. 16-33), stressing that Moses followed the directions exactly. Overall Moses' work is recounted in more elaborate terms than the divine instructions. To follow the instructions exactly does not mean a word-by-word copying of the commands, but following them to the utmost, both explicitly and implicitly. The description does not mention the anointing of the priests commanded in the instructions (vv. 12-15); instead, it substitutes a discussion of the washing of the priests in the water in the basin (vv. 31-32).

The description ends (v. 33b) with an echo of the Genesis creation story: "Moses finished all the work" resonates with the statement that "God completed the work" (Gen 2:2). This echo, like those at the end of chapter 39, may seem slight to readers today, but in the verbally sensitive circles of the priestly tradition that produced both the Genesis 1:1–2:3a creation story and the priestly sections of Exodus 25–31 and 35–40, these verbal links were strongly heard as casting the dwelling in terms of cosmic creation, as

¹²Then bring Aaron and his sons to the entrance of the tent of meeting, and there wash them with water. ¹³Clothe Aaron with the sacred vestments and anoint him, thus consecrating him as my priest. ¹⁴Bring forward his sons also, and clothe them with the tunics. ¹⁵As you have anointed their father, anoint them also as my priests. Thus, by being anointed, shall they receive a perpetual priesthood throughout all future generations.

¹⁶Moses did just as the LORD had commanded him. ¹⁷On the first day of the first month of the second year the tabernacle was set up. ¹⁸It was Moses who set up the tabernacle. He placed its pedestals, set up its frames, put in its bars, and set up its columns. ¹⁹He spread the tent over the tabernacle and put the covering on top of the tent, as the LORD had commanded him. ²⁰He took the covenant and put it in the ark; he placed poles alongside the ark and set the cover upon it. ²¹He brought the ark into the tabernacle and hung the curtain veil, thus screening off the ark of the covenant, as the LORD had commanded him.

²²He put the table in the tent of meeting, on the north side of the tabernacle, outside the veil, ²³and arranged the bread on it before the LORD, as the LORD had commanded him. ²⁴He placed the menorah in the tent of meeting, opposite the table, on the south side of the tabernacle, ²⁵and he set up the lamps before the LORD, as the LORD had commanded him. ²⁶He placed the golden altar in the tent of meeting, in front of the veil, ²⁷and on it he burned fragrant incense, as the LORD had commanded him. ²⁸He hung the curtain at the entrance of the tabernacle. ²⁹He put the altar for burnt offerings in front of the entrance of the tabernacle of the tent of meeting, and sacrificed burnt offerings and grain offerings on it, as the LORD had commanded him. ³⁰He placed the basin between the tent of meeting and the altar, and put water in it for washing. ³¹Moses and Aaron and his sons used to wash their hands and feet there, ³²for they washed themselves whenever they went into the tent of meeting or approached the altar, as the LORD had commanded Moses. ³³Finally, he set up the

---

found in other creation and tabernacle/temple-building accounts ("He built his shrine like the heavens, / like the earth which he founded forever," Ps 78:69). These resonances indicate that the completion of the tabernacle is to be understood as an event of cosmic importance.

The final act of Exodus now takes place (vv. 34-38). With the work completed, the divine cloud covers the meeting tent, and the divine glory fills the tabernacle. The wording corresponds to the description of the divine glory on Mount Sinai (24:15-17; see also Lev 1:1; 9:6, 23-24; cf. 1 Kgs 8:10-11; Isa 6:3). The new tabernacle replaces the divine mountain by providing a mobile mechanism for divine presence and communication. The cloud replaces the older pillar of cloud and pillar of fire (see 13:21-22; 14:19-20; 33:7-11), which will indicate when and how long the Israelites will encamp

court around the tabernacle and the altar and hung the curtain at the gate of the court.

Thus Moses finished all the work.

God's Presence in the Tabernacle. [34]Then the cloud covered the tent of meeting, and the glory of the LORD filled the tabernacle. [35]Moses could not enter the tent of meeting, because the cloud settled down upon it and the glory of the LORD filled the tabernacle. [36]Whenever the cloud rose from the tabernacle, the Israelites would set out on their journey. [37]But if the cloud did not lift, they would not go forward; only when it lifted did they go forward. [38]The cloud of the LORD was over the tabernacle by day, and fire in the cloud at night, in the sight of the whole house of Israel in all the stages of their journey.

(Num 9:15-23; 10:11-28). Just as Moses was promised (Exod 32–34), they will be accompanied by God as they travel in stages to the Promised Land. Absorbing the insights of older traditions, the priestly tradition's new theological creation brilliantly addressed Israel's situation whether at home or in exile. At home it provided a standard for worship in Jerusalem, and it also offered hope of divine presence despite exile and utter loss.

REVIEW AIDS AND DISCUSSION TOPICS

INTRODUCTION

The significance of the exodus *(pages 5–7)*

1. What does human freedom mean in the book of Exodus?

2. What two journeys does the book of Exodus record?

3. In what ways did the early church draw on the exodus for inspiration?

4. How is reading the book of Exodus meant to be a "sacramental" experience?

Historical background of the exodus *(pages 7–9)*

1. Explain the saying "Absence of evidence is not evidence of absence." How does this principle apply to the historical background of the exodus?

The setting of the exodus *(page 9)*

1. In which century do most scholars place the exodus?

2. Why do other scholars prefer an earlier date?

Literary forms, structure, and features *(pages 9–13)*

1. Name the types of literature found in the book of Exodus.

2. Briefly describe the four sources of the first five books of the Bible according to the the Documentary Hypothesis.

3. What is an important theological value in noting the diversity of authors and their styles in the book of Exodus?

4. What picture emerges from the influence of the priestly editors of Exodus?

5. Name some of the hard issues discussed and wrestled with in the long tradition behind the Bible. Are these issues still meaningful today? Why or why not?

The ongoing message of the exodus *(page 13)*

1. What impact has the exodus story had on Jews and in the church's struggle for justice in Central and South America and the United States?

PART I: OUT OF EGYPT

Exodus 1:1–15:21

Chapter 1 Israel's oppression in Egypt *(pages 15–18)*

1. Identify the references to the book of Genesis in the first seven verses of this chapter.

2. How does the new pharaoh of Egypt introduce tension into the opening scene?

3. Examine the "inverted series of parallels," or chiasm, in verses 15-22.

4. How do the two midwives differ from Moses, Aaron, Abraham, Isaac, and Jacob?

Chapters 2 and 3 Introducing Moses *(pages 19–29)*

1. Who are the unnamed women who help Moses survive?

2. Describe the Hebrew and Egyptian origins of Moses' name.

3. How is the birth legend of Sargon related to the story of Moses' birth?

4. Where is the land of Midian, why does Moses go there, and what does he do there?

5. What accounts for calling the mountain of God Horeb and Sinai?

6. Check the references in Judges 6 and 13 regarding angels appearing with fire.

7. Describe the elements in the call stories of Moses, Gideon, Samuel, Isaiah, Ezekiel, and Jeremiah.

8. Explain the alternation of "Lord" and "God" in 3:4.

9. What is the risk in "seeing God"?

10. What point is conveyed in the Lord's being identified as "I am who am" or "He is/will be"?

Chapters 4, 5, and 6 Moses objects, the Lord reassures *(pages 29–38)*

1. Reflect on the point that "biblical heroes are often deeply flawed individuals." What does this say about today's religious leaders?

2. What is signified by the "hardening" of Pharaoh's heart?

3. How might the circumcision of Moses' son be understood?

4. Review the six short scenes in chapter 5 involving Moses' message and Pharaoh's response.

5. What is the difference between a *descriptive* story and a *prescriptive* passage?

6. In 6:4-5, the term "covenant" is introduced. What is the central meaning of this term?

7. What is the point of inserting the genealogy of Moses and Aaron in 6:14ff.?

Chapters 7–11 The ten plagues of Egypt *(pages 38–51)*

1. Note the differences in the plague stories of Psalms 78 and 105. How do we account for these differences, and what do they say about the historical accuracy of the Bible?

2. Taking the plagues one by one, note such aspects as:
    a. natural explanation for the plague;
    b. competition between Egyptian magicians and Moses and Aaron;
    c. plagues as possible attacks against different Egyptian gods;
    d. persistent stubbornness of Pharaoh;
    e. division of the plagues into three sets of three, climaxed by the tenth plague;
    f. characteristics of the tenth plague.

Chapters 12–15 The Passover, departure, and crossing the sea *(pages 51–67)*

1. Describe the basic elements of the Passover meal with emphasis on the sacrificial animal, the unleavened bread and the blood, and the Christian use of the Passover ritual.

2. What are we to think of the 600,000 Israelite men who departed from Egypt and the 430 years spent in Egypt? Are these historically accurate numbers?

3. The "Red Sea" or the "Reed Sea"—which is it?

4. Describe the two versions of the crossing of the sea, the one more supernatural, the other more natural.

5. Describe the three parts of the "Song at the Sea" in 15:1-21.

6. What do the prose and poetic versions of the crossing of the sea tell us about the truth of the Bible? What is the truth to which these versions give witness?

PART II: FROM EGYPT TO SINAI
Exodus 15:22–40:38

Chapters 15–18 On the way to Mount Sinai *(pages 67–75)*

1. Both the book of Exodus and the book of Numbers have Israelite complaint stories. What is the difference between these two books, and what underlies these stories?

2. What exactly is manna, and where do quail come from?

3. How does God answer the Israelites' thirst for water?

4. What prompted the consideration of the Amalekites as enemies when originally they were friends?

5. Identify Jethro and his contribution to Moses' leadership.

Chapters 19–20 Arrival at Sinai and the Ten Commandments *(pages 75–81)*

1. Why does Sinai "loom as the Mount Everest of the covenant and torah"?

2. What is the New Testament's connection with the Sinai experience?

3. Where is Sinai located?

4. Identify the expressions of the covenant relationship between the Lord and the Israelites in 19:4-6.

5. Which natural phenomena are used to express the Lord's presence at Sinai?

6. Read Deuteronomy 5:6-21 and compare this version of the Ten Commandments with Exodus 20:2-17. What accounts for these differences?

7. What are the differences between the Jewish/Protestant traditions of the Ten Commandments and the Catholic tradition?

8. Study the Ten Commandments carefully in terms of their background, prohibitions, and positive commands.

Chapters 21–24 The Covenant Code *(pages 82–94)*

1. How does the Covenant Code compare with other law codes of ancient Middle Eastern societies?

2. How do the slavery rules in a patriarchal society show the vulnerability of women?

3. Describe the rule of retaliation (21:23-25) and its relationship to Matthew 5:38-39.

4. How do rules show concern for weaker groups such as noncitizens, widows, and orphans?

5. Examine several rules in this section and consider their relevance for the twenty-first century.

6. Describe the ritual used to ratify the covenant in 24:1-11.

Chapters 25–40 The ark and the dwelling *(pages 95–135)*

1. Give the dimensions of the ark, the purpose of the rings and poles, what was to be stored in the ark, and a description of the biblical cherubim.

2. Study other furnishings of the ark such as the altar, lampstand, sanctuary, and courtyard.

3. Describe the priestly vestments of Aaron and his sons such as the ephod, breastplate, the Urim and Thummim, and headdress.

4. What are the three ritual steps of the priestly consecration?

5. Be acquainted with the incense altar and the bronze laver.

6. Note that the sabbath observance is the sign of the Sinai covenant.

7. How can the golden calf be something other than outright idolatry?

8. Describe Moses' role as the mediator between God and the people.

9. What are the connections between Moses' and Elijah's encounters with God?

10. In the second set of the Ten Commandments, what are the three variants from the original set?

11. Explain: "Moses becomes the living icon of the God alive in Israel's life."

12. What do the new Dwelling and the cloud replace that provides the priestly tradition's new theological creation?

13. Name and discuss two or three major highlights and insights of this study of the book of Exodus.

INDEX OF CITATIONS FROM THE
CATECHISM OF THE CATHOLIC CHURCH

The arabic number(s) following the citation refer(s) to the paragraph number(s) in the *Catechism of the Catholic Church.* The asterisk following a paragraph number indicates that the citation has been paraphrased.

Exodus

3:1-10	2575*	20:2-5	2083	29:7	436*
3:5-6	208*	20:2	2061	30:22-32	695*
3:5	2777	20:7	2141	31:15	2168, 2189
3:6	205, 207	20:8-10	2167	31:16	2171*
3:7-10	1867*	20:11	2169	31:17	2172
3:13-15	205	20:12	2196, 2200, 2214*	31:18	700, 2056, 2058
3:14	446,* 2666,* 2810*	20:13	2257	32	210*
4:22	238, 441*	20:14	2330	32:1-34:9	2577*
12:3-14	608	20:15	2400	32:15	2058
13	1363*	20:16	2463, 2504	33:9-10	697*
13:12-13	529*	20:17	1456,* 2513, 2533	33:11	2576
13:22	659*			33:12-17	210*
15:1	2810	22:20-22	1867*	33:18-19	210
15:26	1502	23:7	2261	33:19-23	2583,* 2666*
16:19-21	2837*	23:12	2172		
16:19	2836*	23:20-23	332*	34:5-6	210
17:1-6	694*	24	2060*	34:6	214, 231, 2577*
17:2-7	2119*	24:7	2060		
17:8-13	2577*	24:8	613*	34:7	211
19-20	708*	24:15-18	697,* 2085*	34:9	210*
19	751,* 2060*			34:28	2056
19:5-6	709,* 762,* 2810*	25:10-22	2130*	34:29	2058
		25:16	2058, 2058	40:1-2	2058
19:6	63,* 1539			40:36-38	697*
19:16-25	2085*	25:22	433*		
20:1-17	2056*	29:1-30	1539*		

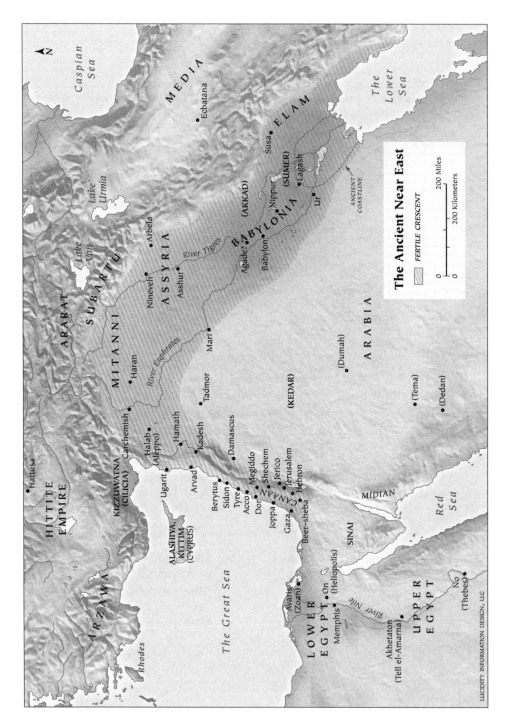

The Ancient Near East

FERTILE CRESCENT

0   200 Miles
0   200 Kilometers

N

Caspian Sea

MEDIA

Ecbatana

ELAM

Susa

The Lower Sea

ANCIENT COASTLINE

Lake Urmia

Lake Van

ARARAT

SUBARTU

Arbela

ASSYRIA

Nineveh

Asshur

River Tigres

(AKKAD)

Agade?

Babylon

BABYLONIA

Nippur

(SUMER)

Lagash

Ur

MITANNI

Haran

River Euphrates

Mari

Tadmor

ARABIA

(Dumah)

(KEDAR)

(Tema)

(Dedan)

Carchemish

Hamath

Kadesh

Damascus

Halab (Aleppo)

HITTITE EMPIRE

Hattusa

KIZZUWATNA (CILICIA)

ARZAWA

Ugarit

Arvad

Berytus

Sidon

Tyre

Acco

Megiddo

Dor

Shechem

Jerico

Jerusalem

Hebron

CANAAN

Joppa

Gaza

Beer-sheba

ALASHIYA KITTIM (CYPRUS)

Rhodes

The Great Sea

MIDIAN

SINAI

Red Sea

LOWER EGYPT

Avaris (Zoan)

On (Heliopolis)

Memphis

River Nile

UPPER EGYPT

Akhetaton (Tell el-Amarna)

No (Thebes)

LUCIDITY INFORMATION DESIGN, LLC

142

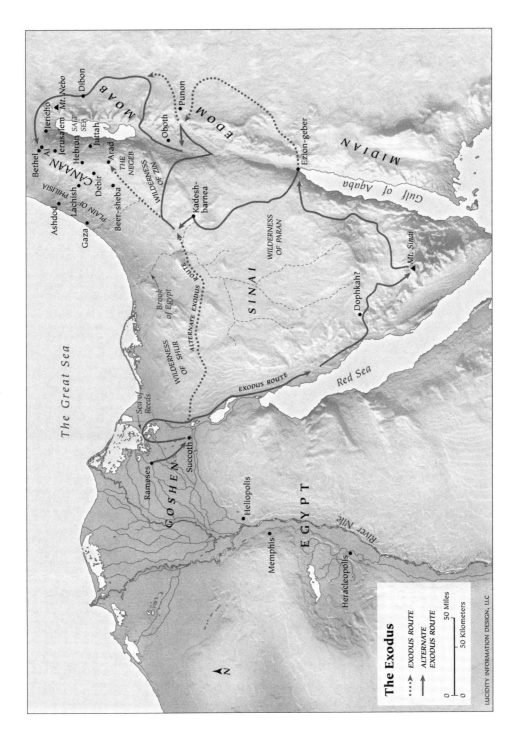

The Exodus

EXODUS ROUTE
ALTERNATE
EXODUS ROUTE

0   50 Miles
0   50 Kilometers

LUCIDITY INFORMATION DESIGN, LLC

143

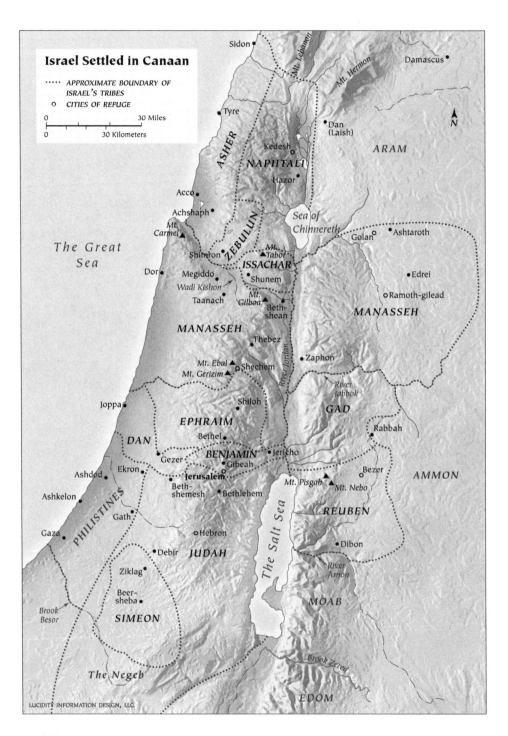

Israel Settled in Canaan

····· APPROXIMATE BOUNDARY OF
ISRAEL'S TRIBES
○ CITIES OF REFUGE

0   30 Miles
0   30 Kilometers

Sidon

Damascus

Mt. Lebanon

Mt. Hermon

Tyre

Dan
(Laish)

ARAM

Kedesh
NAPHTALI

Hazor

ASHER

Acco

Achshaph

Mt.
Carmel

ZEBULUN

Sea of
Chinnereth

Golan
Ashtaroth

The Great
Sea

Shimron
Mt.
Tabor

ISSACHAR

Dor

Megiddo

Shunem

Edrei

Wadi Kishon

Taanach

Mt.
Gilboa

Beth-
shean

Ramoth-gilead

MANASSEH

MANASSEH

Thebez

Zaphon

Mt. Ebal
Mt. Gerizim

Shechem

River Jabbok

Joppa

Shiloh

GAD

Rabbah

EPHRAIM

Bethel

DAN

Gezer

BENJAMIN

Jericho

Gibeah

Bezer

AMMON

Ashdod

Ekron

Jerusalem

Ashkelon

Beth-
shemesh

Bethlehem

Mt. Pisgah
Mt. Nebo

PHILISTINES

Gath

REUBEN

Gaza

Hebron

The Salt Sea

Dibon

Debir

JUDAH

Ziklag

River
Arnon

Beer-
sheba

MOAB

Brook
Besor

SIMEON

The Negeb

Brook Zered

EDOM

LUCIDITY INFORMATION DESIGN, LLC

144

SIMON RAVEN

Simon Raven was born in London in 1927. He was educated at Charterhouse and King's College, Cambridge where he read Classics. After university, he joined the army as a regular officer in the King's Shropshire Light Infantry and saw service in Germany and Kenya where he commanded a Rifle Company. In 1957 he resigned his commission and took up book reviewing. His first novel, *The Feathers of Death*, was published in 1959. Since then he has written many reviews, general essays and plays for radio and television as well as the scripts for a number of successful television series including *Edward and Mrs Simpson* and *Love in a Cold Climate* plus a host of novels. The highly acclaimed *Alms for Oblivion* sequence takes its title from a passage in Shakespeare's *Troilus and Cressida*; it has been referred to as 'a latter-day Waugh report on another generation of Bright Young Things' and has been compared favourably with the *romans fleuves* of Anthony Powell and C. P. Snow. With the publication in 1984 of *Morning Star* he began a new novel series under the title *The First-Born of Egypt*. It is a sequel to *Alms for Oblivion*. Simon Raven lives and works in Deal, Kent.

SIMON RAVEN

The Troubadour

The First-Born of Egypt: Volume 7

HarperCollins*Publishers*

HarperCollins*Publishers*
77–85 Fulham Palace Road,
Hammersmith, London W6 8JB

This paperback edition 1993
1 3 5 7 9 8 6 4 2

First published in Great Britain by
Hutchinson 1992

ISBN 0 586 20022 3

Set in Palatino

Printed in Great Britain by
HarperCollinsManufacturing Glasgow

This book is dedicated to my old friend

DESMOND BRIGGS

who, as editor of the ten volumes of
Alms for Oblivion and the seven volumes of
The First-Born of Egypt, has discharged this office
with enduring patience and percipience over
the last thirty years.

S.R.

Passa la nave mia colma d'oblio
per aspro mare a mezza notte il verno
enfra Scilla et Caribdi, et al governo
siede 'l signore anzi 'l nimico mio;

à ciascun remu un penser pronto et rio
che la tempesta e 'l fin par ch' abbi a scherno;
la vela rompe un vento umido eterno
di sospir, di speranze et di desio;

pioggia di lagrimar, nebbia di sdegni
bagna et rallenta le già stanche sarte
che son d'error con ignoranzia attorto.

Celansi i duo mei dolci usati segni,
morta fra l' onde è la ragion et l' arte
tal chi' i' 'ncomincio a desperar del porto.

Petrarch: *Rime sparse*; 189

PART ONE

The Oracle

So, on I went. I think I never saw
   Such starved ignoble nature; nothing throve:
   For flowers – as well expect a cedar grove!
But cockle, spurge, according to their law
Might propagate their kind, with none to awe,
   You'd think; a burr had been a treasure-trove.

No! penury, inertness and grimace,
   In some strange sort, were the land's portion. 'See
   'Or shut your eyes,' said Nature peevishly,
'It nothing skills: I cannot help my case:
''Tis the Last Judgment's fire must cure this place,
   'Calcine its clods and set my prisoners free.'

If there pushed any ragged thistle-stalk
   Above its mates, the head was chopped; the bents
   Were jealous else. What made those holes and rents
In the dock's harsh swarth leaves, bruised as to baulk
All hope of greenness? 'tis a brute must walk
   Pashing their life out, with a brute's intents.

As for the grass, it grew as scant as hair
   In leprosy; thin dry blades pricked the mud
   Which underneath looked kneaded up with
blood . . .

   Browning: *Childe Roland to the Dark Tower Came*;
                                             X to XIII

'Sarcophagi,' said Fielding Gray, as Jeremy Morrison and he surveyed the avenue of the Alyscamps: 'the specialty of Arles.'

'Sarcophagi,' echoed Jeremy: 'eaters of the flesh. These have long ago eaten the flesh consigned to them – two or three times, one is told. First they ate the Roman colonists, then their Christian successors. The finest examples had pagan carvings on one side and Christian on the other.'

Fielding Gray looked, with his one eye, along the row of stone coffins that lay to the left-hand side of the avenue, all the way from the gate to the ruined church three furlongs away, while Jeremy inspected the right-hand rank, his round eyes bulging out of his round face.

'Of course,' Jeremy went on, 'you won't see any finely carven coffins round here. The best of them were either given to visiting notables, of whom something dirty or confidential was required, or, later on, displayed in a museum. To tell you the truth, old man, I'm getting a bit sick of tombs. After all, we've just been within measurable distance of installation in our own.'

'Oh no. There was to be no tomb for any of us,' said Fielding, 'on the island of Palus Dei. Raisley Conyngham was just going to leave us to rot where we fell . . . dead of hunger or exposure . . . in the shifting dunes or the long ripple washing in the reeds.'

'*Nunc me fluctus habet*,' said Jeremy, '*versantque in litore venti*. Poor old Palinurus speaking: "Now the wave has me and the winds wanton with me on the

3

shore.'''

'And that is what bloody Raisley intended for us. The mire on the shore of that lagoon. . . . '

'But as it was,' said Jeremy, 'darling Milo came back and led us to safety through the quagmire. When Raisley realises what has happened, he will be somewhat less than civil to Milo.'

'He has expelled me,' said Milo Hedley, coming up the avenue behind them, 'with bell and book.' He drew level and walked between them, smiling his young, ageless Greek smile and taking an arm of both. 'I have lost my Master, my Sorcerer, for ever.'

'And he,' said Fielding, 'has lost a very capable apprentice. How did you find us? Through what remains in you of Raisley's art?'

'Magic was not required. The people in your swish hotel at Barbazan told me that of your group Mademoiselle Salinger and Signor Caspar had booked flights back to England from Toulouse, while the Honourable Morrison and M'sieur le Commandant Fielding Gray had asked them to book two rooms by telephone at the Jules César in Arles. When I arrived there just now, the girl at the desk said that she had overheard, as you left your keys, a mild dispute between you about the quickest way to Les Alyscamps. So here I am.'

Jeremy kissed him on the lips.

'You saved us,' he said.

'Demonstrations of love are ill advised in the Alyscamps,' said Fielding. 'A French poet wrote a poem warning lovers to beware of upsetting the ghosts here. Carnal contacts make them envious, you see.'

Sobered by this consideration, they walked on in silence through the tombs and towards the broken church.

'The party's over then?' said Milo. 'Carmilla and Piero are gone. . . . '

'They had their answer,' said Jeremy. 'All four of us

have had it. It was time for them to go home and attend to the affairs of Lancaster College.'

'What exactly,' enquired Milo, 'was the answer that you all received?'

'That Raisley Conyngham,' said Fielding, 'is subtle, sinister, and, if it suits him, homicidal.'

'You knew that already.'

'In a general way, yes. We know now of one particular area in which he operates – the Cathar provinces here in the Languedoc – and we know the precise nature,' said Jeremy, 'of his operation: present and practical diabolism.'

'And how,' said Milo, 'do you propose to prove this singular assertion? How can you use your knowledge to discredit Raisley? That's what you want, isn't it? To get the man out of the way, and especially out of Marius Stern's way, by branding him as an agent of evil and corruption, totally unfit to instruct the young at a great English public school – or indeed anywhere else. *That* is what this entire business is about.'

'Right,' said Jeremy and Fielding together.

'So you came here to find out what he was up to, and now you know. But you can prove nothing – nothing even remotely injurious to Raisley Conyngham. Yes, he will say, indeed I was in the Languedoc early this year. I have been there many times – ever since nineteen fifty-one, when I first went with the lady who taught me the Classics at Brydales. It was she that first instilled into me a love of the Languedoc and its history . . . so great a love that for the last thirty years I have been conducting research into its people, its customs, its religion. My efforts as a scholar in this line have been recognised by my old college – Marcian College, Cambridge – the council of which subsidised and strongly encouraged my research during the sabbatical year (nineteen seventy-five to six) that the school where I teach awarded me in order to pursue it. As for my most recent visit, on which my accusers set so uncharitable a construction, I had urgent cause to check previous findings with a view to their forthcoming publication. The fact that their vulgar curiosity in some matter or other led them to lose themselves in the swamps of Aigues Mortes is nothing to do with me.'

'But you could put the record straight about that,' said Fielding to Milo: 'you could tell the world what Raisley tried to do to us.'

'And what I too tried to do to you as his accomplice,' said Milo. 'Yes, yes, I know I thought better of it and came back to rescue you. The fact remains that I willingly helped Raisley to trap the four of you in the middle of that abominable bog, and it is not a matter which I wish to discuss with the authorities.'

'That's the trouble with Raisley,' Jeremy Morrison said: 'no one can accuse him of anything or ever could. Either the evidence is too flimsy, or the charge would also destroy his accusers.'

'That's what Raisley said to me when he excommunicated me,' said Milo. '"You can prove nothing that any sane man would believe," he said, "and if you try, you will be the first of your own victims. Now get out, you nasty little toad; and remember that though those glands of yours are throbbing with poison, you can never dare to spit. I hope the surfeit kills you." But,' continued Milo Hedley, 'that wasn't quite the end of the interview – or not as far as I was concerned. Just as I got to my own bedroom, the telephone rang in Raisley's. You know how thin the walls of French hotel bedrooms are – you hear every quaver in the sexual scale from opening squawk to the final squeal – so with a bit of concentration I was able to listen to Raisley's telephone talk. And what it was all about was this: Raisley had been rung up by Mrs Maisie Malcolm's lawyer, John Groves he's called – '

' – "Young" John Groves,' said Fielding; 'heir to the secrets of half the peerage. One of Maisie's smart

6

clients must have put her on to him. Perhaps "Young" John Groves was one of her clients,' said Fielding speculatively, 'when she was still a swish whore . . . so she became one of his – '

' – Anyway, it seemed that he'd made her will for her. And was executor, and so on. He'd traced Raisley to Lourdes, where he'd missed him, and now on to Sète, to tell him about a codicil in this will, made in the spring of 1981, which appointed Raisley to be guardian to Tessa (properly called Teresa) Malcolm in the event of Maisie's dying before Tessa came of age.'

After a silence, Fielding said:

'Of course it was sensible of Maisie to name a guardian in succession to herself . . . if only because little Tessa will now be very rich. She will own Maisie's half of Buttock's Hotel. As it happens,' he added with a puzzled air, 'I own the other half. The question is, what to do with it. The place is now worth millions – but old mother Buttock bound her heirs in honour not to sell it. She knew, you see, that developers would just pull it down and put up some cheap and modish obscenity on the site – like what happened to the dear old Cavendish. Although one sees the old bag's point, Buttock's can't just go on being fossilised by mortmain. It was – it is – an attractive hotel of its kind, but if it's not pulled down soon it's going to fall down. It will be pertinent to find out what view Tessa is going to take. . . . '

'That will depend,' said Milo, 'on what view Raisley Conyngham takes. While he's her guardian, he can presumably pre-empt her decisions.'

'Only until she is eighteen. Is he in charge of her money as well as her *mores*?' Fielding asked. 'I should imagine there's a financial trustee as well as a guardian . . . in which case they would both have to be in agreement before anything radical was determined.'

'I don't know about that,' said Milo. 'All Raisley seemed to be getting was the basic news – that he was

7

to be Tessa's guardian.'

'Which raises some interesting questions,' said Jeremy, 'quite apart from what is to be done with the hotel. For instance, I've often wondered by what authority Mrs Malcolm became Teresa's guardian in the first place; and now one asks, by what authority can she bequeath the guardianship? She purported to be Tessa's aunt and her nearest living relative; but the welfare nargs can't have been too happy about handing Tessa over to a rackety old number like Maisie, even if she did own half a hotel. And come to that, she must have adopted Tessa long before she ever went to Buttock's.'

'All that's easily explained,' Fielding said. 'Although Maisie masqueraded as Teresa's aunt, it is now an open secret that she was in fact her mother. And now Maisie's dead nobody can reasonably question her wish that her daughter should be under the care of a respectable schoolmaster at the school where Tessa is a contented and promising pupil.'

'*We* can question that wish,' said Jeremy, 'knowing what we do about Raisley. Why on earth did Maisie choose him?'

'As far as Maisie was concerned,' said Milo, 'Raisley Conyngham was a rich and cultured gentleman, who had kindly invited Tessa along with Marius Stern (and, as it happened, myself), to spend her holidays in the spring of nineteen eighty-one in his country house, Ullacote, on his delectable estate. He was also, for good measure, a senior and successful dominie.'

'Some pretty nasty things happened at Ullacote that spring,' said Fielding: 'Tessa took off home.'

'But only towards the end of her stay in Somerset,' said Milo; 'and being the nice, kind girl she was, she didn't sneak to Auntie Maisie. Now what could have been more natural, if Maisie had a twinge or two in her ticker about that time and thought she'd better check up on her will, than to appoint the egregious country gentleman, who could easily have lived at leisure but thought it his duty to be of some use in the world, as dear little Tessa's guardian?'

'It would have been more natural,' said Jeremy, 'to make someone like "Young" John Groves her guardian.'

'Maisie probably thought that lawyers were a stuffy lot,' Milo said, 'and wanted something a bit jollier for her Teresa.'

'But Maisie never even met Raisley.'

'They'd corresponded,' said Fielding, 'before Tessa's visit to Ullacote. Raisley writes charming and plausible letters. John Groves probably writes pedantic and ponderous letters (and charges fifty guineas a go). Provided Maisie never heard about the goings-on at Ullacote, she might well have decided that Raisley was a most admirable man to have charge of Teresa for a year or two – in the unlikely event of her own death.'

'Whatever the whys and wherefores,' Milo said, 'Raisley is now Tessa's guardian – if I can believe my ears – and that's all about that. Clearly he is in a position to promote more injury and corruption than ever.'

'So what do we do,' said Jeremy, rather feebly, 'to stop him?'

'We take counsel once more,' said Fielding, 'with Carmilla and Piero.'

'When we get home,' said Jeremy, and all God's creation that lay near to them seemed to connive in blessing his indulgence. The sun shone on the Alyscamps; the birds chattered along the branches; and even the crooked church gave them good time of day as they approached it.

'Yes,' said Fielding: 'when we get home. *Ver purpuratum exiit.* "The coloured spring will soon be forth." Time for pleasure.'

Where, he thought to himself, had he last heard that line of Latin which had so suddenly come to his lips? It was from one of the songs in the Cambridge Collection

9

. . . yes, that was it, yes, it was his Headmaster, many years ago, who had quoted the entire verse:

Ver purpuratum exiit,
Ornatus suos induit,
Aspergit terram floribus,
Ligna silvarum frondibus.

That time in Wiltshire, in 1945, over the grave of the Troubadour Knight, Lord Geoffery of Underavon, who, the Headmaster had conjectured, while he could not have sung that particular song, would have sung something very like it. 'The coloured spring is forth': time for pleasure. Lord Geoffery, the Headmaster had explained, had had altogether too much pleasure, with local wives and daughters. Six black, vengeful knights had lain him low in a meadow, while his page fled into the forest and his dogs whimpered among the flowers.

'You don't seem very urgent, you two,' said Milo. 'Very soon now Raisley, fresh from his sabbatical excursion among the Cathar tombs, will return to the school on Farncombe Hill and come close, once more, to his prize pupil, Marius Stern, and his virgin ward, Teresa Malcolm.'

'Raisley will be more cautious for a while,' said Fielding slyly. 'Knowing that we have escaped him, knowing what we now know about him, he will take pause.'

'And meanwhile,' said Jeremy, 'I have a mission to complete. My instructions are plain and the journey will not take very long, unless we loiter. Shall we loiter?'

'What mission?' said Milo.

'You will see, *carissimo*, if you care to come on it with Fielding and me. I shall be your host, Milo, you my sweet guest. When do you have to be back in Cambridge?'

'Mid-April.'

'Then you have plenty of time. But I think,' Jeremy said, 'that we shall not be lovers any more, my darling. You will have heard that there is now a shadow hovering over the realm of Eros. *Semper aliquid novi ex Africa vel ex America*: always something new out of Africa or out of America: in this case, I gather, no one is quite sure out of which. But out of one or the other – this they know – a spectre ten times more vicious and spiteful than that loathly damsel, the pox. For all I know, that spectre may have tweaked me with his finger, and I would not pass his slime on to you.'

Milo nodded, then waved a hand towards the church.

'Thank you, God,' he called, 'for your bounteous mercy and loving kindness to us, your creatures.'

After dismissing Milo Hedley, Raisley Conyngham paid the bill for both of them at the Alberge des Langoustes at Sète, and drove himself west by south towards Narbonne.

'How odd,' he said to the driving mirror as he was passing Béziers on Autoroute Nine, 'that Milo should behave so sentimentally. Never trust a sentimental man; sentimentality is often the motive of treachery; we have a prime instance here. This aberration has been particularly conspicuous since E. M. Forster remarked that he hoped he would have the courage to betray his country before his friend. I really am amazed that they gave Forster a Companionate of Honour, let alone the Order of Merit: if a few more people followed his precept, England would become ungovernable.'

And at about the time he was turning off the A9 for Narbonne-Est, Raisley remarked to his face in the mirror:

'Of course, Milo was a very attractive boy with that sly adolescent smile and those long, loose limbs. But since I am mercifully exempt from any form of sexual desire, his appeal to me was merely aesthetic or, at the most, sensuous. Like Marius's appeal, come to that; though Marius is an altogether more serious matter, and it would certainly not do to lose him ... particularly just now, when the influence – the authority – which I have just been granted over Teresa Malcolm, combined with the loyal obedience which I have long elicited from Marius, has a very grave (if also piquant) potential.'

When Raisley had managed to park his car (a tedious proceeding) in Narbonne, he went to the Museum of Antique Sculpture, which is in the Priory Church. There he spoke to the curator, a smooth-faced, spiky-nosed, husky Frenchman of the Midi called Jacques-Emile Gagneac, who sat behind a fine sarcophagus as if it had been a desk in the chantry which he used as an office.

'I have two reasons for coming to see you,' said Raisley Conyngham. 'First, to assure you that you need fear no complaint against you from the four antiquarian investigators in whose discomfiture you assisted me by decoying them to Palus Dei. They are not interested in you or your breach of the laws of France, only in me and my destruction.'

'So I supposed,' said Jacques-Emile Gagneac; 'still, from several points of view it might turn out to be a pity that they were allowed to return whence they were taken.'

'Indeed it might,' Raisley Conyngham said. 'Secondly, therefore, I think it would be wise to postpone all acts of worship or celebration at Palus Dei or anywhere else in this area until further notice. It is now known, by four highly intelligent and articulate people, exactly where the island of Palus Dei is situated and exactly where the monument on it is to be found. Quite apart from being my enemies, they are people of scholarly interests and intellectual repute; if

12

they should start talking about the island, men of standing will listen to them. It is therefore desirable that none of our brethren should leave traces of any kind on Palus Dei that might indicate recent ceremony or rite. Agreed?'

'Agreed,' echoed the Curator Gagneac.

'I shall now go briefly into Spain and Italy, in order to inspect our congregations there and to warn our brothers and sisters of a need for discretion. I shall be back at my address in England shortly after the middle of March.'

'Back teaching at that school, Maître?' said grinning Gagneac. 'Oh happy boys and girls that have such a peerless minister.'

'The quarter, that is the term, will be just about over,' said Raisley, ignoring Gagneac's sarcasm, 'but I shall be in time to talk with two pupils of whom I have high hopes. One has just become my ward; the other has long since been my creature. Their services will one day be acceptable in the sight of Our Lord. Fairly soon now – but not yet, not yet – I shall bring them closer to the Rule and Commands of the Demiurge and explain their destiny.'

When Raisley had gone clear of Narbonne, he rejoined the A9, but now he was heading east, for the Italian border. On his way home, he told himself, he would cross the Pyrenees by Roncevalles for a brief circuit of the congregations in northern Spain.

'And then back to school on Farncombe Hill,' he told his face in the driving mirror, 'to attend to Teresa and Marius. As I told Gagneac, it will soon be time for them to learn about the latter day resurrection of Cathars in the Languedoc, Navarre and Lombardy, and how they must both serve its purposes. Soon; but not yet.'

'How did you get on?' said Marius Stern to Tessa

13

Malcolm, as they walked away from the examination centre (as it had recently been re-named) at their school on Farncombe Hill.

'I did not like the ancient history paper,' said Tessa; 'it was too woolly.'

They had just been sitting their O levels, which had been postponed (because of 'strike action' by examiners in protest against the failure rate among 'deprived' (i.e. illiterate) candidates from Midsummer's Eve of 1981 to Hallowmas to Advent to Ash Wednesday of the following year, until now, on the Ides of March, they were finally done with.

'The questions were too vague,' glossed Tessa: 'as if they were an invitation to write about anything one wanted to.'

'They were,' said Marius. 'The idea is that nobody should be allowed to fail and nobody to excel. Imprecision in questions makes for imprecision in answers, which enables the examiners to penalise talent as misapplied and excuse stupidity as misunderstanding.'

'I wasn't at my best anyhow,' Tessa said, as they walked through the northern entrance to a little cloister, then paused to listen to the midday chime. When the last stroke had faded, Teresa went on:-

'I've heard from my solicitors – from my mother's solicitors – Groves and Groves. They say that my mother appointed Raisley Conyngham as my guardian, until I came of age.'

'Groves and Groves?' said Marius, astonished into repetition. 'They're my lawyers too,' he said, pulling himself together; 'I deal with "Young" John Groves, who is rather sympathetic in a cynical sort of way. He helped me stop my mother from interfering with my allowance.'

They walked on, towards the Domus Vestalis (the Vestal or Virginal House) in which Tessa and other girls lived, safe, as was supposed, from masculine attentions.

'My letter was signed by a John Groves,' Tessa said. 'I don't think he can be of any help to me. He just said I was Mr Conyngham's ward. And that would appear to be that.'

'Your mother must have thought you liked him. After all, we both stayed with him at Ullacote a year ago.'

'She didn't know what happened there. When I went home early, I told her it was because I was missing her. Which of course I was ... though not as much as I pretended. I said it to please her. That was when I still thought she was my aunt, who'd done everything for me when she needn't have. So you see I was anxious to thank her; and the last thing I wanted to do was upset her, by telling her how horrible Mr Conyngham and Milo had been. And now this is my reward for trying to be considerate: I get landed with Raisley Conyngham as my guardian.'

'The bond is not a tight one,' said Marius, 'and it will only last two years, until you are eighteen. I may be bound to him – and very closely bound – for life.'

'Why should you be? You will grow up, go away from here – '

' – I am bound by love, of a special kind. By love, and by custom, and by fear.'

'Love will die when you see through him, as soon you must, for the repulsive man he is. Custom will soon be staled.'

'And fear?' said Marius.

'You are clever and strong. You can conquer fear. You must begin as soon as Mr Conyngham returns ... from his research. Do you think it is really that?'

'Why not? He is learned – and inquisitive. But you are right,' said Marius, halting as they came near to Tessa's Domus. 'Fear is to be conquered.' He paused. 'I think Jeremy Morrison will help me.'

'How?' said Tessa.

'Fielding and Jeremy are going on from France to the

Peloponnese. I have given him a message to take to my father. Not exactly a message: a greeting from me, as his son.'

'How can anyone greet your father, who is dead?' said Tessa, being of logical and literal inclination. 'Or is he searching for his ghost?'

'He is simply representing me, in paying the respect required by *pietas*, by loyalty and loving memory. *Pietas*, if it be sincerely felt and practised, can help a man conquer fear. If my father . . . should make any kind of answer . . . it would strengthen *pietas*.'

'How can your father make answer?' said prosaic Tessa.

Marius shrugged and turned. Tessa went to her Domus.

The Jewish Burial Ground on the island of Zacynthos is on a hillside which commands a fine view of the harbour and thence over the sea towards the castles of Clairmont and Glarentza on the mainland of the Peloponnese. Sheep graze and loiter on the green grass among the tombs, which are simple stone slabs, standing fast and upright, often engraved with the coronet of an Ionian baron. No Jews, however, or none in this gallery, appear to have been created counts or princes. No sarcophagi are visible above ground (as they are in so many pagan or early Christian graveyards): Jews, once buried, have the good manners and good sense to stay below.

On one slab there are the words:-

I
GREGORY STERN
RODE WITH THE KING'S MEN

'It seems,' said Jeremy Morrison to Fielding Gray and Milo Hedley, 'that he was very proud of his service with the Household Cavalry.'

'I wish I could be proud of my service,' Fielding said: 'I was a rotten soldier.'

'You were wounded with your face towards the enemy,' said Milo, 'and honourably discharged.'

'What do you know about it?'

'I have made enquiries. It was when you were serving with your regiment in Cyprus. It was there that you lost your eye.'

'I had made a truce with the terrorists.'

'And they broke it.'

'I should never have made it,' Fielding said; 'or having made it, I should have been the one to break it. All terrorists should be killed on sight, even if you shoot them in the back. Filth. Scum. Vermin. *Faeces*.'

'Steady,' said Jeremy, as the rage twisted the cicatrix that was Fielding's mouth. 'Steady, old love. . . . Attention, both of you. Some time ago, Marius told me his father was buried here by his own request, which was in a late codicil to his will . . . made after a visit here with Isobel, his wife. Now, for many months after his crucifixion on Buranos[*] the Italian police kept his body on ice. But at last they let it go, and then, by permission of the Zantiot Jews, who were inclined to honour the petition of a brave man, it was buried here. When I wrote to tell Marius we were going to make a tour of the Peloponnese before coming home, he telephoned to me at the Júles César and said: "Go to Zacynthos and greet my father for me." "What shall I say?" I said. "What you will." So now, my friends, what shall I say to the man who rode with the King's Men?'

'And published my books,' Fielding said.

Two lightly clad figures, a leggy ephebe like Bronzino's Eros and a maiden who might have been his sister, were walking towards them up the hill.

[*] See *The Face of the Waters*, by S.R. Muller, Blond & White; 1985

'Surely,' said Milo, 'those are the twin children of Jacquiz Helmutt? I saw them when I stayed with Tom Llewyllyn at Lancaster last summer. Striking. They've grown.'

'We saw them – Jeremy and I – in Italy last autumn,' Fielding said. 'As you observe, they have grown.'

'They seem to favour the Mediterranean coast,' Jeremy said. 'You two,' he called in a familiar and almost paternal voice (for, after all, he had seen them not only last autumn at Bari[*] but often when they were much younger and he himself was a boy at Lancaster), 'you two twins, here is Gregory Stern, who was the friend of Tom Llewyllyn, who was Provost, before he died, of Lancaster College, of which your father is now Provost. I am charged by Gregory's son, Marius, to bear greetings to his father here. What shall be my words?'

'They say those children never speak,' said Fielding, 'except perhaps to their parents.'

'Maybe they will speak now. Gregory went often to Lancaster and Marius with him, a tall dark man and a tall bright boy. These two must surely remember them. What shall be my words,' Jeremy repeated, as the twins came nearer through the stones, 'to Gregory, father of Marius Stern?'

The ephebe beckoned with a curious circular motion of the wrist and arm, then turned with his sister down the hill towards the harbour.

In Cambridge Piero Caspar and Carmilla Salinger met for dinner, some three weeks after they had returned from the Languedoc. The cooking in their college, Lancaster, had declined very noticeably of late, along with the decline of Balbo Blakeney, the Steward; so they had decided to dine outside the college, at a new and

---

[*] See *Blood of My Bone*, by S.R. Muller; 1989

fashionable restaurant called the Caring and Sharing.

'Time to discuss what happened in those marshes near Aigues Mortes,' Carmilla said, 'and draw our conclusions. We may properly omit any element of the supernatural, I think, and confine ourselves to human action and reaction.'

'By which you mean "the facts". It is not like you, Carmilla, to talk jargon.'

'I'm sorry, Piero. It comes of reading too many bad books in the course of research. Very well. The facts of our adventure were simple. Raisley Conyngham, Milo Hedley, and that Frenchman Gagneac conspired to trap us on that island in the hope that we should die there in total isolation. Then Milo thought better of it and rescued us – more for Jeremy Morrison's sake than for any other reason.'

'But rescue us he did, Carmilla, for whatever reason.'

'These blinis are soggy.'

She beckoned the head waiter, a grinning, bustling sycophant, and asked, none too politely, for a new lot properly cooked.

'Our conclusion,' said Piero, 'must be as simple as the facts. Raisley wants us out of the way so that he can get on, unimpeded, with the corruption and exploitation of Marius Stern. Not sexual corruption or exploitation; far worse. He wants to possess Marius's mind, his intellect and his soul. He wants morally and spiritually to enslave him.'

'And now he has a bonus coming his way: that imbecile mother of Tessa Malcolm's has made her Raisley's ward in her will.'

'I don't think she quite understood the position,' said Piero, 'before she died.' His pretty Sicilian face, which had successfully defied the years (usually so cruel to Latin beauty) of his early and middle twenties, now suddenly shrivelled in pain. The cold of the fenland winter always made a long, clammy ache in his crippled foot and from time to time tightened its grip to cold fierce torture. 'I don't think,' he said, willing the agony away, 'that she understood anything of importance. Imbecile, as you say. Her conception of wickedness envisaged nothing worse than the physical molestation of children or deliberate transmission of the pox. Her notions of evil did not comprehend the seduction of the psyche.'

'In Teresa's case it might have to be rape – if he wants to dominate her psyche. He will not have time for the long and gentle process he used on Marius.'

'The problem of Tessa increases the urgency for action,' said Piero: 'it does not change the nature of that action. Our only solution must be to destroy Raisley Conyngham. Not just to discredit him, as we once thought. We know now that he is powerful enough to take his disciples with him (despite the surprising defection of Milo Hedley) however deeply he might be disgraced. Nothing which anyone has been able to think of, and no degree of foulness in Raisley himself, has so far detached Marius from him. Mere exile would never achieve this. There is only one answer: Raisley must be altogether . . . taken out, in the tactful new expression.'

'Might he not take his disciples with him even in death?' Carmilla said. 'If only out of spite?'

'That is a risk that must be run.'

'Another thing,' said Carmilla. 'I do not think Jeremy and Fielding understand quite how immediate the danger is. They are simply footling around in the Peloponnese, with Milo as I now hear. Meanwhile, Raisley Conyngham will be putting time and effort to endeavour.'

'Not, at the moment, in England.'

'He will be in England before long, I think.'

'When he gets back to that school, Tessa and Fielding will be on holiday,' said Piero, 'unless he comes almost at once.'

'Raisley Conyngham will whisk them back with a flick of his fingers – if it suits him.'

'Look,' said Piero, after a pause during which Carmilla waved her beautiful bare arms around out of her sleeveless tunic, signalling to the head waiter for her blinis; 'look, Carmilla, my tall goddess, my Athena of the Cam. I do not think that Fielding and Jeremy are necessarily wasting their time. While we were on our journey in France, they told me a story. It seems that during their voyage along the Mediterranean coast from Ithaca to Brindisi last autumn[*] they met Jacquiz Helmutt's twin children, who are now apparently on the loose in that part of the world.'

'There is something odd about them,' said Carmilla. 'There are some curious tales of their birth – and conception. Balbo Blakeney knows something of all this, but he never speaks of it.'

'Nor will he . . . if his illness does not let go. Poor Balbo.'

'Never mind him now. Those Helmutt twins – their growth has been unusually swift; their beauty is breathtaking. Their mother, Marigold, won't even discuss their whereabouts. She just smiles sadly.'

'However peculiar their circumstances,' said Piero, 'there is no doubt but that the Helmutt twins are in full control of them. Jeremy and Fielding saw them in the basilica at Bari. Later they saw them again – or so Jeremy and Fielding both think. It was when they were in bad trouble on the sea between Bari and Brindisi. A boat appeared, out of a squall, with two figures aboard it, and led them to safety.'

A lugubrious waiter arrived with Carmilla's blinis.

'They're burnt,' said Carmilla, to the back of the receding waiter. 'Two figures?' she said to Piero. 'Lend me some of your toast to go with my lumpfish roe.'

'At first,' said Piero, passing a dismal slice of toast,

[*] See *Blood of My Bone*, by S.R. Muller; 1989

'they thought the two figures were the Dioscuri, the twin gods that bring sailors to haven. When they calmed down, they knew this must be rubbish; and since Fielding recognised a certain gesture of the hand and arm with which one of them signalled, and Jeremy was convinced that one of them was female – something to do with the way she held herself in the storm – they decided the two figures must have been the Helmutt twins.'

'Why on earth should they have been?'

'Their demeanour; the way they had waved in the basilica earlier on; somehow it made Jeremy and Fielding feel that they were being watched for their own good – protected. And then the two figures in the storm . . . even though their faces were hidden by oilskins . . . the way the whole thing happened . . . the other boat coming out of nowhere just when it was needed – the sum of it was, Carmilla, that Fielding and Jeremy, when they discussed it all later, much later, were visited with a kind of revelation, that the Helmutt twins were their good daemons who had been sent to preserve them.'

'How conceited men can be. First they thought Castor and Pollux had come to rescue them, then they thought that the Helmutt twins, endowed with extraordinary powers on sea and land, had followed them and hovered about them all the way from Dalmatia to Apulia. As if those children had nothing better to do.'

'Well,' said Piero, 'what had they got to do?'

'Further their education,' said Carmilla; 'presumably that's why they were sent down there in the first place.'

'But is it not just possible,' said Piero, 'that if the twins *were* to be encountered again – in pretty much the same area – they might again be of assistance? And that, if only subconsciously, Jeremy and Fielding realise this?'

Carmilla chewed and discarded her deplorable

toast. The lugubrious waiter removed it, with an air of paranoia and brought gnocchi in tomato sauce for both of them. When Carmilla had unstuck her jaws from her first mouthful of gnocchi, she said:

'If I grant your absurd hypotheses, Piero, will you kindly tell me just how those pretty twins are to help Fielding and Jeremy solve the problem of . . . *taking out* . . . Raisley Conyngham, without at the same time destroying or alienating Marius Stern and Tessa Malcolm?'

'Your trouble, darling,' said Piero, 'is lack of imagination. That's why your research into mediaeval diseases is now going so badly. You understand symptoms and processes of infection; you do not understand the suffering of the sick or the special insights required for diagnosis.'

'Oh,' said Carmilla, bitterly hurt.

'Lack of imagination leads to lack of tolerance,' Piero pursued crossly as he surveyed his dish of lank, dank gnocchi, 'and lack of tolerance explains your utter failure to sympathise with (say) Jeremy's pathological addiction to being sodomised or Marius's yearning to find a way (other than sodomy, which Marius would abominate) to love and comfort him.'

'At least I understand why Marius is obsessed by Raisley Conyngham,' Carmilla said: 'Marius is weak and longs for a master. Particularly now he has no father.'

'That is about half the story,' Piero said. 'The other half lies in the same realm as Jeremy and Fielding's belief in the powers of the twins to guard and guide them, something you will never understand, my long, lovely goddess of Wisdom, if you live to be a thousand. That is why Jeremy and Fielding told *me* the tale of the twins' appearance to them in the troubled waters of the Adriatic only when they knew that *you* were safely out of the way at the hairdresser's.'

*

As Jeremy, Fielding and Milo followed the Helmutt twins through the sheep and out of the Jewish Burial Ground, and then along the shabby and attractive streets towards the harbour of Zante, Milo said:

'Still not very chatty, those two.'

'When I was up at Lancaster,' Jeremy said, 'their mother, Marigold Helmutt, used to say that when they wanted something they would ask for it by some sort of thought transference which was so clear that it actually sounded in her brain like a voice. It was only when she looked at them, in the course of a "conversation", that she realised they couldn't be talking because their mouths never moved.'

'How old are they?' said Milo.

'They can't be more than ten,' Jeremy said. 'They were born early in the Seventies. Marigold came back preggers (so I've been told) after she and Helmutt had been to Greece,[*] on that expedition which got him his knighthood.'

'I thought,' said Milo, 'that he'd been knighted, like most of 'em, just for growing old without putting his prick in the wrong place or his fingers in the money pot.'

'He discovered a legendary necklace of rubies,' Fielding said, 'the so-called Roses of Picardie. I think Balbo Blakeney was in on it all. That's why Balbo's still a Fellow of Lancaster. He'd been sacked for the drink, but was such a help to Jacquiz Helmutt in tracking down the necklace that he was restored, as Fellows' Steward. Or perhaps that was a bribe – to keep him quiet about something.'

'Like who was the real daddy of these twins?' suggested Milo. 'I can't imagine that that old stick, Jacquiz Helmutt, ever had the spunk to get two bouncing beauties like that.'

' – Who look sixteen at least when they're barely

---

[*] See *The Roses of Picardie*, by S.R. Muller, Blond & White; 1979

ten,' said Fielding, 'and are allowed out alone all over the Mediterranean.'

'Apparently Marigold says they just took off,' said Jeremy; 'last summer, after Tom Llewyllyn's funeral.'

The twins halted on the quayside, by a caique which had no name but two eyes painted on the bow, one to starboard and one to port.

'This was not the boat on which they came to us on the sea south of Bari,' said Jeremy to Fielding.

'You're still sure it was them?'

'Aren't you?'

As Fielding, Jeremy and Milo walked along the quay, the ephebe fetched a gangplank. His sister boarded the caique; Fielding and Co. followed; the boy then followed them and drew the plank aboard. The maiden took a length of cord and started a small, smokey, comfortably chugging engine at the rear of the deck. Her brother took the wheel, which was for'ard of a ramshackle erection that resembled a hut on an allotment and was itself for'ard of the vibrating engine.

'No sails, thank God,' Jeremy said: 'one might have been made to help.'

'What does one call you?' leered Milo at the girl, who totally ignored him and went through a doorless doorway into the hut and then down some steps, presumably to a cabin below.

They chugged out of the harbour and turned north.

Fielding and Co. stood about. Since no deck chairs appeared, they then sat about, on coils of rope and life belts and gunnels. After a while, the boy turned and looked at Fielding; and into Fielding's head came the lines, so clearly that someone might have been speaking them, speaking them in the light voice of a fifth-former called upon to read them, nearly fifty years ago at school:-

ἀλλ' ἄλλην χρὴ πρῶτον ὁδὸν τελέσαι καὶ ἱκέσθαι εἰς Ἀίδαο δόμους "But first you must go forth on another journey, and come to its ending at the House of Hades and dread Persephone." ... Ψυχῆ χρησομένους "To seek prophecy of his soul, if perchance the horseman will come forth to you."'

'What's all this about a horseman?' said Fielding to the boy. 'The poet says, "to seek prophecy of the soul of Θηβαίου Τειρεσίαο/μάντηος ἀλαοῦ ... of Theban Teiresias, even of the blind seer." No horsemen in the text just here.'

The boy turned his eyes away and the voice in Fielding's head was silent.

'We are offered a prophet,' Fielding said to Jeremy and Milo, 'a horseman who will perchance come forth to us from the House of Hades and Persephone.'

'Riding with the King's Men, do you think?' said Milo. 'After all, it was that horseman whom Jeremy came to greet.'

Lady Nausikaa (often in slovenly mode pronounced 'Nausika') slept in the first (the larger) night nursery with her nurse, a jolly snub-nosed girl from the Dalmatian coast, who sang and chattered to the infant all the day long. The Marquess and Marchioness Canteloupe came to say goodnight to their daughter, while the nurse, Dobrila, who always dressed as a fisher-boy from her own town of Koviza on the tiny island of Vis, celebrated their arrival with a ballad in English about how the King and the Queen came to say goodnight to the little Princess.

'See, my lord and lady, Nausikaa is asleep,' said Dobrila (who pronounced the name properly and in full) at the end of her ballad.

'Where did you learn that song, Dobrila?' said Theodosia Canteloupe.

'An English lady who lived on our island taught me.'

'That would have been Patricia Llewyllyn's mother,'

26

said Canteloupe to his wife, as they walked across the Great Court, past the Fives Court, towards the Rose Garden, 'and also Isobel Stern's . . . Lady Turbot, wife of Sir Edwin. She left him when Isobel was born, because she couldn't stand the sight of the child, and went to live on Vis . . . lived until she was over a hundred, so Gregory once told me, though he may have been sacrificing accuracy to romance – or to his Jewish love of round numbers.'

'It is funny to think of her,' said Theodosia, 'as old as a Sibyl, teaching that silly little song to Dobrila.'

'She was rather dotty,' said Canteloupe; 'so was Sir Edwin. No wonder Isobel is so eccentric . . . to say nothing of poor, mad Patricia – '

' – And her daughter, poor, mad Baby, who was once your wife.'

'I preferred to call her Tullia. Tullia was never mad, just difficult.'

'The strain was bad,' said Theodosia. 'It is just as well her son, little Tully, died so young.[*] It was a sensible idea, Canty, to arrange for his murder.'

'You knew about that? I tried to keep it from you. Yes, we arranged for his murder – but in the end his death was accidental, however dramatic. Now we have Nausikaa there need be no more plotting. She is a fine child. She should be. She is yours by young Marius.'

'Even Marius is suspect. After all, he is Isobel's son.'

'I say: there shall be no more plotting,' Canteloupe decreed.

'Good,' said Lady Canteloupe. 'You will not ask me to couple, with Marius or another, to get a son? I want your final word.'

'I love Nausikaa. I need no son, by Marius or another, now or ever.'

'Good,' repeated Theodosia. 'Then I shall never

---

[*] See *New Seed for Old*, by S.R. Muller; 1988

know a man with my body again. Teresa shall be all, and all.'

'If she is all you wish for.'

'She is.'

'She won't be yours for ever. She will grow.'

'I shall love her nevertheless.'

'She will wish to marry,' said Canteloupe; 'or at least to fornicate.'

'Never.'

'You must not try to possess her whole being, her whole life.'

'What do you care?'

'If you do try, she will turn, at the last, and rend you.'

'Again,' said Theodosia: 'what do you care? You will be dead by then.'

'So much the more will Nausikaa need her mother – a soft, contented woman, not a wounded virago.'

'I do not care much about the needs of Nausika.'

'Then perhaps, like old Lady Turbot, you should retire for ever to Vis. Find a girl like Dobrila there.'

'I love Teresa.'

'Who *did* find Dobrila for you?'

'Marigold Helmutt. She goes more and more to the Mediterranean Sea, seeking for her two lost twins. She went to all the islands in the Adriatic, and at last she came to Vis. There she sat crying on the shore, when Dobrila came along the sand and comforted her. She asked Dobrila to come to England for a while, and when she heard about Nausika's birth, she sent her to me, to be the nurse.'

'Did Marigold not want to keep Dobrila, her comforter, to herself?'

'Dobrila was pining for her brother and her sister on her island. She was just about to return to them, but her mother wrote to say that they had both died. It was then Marigold sent Dobrila to be Nausika's nurse . . . so that Dobrila might at least have a little sister.'

'A pity,' said Canteloupe, 'that you too cannot love Nausikaa.'

'I am told that mothers often dislike their babies – sometimes murder them. Dobrila will do well enough for Nausika. My love is for Teresa.'

'I have told you. You cannot have Teresa for ever,' said Canteloupe: 'you could have Nausikaa for ever.'

'Nausika too will grow and marry and rut.'

'She will always be your daughter.'

'Teresa will always be – '

' – I have warned you,' interrupted Canteloupe. 'I shall say no more. Do as you please. Publicly, of course, you will show proper affection for Nausikaa. Otherwise you may leave her to Dobrila, and, for as long as I live, to me. As for Teresa, please do not make a tedious fuss in my house when you find she has betrayed you.'

'I told you,' said Theodosia, without spite and even with sorrow: 'you are an old man, and by then you will be dead.'

By the late morning of their second day at sea, Fielding, Jeremy and Milo reckoned (from a crude map in Milo's guide book) that they had now left Leucas behind and to starboard and were still sailing pretty well due north, past Actium and Nicopolis. Since questions to the twins elicited no response other than a distant smile, they put away the guide book and fell to speculating whether or not their hotel in Zante would charge them for the previous night, during which their rooms had been empty.

'Not exactly empty,' said Jeremy; 'our kit was in them. Anyhow, they couldn't let them to anybody else, in case we came back and made a row with the Tourist Board.'

'We shan't be back for tonight either,' said Fielding glumly; 'nor even for tomorrow night by the look of it.'

'What does it matter?' Jeremy said. 'There is nothing we can do about any of that – hasn't been since we embarked. I must say, the twins have done their best to make us comfy. Those bedding rolls in the cabin were soft and warm – I wonder where *they* slept, by the way? – and corned beef hash makes a very decent dinner once in a way. Nice brisk wine; strong coffee and warm rolls at breakfast: a credit to the establishment.'

He waved cheerfully (rather like the Michelin man, thought Milo; tall as he is, it's high time he did something about that blubber) to the passing maiden, who was carrying a bucket of something or other but waved politely back with the other arm.

'It's all very well for you,' said Fielding to Jeremy. 'You're a rich man. It's all very well for Milo – he's your guest. But these days I cannot afford to take rooms in fancy tourist hotels and then not use them.'

'Your entertainment on this boat is presumably free,' said Jeremy. 'That makes up for it.'

'I still resent paying for a room I haven't slept in.'

'Stop grizzling,' said Jeremy, 'as Nanny would say.'

'I mean it,' said Fielding: 'you don't realise how poor I am. I haven't the energy to write as many books as I used – '

' – Too much pleasure,' Milo said.

' – And nobody reads the ones I do write, or if they do they get them out of libraries – '

' – What about the cash you extracted from Canteloupe,' said Jeremy; 'for not letting on about the – er – suspected ellipsis in the line of his inheritance?'

'That was years ago, and anyway you're not meant to know about it. That was the whole point. Canteloupe gave me . . . rather a lot of money . . . to see the secret didn't get out. Who told you?'

'You did,' said Jeremy, 'when you were pissed.'

'Oh, well. The original agreement was to do with some book I was writing – I had to keep it all out of *that*, though it might have been very handy as part of the plot. As it happened the book was quite successful in any case – the last of my books that made any money. It's gone now, of course, as well as Cante-loupe's subvention.'

'Ask him for a new lot,' Milo said.

'That would be blackmail.'

'Oh, would it? And what was it the first time?'

'A friendly exercise in discretion. Anyhow,' said Fielding Gray, 'I understand that Canteloupe now has his own problems about money. Cant-Fun has fucked up.'

'An ugly intransitive use,' said Milo, 'of a transitive verb. Shortage of greens is no excuse for mangling your grammar.'

'Poor Fielding,' said Jeremy. 'I'll have to see what can be done when I get home . . . on the strict con-dition that you sit right down and start writing again, if only to keep you out of mischief.'

'I'm too old for mischief. Like a potted shrimp.'

'Then there's more reason to pass the time by writing.'

'I've got nothing left to say,' Fielding said. 'I haven't had for years. But one learns lots of tricks as one grows old in the profession, so one can go on for a long time dolling up the same old thing to look fresh and attrac-tive. Beef dressed as veal (like all veal these days). But sooner or later one gets rumbled, and anyway I've lost patience.'

They all of them looked at the sea. They seemed to have turned a degree or two to the east: the pretty, broken theatres of Nicopolis were plainly visible, weeping in a wilderness of thorn.

'Nobody goes to Nicopolis any more,' Milo said. 'Raisley told me. There's a fast new road which bypasses it, and no one can be bothered to stop.'

*

Isobel Stern and Jo-Jo Guiscard, each holding one hand of Oenone Guiscard, walked up the hill into St-Bertrand-de-Comminges and turned into the PTT, where they received their correspondence, together with a blast of snotch and a Pompeian shower of cigarette ash, from the postmaster. Isobel bought a technicolor ice cream cornet for Oenone (the only person whom Isobel ever indulged); they walked down a narrow street to the ramparts, and settled on a seat to read the news from England, lifting their eyes occasionally to the massed Pyrenees.

'Marius has condescended to write to me at last,' Isobel said:-

'"Darling Mummy, I dreamt last night that we were all in your Lagonda, driving to Cambridge for Tully Sarum's christening.* You remember? You nearly ran over some old-age pensioners in Barnet, and when Daddy disapproved you said they all ought to be dead anyway."'

'Ha! Ha! Ha!' said Jo-Jo. 'What a lovely caring person you must have been in those days.'

'Was Oenone there?' said Oenone.

'Oenone was at the christening later,' said Isobel in a satin voice, 'inside Mummy Jo-Jo. Mummy Jo-Jo hoped Oenone was a boy.'

'Oenone would like to have been a boy,' Oenone said; 'then she would have had one of those purdy pink prawns *pour faire pé pé* in the gutter, like the little French boys do. Much more convenient than Oenone's cunt.'

'Who taught her to say "cunt"?' said Isobel.

'Mummy did. Mummy said, "This is your twat, prat, quim or cunt. Little boys will want to touch it, and so will bigger boys too, but you mustn't let them."'

'Sex education,' said Jo-Jo. 'I'm not quite such a bad

---

* See *Morning Star*, by S.R. Muller, Blond & White; 1984

mother as you think. Go on with Marius's letter.'

'"Well, the old-age pensioners probably *are* dead by now; Tully Sarum of Old Sarum certainly is, and so is Daddy. Jeremy Morrison – " '

' – I like Jeremy Morrison,' Oenone said. 'When he was here he let me lie in his arms, like I used to when I was a baby. I hoped that he would touch my twat, prat, quim or cunt, but he didn't.'

'" – Jeremy Morrison,"' Isobel went on, '"has gone to the Peloponnesus with Major Fielding Gray and Milo Hedley. Did you see any of them while they were in your part of the world? I don't suppose you saw Milo, because he was in Raisley Conyngham's camp, so you would only have seen the other lot. Milo has joined the other lot now, and has gone on to the Peloponnesus with Major Fielding Gray and Jeremy."'

'Curiously childish style,' said Jo-Jo; 'writing to you must retard him somehow.'

'He liked it when I fancied him as a little boy,' said Isobel: 'he liked being tickled and snuggled and kissed on his eyes and ears. Perhaps he wishes that it could happen again.'

'So it could, if you both wanted it.'

'Stop being inflammatory,' Isobel said. 'The next bit isn't so childish. "The real purpose of this letter is to tell you that I have asked Jeremy to bear my greetings to my father, whose grave (as you presumably remember) is in the Jewish cemetery of Zacynthos. Although you are now one of Sappho's gang, and started your affair with Jo-Jo Guiscard even before my father's death, I thought you might like to know that the pieties are being observed."'

'What are "pieties"?' Oenone said.

'That depends,' said Jo-Jo, 'on who's observing them.'

'"Rosie is very pleased,"' Isobel read on: '"I sometimes think she loved Daddy more than any of us. She is very excited, just now, because Tessa Malcolm has promised to take her to stay with Thea Canteloupe. She is particularly looking forward to talking to Canteloupe about Papa and the time when they were all young together. Love from Marius."'

'So Rosie will be going to Dyke Castle,' said Jo-Jo. 'These coming school hols, I presume. Perhaps Thea Canteloupe will take a fancy to her too.'

'Rosie is very different from Tessa; rather immature for her age; a jet-haired Jewish Jessica. Tessa is auburn going on for ginger – apricots and cream. Besides,' said Isobel, 'one thing I will say for my two children: they're pretty normal. Marius likes girls – though he could have any boy at that school of his for a nod and a wink, and as for Rosie – '

' – She seems very fond of those Blessington girls, Jakki and Carolyn.'

'That's just a sentimental girlie thing.'

'Please,' said Oenone, 'what is Dyke Castle, where you said Rosie is going?'

'A castle with at least one dyke in it,' said Jo-Jo; 'usually more.'

'And what is a dyke?'

'A dyke,' said Jo-Jo, 'is a lady who likes touching other ladies on the twat, prat, quim or cunt.'

'I thought you said only boys like doing that.'

'People often get rather muddled about which they really are.'

'Oh,' said Oenone, and thoughtfully sucked her many-hued ice cream.'

Late in the afternoon, Fielding, Jeremy and Milo realised that the caique was making directly towards the shore. Soon they saw the mouth of a river; and a little later they were chugging very slowly up it, between oozy banks that barely admitted their vessel.

'ἀλλ ὁποτ' ἀν δὴ νηὶ δι' Ὠκεανόιο περήσῃς,' the clear young voice spoke in Fielding's head, '''when in thy ship thou has crossed the waters of Ocean, to a place where is a level shore and the groves of Persephone, with tall poplars and willows that shed their fruit, there do thou beach thy ship. . . .'''

'The rest fits,' said Fielding aloud, 'but where is the level shore?'

The caique turned a bend in the river, and there, on the starboard side, was a mud flat on which the golden helmsman beached his ship.

'What put that in your head,' said Jeremy, 'about a "level shore"?'

'I was just remembering how Odysseus came to a beach, near the marshes with the sad trees where the rivers meet. . . . '

The girl set a ladder from the gunnels down to the 'beach'. She went down first, paused, and beckoned (with the same almost circular motion her brother had made at the cemetery), and led the way across the mud, treading neat and dry, knowing (so Fielding supposed) the best path. Fielding, Jeremy and Milo followed; the ephebe brought up the rear. That boy has the same smile as Milo, thought Fielding, as he turned to survey the file behind him, that certain smile which archaic Greek sculptors bestowed on their striding *kouri*, boys who were not quite youths; they are both smiling it now, as if they were faintly amused (oh, very faintly) at what they know is about to happen.

They stepped from the landing place up on to a shallow bank of grass, which was raised just above the dank, reedy flats on the side away from the river. For half a mile or so they walked along the bank, until they came to a crude wooden bridge with only one handrail. On this they crossed the river. As he stepped off the bridge on the far side, Fielding turned back, once more, and saw a sign that would face anyone who approached the bridge from the other direction. On the sign was written:

35

'The river Acheron,' said Milo. 'It's on my map. Soon we come to another river. Then to a place called Ephyra.'

As evening began to fall, the girl led them away from Ocean, along the north bank of the Acheron, her smiling brother bringing up behind lest any of their three guests should fall or fail.

Leonard Percival, too, was walking down a small river: but he was walking along a dry path over a meadow in blithe midday, not (like Fielding and Co.) along a dyke above a quagmire at sullen twilight; and he was thinking merry thoughts, not, like Jeremy, about how and when he would ever get back to the comfort of his faraway hotel, nor, like Fielding, about how much he would have been charged in his absence. Leonard was thinking about the time when he had hidden in the wood just ahead of him, and had seen Theodosia Canteloupe and Tessa Malcolm as they strained, strong sportswoman's muscled thigh to soft girl's silky crotch, and cried out in an antiphony of love which rang in his old ears yet.

But as the remembered sounds of erotic battle rose higher and higher, his steps were suddenly twisted by arthritic torment, and his thoughts changed from brisk bawdry to sour Stoic care. Time to leave the party, Leonard thought. Conjure these shadows of desire as I may, I can no longer achieve so much as a twitch in my pecker. Like the melancholy poet, Horace (whom Fielding Gray was always quoting), I should reflect that I have eaten enough, drunk enough, laughed and frolicked enough, and must now depart before I become a loathsome old voyeur and a croaking, creaking bore. But of course I already am a loathsome old voyeur and a croaking, creaking bore. Canteloupe tolerates me because I have done the man some service in my time: her ladyship, on the other hand, finds me quite disgusting (oh, how I agree with her) and is at small pains to dissimulate her nausea. Yes; no doubt of it; time to go. Yet I cannot expire simply of my own will; I am not one to fall on a sword or open a vein in my bath; God must take me hence, and God is not biddable.

By now Leonard had reached the copse. He entered and hobbled through the thick undergrowth and the clustered lady birch by the secret path, and came to a tiny pool at the centre, on the margin of which he managed to squat, thinking of Jo-Jo as she had sat there, great with Oenone, boasting of how she would enjoy the male child she expected to bring forth in due season, and of little Tully Sarum, the changeling heir to the Marquessate of Canteloupe, who had lain drowning in the pool one summer's afternoon while his pretty ginger nurse (only moments away, had she known, from her own death) was dallying on the bank with Marius Stern.*

After they had trudged along Acheron for another twenty minutes, they saw that a second river was coming to join it from the north (to their left) and that this would bar their way. But again there was a flimsy wooden bridge, this without even one handrail, little more than a plank. On the ground lay a notice which had fallen from the fallen post beside it:

KOKYTOS

the notice announced.

'ἔνθα μὲν εἰς Ἀχέροντα,' said the young voice in Fielding's head: '"There into Acheron flow Pyriphle-

---

* See *New Seed for Old*, by S.R. Muller; 1988

gethon and Cocytos, which is a branch of the water of the Styx; and there at the meeting place is a rock. . . ."'

Where is Pyriphlegethon? thought Fielding as he teetered along the plank behind the dainty treading maiden. Here is only Cocytos (that notice affirms); yet Homer distinctly states that both Pyriphlegethon and Cocytos flow into Acheron at one and the same place. Ah well: perhaps the geography has altered in the three thousand-odd years since Odysseus came this way.

But the 'rock' was there still, or at any rate a bare hill of stone and scrub, which rose out of the marsh about a furlong further on, just visible in the last of the light. Behind him Jeremy started to whistle: 'Rory Gilpin' he was whistling, the march of the 10th Sabre Squadron, which Jeremy must have remembered (Fielding thought) from that time they had heard it played, by a British cavalry band on tour, in the gardens at Adelaide. It seemed that Milo knew the words:

'"Rory Gilpin far he rode,"' sang Milo softly,
'"Rode among the willows;
By the river Rory rode,
Among the willows his white horse strode."'

The dyke veered left across a hundred yards of bog, and then the path turned into a flinty uphill track.

'"Rory Gilpin far he rode
And came to a town atop a hill;
Through streets and houses Rory road
And up to a tower his white horse strode."'

The houses they passed showed blank walls to the street, though thin lines of light glinted under some of the doorways. They came to a tall gatehouse without a gate. A prominent notice beside the entrance proclaimed, in several languages,

CLOSED

The girl led them on under an arch.

'"Rory Gilpin far he rode,"' sang Milo,
'"He has passed the town and passed the tower;
And now he has come to All Shadows' road;
And down to the pit his white horse strode."'

'That town was Ephyra,' said Milo after a brief silence, 'of which I told you. It used to have a necromanteion – a sacred place below the earth, where enquirers sought oracles of the dead. It is now a tourist attraction, giving welcome employment to out-of-work actors from Athens, who impersonate superior ghosts such as Agamemnon, Clytemnestra, and fair Helen of Troy.'

Sir Jacquiz Helmutt, Provost of Lancaster College, Cambridge, walked with his private secretary, known as Len, in diagonals back and forth across the rear lawn of the college. The diagonal which they were at present following led them from the corner of the lawn by the west end of the chapel to the corner of the lawn by the approach to the College Bridge over the River Cam.

'Marigold,' said Provost Helmutt. 'She hankers, she yearns for those twins of hers. They are so very young, you see.'

'I have spoken to Balbo Blakeney,' said Len, 'who was present when they were got on her . . . as you will doubtless recall.'

'Vividly,' Provost Helmutt said.[*]

'Balbo is very ill and very vague,' said Len. 'As far as I can make out, he thinks, as I think, that there is nothing to be done. That mysterious youth, who was with you in the Mani – he got the twins; "gat them", as the Old Testament has it. They are undeniably his children, not yours, gifts of God or possibly the Devil. Who knows? Such children, once they have gone, do

---

[*] See *The Roses of Picardie*, by S.R. Muller, Blond & White; 1979

39

not come back.'

'Marigold is off again soon,' said Sir Jacquiz. They came to the corner of the lawn by the bridge, executed an elegant about turn (facing inwards towards each other as they pivoted) and walked slowly, heavily and in perfect step back towards the north end of Sitwell's Building and the west door of the chapel. 'This time she is going to Turkey: Antalya, Ephesus, all up and down the coast.'

'As good a place as any to go,' said Len, 'at the approach of the gaudy spring. You can well afford her passage, my fine Provost. Let her go, if it will make her happy.'

'It won't. She will find nothing to her purpose, and she will grieve.'

'So did Ceres and many others in similar circumstances. She is in good company. Those children, egregious Jacquiz, were last seen in the Provosts' Crypt of the chapel towards the climax of Tom Llewyllyn's funeral.* They move, like their father, in a mysterious way.' Len looked down happily at his light green suede booties, the ankles of which were tightly cuffed by his narrow pink trousers; the colours of the Garrick Club, he thought. And aloud, 'You don't, I know, resent the twins' fatherhood, you are not jealous of Lady Helmutt's longing for the twins themselves, these days you do not much miss her when she is gone, and she is, as you know very well, a questionable asset as your official consort. Indeed, the Provost of this college, such is his magnificence, does not need a consort. Do I speak sooth, magnificent Provost?'

'You do.'

'Then just let her go.'

'She is unhappy.'

'Even you, Provost, are not magnificent enough to bring happiness to your wife or any other member of

---

* See *Blood of My Bone*, by S.R. Muller; 1989

the human race. Only God can do that, and he mostly prefers not to, no doubt because he finds the spectacle of other people's happiness rather annoying, as we all do. Shall we let it go at that? And talk of something important and interesting, like the best way of teaching undergraduates from comprehensive schools how to behave as gentlemen? If the college managed to make a gentleman of me,' Len said, complacently smoothing his mauve silk tie, 'it can make a gentleman of anybody.'

About a hundred yards beyond the gatehouse, the maiden halted. The ephebe joined her at the head of the little column. The maiden then went to the rear, and the ephebe began to lead them down a long, steep and narrow flight of stone steps.

'Is Teresa Malcolm coming here for the Easter holidays from school?' Canteloupe said.

'Of course.'

'When will she arrive?'

'Any time now,' said Theodosia Canteloupe. 'She has finished her O levels, which tired her. I have persuaded the head of her Domus to let her go a few days before the end of the term.'

'Of the quarter,' said Canteloupe. 'What's Domus? We didn't have them in my day.'

'I suppose not. A Domus Vestalis is where some of the girls live.'

'How extraordinary. Change for the sake of change.'

'You wouldn't expect the girls to live with the boys?' Lady Canteloupe said.

'Why not? They're always going on about how they're absolutely equal. No distinction or discrimination.'

'Teresa,' said Theodosia, ignoring Canteloupe's

male chauvinist folly, 'will bring Rosie Stern with her. She too is being released early, at my request, although *she* has not been doing her O levels. She is younger than Teresa.'

'So I recall, Thea. Rosie Stern is the little dark Jewy girl with the remarkably thin legs.'

'As good a description as any,' Thea Canteloupe conceded. 'She has been a very sweet friend to Teresa at school, at a very difficult time, just after Maisie Malcolm's death. You will be kind to little Rosie . . . for my sake?'

'For her own sake,' Canteloupe said.

As Fielding followed the ephebe down the steps, he realised that the whole descent was illuminated by a series of dim yellow lights which were glowing from behind thick glass panels (six inches horizontal by three inches vertical) that had been inserted flush with the stone walls. When they reached the bottom step, the boy paced into the middle of a circular arena of sand (say a cricket pitch in diameter) which formed the base of a hollow, round tube which ascended for perhaps one hundred and fifty feet and was open, at the top, to the sky. The wall of this shaft was scattered with lights similar to those that had lit the steps, and the visible disc of sky was decorated by a few large stars and one obvious planet of blood red. No lesser stars were visible; evidently the cloud that had covered the sky since they disembarked from the caique was now much thinner but not entirely gone.

Directed by the maiden, Fielding, Jeremy and Milo formed a line at the bottom of the staircase. The girl herself went to join her brother in the centre of the sand. There was the plangent sound of a lute: after two or three bars, Fielding decided that it was coming through a loudspeaker or tannoy system, no doubt used to purvey information to tourists and to entertain them with special effects. I hope the show is going to be brief, Fielding thought: it is getting near time for dinner, and since Ephyra (if one is to judge from its appearance so far) will certainly provide none, we may have to travel, i.e. walk, a long way to get it.

After the lute came the snorting of several horses, a young male voice screaming in terror and diminuendo, a hysterical barking of at least two dogs, a creaking of upholstery, a rattle of spurs and armour, and the galloping of a single horse. Then a tableau in the middle of the arena. Where the twins had been lay a body in long, soft robes, and by its side a discarded lute. The head was uncovered and split into halves from the apex of the skull to the bridge of the nose, which, with the riven brow, was tilted towards the audience.

Round the body stood six men in cowls and hauberks of chain mail; the hauberks reached nine inches below their knees, while their shins were encased in greaves of plate armour; from their shoulders hung surcoats of black which carried small white Maltese crosses on the chest. The men were sheathing short swords; after a brief look at their victim, they turned away toward some shadowy horses in the background. The horses whinnied as they were mounted by their cumbersome masters; two dogs (a little nearer the spectators and of vaguely heraldic aspect) cowered among pretty wild flowers. The horses wheeled, the dogs whimpered, the tableau faded into nothing.

'Clever optical effects,' said Jeremy to Fielding.

'Not very Greek,' said Milo; 'perhaps it was some incident from the days of the Frankish Empire. Rather recondite for tourists, though: as the guide book suggested, they'd be expecting Achilles and that lot.'

'Lord Geoffery,' said Fielding; 'Lord Geoffery of Underavon, the Troubadour. Murdered in a meadow by six knights. But that was in England.'

'Just what, *darling*, are you trying to tell us?' Jeremy

said.

'Your father knew the story,' Fielding babbled. 'I told him, and Muscateer told him in India – Muscateer was the heir of the last Lord Canteloupe, the one before this one. Muscateer died in India,* and his father died childless after that, which is why Detterling – that's what this one was called – inherited in some labyrinthine way . . . through the female line.'

'Calm, calm,' Milo said. 'Precision and order, if you please.'

'Very well.' Fielding took a deep breath. 'There was once a crusader,' he said, 'called Geoffery of Underavon. In the twelfth century. Possibly an ancestor of the Sarum family, though *they* were nothing until Agincourt and only got the title of Marquis or Marquess Canteloupe in the late eighteenth century. Anyway, while this Geoffery of Underavon was returning to England from the Holy Land, he lingered among troubadours in Provence. The troubadours, for all their talk of pure and ideal love, had naughty habits which Geoffery imported into Wiltshire, whither he went to claim the manor which he had been awarded for his services. The local Wiltshire gentry didn't care much for Geoffery's winning ways with their wives and children, and six black knights waylaid and slaughtered him while he was riding with his page *en route* for a louche appointment.'

'This lot wore Maltese crosses,' Milo said. 'Were all these rural vigilantes Knights Hospitaller? Six knights of St John in *Wiltshire*, all at the same time? I doubt whether they even had the Maltese connection as early as the twelfth century. Malta was the last territory conferred on them, long after Rhodes.'

'I don't know anything about that,' said Fielding. 'It's only a story, at best a legend.

'And this thing just now,' said Jeremy, 'was only

* See *Sound the Retreat*, by S.R. Blond & Briggs; 1971

some kind of charade.'

'Of course,' said Milo, 'you have to remember that some people think a Maltese cross is a sign of ill omen. Do the Sarums, the Canteloupes, think that? After all, you said that Lord Geoffery could have been an ancestor of the house of Sarum, and you also said that Jeremy's father first heard the tale from a dying heir to the marquessate. Leave aside any quibbling about historical accuracy, there seems quite a lot of room for a symbol of ill omen somewhere in this.'

'No one who passed on Muscateer's story ever spoke of Maltese crosses,' said Fielding; 'not as far as I know.'

'An embellishment by the local producer here in Ephyra?' said Jeremy Morrison. 'The Thespian gang always get this kind of thing wrong. More than ever likely to happen if the scene was done by some conceited wretches from Athens.'

'Where are those two children?' said Fielding, losing interest and thinking once more of his stomach. 'We need them to get us out of bloody Ephyra.'

The twins were not to be seen. Fielding and Co. turned uncertainly towards the steps which led up and out – out of the necromanteion at any rate, as Jeremy remarked. As they began to mount the staircase in the dim yellow light, a low, pleasant, cultivated voice whispered down from the walls:

'I owe you my best thanks, gentlemen. You came all the way to Zante to greet me; but of course there is nothing to greet in a grave. This place, however, is something else again; and here I can make some kind of answer. Am I an actor? Actors were traditionally used in this kind of role – but as to that I shall not bore you with tedious speculation, you must simply form your own opinion.

'I too was a horseman. I too was murdered, though I was not riding a horse at the time, and my murderers, too, were unmounted; for as two at least of you will recall, I was in fact crucified. Even so, I feel a kinship with the murdered man whom you have just seen. A troubadour, most certainly. Lord Geoffery of Underavon? That doesn't matter very much. Killed by Knights Hospitaller who sported an anachronistic emblem? That doesn't matter much either. What does matter is that he was a troubadour, a poet and a musician, and, not least, an entertainer.'

They stood still, one behind the other, on the steep stone stairs.

'I see I have your attention. Good. I think my son hoped that I might have something to say when he asked you to come to me, and I should like to be well understood. I cannot tell you all I might wish, of course; no ghost is ever permitted to do that. You will remember that even Tiresias was somewhat misleading. But what I can, I shall now tell you, and shall hope not to confuse you, though I grant you my message is rather difficult to interpret.

'It comes in the form of a riddle. The riddle has to do with a crisis in the life of my son, Marius, which at present preoccupies you and some of your friends. The riddle runs like this:- The struggle will come to an end, though no one will be able to draw an edifying or even a satisfactory moral from its ending, when the following events have occurred: when a silver horseman shall overcome a cerise horseman; and when a gold horseman shall win the sword of the cerise horseman (what a lot of horsemen – I'm afraid it can't be helped) and shall slay, both in innocence and in guilt, a dark horseman from the Vales of the West. So there you are. Let me just iterate the salient conditions that will precede the outcome of the *affaire Marius*, listing them once more at the necessary risk of boring you – so that none of you shall be able to say that you have not been warned. A silver horseman must overcome a cerise horseman, whose sword will be used by a golden horseman to kill, both in innocence and guilt, a dark

46

horseman from the West. As always, in such enigmas, there is only one easy clue, at least for the observant, but also one rather nasty catch. I wonder – don't you? – just what it can possibly be.

'And now, gentlemen, you have had a long day, I fear. You can find a taxi if you knock on the door of the second house on the left down the hill from our gatehouse. Disregard the lack of light: just knock. I advise you to take the taxi to Prevéza, where you will arrive in time for dinner (of a kind) at the Xenia Cleopatra, an establishment of the delta category, despite its promising name. Here you may also spend the night. Do not go searching by the rivers or the seashore for our two young friends and their caique: their part in this affair is now concluded. You may take the public ferry from Prevéza back to Zacynthos at four thirty a.m.; or, if you wish to lie later in the distressful beds of the unheated Xenia, you may hire your own vessel for the equivalent in drachmae of about one hundred pounds sterling.

'Just one more thing before you go, gentlemen: although, as I have indicated, this business of Marius will sooner or later come to a bearable if rather shabby solution, I should warn you that everyone concerned will encounter some very nasty setbacks before it is done with.'

PART TWO

The Interpreters

Sick men's dreams, dreams out of the ivory gate, and visions before midnight.

Sir Thomas Browne

'You'll have to stand back to Zante,' said Fielding to Jeremy at dinner; 'this whole thing is a damnable rip-off.'

'I shall gladly pay your entire passage and refection from here and now on,' said Jeremy, 'if only you will stop bloody well whingeing and whangeing.'

'You use those sort of expressions much too much,' said Fielding Gray. 'It's as good as shouting out loud that you've been in an Australian prison.'

'Everyone bleeding knows I have. You just stop whingeing, whangeing, grizzling and grinding about money,' Jeremy Morrison said, 'and I'll see, as I've already promised, what can be done for you when we get back to England – though bear in mind that I am not offering you life cover.'

'Right, girls,' said Milo: *that's* now settled. May we please discuss the events of the day?'

'Who asked you to stick your nose in?' Fielding said.

'I did,' said Jeremy, 'when I invited Milo to come with us. Besides, Milo knows Marius as well as anyone and his advice will be valuable. Will you please, Fielding, stop going on like a screech owl pissing fish-hooks.'

Fielding took three deep breaths.

'Very well,' he said: 'Fielding's himself again. It would appear, from this evening's *son et lumière*, that somebody or something from somewhere is telling us that when certain things happen, then certain other things will happen, and that these will solve the present problem of Marius Stern. It would further appear that this solution will not be morally uplifting, and that

51

large numbers of "horsemen" will be involved. The expression, "horsemen", is, one may presume, a metaphor of some kind.'

'Why a metaphor?' Milo said. 'Several people close to Marius are known to be proficient on horseback. His father did mounted duty with the Household Brigade in London; his father's friend, Detterling, later Canteloupe, was in Hamilton's Horse, as indeed, Fielding, were you – '

' – Hamilton's Horse,' said Fielding, 'has long since lost its horses – '

' – But still had them when Detterling first joined – '

' – Dear Milo,' said Jeremy, 'you seem to have gone very well into it – '

' – I have,' Milo said. 'I find it all highly entertaining. And if I may continue:- Marius's instructor and bad fairy, Raisley Conyngham, owns a small string of steeplechasers (though he has now given them into somebody else's care) some of which he often exercised in person. Marius himself, come to that, rides beautifully. Horsemen, in short, are all about him.'

'So much so,' said Jeremy, 'that the term is otiose. Whoever was speaking to us – '

' – Purporting to be Gregory – '

' – Might just as well have referred us,' Jeremy continued, 'to Marius's friends and relations, one of whom would do *this* to another who would do *that*, and so on and so forth. The trouble is that whether or not the word "horsemen" is metaphorical, their predicted actions are certainly so. All this talk of "overcoming" and "swords" and "slaying" – what could it possibly mean?'

'Why should it not mean what it said?' said Milo.

'Don't be ridiculous,' said Fielding.

'Nothing ridiculous about it. People do get slain and overcome, even nowadays, with swords or without.'

'The general idea seemed to be,' said Fielding, 'that in whatever case there was nothing much any of us

52

could do. Perhaps that was the message.'

'But who was broadcasting it?' said Jeremy. 'A voice which resembled, and which claimed to be, that of Marius's dead father. An actor of some kind? A con man or mountebank? And what about that scene with the horses? My father has indeed repeated to me, several times, the story of the six black knights in the meadow, as told by Muscateer in India and by others elsewhere; but who on earth would think of re-enacting it? In *Ephyra*, for Christ's sake? Unless Carmilla has been arranging one of her productions – as she did in Brindisi a few months back.* She had those twins to help her then, come to that, *and* she knows some talented actors, any of whom – '

' – Carmilla,' said Fielding, 'has not been back in England long enough to arrange anything so complicated.'

'But those twins,' said Milo, 'as Jeremy has just remarked, were in on the affair at Brindisi, and they obviously know how to get this sort of show together. It could have been their work – not just leading us there but the whole production. The message given to us,' he went on, 'never mind for the moment who was giving it, was that violent horsemen *can and do kill*. There it was right under our noses. The voice then provided a gloss on the tableau, by saying that at some time in the future various horsemen of various colours would kill and be killed, and that this process would somehow solve the problem of Marius, though there was no mention of any kind of evangel or redemption. Nor, for that matter, was there any mention of any action which might or should be taken by us.'

'As I have just said,' capped Fielding. 'Let me repeat that there was an implication, at least, that we simply were not required to interfere.'

'Right,' said Jeremy. 'How very convenient.'

* See *Blood of my Bone*, by S.R. Muller; 1989

'Ghosts,' said Milo, 'or even actors who pretend to be ghosts, notoriously mislead people. Sometimes they stir up unholy trouble about nothing. This was very well known to Hamlet, and explains why he delayed so long before heeding the commands of his ghostly father. On the other hand, ghosts also frustrate and inhibit those whom they visit by counselling inaction when action is urgently needed. This could be the case here.'

'Ghosts or not,' said Jeremy, 'why should any of them bother? This food is the most disgusting I have ever tried to eat. It is, for a start, stone cold.'

'They heat it up,' said Fielding, 'then they let it get cold again, in case the heat should be harmful. That is the modern Greek mentality in one of its more obliging aspects.'

'If that production *was* the work of Carmilla,' Jeremy said, 'I should say that she was saying that she no longer wants or trusts us.'

'Rather an elaborate idiom for such a simple statement,' said Fielding. 'Have I not already told you that it cannot be the work of Carmilla, who has not had time to arrange it? Anyway, Carmilla originally co-opted you and me, Jeremy, because she most emphatically did want and trust us. What have we done to make her change her mind?'

'Nothing,' said Milo. 'Mere time would take care of that, without any provocation from you two. Women are changeable, as every single poet of any perception tells us *ad nauseam*, particularly rich women.'

'If anyone mentions money again,' said Jeremy, 'I shall take all my clothes off and have a fit. Carmilla has the constancy of a man, an honorary man, and in any case common sense and Fielding both tell us, unarguably, that Carmilla could not possibly have arranged this evening's little pageant. God knows who did or how, so we may as well pass to an answerable question: what next?'

'Carmilla is chief among Marius's champions,' said Fielding, 'and you are her first lieutenant. So *you* tell us: what next?'

Fielding, Jeremy and Milo arrived back on Zacynthos early in the afternoon of the day after their visit to the necromanteion at Ephyra. Jeremy went straight to his bedroom in their hotel (the manager of which announced that he was charging them in full for their absence) and telephoned Carmilla, who was busy with her notes on mediaeval diseases in her rooms in Lancaster College, Cambridge.

Jeremy gave Carmilla a brief, general account of what had occurred at Ephyra. Carmilla was, she said, at a total loss to explain any of it. She had not, she added, been feeling very well; a morning's concentration on mediaeval diseases had made her feel much worse; she was about to go to bed with a mug of Ovaltine. In her present view nothing more should or could be done in the matter of Raisley Conyngham until a full appraisal had been made of the likely consequences of his newly inherited guardianship of Tessa Malcolm. This development was so unexpected, its possibilities for evil (or, perhaps, for good) so difficult to calculate, that 'watch and pray' must now be the order of the hour. It was as though, Carmilla said, Raisley had suddenly been handed a rare and fragile hostage, whose vulnerability might encourage him to commit even crueller enormities or, just conceivably, move him to embrace amendment of life.

'And until his choice is clear,' said Jeremy, 'you will not be needing Fielding or me?'

'Just tell me where you are going to be,' Carmilla said; 'and if I want you I shall wire you poste restante.'

'Olympia tomorrow,' said Jeremy, 'for two days; then Corinth, for two days, Nauplion for two days, Monemvasia, Gytheion, Pylos, each for one day and a night. If still not summoned, we may extend our trip to the north: Thebes, Volos, Tempe, Thessalonika, Samothraki and Constantinople. But in that case we should warn you later and more precisely of our movements.'

'Very well,' said Carmilla: 'I've just about got all that. Now please ring off without more ado, because I'm going to the jakes to upchuck.'

Some time later, when Carmilla came back to her sitting room to tidy her notes before retiring to bed, Piero Caspar came in.

'I've been most damnably sick,' Piero said.

'So have I. It must be something we've both eaten. Not just something to cause a bilious attack; something pretty poisonous. I have been . . . racked.'

'So have I. Those gnocchi at the Sharing and Caring? Out of a frozen package that had been improperly defrosted – or refrozen?'

'*The Caring and Sharing*, Piero. I should have thought that at their prices one might have deserved fresh food.'

'No restaurant ever has fresh food these days. The staff are too sluttish. I was once given tinned tomatoes at breakfast in a five-star hotel in Kensington. Christ: here we go again,' Piero said, and threw open the window.

Since the matter which he had to communicate was both solemn and complicated, Jeremy decided that a letter to Marius would be more suitable than a telephone call.

'*Caro*,' he wrote: 'We went to your father's grave in the Jewish Burial Ground on the hill over Zante, and some rather surprising things happened.'

Jeremy then gave a full and accurate account of these.

'I'm afraid,' he concluded, 'that I understand none

56

of them. But I thought (O Marius, *animae dimidium meae*) that you should know of all this. Fielding, Milo (now definitely "ours", I believe) and I myself are now touring round the Peloponnese. We were half expecting that one or other of us would be called home by now, but as none of us has heard anything, we shall go slowly on to the north, possibly as far as Byzantium. Best love, *caro*, from Jeremy.'

Jeremy could think of no good reason for giving the details of their intended journey to Marius, but since he had promised to give them to Carmilla if she had not summoned them home by the time they reached Pylos, and now here they were at Pylos and she hadn't, he telephoned Lancaster College, gave her extension number, and received no answer from it. He therefore walked to the telegraph office near the harbour with Milo (Fielding being asleep on his bed in the Xenia Nestor). There he wired a list of places and dates to Carmilla for her information, and on the way back to dinner at the Nestor enjoyed a zestful conversation with Milo about the curious Gaian rites formerly practised on Samothraki, an island which they hoped to visit in about a fortnight's time.

Marius received Jeremy's letter while Jeremy and his friends were in a small boat on a sick-making sea, being carried to Samothraki. Marius read the letter with great care, and was filled with fear.

Like Jeremy, Marius did not understand the subterranean alarums which Jeremy reported. He had no notion who had been responsible for getting them up, or who could have been using his father's voice, or what the tedious speech about the 'horsemen' was intended to convey in practical terms.

But one thing Marius understood very clearly indeed: the white Maltese crosses on the black overmantles of the six knights boded ill. For Marius, who had loved his mother (perhaps still did) with a soft, sensual love, had honoured, trusted and obeyed his father with the steadfastness of a royal page (this was part of the reason for his later becoming so deeply attached to Raisley Conyngham: when his father died, he had overmuch loyalty to offer elsewhere); and the bond which bound Marius to his father had been the stronger for certain private codes and signals they had between them – one of which was the Maltese cross.

This particular item had been introduced into their code during an expedition to Cambridge, many years before, to see Tom Llewyllyn. When Tom had taken Gregory and the five-year-old Marius on a tour of Lancaster College chapel, Marius had been terrified by a large fissure in a box tomb in one of the chantries. After he was calmed, he confessed that he had imagined that a ghost might at any moment come sliding and hissing out of the crack; and since the crack had been just above a Maltese cross, carved in low relief, this emblem had then and thenceforth been associated by him with irrational suspicion and even terror. Ever since that occasion, if either Marius or Gregory, in writing to the other, drew a Maltese cross on the page, it signified that the news thereon communicated had (in the writer's opinion) a disagreeable and perhaps sinister connotation, whether or not this were at present readily discernible.

It was a sign they seldom used. In fact, Marius could only remember once using it himself, during a bad patch at his preparatory school, when he was being taunted and tortured by boys whom he had thought to be his friends; and he could remember only one occasion on which his father had used it – when Gregory had written him a little note of love before leaving on the journey which he was to finish nailed to a cross.

And now, thought Marius, here is some vision, of whatever origin, which Jeremy has seen, accompanied by, or at any rate immediately succeeded by, a speech in the voice of my father: and in the vision were six crosses of Malta, worn on black backgrounds by murderous knights. My father seemed to be saying, in his speech as Jeremy records it, that matters would conclude more or less well for me, if possibly in mild disgrace at least not in horror or disaster; yet surely those crosses must mean that the road before me is dark and that I shall be pursued and haunted by larvae along the way.

He yearned for Jeremy, that he might talk to him about this; he would have been glad of Fielding Gray, or even of Milo Hedley, who had once been his companion and now, after having been for long an enemy, seemed to have changed, in some fashion, to a companion once more. He longed to speak to Piero Caspar, who had been his watchful guide and tutor across Europe not many months before, and to Carmilla Salinger, his stern patron and doctor in the Art of Love: but Piero and Carmilla were far away from him, farther than any of the others, at Lancaster College, Cambridge, lying in the Fellows' Crypt.

PART THREE

Two on a Tower

We took sweet counsel together,
and walked into the house of God
in company.

Psalms of David: 55; 14

Raisley Conyngham, having completed his tour of inspection and injunction, drove without haste from St Sebastian to Boulogne, where he purchased a copy of the *Daily Telegraph* and caught the next hovercraft to Dover. On his way over the Channel he learned from his paper that the first racquets pair of the school at which he taught would be playing Eton in the finals of the Public Schools Racquets Tournament at Queen's Club that very afternoon. It was lucky, he reflected, that he had chosen the *Telegraph* from the journals available at the hoverport, as every other newspaper, including *The Times*, would have omitted this information on the ground that it was 'élitist'.

In the gallery above the racquets courts he saw, among others, Colonel Ivan Blessington, an old boy of the school who was barely kown to Raisley but now marched boldly up to him and said:-

'Ah, Conyngham. A word with you.'

Raisley bowed from the neck.

'You have been abroad, I understand, on some kind of brief sabbatical. You may or may not know, therefore,' the Colonel pursued, 'that you have been bequeathed the privilege and responsibility of acting as guardian to Miss Tessa Malcolm.'

Raisley bowed again, this time from the shoulders.

'Mr John Groves contrived to telephone me while I was in the South of France,' Raisley said. 'He had something to say of the matter.'

'Did he not mention that Mrs Maisie Malcolm's will appointed myself as financial trustee to Tessa?'

'No. Nothing, Colonel, of that.'

'Nevertheless it is so. My appointment was made in a separate and later codicil, I understand. It is possible that this was at first mislaid.'

Or later forged, thought Raisley: I had an impression that Groves was not enthusiastic about my appointment; he may well have decided to insert his own man through some legal slot in order to protect Teresa's money, or, in general, to hold a watching brief. Annoying for me: very sensible, I have to admit, of Groves. Whether the method used by him for his introduction of Blessington into this affair was proper or otherwise, there is nothing I can do about it, and so I shall accept the situation with good grace.

'We shall have a lot to discuss,' he said to Blessington, bowing a third time and placing his right hand over his left tit: 'the whole future of Buttock's Hotel to begin with.'

Ivan Blessington half opened his mouth in a cautious fashion, revealing some cleverly chipped and stained false teeth, then closed it again before smiling broadly and with candid pleasure as a long figure in black trousers and a black polo-necked sweater leaned elegantly from the verticle and applied its head to his ear.

'I have been playing tennis with the pro,' the figure said. 'He told me he had seen you come up here.'

'Theodosia: this is Mr Raisley Conyngham.'

'I have heard of Mr Conyngham.'

'Conyngham, this is Lady Canteloupe.'

'I have heard of Lady Canteloupe.'

Neither offered to shake hands with the other. There was a silence.

'One of the things I have heard about you, Marchioness,' said Raisley, 'is that you play royal or real tennis. Is that what you meant just now?'

'I play tennis,' said Theodosia Canteloupe; 'the other game should be referred to as "lawn tennis". So the game I have just been playing, with the incumbent professional, was neither royal nor real, but simply tennis. It requires the same knowledge of angles and ballistics as this game of racquets, which is now being indifferently played before this gallery, but stipulates the use of a far more cumbrous racket and a much larger and heavier ball. Most women, therefore, are not strong enough to play it – another instance of the demonstrable inferiority, in sporting matters, of my own sex.'

'But you, Marchioness, are strong enough to play it,' Raisley said. 'Is that attractive black ensemble which you are wearing the customary costume for females when they play at tennis?'

'No. Like men, we play in white. This "ensemble" is a mourning outfit.'

'But it is already afternoon.'

'Conyngham has been abroad,' volunteered Ivan Blessington; 'it is at least possible that he has not seen the newspapers.'

'Not until this morning,' Raisley said. 'When I am abroad, I leave the news to take care of itself.'

'Suppose there were a slump on the stockmarket?' said Ivan, genuinely inquisitive on this point. 'Would you not wish to hear of it?'

'My stockbrokers, bankers and agents have standing instructions against all contingencies.'

'Such people often grow careless, nowadays, if they know a client is away,' said Theodosia, who evidently shared Blessington's concern in this field. 'They resent others who are in a position to absent themselves without care, and although they do not dare to practise deliberate negligence, they are subconsciously motivated to make cretinous mistakes.'

'The last man of business who made a cretinous mistake at my expense,' said Raisley, 'whether his motive was deliberate or subconscious, finished up in prison.'

'His mistake was criminal as well as cretinous?' Lady Canteloupe enquired.

'His mistake lay in disobliging me,' Raisley Conyngham said. 'The standard of play in this contest is, as you observe, poor. It will be improved in a year or two when Marius Stern represents the school at racquets.'

Knowing that Marius, both at school and away from it, was a friend of Ivan Blessington's two daughters (as was Marius's sister, Rosie), and that Marius was both the father of Theodosia's ten-week-old baby (by arrangement of Theodosia) and the lover of her sister, Carmilla (by desire of Carmilla), Raisley now waited to see in what manner his companions would respond to the obtrusion of his name.

'It is a pity,' said Theodosia with indifference, 'that Marius has such thin legs. This, with his circumcised penis, detracts from his aesthetic appeal.'

'You seem . . . intimate with the details of his physique,' said Raisley.

'Oh yes: he was the apprentice paramour of my dead sister, Carmilla. She furnished several reports of his progress.'

'Your *dead sister*?' said Raisley.

'Yes. Her death is one of the items you must have missed by neglecting to procure English news sheets in France. It accounts for my subfusc "ensemble". Another death you must have missed was that of Carmilla's friend and colleague, Piero Caspar. They were both apparently poisoned by a dish of decaying gnocchi served to them at a Cambridge restaurant, the Sharing and Caring.'

'Sorry, Thea,' said Ivan Blessington: 'The Caring and Sharing.'

'I am very sorry to hear this sad news,' said Raisley: 'when next in Cambridge I shall eschew the Sharing and Caring at all cost.'

'The Caring and Sharing,' insisted Ivan Blessington.'

'In either case, I shall shun it. . . . Miss Carmilla Salinger was a fine scholar.'

'How would you know?' said Theodosia. 'Carmilla was an expert on mediaeval diseases. Your line, I'm told, is Latin and Greek, with particular reference to verse composition.'

'True. I have two outstanding pupils, at the moment: Marius Stern, other aspects of whom we have just been discussing, and my own ward' – high time to get this in, Raisley thought – 'Miss Teresa Mal –'

' – None of which entitles you to pass judgements, adverse or favourable, on the forensic, diagnostic or historical scholarship of my dead sister.'

Theodosia Canteloupe nodded brusquely to Raisley, smiled sweetly at Ivan, turned about with the stylish precision of an ensign at gentlemen's drill before the Changing of the Guard, and lumbered smoothly off towards the exit.

'You realise,' said Raisley Conyngham to Ivan Blessington, 'that that woman has an overwhelming and unwholesome influence on my ward and the subject of your trusteeship, Teresa Malcolm.'

'Nothing unwholesome about Thea's influence on Tessa that I know of. You want to be careful of making remarks like that, Conyngham. Unprovable accusations can constitute criminal libel.'

Raisley, unprepared for opposition, let alone rebuke, from this good-humoured and reputedly malleable ex-soldier, gave a poo-poohing pout.

'You forget,' said Ivan: 'I was appointed, by Carmilla and Theodosia, quite a long time ago, to be their liaison officer with the other partners and members of the board of their own firm, including Theodosia's husband, Canteloupe, and with particular reference to senior employees who grew too big for their suede boots – like that slimy bugger, Ashley Dexterside, whose bloody-mindedness was the original cause of my recruitment. Since then, I have come to know those two girls as if they were my own, and to have a very sharp eye for all the turds that float about on (or under) the pools of shit which they must frequently step across. I'm on their side, and I love them, and now Carmilla's dead, God bless her soul, I love Theodosia double. So I despise and abominate, Conyngham, any vile chatter, Conyngham, that may emanate from the filthy throats, Conyngham, of the likes, Conyngham, of you.'

'Commendable loyalty, Colonel,' said the dominie breezily. 'By the way, where *is* Miss Malcolm?'

'Tessa? Down at the school, I suppose. The quarter's not quite over, or my own girls would be home. Dear God, Theodosia's right about that racquets pair. The only way they could have got into this final is by rubbing off their previous opponents in the changing rooms before the game started.'

'And you think they have failed to take that precaution before this match?' Raisley enquired.

'The opposing pair today is from Eton. I expect Etonians are too grand or too fastidious to shag with our lot. Do they still call it "shagging"?'

'I believe so,' said Raisley. 'I must get down to Farncombe Hill. We shall correspond about Teresa's well being?'

'I'll come down and see you at school early next quarter. On the day of the Butterfly Match.'

By which time, thought Raisley as he drove along the Cromwell Road, I shall have done my sums and made my plans, and shall altogether be on firm ground. But I cannot really think of this blunt booby as a serious threat. Did I not hear that he went through a religious phase, not when he was fourteen, which is about par for that sort of nonsense, but well over forty? A retarded religious phase suggests something not far off imbecility. He has, of course, grown out of it, to judge him by his own judgements and the idiom in which he expresses them; and he has also, one may infer from his bombastic bluster immediately followed by his genial and fatuous obscenities, grown into the habit of lunching pretty lengthily. If religion rots the wits, gourmandry rots the guts, and in either case effective action is precluded, whether by mental or visceral liquefaction.

In a chantry off the quire and chancel of the chapel of Lancaster College, Cambridge, Marigold Helmutt knelt on the stone floor, staring at a Maltese cross sculpted on the wall of a cracked tomb, praying that she might find her twins when she resumed her search.

'In two days' time, God,' said Marigold aloud, 'I fly to Istanbul and set off down the Turkish coast. I have not tried the Turkish coast before. I have tried Greece, and all the Ionian and Aegean islands; I have tried Yugoslavia and its islands in the Adriatic Sea; I have tried Bulgaria and Romania and Israel and Egypt; but the Turkish coast – Antalya and Ephesus and Bergamos – I have not yet tried. Please, God, grant that I may come across my twins, or that they may come to me, somewhere on the coast of Turkey, among the dunes of the temples or the pine trees that border the sea.'

'Dear Marigold,' said Len, her husband's private secretary, who had appeared behind her, 'if your twins wished to come to you they would come to you here in Cambridge. If they wished you to come across them elsewhere they would long since have arranged it.'

'I thought they might come when we committed Carmilla and Piero to the crypt. It was by way of the crypt that they left us, when it was opened for Tom Llewyllyn's burial. I thought they might return that way, when it was opened once more for Carmilla and Piero.'

'Tom Llewyllyn was buried in the Provosts' Crypt:

Piero and Carmilla in the Fellows'.'

'The distinction,' said Marigold, 'is academic. The bodies went down through the same hole; the same slab was raised to receive them and lowered to secure them.'

'But their coffins slid along a ramp beneath the slab to a different resting place, a good hundred yards west of where the Provosts of the college lie.'

'Even so, it is in the same crypt. Had they wished to return to it, they could have done so. They know the way. I was about to leave for Istanbul when Carmilla and Piero died. I postponed my journey, thinking that at the funeral the twins might come back to me. Now I have bought fresh tickets and shall leave the day after tomorrow.'

'So I heard you inform God,' Len said. 'Let me repeat, Marigold: if the twins wanted to meet you, they would, without any of your contriving, without any opening or closing of crypts. You will never find them without they wish it.'

'So there is no point in searching?' Marigold said.

'I did not say that; for journeys, of themselves, are good. It does not matter whether you arrive where you intended to arrive, still less whether you find what you are looking for. There are plenty of things to find instead. You should do what the poet Cavafis advises: you should listen to voices and linger in harbours and drink exotic liquids and buy expensive perfumes. Only in the narrowest sense did Ulysses' voyage have anything to do with returning to Penelope. All accounts, even Homer's, if we are to believe the words of Tiresias uttered in Hades, agree that Ulysses very soon tired of his faithful, dreary wife, and decided to journey on – on and away from the Isle of Ithaca, far into the heart of Europe, according to Tiresias; west over the ocean and through the Pillars of Hercules, according to Dante, then south, until, after many moons, he came in sight of a conical island which, though he could not know it, was the mountain of Purgatory.'

'Did he go ashore?' asked Marigold, climbing, with Len's assistance, to her feet.

'That was not considered fitting. When he had seen the island, he sank. His soul was assigned, rather unfairly in my view, to the eighth chasm of the eighth circle of the Inferno, on the ground that he had disseminated evil counsel. But all that is beside the point . . . which is that Ulysses had his marvellous journeys, and never mind what they did or did not achieve. So go to Ephesus with my blessing, Marigold, not caring whether or not you get there and what if anything you may find . . . an attitude conducive to pleasure of the body and peace of the spirit. Did you not tell me, some months ago, that you had dreamt of your twins?'

'Yes. They were leaving a harbour in a ship, and waved to me from the poop as they passed.'

'What more could you possibly want than that? Your dream tells you that they are well and safe; that they greet you and love you; that they too have set out on a journey.'

'Do you believe in dreams, Len?'

'I believe in nothing,' said Len; 'I am therefore fully as prepared to trust dreams as to trust any other source of information.'

They passed out of the chantry into the quire and under the organ to the nave.

'Do you remember when we were lovers?' said Marigold, looking up at the sumptuous windows. 'All those years ago, when you were just a research student and such a ghastly oik?'

'Vividly,' said Len.

'You taught me some really disgusting tricks. I never could make Jacquiz do them.'

'I should hope not. They are not the sort of tricks which Provosts should practise.'

'I'll bet Tom Llewyllyn practised them.'

'Only before he was Provost,' said Len.

'I sometimes wish I had the heart,' said Marigold, 'to find someone to practise them on me again. I know you're too old and lazy.'

'Not so much that. Bored with sex. All that fuss and bother about a quick tickle – a quick squirt of what our grandparents called "jism".'

'I was wondering,' said Marigold, 'whether that appetising little boy, Marius Stern, would be interested, next time he comes here.'

'He came to see his mistress, Carmilla Salinger, or his *amico per le pelle*, Piero Caspar. Carmilla and Piero are dead.'

'Leaving the field open.'

'But now he will not come.'

'I suppose not. That beastly restaurant which killed Carmilla and Piero – have they closed it down yet?'

'No. The kitchens, on examination, were spotless, and there was good evidence they had always been so. Despite what Carmilla and Piero said before they died about the gnocchi, an autopsy revealed not the slightest sign of food poisoning. Anyway, they dined at the Caring and Sharing some days before they fell ill, let alone died. And whoever heard of anyone's being poisoned to death by gnocchi – however rotten?'

'Then what did they die of?'

'Ask me another,' said Len, looking down with pleasure at his orange and violet suede chukka boots.

When Raisley Conyngham arrived at the school on Farncombe Hill, early in the evening of the day of the racquets match at Queen's Club, he sent a servant from his chambers to fetch Marius Stern from his house and Teresa Malcolm from her Domus Vestalis.

Only Marius arrived.

'I'm glad you're here, sir,' Marius said. 'The school is breaking up tomorrow morning – three days early as

72

there's an epidemic of 'flu – and I don't know where to go. I don't want to go to my mother in the Pyrenees, because she's so horribly socialist and *teaching* these days, and I can't go to Carmilla or Piero in Cambridge because they're dead.'

'So you hoped I would put you up?' said Raisley Conyngham.

'I've got plenty of money,' said Marius, 'to put myself up. It's just a question of *where*. I hoped you might make an amusing suggestion.'

'How flattering of you. What's the matter with your family's house in London? I understood it had been kept open.'

'It was. And it still is – but only just. You see, the cook-cum-caretaker, who is a gentleman called Mavis – or Ethel or Hilda, he changes it every month – has been appointed manager – or manageress – of Buttock's Hotel, now that poor old Mrs Malcolm's dead, until someone decides what's to be done with the place. And although he's still in charge of our house in London, he can't be there as much as he used to be, which makes it rather forlorn and means irregular meals.'

'My poor boy. How ghastly for you,' Raisley said. 'But if, as you tell me, you have so much money, you could perhaps go out for your meals?'

'Rotten value, these days, eating out in restaurants.'

'A very percipient and provident attitude, Marius. One should never forget that your father was a Jew.'

'You are not being very agreeable,' Marius said.

'I shall start being agreeable again when you start calling me "sir" again – and tell me what has become of Teresa Malcolm. My houseboy went to her Domus and she couldn't be found.'

'Tessa left early, sir.'

'It seems that you are all leaving early.'

'Tessa left earlier still. Lady Canteloupe wrote to the mistress of Tessa's Domus, and said that Tessa was

73

very tired after her O levels, and could she come down to Wiltshire before the quarter ended? She also got permission for my sister Rosie, who's going there with Tessa.'

'How did Lady Canteloupe know – that Teresa was so tired?'

'Tessa rang her up and said that she was worried about her ancient history paper.'

'How do *you* know that Teresa did that?'

'Because she told me, sir. She'd already told me that she was worried about that paper, and I suppose she got into a state and telephoned Lady Canteloupe. So Lady Canteloupe arranged for Tessa and Rosie to leave before the end of the quarter – '

' – How long before the end of the quarter?'

'Today, sir. They were to take a train to Waterloo after lunch, and meet Lady Canteloupe in London this afternoon, and drive down to Wiltshire all together in Canteloupe's Rolls Royce.'

'I saw Lady Canteloupe this afternoon at the Queen's Club. She said nothing about this.'

'Perhaps she forgot . . . sir.'

'I am, after all, Teresa's guardian.'

'So she tells me.'

Raisley Conyngham bullied the fire with a poker and said:

'Still, whatever plans I may have for Teresa, keeping her away from Lady Canteloupe is not one of them.'

'I'm glad, sir. They wouldn't care for that. And what *are* your plans for – for Teresa? She will be of age in two years or so.'

'I plan to use those two years well, in her interest and ours, Marius. More of this anon. As you are uncertain what to do with yourself, you can spend the school holidays with me . . . if you wish.'

'Can we go down to your house at Ullacote, sir? And ride the horses?'

'The horses have been sent elsewhere. To Prideau

Glastonbury's stable. I thought you knew.'

'I did. I hoped they might be back by now.'

'They will never be back, Marius. Ullacote is – shall I say? – under a curse. Any creature that has been there is endangered. Lover Pie, the horse you particularly cared for, is dead.'

'Oh. Lover Pie. Oh.'

'Captain Jack Lamprey, the trainer, died some time since. Jenny, the stable lass, fell and died a few weeks ago. Carmilla Salinger and Piero Caspar – '

' – What had they to do with Ullacote?' Marius said.

'They went there, in order to make impertinent enquiries, with your so-called Aunt Flo from Burnham-on-Sea.'*

'You have not harmed Auntie Flo, sir?'

'The curse has not harmed her, Marius. Nor will it, if she minds her business from now on. But come, little Egyptian: we are men of the world: we do not believe in curses.'

'Then why did you mention this one?'

'As a manner of saying that Ullacote, and many of its connections, have been shrewdly out of luck. Reason tells us that this is sheer coincidence. And no ill luck has come to you or to Teresa, or even, so far, to Milo Hedley, although he has betrayed me.'

'Then if there is no curse, sir, surely there is nothing to prevent you and me from going to Ullacote this Easter?'

'To an Ullacote with no horses, Marius? Besides, even if there is no curse, we do not want to expose ourselves to this persistent misfortune that must now be associated with the place.'

'You just said that reason tells us that this persistence is mere coincidence. Surely, the laws of chance must prevent any more unpleasant coincidences to do with Ullacote?'

* See *Before the Cock Crow*, by S.R. Muller, Blond & White; 1986

'The laws of chance serve as a useful guide by which to calculate the odds, but they do not forbid or prevent anything, however long the odds they find against it.'

'I suppose not,' said Marius. 'Lover Pie was always winning at long odds. When I was with Jeremy at Newmarket once, years and years ago –'

Marius broke off and looked into the fire.

'What do you see in the flames . . . Marius the Egyptian?'

'I see odds longer than those against Lover Pie could ever have been. I see astronomical odds, sir. I see chains of coincidence which may extend to infinity. . . .'

'Not to infinity, Marius. At infinity, we are told, everything comes to be evenly balanced at last. However long the runs of good or ill luck may be in the world, however long the runs of *rouge* or *noir*, of this number or of that, at infinity . . . if only we could reach it . . . all would attain a strictly equitable average. Every number on the wheel would have turned up exactly as often as all the rest; all the casualties of Ullacote would have been exactly compensated, both in number and degree, by felicitous occurrences.'

'But since we never shall come to infinity,' said Marius, 'we must respect the possibility that runs of misfortune, however long already, may well stretch even longer, far longer, and on no account must we go to Ullacote?'

'Good,' said Raisley Conyngham, filling two glasses of Canary and passing one to Marius: 'you have seen to the heart of the matter. We, who live in the fickle country "beneath the visiting moon", cannot afford to think in terms of the even and frankly rather boring dispensations of infinity. We shall stay here these holidays, and you shall mind your books. If you need a change of air, we shall go for a few days to Paestum, to look at the Greek temples.'

'I once saw them with Piero Caspar.'

'When you see them again, you can reflect on his premature demise, and, by extension, on how very unwise it would have been of us to visit unhealthy Ullacote.'

March winds blew through the Great Court of Canteloupe's pile in Wiltshire, but play was possible in the Fives Court. Theodosia Canteloupe and Teresa Malcolm were playing against two brothers from a neighbouring house. The brothers were Harrovians and persistently cheated, pretending, for example, that one of them had got the ball 'up' when in fact he had taken it half-volley on the second bounce. Thea Canteloupe played in long white (real) flannel trousers, Tessa in short white (real) flannel trousers, and the Harrovian brothers in grey slacks of chemical composition and ugly texture. Since Tessa's pretty freckled legs were the only pair visible, everyone looked at them a lot, especially Leonard Percival, Canteloupe's private secretary, who had braved the cold to stand near the Fives Court, as he always did when a match was playing, to see if any succulent flesh were on exhibition. Tessa's legs weren't exactly succulent, being long and well-muscled, as she was given to many kinds of demanding sports including cross-country running; but they were certainly a sight worth braving the cold for, Leonard thought, as he listened with automatic courtesy to what Canteloupe was saying into his good ear.

'Money's getting tight,' Canteloupe was saying.

'Cant-Fun doing bad? It'll pick up when the summer comes.' Cant-Fun was the 'fun complex' in which Canteloupe entertained the public that visited his 'stately home'.

'No it won't neither,' said Canteloupe, who sometimes employed a double negative when he was vexed. 'Everybody's sick of bloody Cant-Fun. They

77

want something new.'

All this was articulated in Canteloupe's usual clear, easy tones and so was audible, despite the wind, to Rosie Stern, who was watching the fives with the two men.

'Then give 'em something new,' Leonard said.

'What do you think they want?'

'Squealing music. Writhing nautch-girls and black-amoor studs.'

'We do quite well in the tit and cunt department already.'

'These days the young want it jet black,' said Leonard. 'They want priapic bucks to be straddling over open-groin girlies with chain saws and road drills. I bet we haven't got that.'

'They'd probably like a few under-age girls as well,' contributed Rosie.

'Why not?' said Leonard. 'During the last war they had choruses of prancing ten-year-olds in variety shows and pantomimes. Everyone loved it.'

'It isn't mentioned much these days,' Canteloupe said.

'That's because we've lost our innocence,' said Rosie. 'People feel guilty if they like looking at little girls' legs. In the old days it would have been put down to paternal or avuncular affection, like letting them straddle your knee with their knickers showing. Now everyone realises just where that sort of thing can lead. And so they've all got guilty – and enjoy it more than ever when they get the chance.'

'The trouble is,' said Canteloupe, 'that whatever changes we have in the type of amusement offered, we shall certainly have to repair and rebuild. The whole place is a shambles. And if we make alterations in structure, we shall need Balbo Blakeney to come from Lancaster to re-arrange the accoustics. As an amateur architect *and* a scientist, he's a real pro at fixing things so that nasty noises inseparable from proletarian junketings do not penetrate to the private quarters. He set up Cant-Fun years ago in such a way that all the hullabuloo of the space ships and sex saucers was quite inaudible even as close as the Rose Garden and the Grave Ground. But they tell me that poor old Balbo's too ill to move, let alone start designing new pleasure parks. He'll probably be the next to join my sister-in-law in the Lancaster Crypt.'

'And I'll be the next,' said Leonard in a fit of self-pity, 'to join your ancestors in the Grave Ground here – that's if you'll let me into the place.'

'Why not?' said Canteloupe. 'I shall be having a hole here myself when my day comes, and God knows my claims are pretty dodgy. A chancy remainder on the distaff side granted by a mad king –'

' – To say nothing,' said Leonard, 'of that potty by-blow* in the marshes of the Veneto.'

' – If you're going to bring that up again,' Canteloupe said, 'I certainly shan't fit you into my Grave Ground. In any case, that boy – Paolo, was he called? – is now in an island prison in the Lagoon for the criminally insane.'

'But still the rightful Marquess Canteloupe,' huffed Leonard.

'Little pitchers,' said Canteloupe, indicating Rosie, 'have enormous ears.'

'No need to worry about me, my lord,' said Rosie, who was a very formal child in many respects. 'I shan't be telling anyone. Anyhow, the story's perfectly well known to most of your friends by now. Major Gray let it out when he was in drink. Still nothing to worry about, as nobody really believes it: a wicked young lording in exile in Venice raping peasant girls in the middle of a swamp – that sort of thing died with Dumas.'

'I'm very glad to hear it, Miss Rosie,' said Cante-

---

* See *The Survivors*, by S.R. Blond & Briggs; 1976

loupe. 'By the way, since you're a gentlewoman, you call me "Canteloupe".'

'Not "Lord Canteloupe"?'

'No. Still less "my lord". "Canteloupe".'

'With pleasure. And now, Canteloupe, what are you going to do about money? This business of reviving Cant-Fun – with or without the help of poor Mr Blakeney – is absolute rubbish *You* don't need to go on with sucking up to the Jacquerie, like Bath and Bedford and the rest. You've got a huge share in our printing and publishing firm – after all, you and my father founded the publishing half of it – and so has your wife, whose adoptive father founded the other half; and her share will be even bigger now that Carmilla's dead. So if you haven't enough to keep all this up' – Rosie lifted her arms to embrace the Great Court, the Fives Court, the Campanile – 'you go and ask Lady Canteloupe, politely of course, and I'm sure she'll give you what you need.'

'What makes you think that, Miss Rosie?'

Rosie shook out her raven hair, then gathered it about her throat against the cold.

'You see the way those two rebarbative young men are cheating Lady Canteloupe and Tessa?' Rosie said. 'It's so obvious it's pathetic.'

'But neither your wife nor Tessa protests about it. As it happens they're winning easily enough; but they wouldn't make a row even if they were losing. Quite simply, Canteloupe, they are too grand – grand in the best sense, I mean; too generous, too magnanimous. They do not wish to make those two boys look any more squalid and nasty than they look already. They pity those boys – my darling Tessa and your queenly wife. By the same token they are incapable of cruelty or meanness. That is why Lady Canteloupe will give you what you ask, always providing you are civil. And how could you be other?'

'You are cold, Miss Rosie. Their match is nearly

done. I would wish to hear more from you of grandeur and civility. Leonard . . . good afternoon.'

Canteloupe raised his brown racing trilby to Leonard, waved it to his wife and Teresa in the Fives Court, then led Rosie through a door in the wall so low that both of them had to stoop.

Ten minutes later, as Theodosia and Teresa came away from the Fives Court, having trounced the two fouling brothers from Harrow, she said curtly to Leonard, who was still there looking at Tessa's downy legs,

'Tell those boys to have a shower in the room allotted to them, and see that a liberal tea is sent up to them there. Under the circumstances, I do not wish to see them again before they go.'

She turned and nodded to the two boys, who had clearly heard every word she said to Leonard, then strode away across the Great Court; Teresa nodded a little more kindly than Theodosia to the pair, then skipped for a few paces to catch up with her friend.

'Go and change,' said Leonard to the Harrovians. 'Your tea will be coming up by the time you've finished.'

'We know,' they said sheepishly, and went on their way, in the opposite direction to that taken by Theodosia and Teresa.

One more local family we shan't be seeing again, thought Leonard as he watched the two boys slouch away. Theodosia may be too grand to raise a row, as little Rosie was saying, but she leaves no one in doubt as to her opinions.

He started towards the kitchens to order the boys' tea. Out of the kitchen door came Dobrila, carrying a white bundle at her breast. Little Lady Nausikaa, thought Leonard. Dobrila made towards Theodosia and Tessa, and began to hold out the bundle; but Theodosia merely waved perfunctorily, without stopping, while Tessa, although she turned to smile as well as wave, kept pace with the Marchioness.

So Dobrila kept on towards Leonard.

'*Dobro vece, Dobrila,*' said Leonard; '*kako ste?*'

'Well, *hvala*. And you, gentleman?'

'It is a bitter day for the very old and the very young. Lady Nausikaa would surely be warmer in a pram.'

'In my island we do not have prams. We carry our babies everywhere. I do not think the Lady Canteloupe would carry the Lady Nausikaa. I do not think she loves her enough.'

'But Lord Canteloupe loves her,' said Leonard; 'and so do you. As the world goes, she is lucky.'

'But I shall not always be here with her, gentleman. Nor will my lord, I think. What will she do for love then?'

'Doubtless she will learn, as most of us do, to live without it.'

'On my island there would always be somebody to love and to carry her. Even if all her family died (which would not, on my island, be possible) there would still be somebody to hold her and to love her.'

'This is not your island, Dobrila, it is England. Perhaps you should take Lady Nausikaa to your island. Perhaps she would be happier there than she is going to be here.'

'She would be poor there,' said Dobrila; 'here she will be rich.'

'That,' said Leonard, 'remains to be seen. *Laku noč*, Dobrila,' he said as he started again towards the kitchens.

Canteloupe and Rosie observed the events in the Great Court from a small window halfway up the Campanile.

'What do you make of *that*?' said Canteloupe, as the two Harrovians were dismissed with barely a gesture.

'You said she pitied those boys –'

' – And so forbore to humiliate them in public. That is not to say she was bound to gush all over them. Such hypocrisy would have been intolerable.'

'Hypocrisy is the necessary lubricant of good manners,' Canteloupe said. 'Was she not almost cruel, leaving them like that?'

'No, Canteloupe. Merely firm. She put them in their place.'

'I suppose so.' The window was narrow and they were very close. 'And was she putting Nausikaa in her place – striding past her like that?'

'It is just as well that she should stay away from Lady Nausikaa,' said Rosie, 'if she does not much care for her. Women sometimes kill their babies if they mislike them. I am sure Lady Nausikaa will do very well with that jolly girl from the sea.'

'I dare say, Miss Rosie. There's something I want you to enjoy. First we must go higher, to another window.'

'As high as the bells?'

'Not quite as high,' said Canteloupe, 'as that.'

When she left Leonard Percival, Dobrila crossed the Great Court and went down a passage into the Rose Garden, where there wasn't much in the way of roses.

'A bare and dreary garden,' said Dobrila, in her own tongue, to the infant Nausikaa in her arms; 'but soon, when the summer comes, it will be happier. I shall be with you, I think, at least until the summer.'

Lady Nausikaa dribbled. Dobrila put her hand in her trouser pocket, pulled out a very clean handkerchief, and wiped Lady Nausikaa's toothless mouth.

Dobrila walked on through the black bushes. To her right was a hedge, through which a path led into a meadow and along a stream to a little wood of lady birch. Since Dobrila had already been in the meadow, she now looked to her left, where was a grass bank or rampart topped by a high and handsome stone wall beyond which sprang the trunks of Aleppo pines, spreading and flattening into canopies of rifle green. Dobrila saw that there was no way through the wall (which, with the trees and the green rampart, had been designed by Balbo Blakeney to exclude both the crowds and the cacophony that might otherwise issue from Cant-Fun on the other side), and she therefore decided to go straight on.

At the far right-hand corner of the Rose Garden a small area was enclosed by a yew hedge some ten feet high. An arch cut through this admitted Dobrila and her charge to the Grave Ground, in which stood slabs of marble and occasional obelisks, all of moderate size and elegant workmanship. The dates on the stones, still clearly legible because deeply and sharply incised, began on a slab sunk far into the earth with 12 August 1680, and ended (Dobrila saw as she wandered) with an early day of this very year, 1982, on a Grecian altar erected in honour of someone called 'Gat-Toothed Jenny', a person also referred to (Dobrila recalled) on a tablet set in the wall of the Fives Court, in which she had, apparently, fallen and died.

'Why do we walk here, my darling?' said Dobrila to Nausikaa. 'It is a sad place, and the stones tell tales of mystery and disquiet. Who can be this lady with such a name as Gat-Toothed Jenny?* And now, see here: a broken column with a tall plinth, and on that plinth:

'YOU THAT PASS
THINK OF THE BLITHE BOY
MUSCATEER†
WHO SICKENED AND DIED
IN BANGALORE SOUTH INDIA

* See *Before the Cock Crow*, by S.R. Muller, Blond & White; 1986
† See *Sound the Retreat*, by S.R. Anthony Blond Ltd; 1971

AGED BARELY NINETEEN YEARS
ANNO DOMINI MDCCCCXLVI
WHEN THE KING AND EMPEROR YET
REIGNED
OVER THAT UNHAPPY CONTINENT

'FOR MUSCATEER HIS BODY
IT LIES IN THE CEMETERY OF THE GARRISON
CHURCH
OF BANGALORE
BUT FOR HIS SOUL
THE BLACK KNIGHTS CAME FOR HIM TO
TAKE HIM
AS THEY SHALL COME FOR ME AND MINE
AND ALL OF OUR NAME WHO SUCCEED ME
UNTIL THE LAST'

Having read this inscription four or five times (her English being yet imperfect) until she understood it (in so far as she ever would), Dobrila shook her head and crossed herself, clutched the Lady Nausikaa more closely to her (lest the Black Knights should come into the garden seeking one of her name) and ran with her, swift and true, until she had brought her safe to her nursery.

Canteloupe stationed Rosie by an even narrower window than the one which they had previously looked through lower down in the Campanile. Then he stood behind her, put his arms round her waist, and said:

'I think you suffer from vertigo. I can tell by the way you are trembling. Even though there are bars across this window, you fear lest you may fall from it.'

'Yes . . . my lord.'

'Canteloupe. But you feel safe, now that my arms are round you?'

'Yes, Canteloupe.'

'Now look: slightly to the left; and slightly down. What do you see?'

'I see a bay window, and through it a naked back. Auburn hair above it. Tessa. On her back is a small lump, on the right shoulder blade. When she was younger it appeared much larger: we used to make jokes about it, calling it her hump, her Rumpel Stiltzkin, and I took a delight in touching it. Now she has grown but . . . it . . . has not grown. It was, and is, the size of a large marble, no longer of consequence if ever it was. But I see that Lady Canteloupe takes a delight in it, just as I used to. Her hand has come to fondle it.'

'Her delight is different from yours,' Canteloupe said. 'Yours was just childish amusement and curiosity. Thea's is a yearning for a peculiarity of the flesh. Why are you trembling, Miss Rosie? Is it the vertigo again?'

'No . . . my lord.'

'Canteloupe.'

'No. Canteloupe.'

'Is it, then, what you are watching? The desire in action of a woman for a girl and a girl for a woman?'

'No. Canteloupe.'

'Then what is it, Miss Rosie?'

'It is desire for you, Canteloupe, who loved my father and will now love me as my father loved me.'

'But you did not desire your father? Nor he you?'

'No. One may not admit to desiring one's father, or one's daughter. But I may admit to desiring you.'

'I am an old man.'

'One may desire old men. Once the Lord God had given his permission, Lot's daughters desired Lot.'

'No they did not,' said Canteloupe: 'they merely did their duty as the Lord God commanded them, that their race might live.'

'I have seen pictures,' said Rosie, 'in which Lot's daughters are taking a delight in the matter.'

'There are other pictures in which they are not. In

86

any case, these are only pictures.'

'Many young females have desired old men,' said Rosie. 'Aurora continued to desire Tithonus even after he was old.'

'But not when he became impotent.'

'Ah,' Rosie said. 'Tessa has turned. She is standing to Lady Canteloupe as I am standing to you.' Rosie loosed the clasp of the belt round her corduroy trousers, which were an old pair of her brother's. 'Lady Canteloupe is kissing Teresa's little lump. Her hands are where yours are on me. Can they see us?'

'Perhaps. If they looked upward.'

'Lady Canteloupe is looking upward. So is Tessa. But Tessa at least can see nothing. Regard Tessa's thighs. It is as though they were melting wax.'

The cracked bell, Old Mortality, began to chime the half-hour above them. Rosie shuddered violently. Canteloupe lowered his right hand.

'There?'

'Yes. Canteloupe. And down.'

Canteloupe lowered his other hand. Rosie's thin legs jerked and kicked like a merry puppet's.

Raisley Conyngham, wearing the bottle-blue blazer of his regiment, the Blue Mowbrays, with its two ranks of four jade buttons stamped with an earl's coronet, fussed round the columns at the west end of the Temple of Hera at Paestum.

'Fluted with no plinths,' Raisley said. 'No plinths, or soccles as they are sometimes called. Archaic Doric.'

His brown-gaitered legs, tripping and twinkling, gave his lower half a look of Peter Cushing, Marius thought. His head and face, on the other hand, rather reminded one of Christopher Lee. His skull seemed to have expanded of late. No doubt about it: Raisley Conyngham was top heavy.

Marius turned to look west over a wilderness which

became a salt marsh as it approached the unseen sea. Does Raisley really believe there is a curse over Ulla-cote? thought Marius: does he really believe that this curse killed, or helped to kill, Lover Pie and Jenny and Captain Lamprey and Carmilla and Piero? When I was here with Piero, in the autumn, Piero said almost exactly the same as Raisley about those columns, though Piero didn't use the term 'soccles' and did say something about the columns being barrel-shaped. He also said, I remember, that I was an excellent companion, when I chose to be, but was lacking in charity.

'A lire for your thoughts,' said Raisley Conyngham.

Marius turned back to the temple.

'I was thinking of when I was here with Piero Caspar,' he said. 'Piero accused me of lacking charity. Do you think, sir, that the charge is fair?'

'All boys of your age lack charity,' said Raisley Conyngham; 'they have too much else to think about. I have a surprise for you. Just before we left for Heathrow, I received, *sub rosa*, an early and privileged account of your O level results. You had a distinction in every paper you did.'

'No surprise, sir. It is a very easy examination.'

'Don't be arrogant. God might be listening.'

'God knows that I am right . . . about the papers being easy. Tessa was rather worried about the ancient history, but that was because the questions were too woolly to permit of a succinct answer.'

'How did *you* deal with that?'

'I gave a woolly answer, sir, since this was obviously what they wanted.'

'But how did you impart distinction to your woolly answers, as you clearly must have done?'

'The distinction must have lain in the quality of the wool I used. Fine, clean and smooth, sir.'

'Sheer conceit.'

'Piero said, sir, that in the spring there would be asphodel in this meadow. I see none, though early

April must surely be spring.'

'I surmise that the flowers have been destroyed by polluted air from Naples.'

'This is far down the coast from Naples, sir. You don't think . . . that they withered when Piero died?'

Marius turned away again towards the wilderness and the salt marsh.

'There are some fine cypress trees here, sir, to remind us of mortality. Was Piero killed by a curse which lay on Ullacote?'

'No. I have told you. Piero was unlucky, like the rest. He was a victim of a long, unlucky run of coincidence, that is to say, of a long run of fortuitous deaths of those that had recently visited Ullacote.'

'You promise me, sir? There is no malignance here, only bad luck?'

'Turn and face me.'

Marius turned.

'You know very well, Marius, that malignance can kill nobody unless it is translated into deliberate action of a homicidal kind. No such action was observed or reported. Besides, no one bore malignant thoughts towards any of those that have perished.'

'Some of them were your enemies, sir. Or let us say that they were nuisances. You might have wanted them . . . merely as a matter of convenience, without necessarily hating them or bearing malignant thoughts towards them . . . you might, sir, have wanted them out of the way.'

'Let us stop this silly prevarication, Marius. People die when they die. For most of them, though this is not generally acknowledged, death is the greatest possible good fortune. It saves them, almost certainly, from adversity, age, humiliation, from neglect, decay, and ugly, lingering disease. Those whom the gods love, Marius, die young: that is just about all that need be said of death.'

*

When Fielding, Jeremy and Milo reached the remains of Troy, Jeremy said to Milo:

'When are they expecting you back in Trinity?'

'Mid-April,' Milo said.

'In which case,' said Fielding, 'you had better take a bus to the nearest airport and fly home. You must not neglect your education. Here is a tourist office: let us enquire of your best route.'

It transpired that if Milo boarded a bus that was leaving for Ankara there and then, he would probably be able to catch an aeroplane to England in time to be punctually back at Cambridge.

'I do not fancy the bus trip to Ankara,' Milo said.

Fielding and Jeremy made sympathetic noises. 'If you have to spend a night or two in Ankara, you will find it even nastier than the bus,' they averred solicitiously.

'Please, can't I go on with you?' Milo prayed.

'You can't afford it,' said Jeremy. 'I'm not going to pay for you for ever: it is bad for your character and my pocket.'

'Your pocket could not possibly suffer.'

'Your character could,' Jeremy said. 'And as Fielding says, you must not neglect your education.'

'If I get this bus,' wheedled Milo, 'I shan't have time to go round Troy with you. How's that for neglecting my education?'

'We must take the longer and broader view,' said Jeremy.

'There is nothing of excitement or interest to be seen here,' said Fielding, 'unless you happen to be a highly trained archaeologist. If you want the best value out of Troy, Milo, go home and read the poets.'

They got Milo's kit out of the boot of the hired car, and the three of them trailed to the point from which the bus was about to leave.

'What shall you two do now?' said Milo, almost crying.

'We shall go on to Xanthos,' said Fielding, 'unless we are summoned home by Carmilla. At Xanthos – well, we'll see.'

'Does Carmilla know your route?' asked Milo. 'And your dates?'

'I sent her a wire from Alexandroupolis,' Jeremy said, 'just before we crossed into Turkey. However ghastly the Greek telegraph, I thought, it must be more efficient than the Turkish. When you get back to Cambridge, you can tell it to her again, just in case.'

Jeremy wrote a quick list of the places which he and Fielding planned to pass through during the next three weeks. Milo glanced at it and put it in his pocket, then shook hands manfully and climbed on to the bus, which departed vibrantly, making an unusually rancid stench even for an Osmanli vehicle.

'Here's a newspaper stall,' said Jeremy. He swayed grandly and blandly towards it and levered his moon face on his pneumatic torso down over the counter. 'It has a *Telegraph* five days old.'

'Leave it there,' said Fielding. 'We've done very well without papers since we left France. Why should we want one now? It'll only be dripping with unction and cant.'

'And imbecility,' Jeremy said. 'But suppose somebody's dead or something of the kind? My father, for instance?'

'Your knowledge of it would not bring him back to life, but might well nag at your conscience, to the vexation of both of us. Give me easeful ignorance any day,' Fielding said. 'If anything really exigent crops up, Milo will let us know.'

'As I was just saying, my dear, I do not have the slightest confidence in Turkish systems of communication.'

'Don't be silly,' Fielding said. 'You talk as if the Sublime Porte was still running the place. Let us now have a look at Troy.'

'You said it wasn't worth looking at, unless one was an archaeologist.'

'Now we are here,' said Fielding, 'we had better see the bloody thing. It would be rather ill mannered not to.'

They started at the bottom of a hill which was little more than a mound, going round it anti-clockwise like Virgil and Dante on Mount Purgatory. Marigold Helmutt, who had also gone round it anti-clockwise, went out at the place where they had come in some minutes after they had disappeared round the flank of the hill. This was a pity, because Marigold was feeling very lonely and would have been grateful for the diversions which Fielding and Jeremy could have offered her.

Tessa and Rosie had a lovely time at Canteloupe's house. Whenever Lady Canteloupe took Tessa away to her bedroom, Canteloupe took Rosie up the Campanile.

They also did other things.

Canteloupe and Rosie went for long walks with Dobrila and Nausikaa, whom Dobrila always insisted on carrying.

Lady Canteloupe and Teresa went to visit 'Aunt Flo' at Burnham-on-Sea. Aunt Flo had been the aunt of Marius's dead friend, Galahad Palairet, and now considered herself to be an honorary aunt to Marius. She was hurt because Marius had not come to see her these holidays; but Tessa explained that he had been working at his Classics with Raisley Conyngham and had then gone with him to Paestum. She had had a postcard of the Temple of Hera, she told them.

'You should not have allowed this,' said Aunt Flo to Theodosia Canteloupe; 'your sister Carmilla would not have allowed it.'

'Carmilla is dead,' said Theodosia. 'Nothing has been proved to the disgrace or even to the mild discredit of Mr Conyngham. Doubtless Marius was glad of his tuition, which is the finest to be had in that line, and delighted to accompany him to Paestum. What could I or should I have done about any of that?'

'Surely, Thea, there are still several of you who are determined to shield Marius from Raisley Coyngham's attentions?'

'What attentions?' said Theodosia. 'The whole thing – this idea of a sinister threat to Marius – is now fizzling out. What do you think, Teresa?'

'I think Marius is old enough to take care of himself,' Tessa said.

'What about you?' Aunt Flo said to Tessa. 'You are to be that man's ward. Does the prospect trouble you?'

'Not all that much,' Tessa said, 'not now I've had time to think it over. I find him physically nauseating, but I do not suppose that he will touch me. For the rest, how can he bother me?'

'His house at Ullacote is under his own curse,' said Aunt Flo. 'Carmilla and Piero came there with me before they went to France. We saw the curse in action: the place was like Golgotha. Since then Carmilla and Piero have died. You too have been in that house, Teresa, and so has Marius.'

'And so have you,' Tessa said.

'It does not matter what happens to me because I am a bankrupt old woman who only gets by because of the generosity of my darling Thea here. It does matter what happens to you and Marius.'

'A lot of people have been at Ullacote,' Tessa said: 'some have died, for one reason or another, and some have not, and that is all any rational person can say about it.'

Being young, Tessa had forgotten all the noxious things that had happened to her while she was a guest at Ullacote a year before.

'What shall you do,' said Aunt Flo, 'if, despite all your bold talk, that man begins to frighten you?'

'I shall come to Thea,' said Tessa, as Theodosia touched her gently on the right shoulder blade.

'You shall of course go to Lady Canteloupe,' said Raisley Conyngham to Tessa Malcolm on the first afternoon of the new (the cricket) quarter, 'whenever you wish and whenever she invites you . . . though I think perhaps I should be told in future. But in general my guardianship of you will make no difference, Teresa, to your day-to-day life.'

They were in Raisley Conyngham's chambers, where an ample tea had just been spread by a severely clad housekeeper.

'Tea?' said Raisley. 'Scones? Egg sandwiches? Marius is particularly fond of my housekeeper's egg sandwiches.'

'I never eat, or drink, anything at teatime,' said Tessa.

'As you wish, my dear,' said the schoolmaster, helping himself to plain bread and butter. 'Now then. As to money and all that, Colonel Blessington and I will arrange things for the best on your behalf – in consultation, I need hardly add, with yourself. There is only one problem at the moment: what is to be done with Buttock's Hotel?'

'Major Gray and I must keep it, sir. Old Mrs Buttock said in her will that it must not be sold.'

'Her will . . . is hardly binding in the matter. Modern circumstances alter old-fashioned cases.'

'Her will is binding in honour,' Tessa said.

'Major Gray . . . might be glad of some ready money.'

'So might I. Nevertheless, Mrs Buttock's wish is mandatory.'

'We do not have to take any decisions just now, Teresa.'

'Nor, indeed, until I am of age, sir, when I shall

make them for myself.'

Raisley Conyngham smiled.

'If no decisions are required before then,' he said, 'none need be taken. At the moment, there is only one thing I must impress upon you. Although, as I have said, I shall not use my authority as your guardian to impose any rules upon you from day to day, I shall make one definite request for your cooperation, in one specific matter, before many weeks have elapsed. In this one case I shall require your absolute obedience. Shall I have it?'

'How can I say, sir, before I know what your request will be?'

'I can tell you that it will be simple, reasonable, and easy to comply with.'

'Some people's notions of what is simple, reasonable and easy to comply with,' said Tessa, 'are not necessarily those of others.'

'It is all that I shall ask of you, Teresa.'

'And if I refuse you, sir, when you ask?'

'It might then occur to me that Lady Canteloupe was, after all, a dangerous and corrupting companion for you, that her influence had rendered you disobliging to those set over you, and that Lord Canteloupe's house was, in any case, no place for a respectable young lady to frequent.'

'As to that, sir,' Teresa told him, 'we had better wait and see what happens when and if you make your request.'

'Yes,' agreed Raisley Conyngham in an easy voice, 'we had better do precisely that. By the way, Teresa: your O level results – '

' – Oh, sir. Are they out already?'

'Not already, Tessa. Not officially. But I am in a position to assure you that they are admirable. Particularly your ancient history paper. A starred distinction. Even Marius did not achieve one of those.'

*

As soon as he was back in his rooms in Trinity and had unpacked in his usual methodical fashion, Milo Hedley walked round to Lancaster in order to deliver to Carmilla Salinger the Turkish itinerary which Jeremy had written out at Troy.

When he came to Carmilla Salinger's door in Sitwell's Building, he found that somebody else's name was over it; he therefore went to Piero Caspar's set of rooms, near the river, where he found that the oak was sported and that there was a black blank above it where Piero's name should have been in white.

On his way back to the porters' lodge at the entrance of Lancaster, Milo met Len, the Provost's private secretary, who remembered Milo from his visit to the previous Provost during the previous summer.

'I have important news for Carmilla Salinger and Piero Caspar,' said Milo, when their perfunctory greetings were done, 'but they seem to have gone.'

'Gone to earth,' said Len.

'Dead?'

'Dead.'

'How . . . dead?' asked Milo.

'Poisoned . . . in one form or another. Most unhelpful, or so the Provost felt – the press and so on, don't you see? So he used his powers as coroner – sovereign coroner by royal grant within the college boundaries – to pronounce death by misadventure. They are buried in our crypt and no power on earth can get them out of it. So although your news can be of no interest to them, it might be of interest to me, as I am interested in news of any kind, particularly news intended for others.'

'It is simply a list of places which Fielding Gray and Jeremy Morrison will be visiting in Turkey during the next few weeks . . . in case Carmilla should want them.'

'Well she won't,' said Len, 'will she? Neither will anyone else that I know of. They may just as well go drifting on through the Levant for ever and ever, amen. They *might* meet Marigold Helmutt, who is thought to be in that area. Then they could have dinner together, for what good it would do them.'

'You seem rather morose this afternoon,' Milo said.

'So would you be if you lived in a college like this. With the exception of the Provost, there is nobody left in it who is remotely conversable. All the pleasant or amusing people are either dead, like Carmilla, away, like Marigold, or dying, like Balbo Blakeney. The rest are inorganic chemists, vegetarians or Maoists, or all three.'

'Thank God I was warned not to come to Lancaster.'

'By Raisley Conyngham, I suppose? As usual, he was right. I do not understand why Carmilla and the rest got into such a taking about his supposed influence over his pretty little moll, Marius Stern. His advice, from what I hear, is infallibly excellent.'

'Raisley is not really a very agreeable man.'

'At least – from what little I know of him – he is more entertaining than inorganic chemists or Maoists.'

'He is undeniably that,' said Milo. 'As crafty and poisonous as a viper, of course, but no one can say that either trait is dull.'

Musing on what to do, Milo decided that he would send a telegram to Jeremy c/o poste restante at Ephesus, where Jeremy and Fielding should arrive on the next day but three. He would tell them that Carmilla and Piero were dead, and that they should come home pretty soon to look after Marius's interests, since serious attention to the boy's plight seemed to be fading rapidly with the demise or absence of his supporters. The truth was, Milo suspected, that people were bored with the topic. As Marius grew, he was inclining to gawkiness, and there was even a hint of a pustule here and there. Whereas gawkiness could be seen as ranginess and so pass as not unattractive, there was nothing quite like pustules to diminish prior regard.

Nevertheless, thought Milo loyally, there is a duty here. He therefore did a sharp right turn at the Senate House, and walked across the Market Square and on towards the central post office, where he wrote a foreign cable:-

CARMILLA AND PIERO HAVE BID THIS
WORLD GOODNIGHT STOP INTEREST IN
MARIUS FAST EVAPORATING STOP MUCH
LOVE FROM MILO STOP

He would have saved a lot of money if he had been less pedantic about punctuation and had substituted DEAD for the half line from *Richard III*, but he felt that Carmilla and Piero would have enjoyed this, to say nothing of Jeremy and Fielding.

Not that they were to have any pleasure from it. The cable, by predictable inadvertency, was relayed from Smyrna to the post of tourist information (instead of the poste restante) which was a kiosk just outside the ruins at Ephesus. The man in charge of the kiosk consulted friends, who could make nothing of any word save MARIUS, which they misconstrued as MARIA. They therefore opined that there was some import of infidels in all this; and the kiosqueur, though not a very enthusiastic Moslem, felt that here was a safe and easy chance of securing favour with Allah and used the cable as rear bumph (a rare commodity in Ephesus), conscientiously improving the occasion by applying Milo's message strictly with his left hand.

'Dearest Mummy,' wrote Rosie to Isobel, who read the letter to herself while sitting in the Café Albigeois in the main *place* of St-Bertrant-de-Comminges,

Tessa and I had a very happy stay in Canteloupe's

palace (for it is no less) in Wiltshire. Tessa played Eton Fives a lot with Lady Canteloupe. At first they played against two boys from Harrow, who lived nearby, but later on they taught some of Canteloupe's peasants' sons to play with them instead, as the two boys from Harrow turned out to be very common and cheated rather a lot. Canteloupe said that most boys from Harrow behave like that so it was silly to invite them in the first place.

Canteloupe and I went on lots of walks with the new baby, Lady Nausikaa Sarum, and her nanny, who is a funny girl from Yugoslavia, in rolled-up trousers, called Dobrila. Dobrila likes Canteloupe a lot. So do I. Sometimes we went up his Campanile, to hear the chimes strike right above us, which was more exciting than I would have thought possible.

I think Canteloupe is having worries about money. Apparently Cant-Fun, his stately home apparatus, is old-fashioned and doing badly. I heard him telling his private secretary, Leonard Percival, about it. Mr Percival didn't pay much attention, as he was concentrating on Tessa's legs. Mr Percival looked *hungry* for legs. I think he would even have looked at mine, only I was wearing Marius's old cords.

But whether Mr Percival heard or not, Canteloupe was saying that he was short of money. I told him he ought to have enough, one way and the other, and that if he didn't Lady Canteloupe would give him some, as she is very rich in her own right, owning goodness knows how many of the shares in our printing and publishing business, and now all her dead sister's as well.

He is so super, Canteloupe, that I'd gladly give him some of my money, but I really can't think that that will be necessary.

Now we are back at school, and Tessa has been to see Mr Raisley Conyngham, the Classics master, who is her new guardian. Some people think Mr Conyngham is too worldly and has a bad influence on Marius. I think he is just rather silly and pathetic – but of course silly and pathetic people can be quite as dangerous as worldly or wicked ones. Tessa says that Mr Conyngham says that he will make no attempt to interfere with her personal affairs, provided she will obey him in one important matter the nature of which he has not yet disclosed. I wonder what *that* can be? Tessa says there is no point in worrying about it until he tells her what it is. She says it is certainly nothing sexual, as Mr Conyngham is sexless, and that it cannot be to do with money because Colonel Blessington is her financial trustee.

Myself, I think it will probably turn out to have something to do with Marius, but it is hard to imagine what, as Marius will do whatever Mr Conyngham asks without any additional pressure from Teresa. And what else could Mr Conyngham want of her?

Love to Jo-Jo and Jean-Marie and especially to Oenone.

Love from Rosie.

'If you ask me,' said Jo-Jo Guiscard, after she had been allowed to read the letter, 'Rosie has got a pash on Canteloupe.'

'Better him than some silly young boy,' said Isobel. 'Canteloupe will know exactly what if anything to do with her, and the thing will be quite harmless.'

'I thought,' said Jo-Jo, 'that in your adopted role of socialist you disapproved of Peers of the Realm?'

'The fact remains that Canteloupe will know how to manage Rosie.'

'I wish,' said Oenone, 'that somebody would read

Rosie's letter to me.'

'Ah,' said Jo-Jo: 'at last she is beginning to stop referring to herself as Oenone and to use the personal pronoun.'

'Oenone is very hurt,' said Oenone, 'that Rosie did not come here last holidays but went to stay with Canteloupe.'

'You must get used to that kind of disappointment,' said Jo-Jo.

'I thought Rosie loved Oenone.'

'She does. But she has other things to fit into her life.'

Oenone thought about this.

'Then from now on I shall have other things too,' she said.

'That's the spirit, girl,' said Isobel.

'She's really becoming quite intelligent,' said Jo-Jo. 'I see I shall have to take more interest in her from now on.'

'I'm not quite sure, Mummy,' said Oenone to Jo-Jo, 'that I shall be able to fit you in. Isobel has always been much kinder to me than you have.'

'At this rate it will soon be time,' said Isobel, 'to send her to school in England . . . as you've always wanted.'

'I've always wanted to be rid of her,' said Jo-Jo, 'if that's what you mean. But now,' she said, lifting Oenone on to her knee and kissing her for the first time since she was born, 'she's beginning to be amusing. I wanted a boy, but there's no doubt that girls can have piercing insights.'

'She must be given things to learn and tasks to perform,' said Isobel severely; 'otherwise her mind will atrophy.'

'You yourself said that no proper school in England would take her as a boarder until she was at least eleven. Between the two of us we can surely educate her until then. The main thing is that she should learn to read and write.'

'Don't go getting any fancy ideas,' said Isobel, 'about Oenone.'

'I'm her mother when all is said,' said Jo-Jo, kissing Oenone again.

'Better ignore her, as you have always done, than devour her . . . if only with kisses.'

'It is rude to talk of me in this way in front of my face,' Oenone said.

'Another valuable lesson,' Isobel told her: 'all women behave immoderately in matters of emotion.'

'I should prefer nobody to behave immoderately in the matter of me,' said Oenone. 'I shall now walk down to our church and talk to poppa Jean-Marie. He will not behave immoderately. I shall walk there alone as I know the way.'

'Your father is busy,' said Jo-Jo.

'If he is busy,' said Oenone, jumping to the ground, 'then I shall just sit there with him.' She skipped to the door of the café and turned. 'That will be very restful,' she said. 'It is never really restful with you two, or even with Rosie. But with Jeremy it was restful, and it will be with poppa.' She opened the door and was gone.

'The brush-off,' said Isobel, 'for both of us.'

'She is quite right,' said Jo-Jo: 'women as idle as us are a pain in the neck. So are men, come to that. Jean-Marie has something to do, knows how to do it, and does it. So Oenone finds him restful. Perhaps we should both have a hobby.'

'We have each other,' Isobel said.

'Not enough, after all this time.'

'Educating Oenone could be a hobby. Your suggestion. We both have a lot to offer.'

'Yes,' said Jo-Jo. 'I still wish Oenone was a boy. I should have so much more to offer a boy. But I suppose one should make the best of what is to hand.'

'You had better be quite clear from the start,' Isobel said, 'that we are talking about what we have to offer,

102

not about what is on offer to us.'

The first important cricket matches of the season were the School 1st XI v. the Butterflies CC and the Girls' XI v. Benenden, both matches being played on the same day. The 1st XI played on 'Green', below an elegant terrace at one end and above a toy valley at the other; while the Girls' XI played on 'Harlequin's', a small, rectangular ground which was flanked on three sides by Surrey pines and overlooked on the fourth by a statue of the Founder, who had been a Jacobean crook. The two grounds were separated only by the Old School Chapel, which was now a medical and psychiatric complex, and a lawn, in the middle of which was a fountain on top of which was the Founder who had a shapely leg under his hose and carried (if only by courtesy of the sculptor) a rapier at his left hip and a dagger at his right.

'He had himself written "esquire" on the strength of his enormous profits,' said Raisley Conyngham to Ivan Blessington.

'I know,' said Ivan Blessington, who was an old boy of the school.

'Most people think he was a knight,' said Raisley. 'The Headmaster wrote of him as such in the last number of the school magazine.'

'Did he?' said Ivan, who was looking for his two girls, Jakki and Carolyn, who would be playing, with Tessa Malcolm, for the Girls' XI on Harlequin's – and here they came now, all three, and loitering just behind them little dark Rosie, clutching the score book. How pretty they would look if they all curtsied, thought Ivan, the cricketing girls in their short white skirts, and Rosie in her inappropriate kilt. (Girls were not allowed to wear trousers, let alone their brothers' old cords, while they performed an official function such as scoring.) But of course, Ivan thought, girls do

not do anything as decorative and subservient as curt-
sying these days. Nor did they. What they all four did
was to kiss him heartily instead; after which they
bowed coolly to Raisley and went on their way to the
pavilion, which resembled a log cabin.

'I suppose Marius Stern is playing for the First
Eleven on Green?' said Ivan.

'Yes,' said Raisley. 'He made a hundred before
lunch.'

'But the girls' cricket match is afternoon only? God, I
wish one of my girls could make a hundred before tea.'

'I think,' said Raisley, 'there is only one thing we
need discuss in the matter of Teresa's money. Do you
propose to sell Buttock's Hotel?'

'Tessa does not wish it.'

'Then what will she have for ready money?'

'Her share of the takings of the hotel, which is
almost everything that comes in after running ex-
penses have been met and after taxes. Fielding Gray,
who owns the other half of the hotel, has long since
settled for the use of a suite, and full board and service
as and when he requires them.'

'It would be nice for my ward,' said Raisley Conyngham, 'to have some liquid capital.'

'Mrs Malcolm also left her about a hundred grand in
blue chips and ten grand in a deposit account. I do not
think, Conyngham, that there is any present need to
sell the hotel. Tessa is keen to respect old Mrs Buttock's wishes.'

'What are Fielding Gray's wishes?'

'Fielding won't starve,' said big, bluff Ivan, 'as long
as he has Buttock's to retreat to.'

'He might like some ready money,' Raisley said.

'Fielding always likes ready money. It is best that he
should not have it. If he really needs it, he can sell his
house down at Broughton Staithe.'

'I don't think he'll do that,' said Canteloupe, who
had come up behind them. 'That's where he writes his

104

books.'

'He hasn't been writing many just lately,' said Ivan Blessington.

'Then he'll have to start,' Canteloupe said. 'He must be in pretty low water by now. Time to do some work, instead of swanning around Asia Minor with Jeremy Morrison. He sent me a postcard of the Blue Mosque, by the way. I wonder he can even afford the stamp.'

'Jeremy Morrison will probably see him all right if he's short,' said Theodosia Canteloupe, as she came up after her husband. 'They're pretty thick.' She started clapping as the opening pair of the Benenden XI (the Captain of which had won the toss) came to the wicket.

'This is not,' said Raisley Conyngham, 'a committee meeting about the welfare of Fielding Gray. It is a discussion, between Colonel Blessington and myself, to determine what will be in the best interest of my ward, Teresa Malcolm.'

'Point taken,' said Canteloupe; 'we'll go and talk to Rosie in the scorers' box, Thea.'

'You go,' said Theodosia. 'I shall remain here, as I have one or two things to say to Mr Conyngham about his ward, Teresa Malcolm. . . .'

Marius Stern, out soon after lunch for 117 and thinking that it would be at least an hour before he must take the field, decided that he would go to watch Tessa's match on Harlequin's for a while. As he rose from his deck chair by the boundary, the Captain of Cricket threw him a 1st XI cap. He put it on, amid applause, walked round the boundary and up on to the terrace, then round the west end of the medical and psychiatric complex and on to the lawn – to cross which was one of the privileges of a Major Blood, a title that came to him with his 1st XI cap.

When he saw Thea Canteloupe, who was standing

with Raisley Conyngham and Colonel Blessington on the far side of the Founder's statue, he backed off quickly and entered the complex by the north door into what had once been the narthex of the Old Chapel. Then he realised that he could not avoid Theodosia in this way, no matter how ungracious her behaviour had been towards him before the birth of their daughter, Nausikaa, nor how churlish his had been towards her soon after it. He came out, crossed the grass, removed his cap as he approached the group, and bowed with his head only, as to the Queen, to Theodosia Canteloupe.

'My lady,' he said, bending to kiss her hand; and then to the two men: 'gentlemen.'

Canteloupe stood behind Rosie and the Benenden scorer in the little scorer's box at the end of the pavilion.

'Scoring is torture,' he said. 'I promiose not to say a word.'

Nor did he. He merely placed his hands on Rosie's shoulders, knowledgeably applauding and tutting over the play. Rosie, eyeing the Benenden scorer, nearly burst with love and pride, until the Benenden scorer, a snub-nosed girl with blonde hair cut like a boy's, said in a sharp voice:-

'My two brothers came to play fives at your house, Lord Canteloupe –'

' – Say "Canteloupe" –'

' – And they were snubbed by your wife. I shall now go and score in another part of the pavilion.'

Which she did.

'Ah well, Miss Rosie,' said Canteloupe, easing his hands gently down Rosie's body, 'we can do pretty well without her.'

*

Marius, having been sincerely congratulated on his Colours by Theodosia, Colonel Blessington and Raisley Conyngham, sensed that, though much admired, he was *de trop*. Having kissed Theodosia again (this time on the cheek, a privilege readily accorded to a new Blood) and smiled at the two men, he replaced his cap and proceeded slowly along the boundary towards the log cabin pavilion. Rosie and Canteloupe, in the scorers' box at the far end, did not see him coming; but luckily he went behind the pavilion to have a pee in the pines, and then, hearing distant applause from beyond the medical and psychiatric complex, realised that the School XI had declared earlier than he had expected and therefore started running back over the lawn, from which Theodosia, Blessington and Conyngham had now vanished, towards Green, doffing his cap to the Founder as he ran.

Ivan Blessington, having settled for the time being with Raisley that nothing need be done about the selling of Buttock's Hotel, took a seat on a bench on the boundary of Harlequin's, as far as possible from the pavilion since he wanted to watch his two daughters and Tessa in absolute peace. The bench, he noticed as he prepared to sit, had Jeremy Morrison's name carved on the bar at its back. He waved distantly to Canteloupe and Rosie in the scorers' box, and they waved distantly back, Rosie with her left hand and Canteloupe, a few seconds later, with his right. He then settled down to watch, gently whistling 'Rory Gilpin' between his teeth, trying to remember the name of the familiar tune and when he had last heard it.

The Marchioness Canteloupe was shown by Raisley Conyngham into an ugly little room at the east end of the Old Chapel.

'This is the personal relations laboratory,' said Raisley Conyngham. 'Boys and girls are allowed to sit here together, holding hands and talking of love. They fill each others' heads with a great lot of nonsense. What did you want to say to me about Teresa?'

'She tells me, in her letters, that you do not intend to interfere with . . . her personal relations . . . with me, provided she obeys you absolutely in one other matter. What is that matter, Raisley Conyngham?'

'I shall require her help with a cherished plan, Theodosia Canteloupe.'

'What plan?'

'It is quite harmless from your point of view. Teresa's part will be simple and easy. There is no need whatever for you to know about it.'

'And yet,' said Theodosia, 'she tells me that there is a heavy sanction should she refuse.'

'Let us then trust that she will do no such thing.'

'But if she should refuse, you would keep her from me?'

'Yes,' said Conyngham. 'You might find that quite a lot of people disapprove of marchionesses who seduce schoolgirls. To say nothing of allowing schoolboys to get children on them because their husbands are too feeble.'

'I see now,' said Lady Canteloupe, 'what old Florence meant. I was beginning to think that Carmilla and the rest were absurdly exaggerating your . . . ill offices . . . and so I told Florence. I owe her an apology. Good afternoon, Mr Conyngham.'

A little later, after Theodosia had left Raisley Conyngham, she walked to the log cabin pavilion on Harlequin's, where she was met by Canteloupe, who was just then emerging from the scorers' box, lest his being too long alone in it with Rosie should cause comment on the cricket ground. Without saying anything, Theodosia took her husband by the arm and started to walk him very slowly along the boundary towards the bench on which Colonel Blessington was still sitting.

'Before we reach Ivan, old girl,' said Canteloupe, 'I want a very brief word in your ear.'

'Speak, Canty.'

'Money is running low,' Canteloupe said.

'So I had supposed.'

'If things get too tight, you will pass over some of yours? Rather a lot of yours?'

'I shall assist you to my last penny, Canteloupe.'

'That's my good girl. Not but what I knew already. Rosie said you'd say something of the kind.'

'You have been consulting Rosie?'

'She overheard something.'

'Very sharp ears and eyes, that little girl,' said Theodosia.

'She wasn't prying or eavesdropping. I was talking too loud to Leonard – when you were playing fives that day. Rosie was watching too. She just said that you'd give me what I wanted because she knew you were a brick.'

'How did she know?'

'Because Tessa had told her, and because of the decent way you behaved about those two Harrovians – not showing them up in public when they were chizzing. Their sister is here, by the way.'

Canteloupe turned back towards the pavilion and indicated the hawk-nosed girl with the short blonde hair, who was now rejoining Rosie in the scorers' box.

'An improvement on her siblings.'

'And loyal to them,' Canteloupe said. 'She wouldn't sit in there with me because my wife, she said, had snubbed her brothers.'

'I never snubbed them, Canty.'

'You packed them off pretty sharpish after the game. . . . I'm glad you'll be a brick about money, Thea, like Rosie said you would be.'

'There will be a few conditions – let us say, suggestions for sensible economies. About those I shall be telling you later.'

'When?'

'When I have thought about the matter,' Theodosia said.

'Have a nice time with Canteloupe?' the Benenden scorer said, without any malice, to Rosie.

'A nice time?'

'It was pretty obvious. You could hardly sit still from the moment he came in. That's why I left you two alone. Not because her ladyship high-hatted my silly louts of brothers, but so that you and Canteloupe could have the place to yourselves.'

'That was very kind of you. We did have a pleasant talk.'

'Canteloupe said there wasn't to be any talking. Scoring was such torture, he said. But as long as you kept your book straight. . . . '

'Oh yes. I kept it straight. Canteloupe was a very keen cricketer, you see. He played for this school for a start. Someone once told me that he cut the ball later and finer than any man in England. He would have played for his county – for his country, perhaps – if it hadn't been for the war. So he was watching all the time,' babbled Rosie, 'and when I made a mistake, he put it right.'

'Like there?' said the girl, leaning over Rosie's scoring book and pointing to a line of Quink which wavered, wobbled, and then ran straight off the page. 'You be careful. You're still throbbing a bit.'

'The new bowler at the far end is called Carolyn Blessington,' Rosie said.

Canteloupe and Theodosia sat down by Ivan Blessington just as Carolyn started to bowl. Ivan would very much have resented the arrival on his bench of anybody else, but he adored Theodosia (quite apart from having been made a rich man by her patronage) and he had served in the same regiment, and for a time in the same squadron (though much the junior), as Canteloupe; so these two, of all the world, he was very glad to see.

Carolyn's first two balls (off-breaks) were swept over square leg's head for four. The third ball kept straight on and toppled the batsman's leg stump.

'That's my good girl,' Ivan Blessington said.

The three of them on the bench clapped happily, while Carolyn stood bashfully by the umpire, waiting for the next batsman to come in.

'What did that brute, Conyngham, have to say?' said Ivan to Theodosia. 'Do you think he'll keep on banging away at me about selling Buttock's Hotel? I know Tessa's against it.'

'In so far as he does go banging on about that,' said Theodosia, 'I think it is because in that respect and most others he is genuinely anxious to do his best for Teresa. Thus he is very keen, she tells me in her letters, that she should have enough ready money and not be wholly dependent on her income from the hotel.'

'I put his mind at rest about that,' Ivan said.

'But over one thing,' said Theodosia, 'he is getting ready to turn nasty. He has some plan, he tells me, in which he has allotted a simple but essential role to Teresa. This plan is harmless from my point of view and Teresa's – or so he assures me – and her part in it is an easy one. But if she should disoblige him in this matter, he will keep her from me.'

'Why should she disoblige him?' Canteloupe said.

'He refuses to say what the plan is; but one thing is evident – that he envisages the possibility that Teresa might refuse to assist him. The plan itself, therefore, must be shady, and he himself must be in doubt about the propriety, from Tessa's point of view, of her co-optation.'

'But if the plan is harmless – ' began Ivan.

' – Why is he keeping it secret?' said Theodosia.

'For the same reason, perhaps, as one keeps an agreeable surprise a secret,' Canteloupe contributed.

'Perhaps,' conceded Theodosia. 'But why, if the thing is agreeable, is he afraid lest Teresa should reject her role in it?'

'The role could be in some way burdensome even if the plan itself were designed to bring happiness.'

'Teresa would never refuse drudgery or boredom,' said Lady Canteloupe, 'if they were a necessary condition of bringing good to another. But when was a plan of Raisley Conyngham's ever designed to bring good to anybody?'

Carolyn's first over had ended without further incident. Her second brought two wickets, both clean bowled, in the first two balls.

'Conyngham is well known as a superb teacher,' said Canteloupe when they had finished clapping the second wicket. 'That way he must bring good, and plan to do so.'

'Do you mean that he gets good examination results for his pupils,' said Ivan, 'or that he lights a fire in their breasts which will not be put out?'

No one really knew the answer to this, for it was a question that required a lot of notice. All prudently said nothing, until,

'I wonder whether Carolyn will get her hat-trick,' Theodosia said.

But even as she wondered, the Captain of Benenden, a high and spindly girl with a fierce, pocky face, stalked out of the pavilion waving a declaration, and the girls left the field slowly and sedately, as at the command of a Priestess of Mysteries.

*

A few minutes later, Jakki, Carolyn and Tessa, wearing the pink blazers of the Girls' XI (conferred, out of deference to their sex, on invitation to play, not fought for and awarded, like Marius his cap), came walking over Harlequin's, all in line.

'Tea. Tea, tea, tea,' they said.

Jakki and Carolyn took one arm each of their father, and Tessa took one of Theodosia's. Canteloupe could have taken the other, had not Teresa and Theodosia moved off together too deftly, leaving Canteloupe spare.

But only for a moment. Soon came Rosie and the hawk-nosed girl, to claim him.

'I'm sorry I was rude about your wife,' said the hawk-nosed girl. 'Rosie will explain to you later.'

The order of march was now as follows: Theodosia and Tessa in the lead, then Canteloupe, Rosie and the boyish Benenden number, and Blessington with his daughters (who had loitered over family photographs) last. They all made for the terrace above the 1st XI ground, because tea for the Girls' XI was to be served in the 1st XI pavilion on the far side of Green (there being no room for refections in the log cabin by Harlequin's) before the 1st XI and the Butterflies had theirs, which would not be for another half hour.

As Canteloupe and his chums came along the terrace, the Captain of the School XI, which was now fielding, held up his hand to suspend play, came up the steps from Green to the terrace, took off his cap, and said to Canteloupe:

'You are Lord Canteloupe.'

'Pray, sir, call me "Canteloupe",' Canteloupe replied.

The rest of the 1st XI, both batsmen and both umpires, and the Butterfly men who had been watching on the boundary came up the steps after the Captain of the School XI.

'Canteloupe,' said the Captain, a round and laughing boy called Robert Oliver, 'that was once called Detterling; who many years ago made 222 on this ground. We have often heard of it from the Senior Usher, who died last year, and there is a plaque in the changing room, recording that you are the only boy who ever made a double century on Green in a school match. And so now . . . Canteloupe that once was Detterling . . . we ask that you will walk across Green with us, you with the two ladies you have on your arms, and the other ladies and gentlemen of your company.'

The School 1st XI and the Butterflies made a half circle behind Canteloupe and his friends, and walked with them across Green to the 1st XI pavilion, gently clapping as they went. Then Canteloupe said, 'Thank you, gentlemen; I shall remember your courtesy', and led his party into the pavilion for tea, while the cricketers replaced their caps and ran back on to Green at a smartish pace, in order to make up for lost time.

Raisley Conyngham had observed this scene from a bench halfway down a long row of trees which began just below the terrace. It gave him nothing but pleasure, as he approved of this kind of compliment when paid to the old, the distinguished, and the noble. The Headmaster, who was sitting with Raisley, did not approve, as he was not only progressive but meanminded with it. What a good thing, thought Raisley, that this time next year this disagreeable man beside me will be at Brydales. Brydales was a crank school, at which, oddly enough, Raisley himself had been educated, somewhere in the West Country; and Raisley knew, though his companion and Headmaster did not, that he (the Headmaster) had been chosen from the short-listed applicants to take up the 'Eldership' of Brydales from the following September. Had the telegram service still operated, the Headmaster would already have known this himself; but as it was he had been sent an express letter (the Brydales telephone line having been cut by one of the many delinquent pupils) which he would receive, with a bit of luck, next morning.

How then did Raisley Conyngham know of this decision?

He had bribed several members of the selection board, with whom he had been acquainted since his school days in the place, to ensure precisely this result, some ten days before.

Money well spent, Raisley was now thinking; rather a lot of money (it was amazing how avaricious the alumni of high principled establishments like Brydales could become) but unquestionably well spent, had it been four times the figure. This sanctimonious and prying fool will be out of the way by the beginning of next Oration (Michaelmas) quarter. Why any man (Raisley thought) should wish to be 'Elder' of Brydales, rather than Headmaster of this ancient and civilised school, must pass rational comprehension; but so it is, and it suits my purpose well enough. If all goes to plan, I shall be in a position to have the medical and psychiatric complex (*and* the personal relations laboratory) dismantled before next Christmas, and an attractive museum devoted to pagans, apostates and heretics (with a particularly enticing presentation of Catharism) set up instead.

When Jeremy and Fielding reached Xanthos, Jeremy said:

'Very odd that Carmilla hasn't sent us a single word all this time. Do you suppose that Milo forgot to tell her which places we were going to?'

'No. Milo is much too keen on sucking up to forget to deliver a message.'

'Of course you're right,' said Jeremy, 'though I wish you wouldn't put it so balefully. . . . But if she knew where we were going to be, she might have sent us a nice, *newsy* letter, even if she didn't want us, just to keep us in touch.'

'Perhaps she hasn't got any news for newsy letters,' Fielding said; 'or perhaps she's too busy with her mediaeval diseases.'

'Isn't that Marigold Helmutt over there, getting on that bus?'

'I don't know,' said Fielding. 'I was just looking at this tomb. The inscription says that the incumbent was a witch who gave birth to triplets at the age of seventy-four.'

'Are you sure you've done the Greek arithmetic right? Damn. That bus has gone. Now we shall never know whether or not that was Marigold I saw.'

'Does it matter? You were right about the arithmetic. I read *hepta* for *hexa*. She was only sixty-four.'

'I think it *does* matter,' said Jeremy, 'about Marigold. I think her appearance is a sign from the gods that we ought to go home.'

'Why?'

'Because we associate her with England.'

'But you're not even certain that it *was* Marigold.'

'Whoever it was made me *think* of Marigold.'

'Obviously you're going to give me no peace,' said Fielding, 'until I agree with you. So let's go home. I am getting very tired of Turkish food. How shall we go? We're rather out of the way here in Lycia.'

'Dump the car for collection, take a ferry to Cyprus, and then fly.'

'Suits me,' said Fielding. 'After all, you're paying. Can we go to the Castle of Buffavento, in the Kyrenia Mountains, before we catch our plane from Cyprus?'

'Why do you want to go to Buffavento?'

'Many years ago I spent an interesting afternoon there,'* Fielding said. 'I don't remember it too clearly

---

* See *The Judas Boy*, by S.R. Anthony Blond; 1968

now, but I do remember that it was absolutely breath-taking. If I retrace my steps, I may recall just what I found so exciting ... and find out whether it still excites me.'

'Well, and why not?' Jeremy said. 'Marigold or no Marigold, I don't suppose the gods are so urgent that a day or two makes any difference.'

Raisley Conyngham and Giles Glastonbury sat together behind the dedans of the tennis court at Lord's, watching a spry but elderly member play with the junior pro.

'Bloody boring, this,' said Glastonbury.

'Not as boring as the cricket. And much warmer. Anyway, I've got something entertaining to tell you.'

'What's that going to cost me?' said Giles Glastonbury.

'A word or two in somebody's ear when the time is ripe.'

'Well up, Mr Kark,' called the junior pro.

'Kark; unusual name,' said Glastonbury, who was beginning to go to pieces and was now unable to concentrate on one thing for very long. However, he still enjoyed a good intrigue, in fact it was about the only thing he did still enjoy, so Raisley was letting him in on this one partly to do him a kindness (for Raisley could be kind) and partly because Giles could be of real if marginal assistance.

'Listen carefully to me,' prompted Raisley, 'and you will hear something to your advantage.'

'That pro just called a hazard chace wrong,' Glastonbury grumbled; 'can nobody get anything right these days?'

'Listen to me,' repeated Raisley in a soft, comfortable voice. 'For some time I have known that the Headmaster of my school has been hankering to go to somewhere else more modern and trend-setting.'

'Your place is bad enough in that way,' said Giles. 'Those damned girls all over the place.'

'Girls are nothing these days,' Raisley Conyngham said. 'Really trend-setting schools have pygmies, heroin addicts, pregnant twelve-year-olds, and homicidal teenage rapists. My man is going to a relatively moderate one, Brydales, where they are wary of the addicts and the rapists – though reputedly tolerant of vampires.'

'Vampires, Conyngham?'

'A new affliction, recently the subject of a celebrated television programme. Quite ordinary children suddenly wake up one morning and start chewing each others' throats in a manner that ranges from the affectionate to the severely injurious.'

'If I were your man, I wouldn't care for that. Don't know where you are. Better a homicidal rape, and done with it.'

'However that may be,' said Raisley, '*going he is*, and that pretty soon, and I propose to replace him in the headmastership myself.'

'Surely that will interfere with all the things you enjoy – like teaching the Classics and taking long sabbaticals?'

'There will be compensations for that. You should know, Glastonbury, that I am gradually assembling . . . a special community of deeply committed people to serve certain of my ideas and purposes – '

' – A sort of private intelligence network? – '

' – You might call it that – '

' – Max de Freville used to have one. Damned expensive.'

'But not so expensive,' said Raisley, 'if you recruit your rank and file from the adherents of a religion or sect which has some very special appeal for them, and convince them that by serving you they serve the sect. Then they come quite cheap. And the whole business becomes positively economic, as well as far more efficient, if you procure your officer corps, Giles, from some well found and wealthy organisation, Giles, such as a major public school. You then have leaders who are largely self-financing, as they are either affluent by birth, or well placed in profitable professions, or both.'

'Ahhhhh,' said Giles, loving this: 'So you propose to choose some of the more suitable lads and lassies from that school of yours –'

' – Rather a lot of them, I hope; then give them special treatment and training, for which I have one excellent prototype already: Master Marius Stern. I had hoped for Milo Hedley and Teresa Malcolm as further shining examples and fuglemen, so to speak, of my methods. But Milo has gone off the rails and Teresa rebelled almost from the start. But Marius I absolutely possess –'

' – And if once you have control of the school, there will be many more Mariuses?'

'Right,' Raisley Conyngham said.

'But first, old man, you've got to get yourself made Headmaster.'

'Right,' Raisley Conyngham repeated. 'Now, I have here a list of members of the governing body. Some will respond to a direct gift of money, others to suitable kinds of flattery, others again to recommendations in my favour from highly placed and connected people, such as yourself' – for although Glastonbury was deteriorating mentally, he had quite a long way to go, was a distant cousin of the Monarch, and would so remain however far he went.

'Call me when the time comes.'

'Thank you, Giles. But there is one great big buzzing bluebottle in this delectable ointment. I refer to Luffham of Whereham.'

'Peter Morrison as was? Young Jeremy's father?'

'Peter Morrison as was. Young Jeremy's father. He mistrusts and dislikes me very much indeed, and has great influence in the affairs of the school. A distinguished and ennobled old boy, he was recently paid the highest honour which the school can offer to one of its alumni: he was arrayed in the purple gown of honour as *Honorabilis et Honoratus*.'

'Some schools,' said Glastonbury, who had been at Eton, 'don't half give themselves silly airs.'

'The fact remains, Glastonbury, that Luffham of Whereham is greatly *honoured* by and at the school of which I wish to be Headmaster. He will do and say everything he can to prevent the appointment. He will be followed, heard, and obeyed. Therefore my first step must be – '

' – To rub out Luffham of Whereham.'

'Don't be so coarse and offensive, Giles.'

'We'd have thought nothing of it when I was serving with Special Intelligence in India.'

'Luffham of Whereham is *white*, Giles, and a Peer of the Realm. He cannot be . . . rubbed out . . . like some babu.'

'Just after the war, we settled the hash of several princes and maharajahs who were being difficult.* Surely a brown maharajah counts as high as a white life baron?'

'All that is necessary, Giles,' sighed Raisley Conyngham, 'is to *dishonour* Luffham of Whereham. He has been gowned, and incidentally enthroned, by the school as *Honorabilis*. Now it must be firmly demonstrated that he is not.'

'I s'pose that'll do the trick. How shall you arrange it?'

'His son, Jeremy. Not a respectable person.'

'Everyone knows that already. Jeremy was in quod in Australia.'

'That,' said Raisley, 'was not, nor will be, enough to dishonour his father. Lots of peers' sons go to prison

* See *Sound the Retreat*, by S.R. Anthony Blond; 1971

120

every day for dope.'

'Jeremy went to prison for buggery.'

'No. For making an immoral proposition; and anyway that was in another country which is known to consist of yobs and philistines, and where even the judges have comic accents. No one will give Jeremy's conviction in Australia a second thought, Giles. But they will give it a first thought, and this will tell them that he is not quite the thing. I have that on which to build an engine of infamy powerful enough to bring even Luffham of Whereham into the dust.'

'Tell.'

'In the course of his career, Jeremy has been the lover of Carmilla Salinger and could have been the lover of Piero Caspar. Both of them are dead – not of food poisoning, as was originally thought, but of some unknown cause. I am going to have it put about, in a few weeks' time, that they committed suicide by overdose because they found that they were infected with this new and incurable sexual disease . . . the one that comes from America, or from Africa, nobody seems certain of its *genesis*, though they do know its immediate cause, which is sodomy active or passive. So. I am going to have it put about, I say, that Salinger and Caspar did their own *quietus* make because they were infected with this disease by Jeremy Morrison, who is now generally recognised, though never convicted, as a sodomite – and who still lives to spread the infection. And at the same time it will also be put about, Giles, that Luffham of Whereham has been using his power and influence to have the whole thing – the infection *and* the suicides *and* the loathsome part of his son Jeremy in all this – *to have the whole thing*, Giles, hushed up and buried, deep down and for ever.'

'I see,' said Glastonbury, with admiration. 'But you will require at least a modicum of evidence to support your story.'

'Marius Stern. Another lover of Carmilla, a close

friend of Piero, and from childhood an idoliser of Jeremy. He is in a position to report on things he has seen and heard, things, he will say, that sent him post, post haste to Doctor La Soeur, who was mercifully able to report that in his case there is no sign of infection. (As it happens, he has recently been to La Soeur for a general check-up, so that part of the story is as true as it needs to be.)

'Now, the fact' (continued Raisley Conyngham) 'that Marius himself is so far safe does not, of course, prejudice the credibility of what he claims to have seen and heard. Nor need his utterance be specific. My purpose is to stir up a poisonous miasma of RUMOUR, Glastonbury, not to present chapter and verse.'

'Marius, I am told,' said Glastonbury, 'very much loved Carmilla and Piero, and, as you yourself say, idolises Jeremy Morrison, never mind his prison sentence. Marius will never consent to spread such a story, in however vague a version, and however hard you try to persuade him.'

'No,' said Raisley, 'he will not.'

There was a long pause.

'That will do for today, Mr Kark,' from the junior tennis pro. 'Your game's coming along nicely, sir.'

'Teresa, often known as Tessa, Malcolm,' Raisley Conyngham said, 'is now my ward.'

'The more fool poor old Maisie.'

'Nevertheless, Teresa is my ward. Teresa has known Marius from a child. She is, although she doesn't yet know it, Marius's half sister. There are two ways at least in which *she* could persuade Marius to do my bidding.'

'Proceed. Two ways at least, you said.'

'I'll tell you about the two I have in mind when I decide which one of them to use. Nothing like a little suspense to hold one's audience, Giles. I'll tell you how I shall require Teresa to proceed at the same time as I tell you whom to talk to when recommending me for the headmastership and what to say to them.'

'Very well,' said Glastonbury, looking into the black tennis court, which appeared to him (just for a moment) like a huge tomb waiting for a monstrous cadaver. 'Just one more question. Whatever it is you want Tessa to do, in order to make Marius sing his dirge of death by Eros, how can you be sure – *can* you be sure? – that she will do it? She don't like you, Conyngham, not one bit.'

'If Teresa does not do as I ask her in respect of Marius, I, as her guardian, shall prevent her from ever again seeing Theodosia Canteloupe, whom she worships with her whole soul and her whole body.'

Giles Glastonbury shuddered.

'Ever again? She will be free of you in two years.'

'By the time she is of age, she will not wish to see Theodosia Canteloupe . . . or to be seen by her. *Verb. sap. sat.*, as the grammar books have it.'

Giles Glastonbury shuddered again.

'What makes you think,' he said, 'that I shall keep this to myself?'

'Because of two or three dainty tales I wormed out of Doctor La Soeur . . . about your private habits and their consequences . . . the most untidy of which he used, on occasion, to clear away for you.'

'La Soeur has always hated you. He would tell you nothing.'

'Now Doctor La Soeur has retired,' Raisley said, 'he finds, as others do, that he has sadly miscalculated the amount of money required for *otium cum dignitate*. In the circumstances, he is prepared to put aside his former distaste for me providing I come bearing precious gifts. But you need have no fear at all, Giles, of *your* being dishonoured, so long as you keep my confidences and speak as I shall ask to your friends and relations in the matter of this headmastership.'

'Which is so important to you that if necessary you will make these heartless and horrible demands of

Marius and Tessa?'

'I have not yet told you precisely what I shall demand of Teresa.'

'You have told me the penalty you will impose if she refuses. That is enough to be going on with. By the Prophet, Raisley, though we did some atrocious things in Special Intelligence in India, we were lily-white boys, "clothed all in green-ho-ho", compared with you.'

As Fielding and Jeremy climbed winding steps and then walked along a track towards the eastern gate of the Castle of Buffavento, Fielding, who had envisaged the visit as a feast of memory, began perversely to think of money instead.

He had done little serious work of late. He had long ago spent every single penny that he had had from Canteloupe in return for 'exercising his discretion' about Paolo Filavoni, the orphan hobbledehoy from the marshes near Oriago, who could, if properly informed and supported, have claimed Canteloupe's coronet; and now Fielding's quaint honour prevented him from demanding more. Or again, some time since he had raised a considerable sum from Ptolymaeos Tunne for the sale of some 'curious' documents that had to do with the scabrous Venetian antecedents of the Filavoni business; but almost all of that was gone, and Ptolymaeos, from whom he might have wheedled a further fee *ex gratia*, was now dead of a surfeit of laughter for more than twelve months.* There was no question of it, he told himself, as Jeremy and he walked across a stone court and under an arch and then into the refectory of the castle, no question at all: once back in England he must either set himself to work again, or raise a large loan, preferably interest

* See *Before the Cock Crow*, by S.R. Muller, Blond & White; 1986

124

free, from Jeremy, on the strength of his holding in Buttock's Hotel.

This despondent sequence of thought was interrupted by a cumbrous nudge in his left lung from Jeremy's pudgy elbow and a low but querulous rebuke from Jeremy's huge, round face.

'Since it was you that wanted to come here,' Jeremy complained, 'and since we have delayed our journey home by three days in order that you should, you might at least pay some attention to this castle and to me.'

So Fielding raised his head and paid some attention to both. Out of the windows to the left and south of the refectory he saw a vertical drop to the car park, and below that a long sweep, first almost sheer, then merely steep, then gradually gentler and gentler, of wooded mountainside, which at last subsided on to a coloured plain. From the windows to the right, he saw trees and stones descend in a cascade to a narrow belt of shore, against which lay a blue, still sea.

'That was what excited me last time,' he said to Jeremy. 'We are on the spine of the ridge. Where we are standing, the Crusaders stood, far from England and far from Jerusalem, and longed for home. But there is something else; I know there is something else.'

They went through the refectory, along a gallery which ended with a sharp right turn into a brief, dark corridor and then down a narrow, plunging staircase. At the bottom of this they emerged into a grove of pines, in the middle of which was a tiny garden of dingy flowers and surly shrubs. Through these a path led crookedly to the end of the garden, where, in a plot of yellow grass just under the encircling pines, were two upright slabs and a box tomb.

Fielding backed away. 'We should not have come,' he said; 'I should not have persuaded you to come. I remember this place now.'

'Rather pretty,' said Jeremy: 'shabby, yet pretty.'

'That tomb. Bad joss.'

'What sort of language is that?' Jeremy said.

'I once had a friend – I still have, I suppose – called Leonard Percival. He was a soldier and a spy and a lot of other things, all over the world. That was his phrase: "bad joss". Chinese, I think.'

'Meaning bad luck?'

'Meaning much more. Meaning an evil influence that clings. Once you are infected with it, as I was by that tomb, the bad joss clings, defiles, corrupts ... consumes.'

'Then let us turn round and go away from it.'

'It may be too late. Now that I have seen it again.'

'There is some writing on it. The characters are Hebrew, I think. Shall I –'

'NO. Turn, as you say. Turn and walk.'

'How long did the bad joss cling last time?'

'For many weeks.'

'But on that occasion you went closer, I think. .... Evidently it is not lethal.'

'No. It just creeps over you like a film of pus, making you so slimy and filthy and miserable that you can think of nothing else.'

'What finally gets rid of it?' Jeremy said.

'In my case, last time, an act of human charity performed by another towards me.'

'Then I shall have to see what I can do for you in my way,' said Jeremy lightly as they went back through the refectory, 'if needed. Incidentally, old thing,' he continued as they descended the steps to their taxi in the car park, 'do you know who or what was in that tomb?'

'A Graeco-Cypriot-Jewish schoolboy, who had been ripped in half by EOKA terrorists.'*

*

* See *The Judas Boy*, by S.R. Anthony Blond; 1968

Tessa Malcolm came down to Green to watch the 1st XI at practice in the nets. When they were done, she raised her arm to Marius, who joined her presently.

'Sad news,' Teresa said: 'Thea writes that Canteloupe is ill. *Anno Domini*, she says.'

'*Anno Domini*? But Canteloupe is not an old man as these things are reckoned nowadays.'

'I know. She means wear and tear, I think.'

'Wear and tear?' said Marius. 'He saw hardly any action during the war – or so his friends have hinted. He was under no great strain in the House of Commons. My father did almost all the work in their publishing firm, Stern and Detterling. What is all this . . . wear and tear?'

'Guilt for a wasted life – and a selfish one. Canteloupe has not done an action which he can be proud of since he made his double century on this ground in the Thirties. Even his cricket came to very little.'

'He is said to have cut the ball finer than any man in England.'

'As often as not straight into the hands of first slip. Theodosia says,' said Tessa, 'that he played some county matches when he was in the Army before the war, but only a very few after it . . . and in either period made no real impression. He was too flashy – so Thea's father used to say – too inconsistent, even at his best artistic rather than effective. . . . And once he was in Parliament, though he was not, as you say, under much of a strain, he could only get away for club matches at weekends. Anyhow, by then he wasn't asked to play in anything better.'

'And so now he is a sick and disappointed man?'

'The collapse of Cant-Fun hasn't helped.'

'Theodosia will give him money.'

'He would sooner have his own. That . . . celebration . . . he received during the Butterfly Match – it was like a last gift of the gods before the shades began to gather.'

'It is too soon to say that, Tessa. He may very well recover.'

Marius started to walk across Green towards the wicket at its centre (his privilege as a Major Blood) and invited Tessa to walk with him.

'There is another problem,' Tessa said: 'Rosie has become infatuated with Canteloupe. Who is to tell her?'

'Tell her what?'

'That Canteloupe is sinking. "Sinking" was one of the words which Thea used in her letter.'

'You, as her friend, must tell her.'

'Not you as her brother?'

'Brothers should have nothing to do with sisters' infatuations. You tell her, Tessa. Please.'

'Very well, Marius.'

'Shall you go down there at half quarter, you and Rosie?'

'I do not know. Theodosia has said nothing about that. The house is very sad, she said. The old man, Leonard Percival, is visibly decaying. In the Campanile, the crack in Old Mortality widens daily and makes the chime more and more harsh . . . malignant. Canteloupe lies in bed, and the men about the grounds neglect their work, shaming and wasting the gifts of summer.'

'Could not Theodosia see to that?'

'Theodosia is grieving for her sister.'

'She seemed all right,' said Marius, 'when she was here for the cricket.'

'Often people do not take in the finality of death until days or weeks have passed. Only then, perhaps, do they recall how they ignored or hurt the dead person, and feel the hideous remorse that must come when one can no longer beg or earn that person's forgiveness. I know, Marius: my mother died in January: I am now tortured that I cannot soothe, explain, make up. Prayer is no use; one yearns to speak to the dead, not to God. The only cure is love.'

'Then surely . . . you and Theodosia might cure each other.'

'I doubt it. I must tell you, Marius: Theodosia has begun to fall in love.'

'How can you tell?'

'There is a girl from an island in the Adriatic – she came to take care of Nausikaa. When we were there, she was Rosie's friend rather than mine. Rosie and Dobrila – that is her name – went on walks with Nausikaa. Canteloupe, who loves Nausikaa, usually went with them, but he would tire with walking, and would rest at some convenient point while they went the long way round. Thus Rosie was often alone with Dobrila – not counting the infant Nausikaa – and they became close. Now Dobrila has written, with what little skill in English she has, to ask Rosie's advice. It seems that Theodosia is now . . . making up . . . to Dobrila, who does not understand what is happening. She is a very simple girl, you see. So what is Rosie to tell Dobrila? And what am I to tell Rosie about Canteloupe?'

'If it is any comfort to you,' Marius said, 'Theodosia is probably seeking distraction from grief . . . and from the cruel remorse you have just described to me.'

'It is of no comfort, Marius.'

'I suppose not. I do not know what anyone is to tell anyone, Tessa. "Thou woulds't not think how ill's all here about my heart."'

'"Nay, good my lord,"' said Tessa softly, taking Horatio's part in the exchange and touching Marius's arm.

'Raisley Conyngham is up to something,' Marius said. 'I do not know what. He is glittering with excitement. I know that whatever is to happen will involve me. He spoke me fair and spoiled me during the holidays: now I shall have to pay.'

*

129

When Jeremy Morrison arrived home at his house near Luffham in Norfolk, the front door was opened by the 'Chamberlain', an ancient and interfering family servant, who, for the first time since Jeremy could remember, uttered nothing save a bare and formal greeting. When Jeremy attempted (for he was fond of the old man) to engage him in talk, the Chamberlain grunted and led Jeremy straight to his father.

'Ah, Jeremy, dear boy,' Luffham of Whereham said; 'two things have cropped up in your absence. First, your little spree abroad has cost you four fifths of the money which I handed over to you, some time back, when making over the house and the estate. It seems that you left the brokers without instructions in the event of emergency. They will acquaint you with the sad details.'

There was a long silence, while Jeremy shuffled about.

'The land is still ours?' said Jeremy at last.

'Just. Secondly, I have seen fit to procure a place for our Chamberlain in an alms house in Norwich which grants easy admittance to old soldiers.'

'But why, Father? This will break his heart.'

'It is, as you will soon discover, a necessary economy. His keep was substantial; his depredations from household supplies – or what should have been household supplies – positively criminal. He is lucky to get off with an alms house in Norwich.'

'Couldn't you have sent him back to Canteloupe? He was Canteloupe's soldier servant, you remember, and it was Canteloupe who recommended him to us.'

'Having been away, you will not know that Canteloupe is in no position to start taking on extra staff. Canteloupe himself is ill, Theodosia is stricken by the death of her sister –'

' – CARMILLA, sir? – '

' – Carmilla, sir. There, too, is need of economy and no need of one more thieving house servant.'

'What did Carmilla die of?'

'Nobody appears to know. Her friend, Piero Caspar, died at the same time – '

' – Oh. Oh. Is anyone left alive?'

'Yes,' said Luffham of Whereham. 'I am for one, and you, sir, for another; and so you'd better settle down to some hard work and close supervision of the estate . . . which is just about all we've got left.'

Tessa Malcolm and Rosie Stern were sitting on the boundary of Harlequin's, on the same bench that Ivan Blessington had sat on during the girls' match versus Benenden. Today there was no match of any kind; but it was a pretty and peaceful place in which to converse.

'But what has Canteloupe actually *got*?' Rosie was asking.

'A bad fit of depression, to say nothing of guilt.'

'About anything . . . in particular?'

'No. About his life in general.'

'Ah,' said Rosie, somewhat reassured. 'No good worrying then,' she went on sensibly. 'Meanwhile, what am I to tell Dobrila? About Theodosia's advances? It appears that ladies never behave like this on the island of Vis, and poor Dobrila is absolutely at sea . . . so to speak. I think the best thing would be to write to Marigold Helmutt, who first brought Dobrila to England.'

'Marigold is on her travels,' Tessa said. '*You* will have to cope. Tell Dobrila that in civilised countries ladies often fancy other ladies and enjoy a bit of physical contact . . . which sometimes goes deeper than mere contact. If ladies masturbate on Vis, she will know what you mean.'

'I shouldn't think ladies *do* masturbate on Vis, should you?'

'No. How silly of me,' said Tessa, 'to suggest that

131

they might. No doubt they are too busy carrying babies about and gutting tuna fish.' Jealousy was not improving Tessa's character. 'Look,' she said. 'Tell Dobrila that in England milords and miladies have the absolute power of ordering common girls like her into their beds. Then perhaps she'll panic and bolt and leave the field to me, once again.'

'I think you might be a little more charitable,' Rosie said. 'Dobrila is very fetching – with those rolled-up trousers and everything.'

'Whose side are you on?'

'Darling, darling Tessa,' Rosie said: 'I'm on your side now and for ever. I shall tell Dobrila exactly what Theodosia will try to do to her, and since she is a simple innocent sea-girl she will be very shocked and go straight home to her mother. So tell me, darling Tessa: to judge from your experience, what *will* Theodosia try to do to Dobrila?'

When Fielding Gray had parted sadly from Jeremy at Heathrow, he went to ground in his suite at Buttock's Hotel, and waited for Jeremy to let him know how much money he could 'lend' him without interest or inconvenience. When Jeremy, funking the telephone, sent a letter which said that he couldn't 'lend' Fielding anything at all, and explained the dreariness of his new circumstances, Fielding was very put out, mostly because he was sorry for himself, but partly, to be fair, because he was sorry for Jeremy too.

After he had read Jeremy's letter, he sent for the acting manager (ess), the transvestible M/S Hilda Geddes.

'Good morning, Hilda,' Fielding said.

'Good morning, Major Gray, darling. I've decided to be *Missis* Lucretia Geddes, divorced, from now on. Hilda is, after all, rather plebby. Lucretia is serious and sombre, conferring and conveying authority, and the status of divorceé will give more credulity to my role.'

'Remember that Lucretia was raped,' Fielding said. 'If anyone starts raping you and gets as far as where your cunt ought to be – '

' – Don't be coarse, darling. Do you think I ought to have the operation?'

'No. It would leave you with a nasty little slit which is no good to anyone. If you have the operation, I shall see to it that you are sacked.'

'Still so masterful, darling. Now, what did you want to see me about?'

'First, to congratulate you on the way you seem to have managed the hotel in my absence. Secondly, on a simply delicious dinner last night – I gather you still do a lot of the cooking yourself. And thirdly, to ask whether you have talked with Miss Tessa Malcolm.'

'Yes, darling,' said Geddes. 'She came in for a word on her way back to school . . . quite a while ago now.'

'Is she thinking of selling her half of the hotel, would you know?'

'She assured me she wasn't. She said old Mrs Buttock hated developers and all those sort of crap, and nothing would make her sell Buttock's.'

'Good for Tessa. But the trouble is, Hi – Lucretia, that I need money. My half of the hotel is potentially worth millions, but if Tessa won't sell her half, bless her heart, I can't sell mine.'

'You can live here for nothing,' Lucretia said.

'As I grow older, I more and more detest London. Full of terrorists and foreigners and whores.'

'Getting faddy, are we, Major Gray?'

Geddes had been the Squadron Barber of the 10th Sabre Squadron, when Fielding was Captain Commanding it, of Hamilton's Horse (Earl Hamilton's Light Dragoons). This was a regiment which had permitted very frank exchanges between all ranks, so long as everyone knew and kept his place.

'Getting poor, sweetheart,' Fielding said.

'You've got a house down at Broughton Staithe by the Wash, someone told me, where you write your heavenly, rubbishy books.'

'Yes.'

'Go and live there, then, for a time anyway. I'll lend you my savings, if you're short. For years I've been living quite free in the Sterns' London house as caretaker. Thanks to lovely Marius, I was – and still am – very well paid for the job. I've got plenty of money, O Captain, my Captain. Take what you wish. *Res Unius Res Omnium*, as we used to say in the old days.'

Fielding started to blink and sniff a bit.

'Come along, darling. No waterworks in front of Lucretia. But as you see, I do remember Captain Gray, leader of the Tenth Sabre Squadron, who looked like Hermes – if occasionally rather red in the face. And now that Major Gray has no face to speak of, and only one little pink eye, and a slit of a mouth (like what I should have between my legs if I had the operation), and is as gross (not to mince the matter) as Silenus, he still commands my loyalty and my love.'

'Thank you,' Fielding said. And then, pulling himself together, 'There is no immediate urgency for me to decide anything. But I shall not forget your offer . . . Lucretia. Rather a good name, I think.'

Lucretia rose, kissed Fielding on his scaly forehead, adjusted her grey skirts, which reached to the floor, and then moved towards the door as if on castors.

Tessa was in the school chapel, praying that Canteloupe might recover his health and that she, Tessa, might recover Lady Canteloupe's love.

'Please, God, let her still desire me, as I desire her,' Tessa prayed.

Raisley Conyngham sat down beside her.

'I have had a letter from the Marchioness Canteloupe,' he began. 'She asks me, as your schoolmaster and your guardian, that I should obtain special leave for you to go to her in one week's time and stay for some while, to help her with her little daughter. I gather that she had a foreigner for a nanny, who has now, suddenly, gone.'

Her prayer in part answered already.

'Why in a week's time?' she said. 'Why not now?'

'Because Lady Canteloupe and the child must go into hospital. There are some minor surgical adjustments to be effected on both of them, as a result of lesions caused by the rather irregular manner of the birth.'

'Nothing serious, sir?' Raisley shook his head. 'You promise me, sir?' Raisley nodded. 'Then why has she not written to me?'

'I believe she has – about the visit to the hospital. You should have a letter about that tomorrow at the latest. As to this other matter – well, to take you out of school for an indefinite period in the middle of the quarter is obviously an unusual and difficult proceeding, and she felt, quite rightly, that I was the person to deal with that.'

'You will let me go, sir? My O levels are done with, and I can easily catch up with my work for A levels later.'

'And your cricket?'

'Not as important . . . as some other things.'

'Then of course you shall go, Teresa – on one condition.'

'Sir?' said Tessa, still on her knees.

'In some five days' time, Teresa, I have an important request to make of Marius Stern. It is possible that he will accede to it immediately, in which case you will hear no more of the matter. But if he does not, I shall be compelled to ask you, Teresa, to teach him his manners and enforce his obedience to me.'

'And this, I suppose, is the "simple and easy" task of which you warned me? The task I must perform on

135

pain of my being forbidden to go to Theodosia Cante-loupe?'

Raisley Conyngham nodded gently.

'What do you want of Marius, sir?'

'That need not concern you,' Raisley Conyngham said. 'All that concerns you is to compel him – should compulsion prove necessary – to obey me.'

'And how am I to compel him?' Teresa said.

'By threatening to make public the criminal be-haviour of his father Gregory, whose memory he adores.'

'What criminal behaviour?'

'Do you not remember,' said Raisley Conyngham lightly: 'how Gregory Stern used to come to you in the night sometimes . . . when you were a child staying with Marius and Rosie? The house was large, and all the children in it had their own bedrooms, which made it easy for Gregory to visit you. How you dreaded those visits! How you longed for them! For Gregory was very kind and gentle with you. He didn't hurt or rape or rip you, he just fondled you to the point of delight . . . and encouraged you to fondle him. Perhaps you did not need much encouragement; after all, you were an inquisitive child. But in any case, however much you enjoyed Gregory's attentions, and however willingly you reciprocated them, there can be no doubt that it was he who tempted you, defiled your innocence, took advantage of your precocity.'

'Gregory Stern is dead,' said Tessa.

'Yes indeed, Teresa. Nothing can harm him now. That is why your task is so easy. You will say to Marius, "This is what your father did to me when I was a child. I think, now, that certain others should know if it, Marius," you will say: "not only you, but your mother and Rosie and many other people who admired him – Major Fielding Gray and Lord Cante-loupe, for example. It is wrong that they should vener-ate his memory as they do." And Marius will say, "I loved my father and love him still; please do not tell people those things about him, Tessa." And you will say, "Nor shall I, Marius, if you will only do what Mr Conyngham requires of you."'

'But I should have been lying to Marius, sir. Gregory Stern was always wholly courteous towards me in every particular.'

'Precisely. That was why you enjoyed his visits so much. Please do not be naive, Teresa.'

'If I told Marius this wicked tale, it would ruin his image of his father, and it would make him hate me.'

'You may not have to tell him anything. If he consents to do what I shall ask him, without further ado –'

' – And if he doesn't, and if I try to force him by this blackmail you describe, and if he *still* refuses to do what you ask?'

'Then you will have done *your* part in good faith, Teresa, and you may go to Lady Canteloupe, to help her with Lady Nausikaa, for as long as you are needed.'

'And what shall you do to Marius?'

'That need not concern you,' Raisley Conyngham said.

'When will you tell me whether or not I must deceive Marius in this horrible way?'

'As I have told you, Teresa, I shall put my request to Marius in five days' time. If he is . . . compliant . . . you will hear no more of this; if he is not compliant, I shall come to you immediately. But if I have not come to you by six in the evening five days from now, you will know that Marius and I have been able to agree, and that you may join Lady Canteloupe, without further discussion with anybody, on this day week.'

Raisley Conyngham and Giles Glastonbury met for dinner, by Glastonbury's invitation, and in Glastonbury's second London club. (The first was much grander, which was why he used the second when engaged in seedy intrigues.)

'Well?' said Glastonbury greedily. 'What have you to report?'

'I have lit the fuse,' said Raisley.

'Excuse me,' said Glastonbury. He rose and hurried out to the lavatory. When he came back, he said:

'When do you want me to start doing my bit? Talking to people?'

'Very soon now. Very soon indeed. I had an especially good opportunity to bring pressure to bear on Teresa Malcolm, and I took it. I am now confident that she will make Marius do what I require of him – should he prove reluctant.'

'Tell,' said Glastonbury, who wished to savour every drop of pleasure in the matter.

Raisley told.

'You said that you had thought of *two* ways of using Teresa to compel Marius,' Glastonbury persisted. 'What, as a matter of interest, was the other? – Wait till I've had a pee.'

'Have you thought of having an operation on your prostate?' said Raisley when Glastonbury returned.

'No. What was your second idea for dealing with Tessa Malcolm?'

'Under threat of keeping her away from Theodosia for ever – as with the scheme I am actually using – I was going to order her to seduce Marius. What she doesn't know and Marius does is that she is his half-sister – got on old Maisie Malcolm, when in her prime as a whore, by Gregory Stern on an uncharacteristic night out while Isobel his wife was in hospital. I should have kept Teresa in ignorance of this during the period of seduction, and later made her pretend to Marius that she was pregnant – which for that matter she well might have been. Marius, thinking he had made his half-sister pregnant, would have been rather desperate, I apprehend. I should then have offered to tidy up the entire mess – provided Marius was malleable.'

'What a swine you are. Why *didn't* you do it that way in the end?'

'It would have taken so much longer. Seductions and pregnancies and that kind of carry-on – weeks and weeks. As it is, I expect to get Marius to start spreading the word – '

' – About Jeremy Morrison contaminating his lovers and causing those suicides,' said Giles with glee, 'and about Luffham's hushing the coroner up – '

' – I expect to have Marius blurting all that round the place in only a few days. Then, when Luffham is no longer in a position to speak against me as candidate for Headmaster (or even a little earlier), I shall give you details of what to say *for* me and to whom to say it.'

Glastonbury chuckled in a senile fashion and went out to the lavatory. There was a large patch of damp, Raisley noticed, round the crutch of his companion's trousers. Well, Raisley thought, at least I've given him some pleasure, and if he lasts a week or two longer he will still be a useful supporter – at any rate when sober and continent, i.e. between nine a.m. and noon. I do not think I shall be seeing much of Giles Glastonbury, here or elsewhere, once I have become Headmaster of the school.

Canteloupe lay supine and sweaty on his huge canopied bed as the cracked bell from the Campanile chimed midnight. The door was opened from outside and Leonard Percival came in. Behind him Lady Canteloupe, stiffly and awkwardly carrying the infant Nausikaa, stalked into the room and towards the bed, while Leonard closed the door and then followed.

'Both Nausika's operation and mine have been successfully completed,' Lady Canteloupe announced, 'so

I have brought her home.'

'Three days early, Theodosia?'

'In the end she only needed a tiny skin graft.' Theodosia lifted the baby's robe and showed her father a small and very white patch on the left thigh. 'It was little more in my own case.'

'I'm delighted to see you both,' said Canteloupe feebly; 'but isn't this rather an eccentric hour for a home-coming?'

'I was going to wait in the nursing home until tomorrow morning. But then I decided I couldn't stand the place a moment longer. Even though it is a private affair for private patients, the nurses behave as if they were somehow set in authority over one. They never come when you ring the bell, they infallibly disturb you with some trivial piece of routine just when you are comfortably settled to your book.'

'Well: I am pleased to see you both,' murmured Canteloupe: 'we have matters to discuss.'

'If you say so, Canteloupe; but I'm tired of carrying the child.'

'She handed the baby to Leonard Percival, causing him to drop his stick, which she picked up and hooked on to one of his arms. 'Take the child to the night nursery, Mr Percival. I'll join you as soon as possible.'

Theodosia opened the door. Leonard hobbled out, glancing briefly back towards Canteloupe; his long hooky nose, as so often at times when he was amused, seemed to penetrate with its tip the ill-shaven cleft in his chin. Nausikaa, who appeared to be content with the arrangement, nestled her head into his shoulder.

'Thank God,' Theodosia said when she had closed the door, 'that Teresa will be here to help me with that child in three days' time. I think I can just bear it until then. I know you love Nausika, Canty –'

' – Nausikaa –'

' – And for your sake I'm prepared to do my best for her. I shall sleep these next nights with her until

Teresa comes, and then Teresa and I will sleep there in the night nursery until a proper nurse is found by the agency. But if that's not pretty soon, I shall telephone old Florence at Burnham-on-Sea and make her come and take a turn. Now then: what did you want to discuss?'

'Money,' whispered Canteloupe.

'Simple. You shall have what you need to keep this place going – on two conditions. The first is that you get rid of your private secretary.'

'Leonard? Why? You've just entrusted Nausikaa to him.'

'He is perfectly trustworthy. He is also odious. He's a *memento mori*, a death's head.'

'Not the only one round here,' said Canteloupe.

'Don't talk such rubbish, Canty. As for Percival, you can pension him off comfortably enough in one of those retreats for elderly gentlefolk. Or there are old soldiers' homes – there's a famous one in Norwich, where ex-officers, as I must presume Mr Percival to be, are carefully segregated at meals and so on from the ex-other ranks.'

'I shall miss Leonard.'

'Better that than have him die on us – and depress us to death in the process.'

'And your other condition?' Canteloupe said.

'That Campanile must come down. The cracked bell grates and grinds like the hammers of Mulciber.'

'We could have the bell . . . Old Mortality . . . taken away. Cheaper than bringing the whole Campanile down. We could even have another put in if you would pay, Thea; one of those marvellous deep bells, like Old Mortality used to be before it was flawed, like the Marangona in Venice.'

'No, Canty. The whole tower must come down.'

'Why? It isn't dangerous.'

'Because you, and Rosie, and others, for all I know, have looked out from it at Teresa's nakedness.'

141

'And yours,' chuckled Canteloupe. 'What does that matter? Rosie and I enjoyed looking at you both. You were a fine sight, Thea.'

'And suppose Leonard Percival has used it for the same purpose?'

'You really have got poor Leonard on the brain. You surely wouldn't grudge the poor old wreck a little pleasure? He can't even toss himself off any more, he told me. Don't be such a *prude*, Thea.'

'I sometimes suspect, Canty, that you are morally derelict. No point in discussing it any more. My conditions for coming to the rescue are absolute: Percival goes and so does the Campanile.'

'I'm in no position to object, Thea.'

'You do not look well, certainly. You'd better get some sleep. I shall now go and take over Nausika –'

' – Nausikaa –'

' – From Leonard Percival.'

'I wonder you've trusted him so long if you hate him so much.'

'As I have already said, and as we both know, Percival is trustworthy.'

'But hardly suitable for his present office?'

'You don't understand, Canty. There *was* no one else. Leave aside the time of night, we have almost no servants left.'

'Come, come. We – you – can still afford them.'

'It's not that, Canteloupe. They are all well and regularly paid, and would always be. But they are . . . sneaking away. I think they cannot bear the sound of the ruined bell any more. They appear to have . . . sensed something about the place. The men will not do their work in the grounds. Or perhaps cannot. There is wasteland everywhere, Canty. There is a chill cloud which comes lower every day.'

'My sickness, perhaps. Yet you have returned, Thea. And will remain, I think.'

'Because I love you, in my way. I must go to the

child. Goodnight, Canteloupe.'

'Goodnight, Theodosia.'

Theodosia kissed his damp forehead and left.

Canteloupe, as he lay, thought of the stream that flowed through the meadow and made a pool in the centre of the copse of lady birch, then flowed on to the river. By the river were other, wider meadows, separated by other, deeper woods. From one of these meadows came the sound of a lute; along the river, back up the stream and past the copse of lady birch, on up the stream to the orchard and Rose Garden, in through Canteloupe's windows, closed as they were; and with the music of the lute a light male voice:

'*Ver purpuratum exiit* – "The coloured spring will soon be forth."'

Leonard Percival stood up as Lady Canteloupe entered the night nursery.

'Lady Nausikaa is very quiet, very well behaved,' Leonard Percival said.

Theodosia Canteloupe went to the cot, let down one side, and leaned over the child. She moved the sheet down from the little face. After a time,

'This child is dead,' she said.

'I dare say,' said Leonard. 'They often die for no apparent reason. It is called a cot-death. There have lately been several cases in the newspapers.'

'You do not appear to mind very much.'

'I don't. Do you?'

'Canteloupe will mind.'

'Not for long. Soon he will not be able to mind about anything. What would then have happened to the child . . . had she lived?'

'Canteloupe must be told.'

Theodosia picked up the white bundle from the cot.

'Leave her here,' said Leonard.

'Canteloupe must see for himself.'

'Very well. But after that . . . you must leave Lady Nausikaa to people who understand such matters.'

'Here is your daughter, Nausikaa,' said Theodosia, proffering the white bundle to Canteloupe. 'She is dead. Leonard says it was a cot-death.'

'A pretty common affair. Nobody's fault,' Leonard said.

Canteloupe nodded. He looked briefly at the bundle, then turned, with some difficulty, on to his side, and looked away from Theodosia and Leonard towards the closed windows.

'Then go,' said Canteloupe, speaking away from his audience and towards the windows. 'You may go now. I have other matters on my mind.'

'You see,' said Leonard, to Theodosia and the bundle, when they were outside the room. 'He would not have cared for long, whether she died or lived. He has other matters on his mind.'

'Should I go back and stay with him?'

'No. He will not require you. You must return with me to Lady Nausikaa's night nursery. (Let me take her from you; you are tired after your drive.) When we are back there, we will put her to bed again. You yourself will sleep there, as you intended, until the morning. In the morning you will find that Lady Nausikaa has died during the night. You will telephone at once for Doctor La Soeur.'

'He has retired.'

'He will never retire from the service of old friends. The police can be very officious over this kind of thing. Doctor La Soeur will see to it that all the necessary explanations are forthcoming and that there is no unpleasantness. So. There is the child safely in her cot, with the side up, lest she should fall out. You go to bed too, my lady, comforting yourself with the thought that your love, Teresa, red and gold Teresa, will be here with you at the end of the week. I gave instructions about her room in your absence.'

'She will sleep in mine.'

'They always prepare one for her. For the look of the thing.'

'Were there any servants to obey you?'

'One old woman,' said Leonard Percival, 'who has been here for sixty years. She and I prepared Teresa's room.'

'Thank you, Leonard. Goodnight.'

'Goodnight, sweet ladies. Goodnight. Goodnight.'

Captain the Most Honourable Marquess Canteloupe of the Aestuary of the Severn stood on Green before six horsed knights, who wore light silver body armour but whose heads were bare. Each knight was flanked, on the left, by a dismounted page, who supported a shield with escutcheon and carried a helm with crest. By each page was planted in the ground to his right a lance with pennant.

'They said you came in black armour and vizored,' Canteloupe said; 'without banner or crest or coat of arms.'

'We vary our order of dress according to the nature of the occasion,' said one of the knights. 'We decided that you deserved the kind of display which you have always enjoyed, and that if we went bare-headed it would promote a more fluent conversation.'

'Is there anything about which to converse?'

'We wish to clear up a misunderstanding,' said a second knight. 'We feel that we have had rather a bad press, and we should like to put ourselves right with you, as you are an important client, even if you are also an impostor. The various people who have told you about us – Muscateer in India, repeating what his father had told him, or your friend, Fielding Gray, repeating what his headmaster had told him – they have all made one fundamental mistake: they have represented us as murderers instead of benefactors.'

'That troubadour you killed, Lord Geoffery of Underavon –'

'My dear Canteloupe,' said the third knight, 'that was a *prefectorial* action, as many of our actions are. Be reasonable, my dear fellow. That troubadour had seduced almost everybody within ten leagues of Salisbury, of whatever age, rank or sex. It simply couldn't go on. Not that we bothered about the morality of the thing – that's not our line at all – but it was such an infernal nuisance, so untidy. You must be able to appreciate that, after your time with Hamilton's Horse. Even the nobility was rather put out, and as for the lower classes – their self-righteousness was insufferable. The man had to be stopped before there were protest meetings and witch hunts.'

'That's all very well,' said Canteloupe, 'but Lord Geoffery was a troubadour, a musician, a poet. There are too few of those in the world for you to go about "stopping" them just because they are sexually indiscreet.'

'There's another thing,' said the fourth knight, 'about Geoffery of Underavon: he was a rotten poet and a rampant plagiarist. That's how he got his best lines, like the one about "the coloured spring". Otherwise both himself and his verses were extremely boring, he was always cadging half-crowns and drinks, and he was far too pleased with himself.'

'If you say so,' said Canteloupe. 'But then why did you have to make away with young Muscateer in Bangalore? *He* didn't cadge drinks or seduce the whole county: he was thoroughly amiable.'

'Too amiable to live,' said the fifth knight: 'we were doing him a good turn. Like all school monitors (for that is more or less what we are) we *do* have our favourites, whom we enjoy pampering from time to time. It is one of the privileges of our responsible and

146

sometimes unenviable position.'

'And now,' said Canteloupe to the sixth and last knight, 'why have you come for me? I should have expected, what with the miracles of modern medicine, at least fifteen years more.'

'What would have been the point?' said the sixth knight. 'First, you would have become incontinent, like your old brother-in-arms, Giles Glastonbury – so humiliating, Canteloupe, even if you didn't go potty as well. Next, some busybody was very soon going to spread the word that your title was bogus, your inheritance purloined from a peasant,* and your daughter (dead or alive) gat on your wife, as the Bible would put it, by young Marius Stern. Think what a fool you would have looked then. Anyway, you wouldn't have enjoyed life in England for much longer. All this whining and wauling about equality and compassion – not your scene, Canteloupe, as you will be the first to admit. And it's going to get worse, believe me. Margaret Thatcher, strident and hysterical as she may be, is England's last hope – and even a stringy old vulture like her can't last for ever.

'And so, Canteloupe: you've had a very good run for other people's money; now be a man, be a soldier, and be gone.'

The pages handed up the lances. The knights advanced over Green. On every pennant, Canteloupe saw, was embroidered *Res Unius, Res Omnium*. Ah, he thought, as the lances were lowered, the Old Motto of the Old Gang that had once been the Old Regiment, but this time with a different twist: 'The Fate of One is the Fate of All.'

* See *The Survivors*, by S.R. Blond & Briggs; 1976

PART FOUR

Beau Sabreur

Full bravely hast thou flesh'd
Thy maiden sword.

Shakespeare: Henry IV, Pt. I; V iv 132

Teresa Malcolm ran to Raisley Conyngham's chambers and stormed into his study.

'Canteloupe and the child are dead,' she announced.

'So I have heard,' said Raisley: 'Canteloupe of senile disintegration and Lady Nausikaa of infantile misadventure.'

'Lady Canteloupe has asked for me. I must go, sir. Now.'

'You may go, Teresa, just as soon as I have Marius's assurance of his dutiful obedience. I have made that quite clear.'

'The situation has changed. Lady Canteloupe is urgent.'

'Very well,' said Raisley Conyngham; 'then so shall we be. Find Marius and send him here. I shall make my request of him immediately. If his intentions are as I would have them, you may leave for Wiltshire at once.'

'And if his intentions are not as you would have them?'

'You shall remain here,' Raisley Conyngham said.

'How shall you prevent my going?'

'By telling the police what you are going for – i.e. to abandon yourself to the vicious embraces of an older – a much older – woman. I shall request them, as your guardian, to take the whole disgraceful matter firmly in hand.'

'Relations between women are not illegal.'

'Corruption of minors is. Let us not quarrel, Teresa. Send Marius here, and let us settle the matter.'

*

151

Left alone, Raisley Conyngham resumed his reading of Ben Jonson.

'"Madam, had all antiquity been lost,"' he read aloud,

> 'All history sealed up, and fables cross'd;
> That we had left us, nor by time, nor place,
>   Least mention of a nymph, a muse, a grace,
> But even their names were to be made anew,
>   Who could not but create them all, from you?'

Teresa to a 'T', thought Raisley: little nonpareil, little cynosure, little enchantress. I'll warrant she has her way with Marius. This sudden decease of Canteloupe and the brat will make things quicker and easier by a long chalk.

Teresa was directed from Marius's house to the gymnasium, where she found Marius at sword practice with the Sergeant Major instructor who came, twice a week, from Aldershot.

'Good, sir, good,' said the Sergeant Major, who called no one else at the school, except the Headmaster, 'sir'. 'Even sharper than your father when I fenced with him at Windsor in the old days . . . the good days . . . Parry, and riposte. Parry, parry, parry – and riposte. Beat; beat . . . withdraw in feint, beat, beat – and LUNGE. That will do for now, sir. I'll put you down for foil, epée and sabre against the Royal Military Academy next week. I think, sir, you have a friend to see you.'

The Sergeant Major and Marius took off their masks and saluted Tessa with their sabres, kissing the hilt, lowering the point (exposing the wrist), and again raising the hilt to the lips.

'You have been here long?' said Marius.

'Five minutes,' said Tessa, who had known better than to interrupt.

'Just let me change and have a shower.'

'No. You are to come to Mr Conyngham. Straight away. For God's sake,' said Tessa, to the astonishment of the Sergeant Major, 'promise to do what he asks. If you don't, he won't let me go to Theodosia.'

Marius's lips parted in puzzlement.

'Why should you go to her? Just like that?'

'Have you not heard? Canteloupe is dead. And the child.'

'You refer, miss – please excuse me – to Captain the Marquess Canteloupe? Formerly Captain Detterling of Earl Hamilton's Light Dragoons?'

'I do, Sergeant Major.'

'My father knew him in Egypt, miss. A fine cricketer with a firm seat on a horse, but not a good example of an officer, if I may say so. He was arrested, my father used to tell me, as he came in from making the winning hit at a cricket match – arrested for stealing Army petrol.'

'And was subsequently cleared of the charge,' said Marius. You may fall out, Sergeant Major, if you please.'

'SIR,' answered the Sergeant Major, and turned smartly to his right before doubling off into the changing room.

'Tell Mr Conyngham you'll do whatever he asks,' said Tessa; 'then he'll let me go to Theodosia.'

'But – '

' – Don't ask me for details now, Marius. We'll go into the whole thing later, and make a plan if we have to. Go now, Marius. Go as you are.'

Once more Marius saluted Teresa with his sabre; then he placed it in the rack and went.

'So,' said Marius to Raisley Conyngham: 'I think I understand, sir.'

'Tell me what you understand,' said Raisley.

Marius smoothed the white flannel trousers, which he wore for fencing instead of white breeches and stockings, as stockings drew attention to the slight thinness of his calves.

'I understand, sir, that you wish me to put it about that Piero Caspar and Carmilla Salinger, both of them very close friends of mine in one way or another, had contracted this new and incurable disease called AIDS, and that in consequence they committed suicide. You wish me to attribute their infection to congress, former or recent, with Jeremy Morrison, another friend of mine; and to accuse Jeremy of boasting that his father, Luffham of Whereham, used his influence to hush the whole matter up.'

'Right,' said Raisley. 'You need not, you must not, try to be precise as to sexual or medical detail.'

'Why do you want this rumour put about, sir?'

'Because I want Luffham of Whereham discredited, lest he should be able to oppose me in an important purpose. You will do as I ask, Marius?'

'When have I not, sir?'

'Answer my question. You will do as I ask, in this particular matter, NOW?'

'As you say, sir,' Marius said, smoothing his trousers again with his left hand. 'I think that Canteloupe's funeral might be a good occasion on which to start telling people, as so many that might be interested will be there. Meanwhile, sir, I should like to ask an incidental question. How *did* Piero and Carmilla die?'

'They just stopped breathing.'

'Sir?'

'Rather like Lady Nausikaa Sarum, who suffered a cot-death. Infants are sometimes smothered in their cots, I understand, and sometimes . . . they just cease to breathe. That is probably what happened to Caspar and Salinger.'

'Lady Nausikaa was a tiny child, sir. My child, as you know, but that is beside the present point . . .

154

which is, sir, that whereas Nausikaa was an infant, Piero and Carmilla were adult.'

'Adults die of spontaneous combustion, boy. Not only in *Bleak House* but in the real world. Why should they not die of spontaneous congestion, which would seem to have happened here?'

'Both of them, sir? Rather improbable.'

'Highly improbable ... which should assist you, Marius, in convincing people that they in fact committed suicide ... when you tell them so at Canteloupe's funeral, which will be, I agree with you, an excellent time and place to begin.'

Theodosia Marchioness Canteloupe announced a hugger-mugger burial (though this was not the phrase she used) of her lord and master. It was stipulated in *The Times* that only intimate friends of the late Marquess should attend the affair (which would happen three days after Canteloupe's death) and that there would be no refreshments after the interment.

'So that's all right,' said Ivan Blessington to his wife, Betty: 'we needn't go, nor need we disturb the girls at school.'

'You are surely much beholden to *her*?' said Betty.

'That is not the same thing as being an intimate friend of *his*. True, we were once in the same squadron of Hamilton's Horse, but that was very many years ago and even at the time it didn't make us intimate.'

'I remember,' said Betty, 'your sending him special messages* when he was in Parliament and you were an attaché in Washington.'

'I did that for the money, which we sorely needed.'

'But he surely counted as a friend? The girls wrote to

---

* See *The Rich Pay Later*, by S.R. Anthony Blond Ltd; 1964

me that you seemed very pleased to see him at that cricket match at the school the other day.'

'So I was. I like being reminded of the past. And Canteloupe never fails to arouse in me a kind of pleasurable astonishment, that creatures like him are still permitted to exist. But I am not and have never been his intimate, and truth to tell I have always disapproved of him. What was it that Trollope said of the old Duke of Omnium – the one played by Roland Culver in that admirable dramatisation by Simon Raven? "No man should live idly, as His Grace had lived" – something like that. Whether as Detterling or as Canteloupe, this man has lived idly. I doubt if he ever performed a single useful act.'

'Aren't you being rather censorious?' said Betty Blessington. 'For many years he was in publishing as Gregory Stern's partner – to say nothing of his being in the House of Commons before he inherited. Didn't he have something to do with a young England movement – something of the sort – back in the Fifties?'

'Crypto-Fascism,' said Ivan, who was becoming fond of silly clichés in his old age. 'As for being a publisher, he just used it as an excuse for getting foreign currency – you remember, when those Labour johnnies did their damnedest to stop anyone going abroad . . . except for politicians who were going on footling conferences and the like.'

'But Detterling was a politician, or at any rate an MP. So he got a lot of foreign currency anyway.'

'No doubt,' said Ivan; 'but he was still greedy for more, so he used to get a business allowance as well.'

'How do you know?'

'Because it's exactly what I should have done,' said Ivan Blessington; 'only I was a soldier and spent my whole life abroad in any case.'

'Then why are you getting at Canteloupe?'

'I suppose I shall have to own up. The thing is, old girl, that I've become sick and tired of hearing, my whole life long, that he was the only boy at school who ever made a double century on Green in a school match.'

'How very improper,' said Isobel Stern, reading her India paper airmail copy of *The Times* in the Café Albigeois in St-Bertrand-de-Comminges: 'Theodosia Canteloupe isn't providing refreshments at Canteloupe's funeral.'

'So he's dead?' said Jo-Jo Guiscard.

'And pretty well buried too, from what it says here. They're planting him in the Sarum family Grave Ground tomorrow.'

'Rosie will be sad,' said Oenone Guiscard. 'She has a pash on Canteloupe.'

'Who told you?' said Isobel.

'You did. Last time you had a letter from Rosie. Mummy said it sounded from the letter as if Rosie had a pash on Canteloupe, and you agreed, because you said that Canteloupe would be much better than some silly boy, because Canteloupe would know what to do with her.'

'Well, he won't now,' Jo-Jo said.

'So will Rosie get some silly boy instead?'

'Dozens,' said Isobel. 'After her money.'

'And will she give it to them?' Oenone persisted.

'Some of it,' said Isobel, 'if they give good value. She's a calculating little madame. . . . I'm glad, really, that Theodosia is putting on the funeral so quickly. No one can expect *us* to attend at such short notice.'

'The only one of that lot I ever really cared for was Baby Canteloupe,' Jo-Jo said, taking Oenone on to her lap, 'the first wife, Tullia. She cheered me up a lot when I was carrying Oenone. We used to sit by a pool all day, in a copse of lady birch. She wouldn't let anyone else come, except a jolly ginger nurse who brought Tullia's own baby for feeding . . . that disastrous little Tullius. I enjoyed looking at Baby's breasts, and quite often Tullius would get an erection. ... *Lovely* Baby Canteloupe. What a pity she went potty. She went to Africa, you know, and started putting out for the lepers in leper colonies.'

'What's putting out?' said Oenone, amusing herself on her mother's knee.

'An Americanism,' said Isobel: 'it means being intimate with a man. Of course I knew about Baby,' she said to Jo-Jo. 'Do you remember the time she pissed over the floor of that church – the day they crucified my old Jew, Gregory?'*

'Pints and pints of it,' said Jo-Jo dreamily; *'standing up*, with her legs apart. I thought she was never going to stop.'

'And now she's dead and so is Canteloupe. No heir, none at all. So I suppose Theodosia will keep the loot. Such a waste, when she's got such heaps of her own.'

'Will she keep the house?' said Jo-Jo.

'Oh, I expect so. According to that letter of Rosie's, the Eton Fives Court is still in good nick. You don't have the luck to own one of those very often.'

'Is Auntie Isobel still a socialist?' said Oenone to her mother. 'She's been saying a lot of funny things this morning, for a socialist.'

'Well, are you?' said Jo-Jo to Isobel.

'To tell you the truth, I'm somewhat revising my notions. I rather think my socialism was a phase – something to do with the menopause.'

'Oh,' said Jo-Jo. 'Well, thank goodness for that. But was *I* something to do with your menopause? Am *I* going to be revised . . . so to speak?'

'You've got Oenone . . . now. You don't need me.' Isobel rose from her seat. 'So I'll be off,' she said, 'to do my packing.'

'Shall *you* be putting out for lepers at leper colonies?'

* See *The Face of the Waters*, by S.R. Muller, Blond & White; 1985

158

Oenone said.

'I rather think not,' said Isobel. 'I am not quite brave or generous enough. I am going to an island called Vis, off the Illyrian coast. That was where my mother went, you know. She lived happily to a great age.'

'You might just as well go on being a socialist,' said Jo-Jo, 'as live on the island of Vis.'

'I may have stopped being a socialist,' said Isobel, 'but I have not stopped being mean about money. According to my mother's occasional letters, Vis was exceedingly cheap.'

'Only because there wasn't anything to buy there,' Jo-Jo said.

'I have always hated shopping. All those grasping shopkeepers, and lower-class women in one's way with their cheap prams and filthy, unkillable babies. Goodbye, Oenone. I'll have gone by the time you and Mummy get home.'

'Yes,' agreed Oenone. 'We've still got the shopping to do. And today's the worst day for lower-class women and unkillable babies. I think it's the day they collect their free money at the PTT.'

'Goodbye, darling,' said Isobel to Jo-Jo; 'it's been great fun, all things considered.'

'Yes, hasn't it?' said Jo-Jo. 'I wonder if I can churn up Jean-Marie into action again.'

'What do you mean, churn up poor Pappy?' Oenone said.

'Mummy will tell you about all that when you're older,' said Isobel, blowing both of them a smacky kiss from the café door.

'Shall you go to Canteloupe's funeral?' said Len to Provost Helmutt of Lancaster College.

'Nothing to do with me,' said Sir Jacquiz.

'Canteloupe's first wife, Baby, was the daughter of your predecessor, Tom Llewyllyn.'

'The connection is rather tenuous,' Helmutt observed.

'I thought Marigold might like to go,' said Len. 'A bit of an out might cheer her up – now she's back from Turkey with nothing to show for it.'

'Lady Helmutt must do as she pleases,' said Helmutt, who was beginning to be rather grand because he knew he was to be made a baron in the Birthday Honours. Then he repented of his hauteur, being wily enough to know that God might be listening, and said, 'Why don't you take her? She's spending the afternoon with Balbo Blakeney.'

Len went to Balbo Blakeney's rooms in Sitwell's Building.

'Like to come to Canteloupe's funeral?' he said to Marigold, who was watching by Balbo's bed.

'Canteloupe dead?' croaked Balbo. 'You go, Marigold. Represent me.'

'I thought . . . that the twins might come here. I couldn't bear to miss them.'

'They're far more likely to be at Canteloupe's funeral,' said Len: 'that's the kind of thing they really enjoy.'

So Marigold and Len went to Canteloupe's funeral, in Len's Porsche and rather a casual spirit.

Fielding Gray went by train, for driving had long ago become troublesome to his one eye. Fielding did not go in a casual spirit. He had known Detterling since 1945, for more than a generation, and Detterling (or later Canteloupe) had popped up at a great many crises in his life:- when he was a wretched recruit in the Army, and when he was under arrest (or about to be) in Göttingen, and when he was derelict in Yugoslavia, and when he needed money in Venice, and so on and so forth. From now on there would be no more

Detterling (or Canteloupe) to intervene. Fielding would have to pull himself out of his own scrapes and make his own decisions. However, this was going to be a lot easier than it might have been as he had just inherited (so he had been informed that morning) a stiffish sum of money from Piero Caspar. Most of Piero's money (formerly Ptolymaeos Tunne's) had gone to Lancaster College, which did not need it, but some had gone to Fielding, who, as Piero had fondly and fortunately remembered, did.

Fielding could now get out of bloody London and live in Broughton Staithe, writing more books, not because (as things now stood with him) he would need the pittance they would bring him, nor because anybody much would read them, but because one had to have an occupation other than pleasure most of the time in order to keep one sane. Anyhow, he rather enjoyed writing books. The time went much faster when he was doing that than when he was doing anything else. He could dine in the L'Estrange Arms every night and walk among the abandoned gun sites in the dunes each evening to get up an appetite – something sorely needed by diners in the L'Estrange Arms, where the food was uninspired to say the least of it.

He had already asked Geddes if he too would like to come and live in Broughton Staithe. Geddes, somewhat to his relief, had replied that he could not endure the country, not even for hols, and had not spent a single hour out of London ever since he left the Army – a rule which he was breaking today, as he was accompanying Corporal Major Chead (who had been his contemporary in the 10th Sabre Squadron) to Captain Detterling's funeral. Geddes had once cut the hair of Detterling's soldier servant (who was of course coming to the funeral too); while 'Corpy' Chead had once driven all four of them (Detterling, Fielding, Detterling's soldier servant, and Geddes) from Rollesdon Balloon Camp to Salisbury Races, in a 'borrowed' Land

Rover with an illicit work ticket. There could be worse reasons than those, Fielding now thought (with a tiny sob), for attending a man's funeral. It would be pleasant to see Corporal Major Chead again and hear his opinion of the death of his jockey son Danny, whom he hated and who had impaled himself on the spiked rails of the run-in at Regis Priory while riding Prideau Glastonbury's gelding, Mercury.*

Unlike almost everyone else who was going to the funeral, Teresa Malcolm had left (having been released by Raisley Conyngham) pretty near as soon as Canteloupe's death had been announced. This, of course, was because she was going not only to the funeral but to comfort Theodosia Canteloupe first. But although Theodosia had been exigent in sending for her, she showed no interest in her arrival; she merely sent her a note by hand of Leonard Percival to ask her to assist Doctor La Soeur in 'making the necessary arrangements'.

'What arrangements?' said Tessa to La Soeur.

'The child. Nausika.'

'Nausikaa. What about her?'

'Lady Canteloupe wants you to carry the coffin,' said Doctor La Soeur. 'I'm sorry to say that it's white.'

Doctor La Soeur was pinched and neat, the sort of man that wears silk socks with suspenders.

'Surely too heavy for one,' said Tessa, 'whatever its colour?'

'She says that Marius Stern can help you. It will be appropriate, she says. For Christ's sake don't make a fuss, girl. I've had enough trouble, with the police, already. They don't care for cot-deaths.'

'I thought you were Doctor Fix-it,' Tessa said spitefully.

* See *In The Image of God*, by S.R. Muller; 1990

'There's a smart young local police inspector who's after promotion and don't like aristocrats. Name of Oake. Son of a retired general – a lean, mean general, noted for making trouble. Like father, like son. This Oake went to the nursing home where Theodosia and the infant had had minor surgery a few days before. The staff said that when the child left she was one of the healthiest they'd ever seen.'

'Healthy babies do suffer cot deaths,' Tessa said.

'Unfortunately there is evidence that that child could have been dead much longer than Theodosia says. Luckily Leonard Percival served for a time in the same regiment as the general. He took young Oake into a corner and told him a few tales about Daddy's behaviour in India and, more to the point perhaps, about Mummy's behaviour in Germany . . . with a young PT instructor, who may well have been his father. So now this business of Nausika is all right – but only just.'

'Doctor Fix-it.'

'Percival fixed it. Now listen, girl. When this funeral is done, you want to keep your pretty eyes open. Theodosia's been babbling. I gave her something . . . to relax her . . . because I like to know what's going on; and of course she babbled. But not about Nausika, as I'd hoped; about you. She says that Rosie Stern and Canteloupe spied on you and her . . . exciting themselves. She says this has contaminated you. She says Artemis, the Virgin goddess, is angry that a man's eyes have caressed you. There must be vengeance, she says, and there must be purification. But not until after the funeral. It seems that Artemis can wait till then, and anyway you're needed in one piece to carry the baby's coffin. But the moment the first chunk of earth falls on Nausika and Canteloupe, just you watch out for whatever's coming from my lady's corner of the ring.'

'Why does she want me and Marius to carry Nausikaa?' Tessa said.

'Marius, because he's the real father. You, because you were in her company all those months while she was carrying Nausika.'

'I *loved* Thea all those months. How can she wish me harm?'

'It's Artemis that wishes you whatever it is. "Queen and Huntress, Chaste and Fair." Through no fault of your own you've broken the rules. The Queen and Huntress doesn't care for that. Remember Actaeon? But he was a man and a Peeping Tom, and you're a girl that got peeped at, which makes it rather different. All the same, take my tip, and take care you don't end up like dear little Iphigeneia.'

'I must help carry Nausikaa,' said Teresa; 'and I must try to love and comfort her mother, both before the funeral and after it.'

'Well, I've warned you,' Doctor La Soeur said; 'now suit yourself.'

On the day of the funeral, Rosie rose up early and took a train alone. By chance she met Milo Hedley while she was changing at Waterloo. Although she hardly knew Milo, it would have been impolite not to travel with him into Wiltshire.

'I'm gate-crashing,' Milo said. 'I don't know any of the dead, but I'm coming to see what will happen to the living.'

'Why should anything happen?' Rosie said.

'Because a cerise horseman is dead,' deposed Milo. 'I didn't know Canteloupe, but I do know that he was in a cavalry regiment called Earl Hamilton's Light Dragoons. They've been abolished now, of course, because they were too proud and too pretty; but when they were still serving, they wore cherry trousers. Cerise.'

'What has that got to do with anything?'

164

'I recently heard a prophecy,' Milo said, 'that when a cerise horseman was overcome, then a certain matter (which concerns both of us) would soon draw to a close. We are burying that cerise horseman today.'

'My father used to say,' said Rosie, 'that Hamilton's Light Dragoons kept their horses longer than any regiment except the Scots Greys and the Household Cavalry; but even so they had to give them up well before the war.'

'They still had them when Canteloupe . . . when Detterling . . . joined as a cornet. Raisley Conyngham once said that Giles Glastonbury once said that Detterling . . . Canteloupe . . . had the soundest seat and the kindest hands with a horse of any officer or man in the regiment.'

'Yes,' said Rosie: 'I can believe that he had kind hands.'

Len drove his Porsche so fast that Marigold and he arrived far too early for the funeral service (which was to be in an oratory by the Campanile, just off the Great Court) and had to hang about in the area of Cant-Fun, which was shut in honour of the funeral, not that it had been open much lately in any case.

'How poor Balbo would have enjoyed this dismal spectacle,' said Len, having helped Marigold into the fairground through a gap in the rotting fence. 'Just think: he may be dead by now.'

'I fell asleep in the car,' said Marigold, 'and dreamt that he had just died. My twins were with him.'

'Very like, very like,' said Len; 'though I still think that they'd have had a more amusing time here. But they were always fond of Balbo, in so far as they were fond of anybody. They certainly weren't all that fond of you or Helmutt, thought they were usually more or less civil. So now I should think of them, as you say you have just dreamt of them, as the comforter of

165

Balbo in his passing and his courier to the realm of death. Like Hermes, the twins serve as Messengers, Guides and Messengers. Like Hermes, they come to men and women and bid them follow. This is what they will always do. Think of them this last time, Marigold, and then forget them.'

'Very well,' said Marigold, who had always respected Len's judgements and the advice he based on them. She looked round the jagged space ships and sex saucers of Cant-Fun. 'If they're not careful,' she said, 'there will soon be a nasty accident here.'

'I fancy,' said Len, 'that it is now closing time in the playground of Cant-Fun.'

Teresa sent messages to Theodosia by hand of Leonard Percival, who, although Theodosia had formerly loathed him so much, was now the only person whom she would see. Always Leonard came back to tell Teresa that she must occupy herself in helping Doctor La Soeur with 'the arrangements'.

'All the arrangements have been made,' said Teresa; 'you know that. Why was she so urgent that I should come here?'

'I expect she wanted to make sure of you,' Leonard Percival said.

'What for?'

'For the funeral. For your part in it.'

'Never before have I been here and not slept with her in her room.'

Finally, on the morning before the funeral, Leonard brought Teresa a message that she was to come to the Marchioness's apartments as soon as the funeral was over.

'Don't go to her,' said Doctor La Soeur when Teresa told him of this. 'Just go away instead.'

'How can I not go to her?'

'I've told you. If you go to her, you go to someone or

166

something which she calls Artemis. Now you're a clever girl for a girl, girl. You've read about Artemis. Artemis is trouble for a girl, girl. Don't ask me to spell it out, girl: just go away.'

Raisley Conyngham and Marius Stern drove from the school to the funeral in Raisley's BMW.

'I asked your sister, Rosie, to come with us,' said Raisley, 'but she said she would go by train.'

'I think she is sad about Canteloupe, sir.'

'Is that a good reason for riding in British Rail's filthy and unpunctual trains? For enduring the incompetence and the insolence of the black and white trash which British Rail employs?'

'I think,' said Marius, 'that just at the moment Rosie prefers to be alone.'

'So be it. Now, if anyone asks you what *I'm* doing at the ceremony, tell him that I'm representing the school.'

'I should have thought, sir, that Luffham would be doing that.'

'Luffham may be representing the old boys. *I* am representing the body of the school itself – the boys and the masters.'

'As you say, sir,' said Marius, and fell silent all the way from Haslemere to Petersfield, thinking of dead Carmilla and dead Canteloupe, of dead Jack Lamprey and dead Gat-Toothed Jenny, of dead Gregory Stern, his tall and valorous father, and of dead Maisie Malcolm and dead Piero Caspar. Then, as they turned north west toward Salisbury, Raisley said:

'I was at school near here. Brydales.'

'I know, sir. Where our Headmaster is going next autumn.'

'An unattractive appointment, I should have thought, even for him. But evidently he covets it; and his departure will leave the field clear for me.'

'So that's what all this is about, sir? You want to be the new Headmaster, but Luffham of Whereham will oppose you; so I am to discredit him by vilifying his son?'

'You have already consented to do so. You will not go back on your promise now?'

'Oh no, sir. You will never be able to say that I have broken my word to you. I promise you that.'

The purple spring was forth. Along their road the coloured fields of hither Wessex flaunted and flared.

'We hear that there is to be no wake,' said Marius: 'no funeral bakemeats. A pity, sir. I could have spread the word you wish me to spread far more comfortably and effectively at a feast, particularly since it would almost certainly have been a buffet. As it is . . . I shall have to whisper in the ears of the mourners between the oratory and the grave, and between grave and car park. I shall have to move among them as swift and sly as death himself.'

'You will play the role to perfection, little Egyptian. You are the courier who brings a tale of death. Your manner must suit your message.'

The official car park was on the cricket ground, something which Canteloupe would have abominated, as he never allowed a car within sight of the wicket. While Marius, who had played on the ground himself, was explaining this to Raisley Conyngham, a gaitered figure, jet black cap-a-pie and sporting a tall silk topper with flying buttresses, strode across the field and confronted Marius as he climbed out of the BMW.

'Mungo Avallon,' said the figure, raising its topper, grasping and nearly pulping Marius's right hand, totally ignoring Raisley Conyngham, 'Bishop of Glastonbury. I am to conduct the funeral. I knew Canteloupe, you see, in the old days during the war. And since. And since.'

168

'I remember you well, my lord bishop,' said Marius. 'You christened Canteloupe's son, Sarum, in Lancaster Chapel.* There was an interruption.'

'Yes. Canteloupe interrupted to demand that I should use the old and proper form of the christening service instead of some rubbishy modern text. He was, of course, quite right. But at that time I was in the habit of obeying my wife in such matters . . . on pain – er – of marital ostracism. She insisted that I fall in with every progressive fad that a crazed Synod could promulgate. Now she is dead – of spleen at the success of another woman (Margaret Thatcher, who else?) – and I have resumed the traditional and seemly forms of the Church, liturgical and sartorial.' He swelled in his sable accoutrements. 'There will be no fudging of words at this funeral – in which, incidentally, you have a part to play.'

'My lord?' said Marius.

'You are to help Miss Teresa Malcolm carry the smaller coffin – that of the late Lady Nausikaa Sarum. One handle each, one of you on either side. Lady Nausikaa will weigh little enough, I apprehend.'

So, thought Marius, I am to carry my daughter to her grave.

So, thought Conyngham, he will have far less opportunity, at least on his way from oratory to gravemouth, to put about his story. Nothing to be done about that. He will have to make it up on the way back.

'Come,' said Mungo to Marius. 'I must instruct you and Miss Teresa in your duties and movements on the ground itself.'

'My lord,' assented Marius. And to Raisley, 'You will excuse me, sir.'

*

---

* See *Morning Star*, by S.R. Muller, Blond & White; 1984

Just before the guests entered the oratory for the service, a helicopter descended into the Great Court, near the Eton Fives Court. The noise of the engine, reverberating round the Tudor, Carolingian, Georgian and pseudo-Gothic ensemble, sent flocks of crows, pigeons and sea birds (the latter having flown from the Aestuary of the Severn to render their duty at the obsequies of their liege lord) hurtling in panic to the sky.

Out of the helicopter stepped Giles Glastonbury and Luffham of Whereham, Luffham in the robes of a baron of the United Kingdom (with bicorn hat in place of coronet), Glastonbury in the full dress (cherry trousers and tunic of light blue) of a field officer of the 49th Earl Hamilton's Light Dragoons. Glastonbury wore golden spurs of a length appropriate to those of a thirteenth century banneret, with fiercely spiked rowels at the end of them. In place of a sabre he carried an ornamental dagger with a jewelled hilt.

When Glastonbury and Luffham had been helped to the ground – a proceeding which took some time, such was the complexity of their kit – the helicopter rose to the height of the Campanile, then veered away to the west. When the racket had ceased, the birds descended. Many of the sea birds settled on a huge black coffin, which was now being carried, by eight of Canteloupe's tenants, into the oratory (having hitherto rested, according to the custom of the house, in the banqueting room). Behind the bearers of the black coffin walked Marius and Tessa, carrying between them at knee height the white coffin of Lady Nausikaa.

All present then filed into the oratory. They will be named and numbered later; for the present, pray imagine a straggling procession led by Mungo Avallon (now robed in royal purple, with crozier of gold and mitre of green and crimson) and Theodosia Marchioness Canteloupe, who was (somewhat to the surprise of her guests) dressed in a track suit of Cambridge blue, thus nearly but not quite matching Glastonbury's tunic, and a pair of trendy Kickers.

When the mourners were seated in the oratory, Mungo Avallon, with Theodosia as his acolyte, began the ceremonial 'dressing' of Canteloupe's coffin, which lay, massy, black and absolutely rectangular, on a catafalque in front of the altar (Nausikaa's little white box having been placed by Teresa and Marius on a set of Sedilia under the aumbry on the right of the tiny chancel).

The manner of the 'dressing' was as follows. At a sign from Mungo Avallon, the sea birds perched on the coffin flew quietly to the back of the oratory, over the heads of the assembly, and settled on a ledge under the west window, a colourful rather than taste-ful representation of the death of Jezebel. Mungo Avallon then draped the huge black sarcophagus with the banner of St George of England, a red cross on a white background, such a banner as the Christ is often to be seen grasping (though no one seems to know why) in depictions of his rising from the tomb in the garden. After this, Theodosia fetched from the aumbry and placed on the altar Canteloupe's accoutrements and achievements: the coronet bearing the strawberry leaves and low balls of a marquess; the busby, sabre-trache and sabre, which Canteloupe had carried on mounted parades long ago before the Second World War; and also his personal standard, which showed a gold minotaur of Crete against the deep blue never-resting sea, the creature being bonneted, between his horns, with a cerise cross of Malta. Avallon now drew the sabre from its sheath, kissed the hilt and lowered the blade in salute to the coffin; he then placed sabre and sheath, crossed, over the left hand transverse (as seen from the body of the building) of the red cross on the banner, and some way along it; the busby he set upright to the left of the intersection of the axes formed by sheath and sabre, so that it was now near enough over the encoffined Canteloupe's breast; the coronet he placed over Canteloupe's head; and the standard, which was encrusted with heavy embroidery, he arranged just to the front of the busby, its pole bisecting the angle between the curved sabre (on which was embossed in gold along the blade *Hostes Defutantur Mei* – 'Fuck Mine Enemies') and the gilded sheath. When he had made these dispositions, Mungo Avallon gestured peremptorily to Theodosia to join the congregation, which he proceeded to harangue as follows:-

'*Vanitas vanitatum, omnia vanitas*. What other message can I have for you? The daintily decked flesh of this worthless nobleman lies rotting in his mighty coffin, surmounted by emblems of whorish pageantry and lethal hate, each one of these baubles being worth a price in money that would feed an honest labourer and his family for a year.

'*Vanitas vanitatum*. What is here of honour or true valour? Of charity or steadfastness? Of conscience, of purity, of reverence – or even of common use? This lord, this prince, this most honourable marquess has walked among us long enough, and we heartily recommend his carcass to the dust and dung whence it came and his spirit to the boatman – are you there, Old Boatman? – that it may be borne across Cocytus and suffer torment for eternity in the ninth and lowest circle of the Inferno, along with the Grand Master of Betrayal, Harlotry and Fraud.'

Mungo Avallon paused, half turned towards the coffin by which he stood, and raised both hands on high, hooked in execration.

When he turned back towards his listeners, two tears were running aslant his cheeks, and the voice, with which he now continued to address them, was soft.

'And yet, my friends, there have been many worse than Canteloupe. He was idle and trivial, but he was pretty – a pretty toy in a world of much ugliness. He was a man, too, of some slight learning, pagan learning, it is true, but then pagan learning, though vile at its worst, often speaks of sweet reason and comely virtue at its noblest, and was much loved by Augustine, by Jerome, by Aquinas. Again, while Canteloupe did little for others, he expected none to make sacrifice for him. He used his powers of patronage with generosity and, as a rule, with discrimination. He did not pry into the affairs of others, unless this was strictly necessary in the defence of his own. He did not get up trouble and nuisance, whether public or private. He minded his business, such as it was. He was not self-righteous and he was not puffed up. He could be a considerate and entertaining companion; and in his youth, so they say, he sat his horse like a knight of King Arthur, and cut the ball later than any man in England.'

Mungo turned again towards the coffin; this time he raised one hand only and waved it as to a dear friend who is leaving on a boat train for a leisurely tour of the Continent.

He then turned towards the small, white box on the sedilia, and said:-

'As for Lady Nausikaa Sarum, let us be grateful that she has not lived to be served, as no doubt she would have been, with dope and democratisation. Let the bearers take up the coffins, which you will all follow to the place of burial.'

As the great bell, Old Mortality, cracked and crunched its eponymous message from the Campanile, Mungo Avallon, Lord Bishop of Glastonbury, led the way through the Great Court.

Canteloupe's coffin followed immediately after him, borne by the eight tenant farmers, who had remained,

173

and would remain, po-faced through the entire affair.

Lady Nausikaa in her little white box followed the richly caparisoned sarcophagus of her titular father. She was carried by Tessa and Marius, who for their part were as silent, at this stage in the proceedings, as were the bearers in chief.

The sea birds flew low, screeching and keening, over both coffins . . . behind the second of which marched Theodosia Marchioness Canteloupe of the Aestuary of the Severn.

After that, no particular precedence was observed, and quite often the mourners, who were mostly in pairs, overtook each other or walked out on a flank.

The first behind the Marchioness were the Honourable Jeremy Morrison with his friend and some-time lover, Milo Hedley. 'You will observe,' Milo said to Jeremy, 'that the cerise horseman, of whom Gregory Stern spoke in that pit in Greece, has now fallen – I refer to Canteloupe, who, as a Light Dragoon, once wore the same cherry trousers as Giles Glastonbury is now wearing.'

'But was this . . . cerise horseman . . . overcome by a silver horseman?' Jeremy enquired.

'No doubt. Six armoured knights come for the souls of the Sarums – or so the legend has it. I imagine they escort their charges to Charon's ferry – referred to, you will recall, by Mungo Avallon in his address.'

Fielding Gray came next with hobbling Leonard Percival. They spoke of the days when they had been soldiers together (though of very different regiments, Leonard having been a mere fusilier) in Germany, encamped above the City of Göttingen.

'Those were good days,' said Leonard: 'the days of the Tavern and the Garden.'

'There was a viper in that garden,' said Fielding.

'In which garden is there not?' Leonard replied.

Next came Rosie Stern, walking with the girl who had short, blonde hair and had scored for Benenden during the match on Harlequin's. 'I played truant to come,' said the girl: 'I liked Canteloupe a lot, that one time. And I thought you might need a bit of support.'

Len came next, with Lady Helmutt. Marigold was telling Len how she had visited the island of Vis, during the journey which she had made before her more recent journey to Turkey, and had found Dobrila. 'Or rather,' said Marigold, 'she found me. I was sitting on the shore crying, because I could not find the twins.'

Rosie overheard this, and turned her head. 'Funny,' she said: 'my mother telephoned very late last night – they had to fetch me out of bed – to say that *she* was going to Vis because her mother once went there. Perhaps my mother will meet Dobrila.'

'Why not?' said Marigold. 'It's a tiny island. But Dobrila is very innocent.'

'I know,' said Rosie.

'But does your mother know? And will she respect Dobrila's innocence?'

'My mother respects nothing,' said Rosie, 'and never has done. She is an egotist – a bully and a sham. But if she is in the right mood she can be very funny in a coarse fashion.'

'I fear Dobrila has little humour,' said Marigold; 'but she has lots of integrity to make up.'

'Does it make up?' said Rosie.

'Perhaps they could both learn from each other,' said the girl with the very short blonde hair.

Next walked Giles Glastonbury and Luffham of Whereham. Giles was carrying his busby on the crook of his left arm: Luffham was trailing his bicorn between the finger and thumb of his right hand. They were talking of India, of the time when Glastonbury had been a colonel in Special Intelligence and Luffham had been plain Peter Morrison, an officer cadet.*

---

* See *Sound the Retreat*, by S.R. Anthony Blond Ltd; 1971

'Canteloupe once told me,' said Glastonbury, 'in Berhampore - you remember? – that you had a lot of shit in your tanks.'

'I've funnelled it through to my son, Jeremy,' said Luffham of Whereham, 'like a tanker aircraft refuelling a fighter in flight.'

'You think your son is going to do any fighting?'

'No. But he might drop a bomb or two in a cowardly sort of way. At the very least he'll drop the shit I've pumped into him, probably on somebody who's never done him any harm whatsoever – his best friend, I shouldn't wonder.'

After this precious pair came three men in a row, all of whom, like Giles Glastonbury, were wearing the full dress of Earl Hamilton's Light Dragoons, but in their case that appropriate to other ranks – short and sensible spurs of metal, white sword belts instead of scarlet, plain dirks where Glastonbury carried his jewelled dagger. The soldier on the left was Corporal Major Chead, who, as a senior non-commissioned officer, wore a crimson sash from right to left and was palpably (but by no means uncontrollably) drunk. He was telling his companions that he was responsible for the death of his jockey son, Danny Chead (who had been killed riding in a hurdle race), as he had wished him dead so violently that he had developed the gift of the evil eye and had thrown the curse that killed his boy.

'But as I understand it, Corporal Major, you weren't even at the meeting where he was thrown and spiked,' said the soldier to his right. This was the 'Chamberlain' from the house at Luffham, who had once upon a time been Canteloupe's soldier servant and galloper in the rank of corporal, had retired with him into civilian life, and had later been sent to Luffham by Canteloupe 'for a change of air', which for various reasons, none of them very interesting, had lasted until the present.

'I wished him dead,' sobbed the Corporal Major;

'the last time I seed him before that meeting, I looked at him and wished him dead.'

'So you've got worries,' said the Chamberlain: 'now, I'm being sent to a 'ome. A 'ome for old soldiers in Norwich.'

'Really,' said (ex-Trooper) Geddes, who was on the right of the line, 'you are a dismal couple of downers. Here we are on a beautiful sunny day, burying Captain Lord Canteloupe in real style, with lovely Major Gray and spiffing Colonel Glastonbury – '

' – Colonel was only 'is wartime rank,' said the Corporal Major.

' – He was still a colonel in India in forty-six,' said the Chamberlain: 'I know, because I was there with Captain Detterling what's being buried. Detterling was a captain, then as ever, but Glastonbury was a colonel – and a ripe lot of mischief they got up to in their Special-Intelligence-how's-your-father-and-bloody-mother.'

'But he was a major in Göttingen six years later,' said Ethel, Mavis, Hilda, etc., etc., and now Lucretia Geddes. 'He commanded the Tenth Sabre Squadron – you remember as well as I do, Corporal Major – until there was some row about a duel with a Kraut. Then they packed him off God knows where, and lovely Captain Fielding Gray (as he then was) took over.'

'It don't half cheer a man up, having a natter with old chums,' said Chead. 'Please to call me "Corpy", like you did back in BAOR. And why, I wonder, is your "lovely" Major Fielding Gray (as he later became before his face was mashed by them treacherous wogs in Cyprus) not wearing his uniform on this occasion?'

'He lent it to me,' said Geddes, 'and I changed the officer bits into what was proper for troopers. Otherwise I couldn't have come, see, because I've only got skirts and ladies' costumes these days, and I couldn't have come in one of them, now could I?'

'So you're a drag number, are you?' said 'Corpy'

177

Chead. 'Not that I'm criticising, 'cos I always fancied young Lamb in the spare-parts stores, fancied him something fierce but I never quite fancied drag. Makes a man too vulnerable, don't you find?'

'Makes a man free, Corpy, free. Wear a long dress, no knickers needed, you save on laundry and you can piss while you're standing on the pavement – anyway on a wet day . . . which it isn't today, I'm happy to say, sun shining like the young Apollo, see how it flashes on Captain Canteloupe's sabre.'

'I used to keep that sabre as bright as water,' said the Chamberlain (a life-long teetotaller); 'chain mail and Brillo pads.'

Last in the procession came Doctor La Soeur with Raisley Conyngham. Raisley had meant to tag on to Glastonbury, but as Giles was heavily accompanied by Raisley's No. 1 enemy, Luffham, this plan was now inappropriate. In the old days, La Soeur had hated Raisley every bit as much as Luffham did and wouldn't have been seen dead with him at a funeral or anywhere else; but all that had changed since Raisley had begun to be of material assistance to La Soeur in his retirement. And so now,

'There's the Fives Court,' said La Soeur in a friendly way. 'There is an interesting tablet on the wall in memory of someone called Gat-Toothed Jenny.'

'Once a stable lass of mine,' said Raisley. 'She left me and came here. Hit her head on the corner of that buttress, so I'm told, while having a knock-up. Poor Jenny. That fat soldier in front is drunk.'

'Rolling around a bit, I grant you. He's too old to be in uniform, one would have thought. Ah. The Rose Garden. Not far now. Just as well by the look of it. You seem to be sweating up, old fellow.'

'Funny,' said Raisley; 'I don't usually feel the heat. I don't carry an ounce overweight . . . unlike that drunk soldier. I've been a bit seedy the whole morning. Ghastly headache in that horrible oratory. . . . Better now.'

'What did you think of the bishop's address?' La Soeur enquired.

Raisley looked a bit vague. La Soeur repeated his question.

'Can't remember much,' Raisley said. 'That headache in there. Bishop of Glastonbury, isn't he? No relation of Giles, I think. But of course not,' Raisley rambled. 'How should he be? Glastonbury not his name, only his bishopric. Diocese? Bishopric? Dioc – '

' – Steady, old man, steady. Ah. Here we are. The Grave Ground.'

When the bearers reached the graveside, they placed Canteloupe's coffin on the cross-cables prepared for its lowering. While the other mourners arranged themselves round the bottom end of the pit (near Canteloupe's feet, so to speak), with Giles and Luffham prominent and Raisley and La Soeur well over to the right, Mungo Avallon and Theodosia, at the far end, removed Canteloupe's achievements from the coffin and arranged them on a frame nearby: the standard at the foot of the frame; sheath and sabre, still crossed and now supported by a system of brackets halfway up; sabretrache slung above these; the busby placed on a small shelf a little higher; and the coronet, fitted over a wooden sphere at the top of the main vertical shaft, crowning all.

The banner of St George of England, however, remained on the coffin. On this Tessa and Marius placed Nausikaa's small white box. They then moved back behind Theodosia, who was behind Mungo Avallon, who stood at the head of the grave, and now began:

'MAN THAT IS BORN OF WOMAN – '

' – Sorry, my lords, ladies and gentlemen,' said Glastonbury, in an impenitent voice, 'but I can't hold my water these days, and I'm so hemmed in that I can't get out of this crush either, so here we go.'

He produced a huge, floppy, uncircumcised peego and pissed with gusto on to his end of the red cross. 'Sorry, Canteloupe, old chap,' he said as he pissed, 'but I feel sure you'll understand. I'm aiming well short of Nausikaa.'

Everyone turned to watch Glastonbury's micturation, even Raisley, whose half-closed eyes had hitherto been concentrated on Marius.

'I warned him,' said Raisley to La Soeur, 'that he ought to have something done about his prostate.' He sagged sideways towards La Soeur. 'Christ. My head. My poor h – ' he began and never finished, but fell at La Soeur's feet, supine, his head in half, the cutting edge of Canteloupe's sabre now wedged into his lower front teeth and the hilt protruding from his chin.

Marius, who was grasping the hilt, now withdrew the sabre. Glastonbury gave a wry look and went on watering the coffin. Marius kissed the hilt of the sabre, lowered the point (correctly exposing his wrist), raised and kissed the hilt, saluting his dead master from whom he had learnt so much. Then he retired and placed the sabre on the ground, the point towards himself and the hilt at Theodosia's feet.

'Very nice cut, young Marius,' said Glastonbury, as he put away his still-dripping tool; 'but I think you'll have some explaining to do.'

'The golden horseman,' said Milo to Jeremy, 'has possessed himself of the sword of the cerise horseman and cut down the horseman of the west. I shall elaborate the details of this analysis later.'

'Major Glastonbury were right about that cut,' said the Corporal Major: 'classic backhand down-stroke.'

'I like to remember,' said the Chamberlain, 'that it was me that sharpened that sabre. Almost the last thing I did before leaving His Lordship's employment here and going to the household at Luffham. Without my efforts that stroke would never have been possible.'

'That'll give you something to boast of, dearie,' said Geddes, 'when you're shut up with all those senile squaddies in Norwich.'

'I think,' said Luffham of Whereham to Marius, 'that, as Major Glastonbury says, some kind of explanation is called for.'

'Very simple,' said Marius. 'I took the sabre from the frame behind me, and while you were all distracted by Major Glastonbury's performance I walked down the grave and split the skull of Mr Conyngham. I had thought of decapitation, but felt that that would be in bad taste.'

'It is customary in such cases,' said Luffham, 'either to justify one's action, or express regret for it, or both.'

'Very well. I regret the premature demise of a fine Classics master. I justify my part in it by telling you – as Tessa Malcolm here will confirm – that Mr Conyngham was blackmailing me into spreading foul rumours about you and your son Jeremy, who is my friend of many years now, in order to discredit you and destroy your influence with the governing body of our school, to the headmastership of which he is – he was – aspiring.'

Luffham looked at Tessa, who nodded.

'Very civil of you to take my side, Marius,' Luffham said, 'but wouldn't some . . . less spectacular approach to the problem . . . have been prudent?'

'No, it wouldn't,' said Theodosia, who hitherto had been motionless and silent. She now moved to Marius's side. 'Raisley Conyngham was a brilliant scholar (particularly of Greek and Latin verse), a notable connoisseur of dessert wines, and a pretty fair judge of race horses. In every other respect, as you all very well know, he was too bad to breathe. He was a defiler of innocence and a corrupter of the spirit. He was the worm in the apple and the canker in the rose. He was a seducer and besmircher, not of bodies, but of souls. He was anathema, that which is cursed by God, of whom Marius stands as the champion.'

'I do not conceive that many judges or juries will take that view,' said Luffham. 'Sympathetic as it may be to most of those present, some here will feel it their duty' – he pointed to the bucolic coffin bearers, who were standing in a group, with a pair of local undertakers, by the nearby monument to Muscateer – 'to come forward as evidence for the Crown. What is your opinion, Avallon?'

'Very similar to yours,' said Mungo. 'One really cannot allow this kind of thing to go unrecognised. It would lead to anarchy. Much may be forgiven if it is perpetrated in the name of true friendship, but operatic homicide is overdoing it.'

'Miss Rosie?' said Luffham. 'You are Marius's sister.'

'I am delighted that Mr Conyngham is dead,' said Rosie, 'and I hope that you will all have the *nous* to pitch him into that hole with the coffins and bury the whole matter with him.'

'Hear, hear!' said Marigold and the girl with the short blonde hair.

'Impracticable,' said Leonard Percival. 'Enquiries are bound to be made, sooner or later, when he does not reappear at that school. However, I have one or two old friends and colleagues in a special unit housed in Jermyn Street. They might be able to help.'

'I'm afraid,' said Fielding, 'that that unit, Leonard, was a bit too special. It was disbanded by Petty Officer Callaghan.'

'Come on, Len,' said Marigold: 'you're pretty good at greasing out of tight places. Help us – help Marius – grease out of this one.'

'From what I've heard,' said Len, 'the paramount greaser in this sort of area is Doctor La Soeur.'

Everyone, including the bucolics, looked at Doctor La Soeur.

'I'm glad you've got round to me,' said La Soeur. 'You see, although I can't be absolutely certain for the time being, it's about ten to one on in the betting that Conyngham died instantaneously of a stroke – '

' – No doubt of that,' guffawed the Corporal Major, 'and *what* a stroke, as beautiful a backhander as ever I seed in all my service.'

'Now be a good boy, Corpy,' said Geddes, 'and listen quietly to the clever gentleman.'

' – Of a stroke,' resumed La Soeur, 'in the sense of a haemorrhage, probably massive, in the brain. He was describing to me, and exhibiting, the standard prefatory symptoms of just such a trauma all the way from the oratory to this grave. At the very last he complained piteously of his head, and then began to collapse towards me a good half-second before he actually sustained the sabre cut. If I am right, he could have been dead as he started to fall, in which case young Marius is entirely innocent of causing his death. One cannot be charged with murdering a corpse.'

'It will be said,' remarked Glastonbury, 'even if proof of cerebral haemorrhage is forthcoming in autopsy, that Conyngham might not have been finally dead when he fell, or when he received the sabre cut, but was only in a coma.'

'It probably will be said,' replied La Soeur. 'But there must be doubt – enough doubt to exculpate Marius, legally if not morally. As to the morals of this affair, it is not within my competence to pronounce,' he went on. 'Meanwhile, Lady Canteloupe, upon whose ground we stand, will know what to do. I think the solution is pretty simple, Theodosia,' he called down the grave.

Theodosia smiled obliquely. 'Lower the coffins and bury them,' she ordered the two undertakers; and to the tenant farmers, 'Take Mr Conyngham's body,' she said, 'and put it in the oratory, on the catafalque, so that Doctor La Soeur and the police may examine it.'

'Surely, my lady,' demurred the bucolic-in-chief, 'a more convenient place might be found. The police may be surprised that the body has been moved at all, let alone to the – '

' – Oratory. Put it in the oratory,' Theodosia said.

'That's my good girl,' murmured Doctor La Soeur.

Avallon and Luffham looked at each other thoughtfully, then nodded to Theodosia.

'You see,' said Milo Hedley to Jeremy Morrison: 'as Gregory Stern warned us, this solution of the Marius/Conyngham business offers no moral satisfaction to anybody. Lady Canteloupe has proclaimed an heroic victory for Marius; but the blow was cowardly and his pretext altogether too specious and smug.'

'He is, however, in luck,' said Jeremy, 'though *that* is scarcely a moral recommendation.'

'Luck?' queried Milo. 'You mean . . . the way in which Glastonbury's startling exhibition pre-empted general attention? So that Marius could act unnoticed, until it was too late for him to be stopped?'

'No,' said Jeremy. 'I do not mean that – though Glastonbury's incontinence certainly helped him. I mean, Milo darling, that unless I am very mistaken we are about to witness a fascinating phenomenon – the capacity of the English upper class to protect, absolutely and without scruple, one of their own . . . when, and for whatever reason, they consider this to be desirable. You remember the Lucan mystery?'

'You are maintaining,' said Milo, 'that this upper-class lot here is conspiring to extricate Marius. But the whole thing surely depends on the professional . . . plausibility . . . of Doctor La Soeur . . . who is only "client gentry".'

'La Soeur has already conjured enough doubt to compel a verdict of not guilty of murder. But vexatious ancillary charges,' said Jeremy, 'of "criminal intent" or "violating a corpse" might still be preferred. The upper class will now take action to eliminate any possibility of even the slightest nuisance of that kind from the official or the officious. At least, that's my bet.'

Jeremy Morrison paused, and for once his big round face drooped into a lugubrious ovoid.

'But that apart,' he concluded, 'I think that although Marius has undoubtedly rid himself of Conyngham, who can no longer use him to further his own devices, Conyngham, like a dead insect, has left his sting and his poison behind him – in Marius's heart.'

At this juncture, uncertainty spread among those on the Grave Ground, except for those who had received definite orders. The majority of the mourners was doubtful whether to stay put or to move somewhere else in the precincts or simply to clear off and go home. They were, they supposed, witnesses to the unusual event that had occurred by the grave-mouth; and yet they were now assured that, in all probability, what they had seen was merely a commonplace instance of death by cerebral haemorrhage, fortuitously accompanied, or rather succeeded, by a violent attack on a body that was already dead.

In the end, Mungo Avallon and Lord Luffham persuaded the guests to withdraw from the Grave Ground to the Rose Garden and there to await developments. Marius Stern they asked to sit with them (and between them) on a bench by a small fish pool, on the surface of which many of the fish were floating underside up, promoting rather a smell. Before they finally settled in this disagreeable spot, Mungo announced that those with previous instructions, which was to say the undertaker, the erstwhile coffin bearers, and (as she insisted) Teresa Malcolm should be about their business at the double.

So the undertakers lowered the two coffins and began to shovel earth on to them; the tenant farmers, who had carried Canteloupe encoffined, now carried

Raisley Conyngham, not encoffined but seated in a kitchen chair which one of them had procured, to the oratory, and laid him along the catafalque in front of the altar; and Teresa Malcolm waited on Theodosia Canteloupe in her bedroom (whither her ladyship had retreated after rapping out her commands in the Grave Ground), as she had been instructed earlier that day by mouth of Leonard Percival.

Theodosia was doing press-ups on her bedroom floor, still wearing her Cambridge blue tracksuit. When she heard Teresa enter, she jumped to her feet. She was swift and direct in speech.

'Just before Canteloupe died,' she said to Teresa, 'he promised to destroy the Campanile, in accordance with my wish. You and I were defiled by that Campanile, because Canteloupe and Rosie used to gaze from one of its windows upon our nakedness and privacy.'

'But surely – '

' – There is now another reason to destroy it, which you will soon appreciate. Even before this second reason became apparent, I had used the time between Canteloupe's death and the day of his burial to make preparations for the demolition which he had promised but could no longer order or undertake in person. Leonard helped: it was, as you will see very soon, hard work for an old man, but I needed him, as La Soeur was too busy with other matters to spare much time for this. I did not ask you to help because I knew you would try to dissuade me, and I was in no mood for contradiction. As it was, the preparations were a welcome distraction – a therapy, as some would call it – in time of anxiety and grief.'

'But Thea, darling Thea – '

' – Stop whimpering and follow me. We are now going to the Campanile. We shall not cross the Great Court, we shall go to the end of this wing, through the old building, and so into the wing opposite and along it to a short aerial corridor which will take us into the bell chamber.'

Teresa followed Theodosia. They left Theodosia's apartments, climbed some uncarpeted wooden stairs, and walked through a series of interconnected and empty attic rooms. After the sixth of these, they turned right into a corridor which was lit only by small, high, plain rose windows. After sixty yards or so of this, they turned right again into a kind of enormous attic hall, at the far end of which they mounted on to a stage, descended a few yards into what could once have been a green room, and then went through a low door into a tunnel of absolute darkness. Theodosia appeared to Teresa to reach to her left with her left arm, flash a cigarette lighter with her right hand, and ignite a torch or flambeau. This she held aloft to light Teresa and herself along the ten yards or so of the flying passage, which ended in another low door.

Theodosia pushed the door open with her right hand. In front of her Teresa saw Old Mortality, flawed by a jagged, gaping crack that travelled from its apex and down six feet to its rim.

'The bell is operated by various mechanisms,' Theodosia said, 'in its various functions. During the passage of Canteloupe's cortège to the Grave Ground, it was started, then silenced, by a switch on the ground floor which was controlled by an old woman in our service – one of the last in our service. But there is also a switch up here. There: just by the door. Press it.'

Teresa pressed it. Cogs ground. A clapper struck, almost on the crack. A hideous boom filled the bell chamber.

'Down here,' Theodosia said.

They went down a spiral staircase and came to another, an empty chamber.

'This is where they stood to watch us,' said Theodosia; 'Canteloupe and little Rosie. This is where the process of purging must begin.'

She lowered her torch to the end of a rope that

snaked along the floor and down the continuation of the staircase. A flame ripped away from the torch.

'You see, Teresa?' Theodosia said. 'The room below this is full of open cans and buckets of petrol. The floor is soaked with it. It was rough work getting all the containers in place, but we had to make sure. NOW OUT, GIRL, OUT.'

Teresa leapt up the steps by which they had descended. Theodosia followed. Old Mortality clunged and grinded and bawled.

'The mechanism will keep going until the fire mounts up again into the bell chamber,' said Theodosia, as she led the way, torch aloft, along the tunnel: 'that is why it was important to start it by the upper switch to the bell chamber circuit.'

They hurried through the hall and along the corridor and back down the chain of attic rooms through which they had come. When they reached Thea's suite, she dowsed the torch in the hand basin in her bathroom, then returned to the bedroom and hustled Teresa to the window.

'See?' she said. 'The oratory has already taken fire from the lower levels of the Campanile. There will be nothing left of Raisley Conyngham to affront the world or give any evidence to the police that might, after all, inculpate Marius.'

She went to a drawer, took out four pairs of thick, brown leather gloves and a cardboard box.

'Come,' she said. 'There has been vengeance in the Grave Ground to destroy one evil, while here in the tower there is purgation of another. Now that the Campanile is cleansed by fire of the impurities which were wrought in it, the wise goddess will allow a time of celebration and licence. Always remember, Teresa: Artemis, the virgin huntress, was also the goddess of ecstasy beneath the ripened moon.'

The guests in the Rose Garden soon noticed pillars of smoke and fire from the direction of the Great Court. Everyone left it to everyone else to do something about it. It would, after all, have been ill-mannered and presumptuous to thrust oneself forward.

'The police have already been sent for,' Leonard Percival told Mungo Avallon and Lord Luffham and Marius. 'As for this fire, well, there is an automatic alarm through to the fire station, which should be set off there by a serious fire in any room in the house. It will be interesting to see whether it works. If it doesn't, the insurance company will be aggravated.'

'You see?' said Jeremy Morrison to Milo Hedley. 'The upper classes are taking no chances here. There is not even going to be a body about which to prevaricate.'

'Getting our money's worth today,' said the Corporal Major.

'I never cared much for the place,' said the Chamberlain. 'When I was here before Lord Canteloupe sent me to Luffham, I found it a very trying place to be even an *upper* servant in. It quite got on my nerves. There are those that say I've never been the same since.'

'The fall of the House of Sarum,' said Geddes: 'very well timed. Lovely Major Gray says there are no heirs anywhere.'

'There's an heir all right,' said Glastonbury, who now joined them. 'Lovely Major Gray once told me when he was pissed. There's a potty Italian peasant boy in a madhouse near Venice.'

'Come along, Major Glastonbury, dear,' said Geddes: 'please tell us more, sir.'

Marigold, Rosie and the girl with the cropped blonde hair were the nearest to the Great Court, with Len just behind them.

'I wonder how far it will spread,' said Marigold.

'Everywhere,' said Rosie. 'I went over the whole

place with Leonard Percival and Dobrila the nanny while I was staying here last hols. "Once start a fire in this place," Mr Percival said, "and the whole lot will go up in no time." "I hope Canteloupe has taken precautions," I said: "it must be a terrible worry." "Oh, he's taken precautions all right," Leonard said, "but I don't think he's that worried. Canteloupe and I are old soldiers, you see: we know that if it's coming you can't stop it." "If *what's* coming?" said Dobrila – she was still a bit slow at her English. "Just it," Mr Percival said.'

'Here comes her ladyship,' said Len, making a mock curtsy, 'with ginger Tessa. You won't believe this, but I think they're going to play fives.'

'Don't they need two more?' said Rosie.

'Two people can play a singles match of a kind,' said the blonde girl; 'but it's not usual and it's not nearly so much fun. Do you want us to find another pair?' she called. 'I'm not too bad, and there's Rosie's brother, Marius.'

'Oh yes indeed,' called back Theodosia. 'A time of licence.'

So Rosie went to fetch Marius from his bench, and when she had explained to Mungo Avallon and Luffham of Whereham that he was wanted by Lady Canteloupe, and why, they immediately released him.

As Marius and the blonde girl approached the Fives Court, Theodosia cried:

'A celebration . . . that all is purged and Raisley Conyngham is dead. A time to dance upon the toe and cry "Hey Nonny Nonny No". For a while the goddess will indulge us – but not for long. Do as I do.'

There was an edge in her voice and a light in her eye that did not encourage dissent.

She pulled off her Kickers, wriggled her way out of her tracksuit, under which she wore nothing, and put on her Kickers again. Marius, Tessa and the blonde girl watched silently; then the three began to strip. Neither Marius nor the blonde girl could even wear shoes, as theirs were the wrong kind; but Teresa had slippers with rubber soles, so her footwear was more or less suitable. Theodosia distributed the thick leather fives gloves and took a new ball out of the cardboard box.

'A celebration,' she called into the Rose Garden. '"'Tis a splendid thing to laugh and sing/ And turn upon the toe/ And cry Hey Nonny No." Teresa and I shall play a match against Marius and – what's your name?' she said to the blonde girl.

'Eurydice,' said the girl, who had very small but very piquant breasts.

'EURYDICE,' called Theodosia into the garden, from which her guests were now emerging to watch the match.

Since the Eton Fives Court was at the Rose Garden end of the Great Court, there would probably be time for five or ten minutes of play before the fire stopped it. Theodosia was the first to throw the ball up, and was immediately swinged down by Eurydice, who cut elegantly but viciously at the ball while it hovered at the top of its bounce.

'Well played,' said tumescent Marius.

'Such a pretty sight,' the Corporal Major was saying to the Chamberlain and Geddes and Glastonbury. 'The great thing about you upper-class lot, sir, is that we never know what you're going to do next.'

Fielding Gray and Doctor La Soeur joined the military group.

'I've told them about young Filavoni in that asylum in the Lagoon,' said Glastonbury to Fielding; 'I don't suppose it matters now.'

'Did it ever?' said Fielding. 'Christ, those girls . . . Tessa's little gold bush, and Eurydice's little silver bush, and Thea's great, wild, rambling bush – '

' – If that horny little Marius isn't careful,' said La Soeur, 'he'll do himself an injury on that buttress.'

'One of them young ladies would soon kiss it

better,' said the Corporal Major.

Old Mortality continued its single and horrible chime. The palace of Canteloupe continued to burn. The fire brigade did not arrive, as Theodosia had disconnected the alarm while making her preparations before the funeral. Raisley Conyngham's cadaver was consumed like Guy Fawkes'. The police did not arrive, because, although Leonard had sent for them, there was an impassable traffic jam on all roads out of the city of Salisbury, caused by a crash between two ice cream vans and the consequent necessity for complex diversions. So for some time the Celebration Fives Match was able to proceed, warmly applauded by its audience.

'That's another thing I like about the upper classes,' said the Corporal Major: 'the way they face up to disaster, like Nero playing the fiddle while Rome was burning.'

'This is a form of ritual,' said Fielding Gray; 'a ritual rejoicing to announce and encourage re-birth.'

'Whose re-birth?' enquired Geddes pertinently; but his question was either unheard or unheeded.

'It might be advisable to stop the game,' said La Soeur, 'before the police come . . . which I suppose they must, eventually. After all, we've got enough to explain without this rather curious ballistic contest. The provincial police are very puritanical. It comes from being lower class and having no proper officers.'

And indeed common sense now prevailed. Since the fire was getting quite close to the Fives Court, and the first game was just concluded (in Marius's and Eurydice's favour), and the time of licence allowed by Artemis was nearly up, Theodosia led the players out. Following her example, they dressed themselves – and only in the nick of time: for the first police car now arrived in the car park on the cricket ground, just as Old Mortality for ever ceased.

'And that's one more thing about the upper classes,'

said the Corporal Major. 'They know just how far they can go and just when it's time to stop.'

As Theodosia stepped forward, flushed and beautiful in her Cambridge blue tracksuit, to greet the chief superintendent, who had walked across the meadow to the Rose Garden, he could not resist saluting her, though like all policemen he grudged saluting anybody (paranoia). Doctor La Soeur singled out the police surgeon, and started talking to him in a flattering and seductive manner, as one man-of-the-world to another. Mungo Avallon and Luffham of Whereham made themselves agreeable to inspectors and below. Fielding Gray, Giles Glastonbury and the three other ranks walked back to Canteloupe's grave, which was now full of earth. Glastonbury and the others in uniform put on their busbies and saluted, staying at the salute for a long time. Fielding, feeling rather out of it, took off his black silk hat (not quite as tall as the one Mungo Avallon had worn before he put a mitre on his bonce instead), and held it over where he thought his heart was.

'It looks as if everything's going to be all right,' said Fielding at last, 'apart from the house burning down – which is rather a relief in a way, as a lot of awkward secrets have gone with it.'

'Of course everything will be all right, darling,' said ex-Trooper Geddes. 'Everyone here knows the old rule, even those that weren't in the old regiment. *Res Unius, Res Omnium* – the Affair of One is the Affair of All. That means all of *us*, mind, and sod box wallahs, money grubbers, Keyhole Katies, cant artists, and poxy fucking politicians of every poxy fucking party. So God save Her Majesty, gentlemen, and there an end to it.'

'Amen to that,' they all cried; and 'Amen, amen' came echoing back (over Muscateer's column) from the rampart.